The Richest Women in the World

The Richest Women in the World

by KIT KONOLIGE

MACMILLAN PUBLISHING COMPANY
NEW YORK
COLLIER MACMILLAN PUBLISHERS
LONDON

For Lori

Macmillan Publishing Company
866 Third Avenue, New York, N.Y. 10022
Collier Macmillan Canada, Inc.

Library of Congress Cataloging in Publication Data

Konolige, Kit.
    The richest women in the world.

    Bibliography: p.
    Includes index.
    1. Millionairesses—Biography.   2. Women in business—Biography.   3. Women philanthropists—Biography.
4. Inheritance and succession—Case studies.   I. Title.
HG172.A2K66   1985   305.4'89 [B]   85-3067
ISBN 0-02-566610-X

Macmillan books are available at special discounts for bulk purchases for sales promotions, premiums, fund-raising, or educational use. For details, contact:

Special Sales Director
Macmillan Publishing Company
866 Third Avenue
New York, N.Y. 10022

10 9 8 7 6 5 4 3 2 1

Printed in the United States of America

CONTENTS

Acknowledgments

To THE DOZENS of people who contributed in diverse ways without any return, I am much indebted. People such as Alan Halpern, Frank Zachary, Peter Davis, and David Harrop helped by acting as sounding boards for the overall scheme and each provided valuable suggestions. I had invaluable on-the-spot assistance from Cristina D. Carlisle of the *New York Times*'s Buenos Aires bureau, the *Times*'s Madrid correspondent John Darnton, William Claiborne of the *Washington Post* in New Delhi, and other foreign correspondents who preferred anonymity. A large number of aides in embassies in Washington contributed insights into their countries. I was guided by the staffs of the New York Public Library, the Library of Congress, the University of Pennsylvania libraries, and the Free Library of Philadelphia; and also by librarians at the *Philadelphia Inquirer and Daily News*, the *Los Angeles Times*, the *San Francisco Chronicle*, the *Kansas City Star*, the *Houston Post*, the *Jacksonville (Fla.) Times-Union*, and the *Palm Beach Daily News*. And a great deal of the material of the book came from a variety of people who work with and for the subjects of the book.

But of course my greatest thanks must go to the women who agreed to sit for interviews and who thus form the heart of the book: Susanna Agnelli, Mary Kay Ash, Electra Waggoner Biggs, Carolyn Farb, Wanda Ferragamo, Ebby Halliday, Leona Helmsley, Carolina Herrera, Olga Hirshhorn, Minerva Mason, Sarah Pillsbury, Ruth Springer Wedgworth, Marylou Whitney, Candice Wozniak, and Lynn Wyatt. Many of them were quite forthright, and all of them were fascinating.

I would also like to thank my editors, Arlene Friedman and Melinda Corey; my agent, Bill Adler; and Amy Likoff and Gail Gair, who provided typing and transcribing services.

I am lucky to have a group of friends who are also knowledgeable and insightful, and used those qualities to help out informally—Edward J. Martineck, Brian Feldman, Duncan Grove, Bob Simpson, Harriet Shaw, and my brothers Kurt and Peter Konolige.

The greatest adviser and supporter throughout this, as in all else, has been my wife, Lori Zazow; and I'm deeply grateful.

—KIT KONOLIGE
Philadelphia, 1984

Introduction

ONLY IN THE LAST CENTURY has the rich woman emerged as a distinct figure, but she has done it with a vengeance. To be a heroine in American literature was to be rich: the Henry James princesses move in circles of great wealth, and Fitzgerald's Daisy Buchanan had a voice that "was full of money." And the popular press was full of the doings of the greatest of the rich women— first Mrs. Astor and Mrs. Vanderbilt, then, more scandalously, Barbara Hutton and Gloria Vanderbilt. The "poor little rich girl" became a fixture of popular consciousness. Here was a creature who (in almost all cases) was merely born into a fortune, was not expected to take any intelligent interest in it, was thought (until recently) inherently inferior to men, but who nevertheless was capable of exerting immense power over them. The fact that she sometimes fell into servitude or despair only made her situation the more fascinating.

But there are fewer "poor little rich girls" now, victimized by their underhanded intimates and their longing for love. More and more, the rich woman is one who not only inherits her father's money but takes over his business. That development only makes the rich more powerful, and so more interesting. Rich women are especially important in publishing, in fashion, and in charitable foundations (a $60 billion business in the United States)—all of which have a major impact on society. And through their eternal franchise—their sway over rich men—rich women have an impact that goes far beyond the sum of their property holdings.

Being one of the richest women in the world is a full-time job in two ways. One is the truly staggering amounts of time that women of great property around the world devote to their jobs, their husbands, their families, their homes, and perhaps most of all, to their images. Someone like Lynn Wyatt, a Houston department store heiress in her own right and also the wife of one of the richest oilmen in Texas, is eager to describe what she does all day, to show how unfair is the stereotype of the frivolous socialite. Other rich women of an increasingly common type feel no need for elaborate explanations; one thinks of Susanna Agnelli, the Fiat heiress who, after incarnations as a World War II partisan, an Argentine rancher and mother, and a New York socialite, is now an undersecretary of state in Italy. Rich women, who had always occupied themselves with organized charity, are now, some of them, invading the work world.

The second, more subtle, aspect of personal wealth being a full-time job is the sense in which it dominates all other aspects of their lives. Being immensely rich is a condition of the first rank—it has as much to do with forming one's character as being unattractive or being a genius. In this book we will meet women who have tried to give away their inherited wealth; who have denied having it; who have expressed outrage at others' mentioning it; or who have tried to protect their children from knowing about it. Always, sooner or later, they come to the conclusion that it is *part of them*. Some, like Sarah Pillsbury of the flour company fortune, have undergone years of psychoanalysis to understand why they own so much more of their world than their neighbors; some, like Edie Sedgwick and Ethel du Pont, have destroyed themselves amidst their wealth; some, like Candi Wozniak, blame their riches for blighted friendships; many, like the Hunt sisters of Texas or Pamela Harriman of Washington, have taken control of it and used it to carve out for themselves positions of great influence. But all have found that great wealth is something they cannot evade.

How great is great wealth? "Millionaire" has lost its cachet to inflation. Many middle-class people know a number of people worth a million dollars, if only their bosses or their doctors; there are neighborhoods, whole townships, where it is rare to find anyone who is not a millionaire. While the second million may be much easier than the first, $10 million is still a respectable amount of wealth; and it can be attained without too much trouble by all sorts of entrepreneurs, professionals, entertainers, and heirs. It is only when we get to $100 million that we reach rarified air: this is truly great wealth. *Forbes* magazine calculates that there are four hundred people in the United States worth more than $150 million. It is anybody's guess, and nobody's very good guess, how many there are outside the United States; but one imagines that, because of high taxes, nationalization, and paternalistic corporations (such as in Japan), reaching that great a figure is comparatively rare. Still, it is obvious that all developed countries have a number of families of enormous traditional wealth—including, many times, the nobility—and several major entrepreneurs. Third World countries are frequently dominated by a small ruling clique that accumulates immense properties through methods never entirely clear. Anyone who has tried to compete with the foreigners buying up condominiums in Manhattan realizes how much great wealth there is outside the United States. However, only one-fifth of those four hundred richest in the United States are women, and probably a smaller percentage elsewhere. Still, there are always women who marry the rich men or luck into them as fathers, and these women also are of great interest.

This book is not a listing of estimates of wealth or property holdings. Rather, we want to see how rich women live and what drives them to do what they do. For example, Marylou Whitney is hostess in seven different homes around the United States and overseas, each maintained by its own staff. Dominique de Menil has accumulated a $75 million collection of modern art from scratch in forty years. Brooke Astor has given away $130 million in twenty-five years. Nabila Khashoggi, in her early twenties, has already been named president of the Triad Commercial Corporation, the umbrella for her Saudi businessman father's un-countable holdings, and keeps in touch with them via any of the 296 telephones in the eleven suites of the yacht *Nabila*.

As these examples suggest, what great wealth allows more than anything else is excess. From gift-giving and parties through battles over divorces and wills into criminal behavior and self-destructiveness, rich women continue to do it all with verve. If their stories sound unreal, it is because they can literally live their fantasies.

PART 1
GETTING RICH

1 HORIZON TO HORIZON

CAROLYN FARB HAS SOMETHING. She has $30 million, but she didn't start with that—she has something that got it for her. She has a blonde mane, a sweet smile, a beautiful body—and three ex-husbands, one richer than the next, with the last, Harold Farb, one of the richest men in Houston. He's the man perhaps most responsible for the unsettling suburbs-downtown ambience of that bizarre city, having built twenty-five thousand apartment units over the past thirty years, thus making himself $300 million or so from scratch. After Farb made his fortune, he discovered one day that he was pushing sixty and realized: it's time to have *fun*! One thing that was apparently not fun was Shirley, his wife of twenty-seven years. And Carolyn took her place.

What's really irresistible about Carolyn is the voice, which has as much of the sweetness and passion of the old South in it as one can absorb without gagging. Those words just drip off her lips; they are aimed for you, her hearer, and you alone. You are sharing her secrets, her dreams, her joys. As she describes herself, her role in society is to be "like bubbles in champagne."

And yet there will be those who say that Carolyn really has about as much sweetness and passion as a small-town banker. Certainly, she has a formidable amount of information and opinions, which she is forever trying to disburse to as large a public as possible in her chosen field, which happens to be large-scale fundraising at parties. It is the constant fear of such a woman that her charm will be taken for airheadedness, her accommodations for weakness. One does not make such mistakes about Carolyn Farb for long. As she warms to her topic, she speaks with increasing speed and imperiousness. She has, perhaps, thought about fundraising parties in a more systematic way than anyone except the executive committee of the United Way. This, really, is her passion—this and the social acclaim it brings. Carolyn loves to tell you about where she has appeared, where her house, clothes, and (not to be forgotten) her favorite charities have been written about and shown on television.

Carolyn's background begins to explain her. She is the granddaughter of Jakie Freedman, one of the most notorious gamblers of Texas's wild early days. Her husband must have realized early on that he had become attached to something beyond your average spoiled princess. Once she had transformed herself from a twice-divorced secretary into Mrs. Harold Farb, Carolyn wasted no time making it clear that her idea of marrying into a fortune was not to sit at home. Carolyn Farb hit Houston atomically hard with an identifiably Farbesque look. The *Houston Post* described it as "a cross between a Southern belle and a prom queen. The hair is swept up off the shoulders into a loose bun, wispy tendrils fixed into perfect place. The rustling ball gown is full-skirted, low-necked and includes a great deal of ruffles. Large, visible gems are worn. A cheerleader's smile completes the look." Carolyn quickly established a reputation as one of the most outrageously conspicuous consumers in the world. In 1983, in her two-thousand-square-foot closet in the mansion Farb installed her in, Carolyn had sixty hats, ninety pairs of shoes, fifty evening bags, seventy-five gowns, and more than a thousand other dresses and suits.

In her spare time, the flashy Carolyn was transforming her previously ordinary husband into a manic enjoyer of his own money; suddenly, he was entertaining his guests at his $6.5 million baroque Carlyle Restaurant (named after his favorite New York hotel) by singing old standards to them; he was paying the

Houston Symphony $25,000 to accompany him singing Gershwin; he was recording the result and handing out the records as party favors; he was founding *Ultra*, "the magazine for high-fashion, high-profile, high-society Texans."

One of the people he did not succeed in entertaining, however, was Carolyn. By the end of 1982 Harold had had enough; he filed for divorce several times and finally let it ride. In his deposition he complained about the eternal charity circuit, then said, "I really don't know what it would take to satisfy Carolyn. There are only so many clothes and so much jewelry anyone can wear." Apparently, the price of Carolyn is eternal adulation, and that can hardly be expected to emanate from a single man, however rich or peculiar.

Typically, Carolyn shrugs off the marital disaster on the general rich woman's ground that life is basically wonderful and unpleasantness is to be quarantined. "I just have a lot of energy," she reiterates when asked about the suggestion that her hardcore charity didn't begin or end at home often enough to keep Harold. "I think things are negotiable. Certainly, I could've put energy into my marriage in more visible ways. I think it's important to be a good wife and mother. But it is also important for an individual to do things—there are so many things to give your attention to."

Those who are unkind will see a direct relation between the degree of philosophical acceptance of a broken marriage and the size of the divorce settlement. Carolyn's was, well, Texas-sized. Her lawyer, Bob Piro, whose future is now as golden as his celebrated client's, successfully contested the premarital agreement that would have limited Carolyn's reward for her six years of alliance with Harold to $1 million. And what's the use of breaking a limit if you don't really shatter it? The latest estimate of Carolyn's take is $30 million, which shifts her gears well upward from the $1 million annual allowance that Harold had endowed her with. Of course, the income is not quite as large as it appears at first, since the $30 million is not all income-producing; it includes two Rollses, a Jaguar, furs, jewels, ninety pairs of shoes, the six-room closet, and the entire $5 million house that encloses it. However, it was much appreciated by the defendants. In a situation probably not covered by the etiquette books, Piro took Carolyn, her sister, her brother-in-law, and her secretary out for champagne and caviar afterward. Carolyn told Marge Crumbaker, the Houston gossip columnist, "Harold was very generous. After it was ended, we kissed and said goodbye. He's a wonderful man."

Helen Biggs Willingham is in a tizzy in the living room of her mother, Electra Waggoner Biggs. Her son has a rabbit project for the 4-H Club, but he's sick, so she has to go clean out the rabbit cages herself. It is obviously of no immediate importance to Helen that she stands to inherit a substantial portion of her mother's half share of the Waggoner Estate, a share estimated in 1982 by *Forbes* magazine at $150 million. (Mrs. Biggs's cousin Albert Buckman Wharton III owns the other half, and she notes tartly that he doesn't have any heirs to worry about allocating it to.)

Unlike Carolyn Farb, Electra Waggoner Biggs has had no struggle in attaining her fortune. That was taken care of more than a century ago. It is one of the classic Texas fortunes—the sort of production about which Edna Ferber outraged Texans by revealing it to the astonished outside world in *Giant*. In the beginning, in 1849, Dan Waggoner turned twenty-one in Oklahoma and inherited fourteen cattle, twelve sheep, one grey filly, sixteen pounds of wool, one rifle, $3.45 in cash, and 21½ acres of land. He moved south and settled in the Texas Panhandle during the 1850s, when the area was scarcely populated at all. After the Civil War, his son, W. T. Waggoner, drove enough cattle up the Chisholm Trail to come back with $55,000 in his saddlebags. For that you could get a great deal of land in northern Texas, or, for that matter, anywhere in Texas. Pursuing a policy of buying "only the land bordering mine," Tom Waggoner had by 1909 put together more than half a million acres of ranchland. That is something in the range of eight hundred square miles— twenty miles on one side and forty on the other, if it were rectangular. The ranch takes up most of Wilbarger County and large chunks of five counties round about. Before helicopters, the men would spend weeks camping out merely to take care of it. It still takes some four hundred ranchhands to run it, not to mention the engineers and laborers who run the oil operation; and most of them live there.

Needless to say, this is a major enterprise, employing professional managers to run it; R. B. Anderson, the general manager before John Biggs, Electra's late husband, left in 1953 to become secretary of the navy and then secretary of the treasury. Mrs. Biggs told a story to an interviewer: "Once I was driving home and took a shortcut. I drove on and on and it began to dawn on me that I didn't recognize anything at all. I started to call in to the ranch office on my car radio. But I decided I'm not going to admit to them I'm lost! So I drove on and flagged down a pickup truck that was coming toward me. I straightened myself up behind the wheel and, with all the dignity I could muster, said, 'Excuse me. I'm Mrs. John Biggs of the Waggoner Ranch and I think I am lost.' The fellow lifted his hat and scratched his head and said, 'Well, Mrs. Biggs, you're on your own property.' "

The Waggoner Ranch remains the largest piece of land within one fence in the United States, and perhaps in the world. (The King Ranch is bigger, but it is not all in one piece.) Now Electra Waggoner Biggs is heiress to half that land. It is about twelve miles to drive from Electra (named for her late aunt) to Vernon on Route 287, west from Wichita Falls and just south of the Oklahoma border. All the land to the south along that drive, a land of cattle and oil, is the Waggoner Ranch. From Vernon it is an eleven-mile drive south to the grand formal stone entrance to the Waggoner Ranch itself. And from there, Electra Biggs has one of the longest driveways in the world—a full four miles through workers' housing and immense stretches of well-groomed land for the cattle and horses and grain and all the other glories of the empire. (The banking adjunct is in the town of Vernon.) At the end of the road is Santa Rosa Ranch, Electra Waggoner Biggs's seat. The compound commands an artificial hillock that rises in a stately swell from the flatness of the surrounding ranch. The main house, a rambling structure roofed in red brick tile, is approached only through an impressive formal garden planted by Electra's mother; gleaming ponds and pools reflect the sylvan beauty at odd corners. And on the screen door of Santa Rosa Ranch, home of perhaps the richest woman in Texas, are pasted a block of decal bluebirds. A visitor wanders into the kitchen by himself until he runs across a cook, who yodels an alert to Mrs. Biggs in the living room.

That casualness of an immense fortune alongside a steadfastly just-folks approach is one of the hallmarks of Electra Waggoner Biggs. Indeed, it is one of the things that sets her apart from the Carolyn Farbs of the world. While virtually every rich person in the world mentions the names of the famous from time to time, there is less of an edge to Mrs. Biggs's mentions of Mary Martin and Ronald Reagan. She does not even sound boastful when she mentions that the Buick Electra and the Lockhead Electra are both named for her. Perhaps it only seems that way to an outsider, but the woman of immense inherited wealth speaks with more of a right than the upstart rich divorcée. She has a right hallowed by her ancestors' century of possession.

In the current generation, the Waggoner familiarity with money has gone to almost ludicrous lengths. Mrs. Willingham makes a thoroughly unprepossessing heiress: she is wearing jeans and Hush Puppies and a sort of bouffant Elvis Presley–girl friend hairdo that survives only in this nook of the great Southwest. Mother and daughter spend some time kicking around the tribulations of parenthood. When Electra Waggoner Biggs discusses her family, a little later, it is always with great affection and approval; as in most homes of the *dames* who preside over the world's great family fortunes, most available surfaces—especially, here, a piano the size of an aircraft carrier—are thick with the framed photographs of the extended family for generations. With some startling exceptions, the existence of family wealth is one of the great bonding forces in modern life. It doesn't necessarily keep siblings and other relatives friendly, but it does keep them close.

Still, one detects in Mrs. Biggs's references to her daughter an undertone of regret that Helen is not a little more—well, flashy. Electra Waggoner Biggs was once known as "the Doris Duke of Texas"; she went to Miss Wright's School on the Philadelphia Main Line ("I hated it; they were all snobs"), studied sculpture more or less by accident at Columbia and in Paris, then split her time for several years in the late 1930s between casting busts of celebrities and dabbling in nightclub life, occasionally popping up in the gossip columns. Her greatest moment of social glory occurred in 1933, when she married her first husband in St. Bartholomew's Episcopal church on Park Avenue in New York, and a memorable portrait of her by Steichen—a gamine face in an aureole above acres of flowing tulle—appeared as a full page in *Vogue*, which pronounced her "one of the most dramatic brides of the early summer." (The famous $10,000 lace veil she wore, which has since been worn by her daughters on their marriages as well, was a gift from Electra Waggoner I, her aunt, one of the wildest of the early princesses of Texas.) Electra II still enjoys the tea-and-charity circuit, dashing down to Houston in the company plane, for example, to stay in her private hotel suite and drop in on the wide circle of her friends. She is an inveterate world traveler: Florida, New York, and Hong Kong are regular stops on her rounds. Or she brings in ranches full of guests, especially at Christmastime. Mrs. Biggs also retains the guarded flirtatiousness of those brought up to be irresistible but careful at the same time—a particular necessity for rich girls, who constantly meet men who are after money as well as what they're always after.

No one could be less like Carolyn Farb than Helen Biggs Willingham. Electra's daughter apparently has no interest in the lunching-ladies circuit or international travel; her life is encompassed by the spacious boundaries of the Waggoner Ranch and the considerably more confining requirements of a husband and two children. Electra believes her daughter's fundamental shyness, her need to feel herself in comfortable surroundings, her unwillingness to extend herself, are all a product of being rich—of the resentments and cruelties children practiced on her daughter because of the privileged position they thought she was in. Helen herself does not seem to have much sense of being privileged; she would rather forget the whole thing. It is not an uncommon reaction among this generation's heiresses to the great fortunes of the world.

To be fair, while Electra Waggoner Biggs clearly enjoys the benefits of her great wealth, she seems to have retained her disdain for the "society" posturing she came to hate on the Main Line. In the marble ballroom the hushed airiness is relieved by very ordinary plastic flowers and Bic lighters on the marble tables. In the living areas, there are no immediate protestations of great wealth—no spiral staircase, no shuffling butler, no Matisses. A few profoundly plain plastic-covered chairs are scattered in no particular pattern. There are two autographed pictures of President Reagan on the television, conveniently placed for watching while Mrs. Biggs is just sitting around relaxing. (She gave Reagan one of her limited-edition casts of her tabletop version of her well-known sculpture, *Will Rogers*.) As in practically every rich woman's house ever created, the owner's portrait is hung above the mantelpiece. But the portrait is ordinary, the rugs are ordinary, the knickknacks on the shelves are ordinary—Mrs. Biggs is ordinary. Except that she happens to be one of the richest women in the world.

Of all the ways women acquire great wealth, by far the most common is to inherit it. It is also by far the most pleasant: Electra Biggs is one of the most self-assured, cheerfully relaxed people one would ever want to meet. Think in contrast to the anxieties

Carolyn Farb felt during the divorce suit, the talk about her social climbing. On the other hand, there is something to be said for the satisfaction of acquiring immense worldly goods oneself—and do not make the mistake of thinking that Mrs. Farb regrets making her millions "only" through divorce. We will see both kinds of women in this book, as well as the very few who actually possess such vast sums as these two through their own labors in the marketplace.

We will see differences between them, but most of all we will see that their lives have been profoundly affected by their money. It is there, a hovering presence, throughout the span of their lives. Even when Mrs. Biggs is ensconced in her studio, working purely for art and attention, she can hardly escape the physical presences that control her life much more profoundly than do any of the forms she will envision and then cast in metal. Everything in that view, all around the stretched-out horizon, is the Waggoner Ranch. There are rolling hills and scrub—but the most obvious features are the cattle and the oil pumps, both nodding ceaselessly through the unchanging season of moneymaking in Texas.

2 | Who Are They All, Anyway?

Scattered about all the great cities of the world, and in towns the size of Vernon (population, twelve thousand), are women who have made a great deal of money. A few have made it through their own efforts, but by far the bulk have done it by surviving, mainly by surviving rich men—although in some cases of the great family fortunes, such as the du Ponts's, women have become its main bearers. The biological fact that women in general live longer than men leads to the obvious conclusion that they will end up inheriting much of their men's wealth.[1] The predictable result of all that living is the effortless accumulation of great wealth by women, even though they are extremely un-

1. Moreover, it is a happy fact that women in this group live even longer than average. When Metropolitan Life Company studied the life expectations of prominent women—as defined by inclusion in *Who's Who in America* in 1964–65—it was found that women in that group had twenty-nine percent lower mortality than American women in the general population. Mortality among female business executives was seventy-four percent of that of their contemporaries in the general population.

likely to make large fortunes on their own. There does not appear to be any truth to the assertion that women own more than half of all the wealth in the United States; but they do own a great deal of it.

Rich women, as a whole, are older and richer and much more likely to be widowed than rich men—again, the logical result of the fact that men make money faster themselves and then die sooner than their women, presumably from the strain imposed by making it. A study by the Internal Revenue Service based on estate tax return samples for 1981 concluded that there were slightly more than twice as many men worth $500,000 as women—1.2 million men, 600,000 women. However, those women had a combined net worth of roughly $679 billion, while the men were worth $982 billion; that is, the richest group of women was worth over $1.1 million on average, while their male counterparts had approximately $800,000 apiece. Such figures tend to confirm the popular stereotype of the woman of wealth as being older and richer than the rich man. So does the 1981 finding that of the 4.5 million people in the United States worth more than $300,000, 28 percent of the women were widows, while only 4 percent of the men were widowers. And 40 percent of the men in that well-to-do class were under fifty years old, but only 29 percent of the women were.

That said, it is nevertheless true that in the United States, at least, the very pinnacle of wealth is occupied almost solely by men. Two daughters of the outrageous oil swashbuckler H. L. Hunt, Caroline Hunt Schoellkopf and Margaret Hunt Hill, are calculated by *Forbes* magazine to be the only American women with more than $1 billion to their names. Both of them got it by being born into the "first family" of Hunt, which, as we shall see, was an excellent illustration of the hazards and rewards of inheriting an entrepreneur's kingdom. By contrast, there were thirteen men on the 1983 *Forbes* list of the richest Americans worth upward of $1 billion (including two of the Hunt sisters' brothers, amounts that combine to make theirs one of the richest families in the world). The only other women who come remotely close to a ten-figure net worth are the Cox sisters of Atlanta—Barbara Anthony, and former ambassador to Belgium Anne Chambers, who between them own huge shares of the newspapers, television, and cable in Cox Enterprises, and are worth an estimated $1.2 billion altogether—and Jane Bancroft Cook, who is supposed to have the largest chunk of stock in Dow Jones

& Co., worth more than $600 million. Meanwhile, there are several dozen other men worth more than half a billion dollars.

Why should men own almost all the greatest fortunes in the United States, even while women millionaires tend to be considerably richer, on average, than rich men? One reason is that the rich women are almost all fairly old, meaning that their fortunes have had a chance to increase on their own; but on the other hand, they have almost always gotten their money through trust funds, which tend to be conservatively managed. Men of a comparable age are generally still heavily involved in seeking out profitable investments. They got very rich, in most cases, precisely by being adventurous; and if some of their new ventures fail, enough succeed handsomely to produce new centimillionaires every year. There are no women taking chances that compare with those of the great cowboys of the American economy: no sinking $1 billion into an Amazon jungle pulp-farming dream like Daniel K. Ludwig; nobody owning 41 percent of the stock in Wal-Mart discount stores like Sam M. Walton, the pride of Bentonville, Arkansas, who is now suddenly worth more than $2 billion. One can observe the sharp contrast between women's and men's handling of their wealth among the Hunts: Caroline put $250 million of her funds into super-luxurious hotels in Dallas, Houston, and Beverly Hills—safe bricks-and-mortar choices. She and Margaret both deliberately stayed out of the infamous attempt to corner the silver market that has left their two brothers, Nelson Bunker and W. H., paying off a $1 billion bailout loan. On the other hand, the brothers' management of Placid Oil and Hunt Energy is what has created the great boom in their own and their sisters' trusts.

Even more so than in the United States, the women of Europe and South America who are born into families of great wealth tend to have a merely passive role in the family fortune—although there have been some notable exceptions in recent years. For some reason, there are a number of examples of entrepreneurial women, both on their own and taking over from parental fortune-builders, in the Far East, particularly Hong Kong and Taiwan. Nevertheless, the tradition still holds that women outside the United States seldom acquire large fortunes, which tend to go to their brothers; and when they do inherit large sums, they seldom have any substantial say in how they are spent.

Part of the discrepancy in wealth between men and women is due to the fact that a fortune is generally attributed to the entrepreneur who made it, even though in fact his wife and family members, or various private investment companies, frequently own major portions of it for tax reasons. In these cases the women may or may not get money in case of a divorce; but they probably at least have access to a good deal of it while they are married. Further complications arise in the second and succeeding generations, when elements of ownership are broken up even more to conform to estate tax advantages. It is extremely difficult for an outsider to determine exactly who can put their hands on what in such cases—not that it matters much after the first few million.

Outside the United States, the question of personal wealth is even harder to deal with. No other nation has the public-disclosure laws or the mania for information about other people's wealth that obtains in the United States. In most places on the globe it is considered either infra dig, insulting, or dangerous to inquire into the source and extent of a person's wealth. Aside from matters of style or personal annoyance about inquiries, most countries, especially France and Italy, have made a national sport out of dodging the tax authorities. When David Harrop was researching his book *World Paychecks*,[2] he talked with a man in France who noted that his confidence in his banker's ability would suffer severely if he found the banker was so unskilled as to allow his income to become known to anyone.

Although this attitude of hushed privacy about money has been eroded by the populism and informality of the United States—and perhaps by the fierceness of the IRS—it still exists among many of the people who possess the bulk of the resources of the country. Like Mrs. Biggs, who notes that to inquire about how many head of cattle the Waggoner Estate runs is to ask how much money she is worth, Ruth Springer Wedgworth hesitates and makes the same sort of comment before she mentions how many acres of sugar-bearing land she owns in south-central Florida. The point that these facts are either a matter of public record or easily obtainable seems wasted on these people. To them it is a question of style. Money is a very private thing. The *Forbes* listing of the four hundred richest Americans, first published in 1982 and now apparently on its way to becoming an institution, drew cries of outrage from many quarters. Like Mrs. Biggs, those who had inherited money rather than making it themselves seemed

---

2. N.Y.: Facts on File, 1982.

particularly stung. Caroline Hunt Schoellkopf wrote to a friend, "An exercise such as *Forbes* indulged in is not only meaningless, but has the potential to be destructive—not only to the individuals so singled out, but also to the economic system. . . . I fear too many individuals visualize wealth as piles of idle money and possessions rather than . . . potential." Mrs. Schoellkopf's is typical of many rich people's approach to discussing their wealth: she is not embarrassed that she has it, but she doesn't want anybody talking about it. And the reason, of course, is not merely that it might cause her problems (presumably security threats and an inundation of begging letters), but that it is important for the wealth of nations that rich people be allowed to do what they want with their money without anyone commenting on it.[3]

The Richest Women in the World

Fifty-eight women made the 1982 *Forbes* listing of the four hundred richest individuals in the United States. Four of them—Mary Kay Ash, Mary Hudson, Estée Lauder, and Sarah Korein (a little-known dealer in Manhattan real estate)—made the money themselves, although the first three, at least, had considerable help from male members of their family. Four more—Georgia Rosenbloom Frontiere, Yoko Ono, Helen Kinney Copley, and Katharine Graham—could be said to have created, or at least to be operating, substantial fortunes of their own, though they did it by using money left to them by late fathers or husbands. The other fifty had it drop in their laps.

Much of the ownership of the world's riches lies still in the hands of those who have always had it—the nobility of Europe. There are, of course, plenty of exceptions. Europe is littered with the shells of dynastic fortunes; as Americans discovered in the late nineteenth century, the only worth of many coats of arms—all of which were once coexistent with feudal wealth—is to imprint on shoddy New World portfolios. Nevertheless, there remain great fortunes among the nobility. Foremost among them are the royal houses'. Queen Elizabeth of England and Queen Beatrix of the Netherlands are perennial contenders for the out-

3. Malcolm Forbes himself, publisher of the magazine, after siccing his staff on every other centimillionaire in the United States, refused to state his own net worth. "The IRS will estimate it one way, my heirs another," he noted. "I just don't know an accurate figure." (The *Wall Street Journal* put Malcolm Forbes's worth at $200 million; he said "that's a clue.")

right title of richest woman—or even richest human being—in the world. The *Guinness Book of World Records* lists Princess Wilhelmina Helena Pauline Maria of Orange-Nassau as "probably" the world's richest woman; she was queen of the Netherlands from 1890 until her abdication in 1948, and before she died in 1962 her wealth was estimated at more than $550 million. Other candidates for the title of outright richest woman in the world: Christina Onassis, Imelda Marcos, the Hunt sisters, and Princess Ashraf and the former Empress Farah Diba of Iran.

The royals are special cases, for there are difficulties distinguishing between their personal and state wealth. The personal inherited fortune of the royal family of the United Kingdom is estimated at £70 million, or about $100 million against the strong dollar; but that is essentially a meaningless estimate, for if any of the queen's personal possessions could be sold, the provenance would make them virtually priceless. The crown estates, jewels, art, yacht, train, general possessions, and investments, none of which could conceivably be sold, are certainly worth billions. In 1981, Queen Elizabeth was paid £286,000, while Princess Anne got £166,000, and Princess Margaret, £98,000. The queen also received £5,699,912 for the upkeep of the royal palaces and £11,635,000 toward running the yacht, train, and other conveyances—an indication of the huge worth of those items. Queen Beatrix has the usual castles, forty diamond tiaras, fourteen complete services in solid gold, and so on—all, again, literally priceless, for they will never be sold. She is also assumed to own privately a large portion of Royal Dutch Shell. In both cases, the families' huge fortunes and the pressures of public attention have led to classic aberrations among those closest to the throne. The marital and extramarital adventures of Princess Margaret, Queen Elizabeth's sister, have been well documented by the British press. Queen Beatrix herself had caused a storm when, as a young princess, she married a German commoner who had been a soldier in the war; protesters threw smoke bombs at the 1966 wedding. But she has managed to turn herself into a popular queen since she inherited the throne from her mother, Queen Juliana, in 1980. On the other hand, in 1981 her younger sister, Princess Irene, shucked off the obligations of the royal house by divorcing her husband of seventeen years and father of her four children, the Spanish Prince Carlos Hugo of Bourbon Parma; she also abandoned the royal palace of Soestdijk for a more modest villa across the street and does her own shopping in the village.

Demonstrating that royal wealth need not entail royal duties, the Greek royal family has managed to take one of the world's great monarchical fortunes with it into exile. King George I, who was shot in the street by a Turkish fanatic in 1913, had the good sense to keep his personal belongings separate from the royals' state property, and invested a great deal of it overseas. Consequently, the family now has huge real estate holdings all over the world. Moreover, they recently turned down an offer from the Greek government of $200 million for the palaces, estates, and crown jewels that have been held since their exile. Sharing in this potential bounty are a number of women. Princess Irene, sister of ex–King Constantine, lives discreetly in London, occasionally venturing out for a foray among the royalty-loving international glitter set. She has also appeared as a piano soloist with the London Philharmonic and a number of other orchestras on tour. Irene's sister, Sofia, is Queen of Spain, adding her portion of the Greek inheritance to the House of Bourbon. Their niece, meanwhile, Princess Alexia, also lives in England, where she is considering the study of political science at Cambridge.

Very likely the greatest fortune ever taken into exile, but one decked in mystery, is the remaining hoard of the royal family of Iran. Farah Diba conceded in 1983 that she is "still very rich," but she said she continues to struggle with money like everybody else. "I have to worry about bills, traveling, education, health, like any other housewife on a limited budget," she told the *London Sunday Telegraph*. "Of course wealth is relative, and compared to a lot of people, I'm still very rich. But nothing like many other people who don't have my responsibilities and problems." Much like Imelda Marcos and, earlier, Evita Perón, Farah Diba perceived a mission of creating a new and wonderful life for her people once she had managed to marry their monarch. She came from a highly influential and Westernized family—a lineage that did not endear her to the Iranian people—and was educated in Paris before she married the shah in 1959 and was crowned shahbanou. She plunged into the classic improvement projects of strong-minded women who marry strong men in the Third World. "My husband is interested in [Iran's] G.N.P.," she told a reporter. "I am interested in its G.N.H.—Gross National Happiness. . . . The only satisfaction I get out of my life at all is having my people love me. Being a queen, living in a palace, having jewels, mean absolutely nothing to me. It's having the confidence of the people that I care about."

Like her sister-in-law Farah Diba, Princess Ashraf was strenuously devoted to the "betterment"—which is to say, the Europeanization—of Iranian women during the Pahlavi family's time in Camelot. One of the first women in Iran ever to appear in public unveiled (in 1934), she turned into a memorable jet-setter; she was so daunting a manipulator that the French called her *La Panthère Noire* (the Black Panther), her brother exiled her from Iran at one point, and she was nearly assassinated in 1977 (her lady-in-waiting was killed instead in the attack on her Rolls-Royce on the French Riviera, proving once again the value of servants). Since the revolution, Princess Ashraf has been distressed about the reversion to Mohammedan ways in the country her family once ruled. "That breaks my heart," she told the *New York Times*. "I remember how fantastic our women were, how exactly like the European women they were, so well-educated, and now they are becoming so backward again. The Iranian woman is back in the home, and it makes me really unhappy." After the revolution, she retired to a lavish triplex apartment on New York's Park Avenue (previously owned by Charles Revson and Helena Rubinstein), breaking the monotony with occasional bodyguard-laden jaunts back to her house in Cannes.

Like Farah Diba, Princess Ashraf stoutly denies that she is worth much of anything. She says that she has heard rumors that the shah brought a hard-to-believe $75 billion out of Iran, and that she took out $3 billion. "But during this revolution, not one penny has been taken out," she said. "Whatever we had, we left behind. I left about $300 million behind, most of which I made selling land and from a resort in the north of Iran, which had two thousand villas. I became very rich selling land." She describes her current financial posture as "comfortable." The general assumption, however, is that both the widow and sister of the shah have indeed stashed away huge fortunes accumulated during the days of absolute rule in Iran. The *New York Times* has reported that in September 1978, while the Peacock Throne was going down the drain, Princess Ashraf sent a request to the Bank Melli of Iran requesting the transfer of fifty million rials (then $708,000) to her account in the Union Bank of Switzerland, using a code name, Sapia. In 1980, Ashraf admitted to $10 million in assets, but claimed that it was all going to the support of some fifty fellow refugees from Iran. She said she sold her house in Paris ("the one on the Riviera will be the last to go"), that she now buys dresses in boutiques instead of couturiers, and "maybe I'll be obliged to sell my jewels." (At last sighting, she was still wearing staggering emeralds on her fingers.)

The present government of Iran is suing the deposed royal family—Farah Diba, Ashraf, two other sisters of the late shah, a son, and his late mother—for $45 billion, and just as an aside they threw in a suit of $10 billion against the United States government. The claims against Ashraf amount to $3 billion; the Iranian government said in 1983 that it had located $7 million worth of property she owned and impounded it—town houses in New York and land in France and Spain. Another sister of the late shah, Shams Pahlavi, and her husband Pahlbod, were being sued for $6 billion and supposedly had $8 million worth of property impounded so far. Paul O'Dwyer, the former president of the City Council of New York, who has been the lawyer for the Ayatollah's government, says simply that the process of discovery in the lawsuits "will take years." "There are all kinds of crazy stories about what they own," he remarked. In the meantime, they own it. The suit was thrown out of New York courts in the middle of 1984.

In Madrid, one of the world's great inherited fortunes lies in the well-pedigreed and well-guarded vaults of María del Rosario Cayetana Fitz-James Stuart Silva y Falco, the Duchess of Alba. At least since the time of the Grand Duke of Alba—the military genius who managed to knit together, against the centrifugal pull of history, the scattered portions of the sixteenth-century empire of the Spanish Hapsburgs—the family has been one of the richest in Europe. Those who have toured the Liria Palace, the family's Madrid town residence, do not find that hard to believe. The Liria houses one of the great private art collections— and privacy is emphasized, for the family (there are six children) still lives throughout the twenty-two large chambers of the palace except for Saturdays, when thirteen rooms are opened to groups of thirty members of the public who have written ahead to request the privilege. The rooms are jammed with Titians, Fra Angelicos, Rembrandts, Rubenses, Velasquezes, the ship's log of Columbus's *Santa Maria*, and—the greatest pride of a household flush with pride—a Goya portrait of the thirteenth duchess, the great-great-grandmother of the present titleholder, which is much more discreet than the well-known portraits of the same woman (Goya was her lover) in the Prado that go by the names of the *Maja Vestida* and *Maja Desnuda*. Presiding over it all is an energetic, charming woman in her fifties who seems to bear lightly a string of titles that trail behind her like the fabulous trains of past wedding gowns: she is a duchess eight times over, a marquise eleven times, and a countess sixteen. The duchess is known as a socialite on the European circuit; when Henry Ford II in 1980 married his third wife, Kathleen DuRoss, after his scandalous breakup with his second, for example, the duchess threw them a ball when they came to Spain on their honeymoon. Her father is said to have spent $250,000 on her own first wedding. When that husband died, she became the first duchess of Alba to marry a former Roman Catholic priest. Much of Spain was not amused.

Susanna Agnelli, owner of nearly as august a name,[4] has chosen a very different path from the rich woman's rarified jaunt through parties and taste exemplified by the duchess. She has, in fact, engaged in so many different rich woman's careers that she is worth looking at in some detail. With her six siblings, she is heir to the massive Fiat empire. Under her brother Gianni, the current chairman, the firm founded by their grandfather has become the largest auto manufacturer in Europe and the largest private employer in Italy, meanwhile making Gianni into the richest man in the country, according to 1979 income tax figures there.[5] While her brother became what amounted to the David Rockefeller of Italy, in both personal riches and national clout, Miss Agnelli lived in New York in the early 1970s after her divorce from Count Urbano Rattazzi. "Marriage is a very, very difficult thing," she told an interviewer.

But among the taffeta and smiles Marion Javits, wife of the

4. She found out what "nearly" meant when her sister, Clara, married an Austrian noble. Miss Agnelli relates in her 1975 autobiography, *We Always Wore Sailor Suits*, that the man, Tassilo von Fürstenberg, was distinctly concerned about his children's place in the Almanach de Gotha after he married a commoner and had to be assuaged with the assurance that one of Clara Agnelli's grandfathers was a prince. At the wedding, Susanna writes, "the Austrian side was a shimmer of furs and colors and decorations all over their chests and around their necks, the Agnelli side dismally black."

5. Gianni Agnelli's taxable income that year, according to the Milan weekly *Il Mondo*, was the equivalent of $1.12 million. That is small potatoes among American millionaires, not to mention Arabs. Perhaps it is all being reinvested, or perhaps Fiat had a terrible year.

former senator from New York, perceived that her friend Suni Agnelli, as Susanna is known, "never really was a part of fashionable New York," she told the *New York Times*. "She entertained it, but she never really felt it. Once I got to know her I felt she had layers of depths and understanding about life and people and their needs that should be used intelligently. Somewhere deep down, she felt she needed to serve." In fact, Suni Agnelli's need to serve was not that deeply buried. Her autobiography reveals a woman of deep—one would say European intellectual—reflective bent; tellingly, it goes only to the end of World War II and is full of remarks that are normally off the public record among the kiss-on-both-cheeks set. She remarks, for example, that when she came back from boarding school in England, she happened to wander into brother Gianni's room "and I saw that he had become a man." She relates in detail how she became the house naïf when, as a nurse in a military hospital, she would gullibly go from one patient to the next at their request to examine a "scar," which would always turn out to be "an astonishing erection." She and her siblings grew up in a swirl of governesses and footmen and a sort of *Last Year At Marienbad* formality in Turin, grandchildren of the founder of Fiat and therefore among the first families of Italy. Miss Agnelli appears to have never given a thought to her wealth; it was simply there, like the crystalline Mediterranean off Monte Carlo where they spent their summers. Reading her reflections, one gets a distinct impression of the difference between American society and European at the time; while the most aristocratic of American millionaires spent most of their waking hours coming to terms with their money one way or another, among the Agnellis there seems to have been no mulling it over at all. Of course, there was the fundamental understanding that the daughters in the family would not have any control whatsoever over the fortune.

Susanna's father, the sole heir to the Fiat empire, was killed in a freak seaplane accident in 1935. Her mother, Virginia, thirty-five and beautiful at the time, quickly took as a lover an anti-Fascist named Malaparte, who was editor of *La Stampa*, a newspaper owned by the grandfather. This did not sit well with the grandfather at all. He obtained a court order from the compliant police giving him custody of the children. When the mother put them on a train to Rome to try to get Mussolini to overturn the order, police took them off and sent the mother on alone.

Nevertheless, she got the children back by appealing personally to the dictator. During the war, Susanna spent much of her time on hospital ships plying the bloody waters of the Mediterranean. Toward the end, she and her brother Gianni were involved as partisans in a complex game, at one point slipping past German guards from Switzerland into Italy, at another getting Gianni's broken ankle repaired in a pitifully underequipped hospital with Susanna acting as anesthesiologist. At the same time, Miss Agnelli was drifting through the sort of unhappy love affair that all parents warn their rich daughters about. Raimondo Lanza, a devastatingly handsome *avventuriero* who was at one time a fighter for the Republicans in Spain, at another an aide to a Fascist general, was her rather bizarre choice. Confirming all the stereotypes from *La Dolce Vita*, the young heiress lived through a succession of embarrassing scenes that she discussed freely in her autobiography, such as this one:

> Galeazzo came in, sat down next to me, and put his arm around my shoulder. I was rather embarrassed. He told me that Raimondo had quite lost his head over this girl and that I had better forget him.
> Then Galeazzo asked me, "Forgive my being indiscreet, but were you Raimondo's mistress? I mean, did he make love to you?"
> I was horrified, even though I knew that he was trying to be kind. "Raimondo is Sicilian," I answered, "he wants to marry a virgin."
> "Ahh," he breathed with relief, "then it's not so bad. Raimondo is a gentleman. I take my hat off to him."
> I left, walked across the Piazza to a cafe, went to the bathroom and vomited.
> Feelings didn't matter. It was virginity that mattered and Roman society could feel noble again.

Miss Agnelli nevertheless put up with the profoundly crass Raimondo for the rest of the war, until she met her future husband, moved to Argentina, and settled into a life as mother of six children. After they were divorced, she moved into international society in New York. In that whirl of glitter and goodness, she found the rich woman's calling—Doing Something for the People. "What I saw . . . living there from 1970 to 1974 made politics seem worthwhile," she says. "Americans are very community-minded. They all do something for their society."[6] There had been portents even before the fling in New York that Miss Agnelli was not cut from the same cloth as the average frivolous lady who lunches; she had visited North Vietnam on a nursing mission and wrote a widely noticed article in 1969 predicting that the United States would lose the war. She was undeterred by the fact that politics is even less a female avocation in Italy than in the United States, which is perhaps accounted for by the theory that women are smart enough to save themselves from the slough of what passes for government in Italy. Miss Agnelli entered politics out of anger at the "ugly illegal houses" that were defacing the beauty of her retreat in the town of Monte Argentario, along Tuscany's fashionable Costa d'Argento, and was elected mayor in 1974. Activity proved addictive. She was elected to the Italian Senate, served in the European Parliament, and started writing an advice column in the magazine *Oggi*. In 1983, she became under secretary of state for foreign affairs, and her transformation into the Millicent Fenwick of the Mediterranean was complete.

If she showed more initiative than likely for an Italian woman of her era and background, Suni Agnelli is true to her heritage in her political convictions. She is a member of the small, centrist Republican party, which she says represents "clean" government, in contrast to the corruption of the ruling Christian Democrats. She is a practicing Catholic and believes that the church is a functional institution, a unifying force in that fractious country. At the same time, she manages to pull in huge majorities from three different constituencies around the country, and keeps getting reelected mayor by the mostly Communist residents of Monte Argentario, despite her poisonous name. That is an upset on the order of—well, on the order of a Rockefeller being elected

6. As we will see in more detail later, the fashion of sponsoring charitable affairs is a distinctly American one. "Society" in Europe, and even more in South America, has continued to be hedonistic to an extent that went out of fashion in the United States with the excesses of the first flush of capitalist accumulation at the turn of the century. (Indeed there have been exceptions like Barbara Hutton and Doris Duke; but both of them spent a great deal of their time and money in Europe, and Hutton, at least, had a widely unknown streak of philanthrophy.) The great rich-girl's pastime of hosting parties for diseases and museums grew up in, and is still largely confined to, the United States. It has generally not been bred into the European and South American hostesses, but picked up when they jet in and out of New York. As Suni Agnelli notes, some of this is due to the fact that the United States is the only country that allows income-tax deductions for charitable contributions. See Chapters 22 and 23.

governor of New York. "My big campaign argument was that I will do what is best for the country, not the party. Everybody listens to that," says Suni Agnelli in her best high-minded reformer manner. And there is another reason that the people trust her, she believes: "They know I'm not going to steal."

Suni Agnelli is a tall, strong-looking woman with a distinctly non-Italian briskness—a heritage of her English governess—who has combined fortune and the self-confidence that comes with it into a position of power. Her distinguished air is not hampered by the overlay of a British accent on her continental English. Yet she speaks softly and believes other women could profit by her example. She thinks that Italian women are both too aggressive ("people tend to get a bit frightened by an aggressive woman") and "too lazy" to succeed in politics. (She disdains their inability to support a career and still have dinner on the table for their traditionalist husbands.) Though she realizes that her male colleagues are not about to let her make an important political speech, she does not consider that unfairness—nor her youthful suffering at the hands of men—sufficient cause for feminism. "I think feminists always have an aggressive attitude and never have a balanced vision of things," she says. "Of course, men are not simply going to let you have things just because you are a woman. You have to work for it." In fact, it is Suni Agnelli's sturdy bolster of wealth that has allowed her the balanced perspective. It is that condition that makes her different from her compatriots, and ranks her with the international order of wealthy women.

One could hardly leave Europe without mentioning another of the great rich and noble families, the Rothschilds. The women of the current generation have generally confined themselves to a decorative role, happy to grace the openings of their friends' couture showings. None has played a significant role in governing the family's octopus of a fortune, but Baroness Philippine de Rothschild, who lives in Paris, does take a hand in the management of the dynasty's Château Mouton-Rothschild vineyards.

Christina Onassis has a lot in common with other immensely rich women—only more so. Like Nabila Khashoggi, she has a yacht named after her—her late father Ari's 325-foot cruiser. Like the wives of Harry Helmsley and Joseph Hirshhorn, she has made her most recent marriage only after her husband successfully insisted on a weight loss. Like Barbara Hutton and many other too-much-too-soon types, she has been battered by the telltale signs of the loneliness of the top: shattered marriages, general restlessness and uncertainty. But since Christina is so much wealthier than any of them, and perhaps just because she is Greek, her story has a superhuman intensity that makes it a leading candidate for an operatic treatment.

Where should one put the emphasis? On Christina's birth to Tina Livanos, who was herself the heiress to a shipping fortune, married a shipping tycoon in Onassis, and then, after an interval with a British peer, married his bitter rival Stavros Niarchos? On her position as an idolized daughter who nevertheless found herself competing first with Maria Callas and then with the despised Jacqueline Kennedy? On the death of the adored elder brother, Alexander, in 1973, which made it clear that Christina, then twenty-three, would inherit the bulk of the immense fortune her father had built? On the symptoms of the rootlessness that all produced—the pills, the haunted look, the bulbous weight, the three failed marriages?

Perhaps one had best just concentrate on the money. When Onassis died in 1975, Christina inherited half his estate, a share estimated at $400 million at the time; the remainder went to a foundation. She also got control of the business decisions of Olympic Maritime, the corporate umbrella over the tanker fleet. After taking care of the emotionally charged personal business— settling financially with her mother and with Jackie—Christina took on the high-stakes tanker game with a vengeance. Reports coming out of the boardrooms of oil companies like British Petroleum and Royal Dutch Shell indicated that she moved in with Amazonian determination to inform men thirty or forty years her senior that from that point on they could damn well deal with her. In the unsettled wake of the Arab oil embargo and the consequent worldwide recession, however, the tanker business was a giant crap game. Christina won one throw when she impulsively flew to Moscow against the advice of her father's inner circle of advisers, and came away not only with a prescient agreement to rent the Russians five bulk carriers for three years, but also, extraordinarily enough, a Russian lover and future husband—Sergei Kauzov, head of Sovfracht, the shipping agency. Before the world knew about Kauzov, Christina had put aside her seemingly appropriate but actually untenable second mate, shipping heir Alexander Andreadis, and declared, "I'm through with marriage and romance. I won't let anything stand in the way of running my business now. That's the one goal in my life."

Not likely. Soon gossipmongers were treated to the spectacle of one of the world's richest capitalists marrying an important Communist—an alliance that produced some stomach upset among intelligence agencies in the West. Fortunately for them, Christina had little time to unburden herself of significant secrets before she deserted cheerless Moscow four days after the wedding in favor of golden Skorpios. When she divorced Kauzov in 1980, however, she endowed him with a tanker as a parting present. That was indicative of how her much-bandied seriousness about the business had waned as she grew into her late twenties. While staying in touch with the panel of advisers and not doing anything foolish, she increasingly took emotional refuge on Skorpios, and other landfalls within yachting distance, from the consistent series of disasters in her emotional life. The downward spiral accentuated when Jean-Jacques Cornet-Epinat, her entertainment on the rebound from Kauzov, died in a fall from a polo pony in 1980 (an accident that only rich girls have to worry about). The Aegean life was a series of revels—sleeping till noon, world-class eating, and champagne-drenched dancing into the night.

And then, finally, came the man for whom she would make the ultimate sacrifice, losing weight: Thierry Roussel, heir to a French pharmaceutical fortune of some $100 million. The decision to abandon the world of business and let him take over the reins was doubtless made easier by the rapid fading of the Onassis fleet, together with the nearly $60 million settlement she made in 1983 with the Greek government over her father's estate. Christina, now, wants a daughter more than she wants her business clout. She still gets telex reports from the advisers in the couple's hideaways in Paris, St. Moritz, and Skorpios. And the advisers never forget to send the dividend checks of millions a year. Which is just as well, because all Christina herself wants now, she tells people, is "to take care of our home, and have a family, as Thierry wants."

A fortune founded first on frozen whitefish in central Manitoba, and then on cutthroat bootlegging during Prohibition, the Bronfman empire is a television miniseries of a family saga that sweeps across continents and trumpets forth the inspiring truth that money can, indeed, buy respectability, at least in the third generation. The two daughters of "Mr. Sam" Bronfman, the man who ran the world's largest liquor business (sales now approaching $3 billion a year) until his death in 1971, illustrate very neatly the uses to which incredible wealth can be put when it comes time to do something with one's life. Both of them have large interests in the family business—hundreds of millions of dollars apiece, which places them among the wealthiest of heiresses anywhere on the globe—and both take some more-or-less-active role in Cemp, the trust organization that administers the family's personal holdings.

The eldest of the two, Phyllis, a divorcée now in her middle fifties, lives a somewhat Bohemian life on the three floors of a converted peanut factory in the old quarter of Montreal. There she sleeps in the loft, rents out part of the ground floor, and works quietly in a studio decorated with her toy-car collection and her "Stop the Seal Hunt" buttons. With a staff of eight assistants, she is carrying on her private effort to catalogue the old city's architecture. This brings her into constant conflict with the Viger Commission, the official body responsible for the area's development. In the sort of ironic shift that we will see again and again among the very rich, Phyllis Bronfman has turned into the champion of the rights of the poor and downtrodden of the area, charging the Viger Commission with the "elitist" intention of turning *Vieux Montréal* into a tourism money-maker at the expense of the area's inhabitants. The members of the Viger Commission have constantly, and understandably, screamed about the injustice of one of the world's richest women calling them elitists.

Phyllis's little sister Minda makes no bones about what side her sympathies lie on. With the sort of single-minded devotion to familial duty that all rich parents pray for, Minda unearthed a young man named Baron Alain de Gunzburg on a blind date while he was studying at the Harvard Business School. Talk about natural matches: the de Gunzburgs were genuine, if remote, relatives of the Rothschilds, among the few real Jewish aristocrats, and the possessors of their own series of august private banking interests in France. Not only did the baron's personal wealth guarantee that he was not a dreaded fortune hunter, and not only did his family title add the dash of class that the Bronfman's humble beginnings had prevented in Mr. Sam's day, but his own business training made him a valuable ally in such business adventures as Seagram's complicated acquisition of G.

H. Mumm & Cie and Champagne Perrier-Jouët in 1963. The nice Jewish girl from Montreal with the degree from Smith, the master's in history from Columbia, and the dutiful apprenticeship in the workaday world as a sixty-dollar-a-week researcher at *Time* magazine now revolves in the tight and nearly invisible cosmos of the Parisian *haut monde*—shopping for designer originals, hosting parties that attract leading aristocrats and politicians, dining at the fabulous restaurants of the Right Bank, and drifting through the lazy summers aboard Alain's yacht in the Mediterranean. She has, in short, achieved heiress nirvana.

In the United States—perhaps in the world—the most lavishly rich dynasty ever created is the du Pont family. The two main branches of the family seem to be worth something in the range of $20 billion altogether—a sum sufficient to buy outright most countries in the world. The family fortune began, as all fans of fortune-building know, with French munitions-makers. They came to Delaware somewhat before the American Revolution, founded E. I. du Pont de Nemours & Company to manufacture gunpowder, survived several nasty explosions endemic in those experimental days, converted from Catholicism to the Episcopal faith, did even better during the Civil War, made a huge fortune in World War I (one-fourth of all the munitions expended were manufactured by Du Pont), and then further expanded the fortune by buying into General Motors. Even after two hundred years of fecundity, resulting in thousands of present-day du Ponts, the fortune is large enough to make literally hundreds of the family millionaires—and many of them much more than millionaires.

According to *Forbes*, no fewer than seventeen of the fifty-eight women in the United States worth more than $100 million in 1982 were du Ponts. The du Pont women have not, in general, achieved much; they are the classic examples of women who marry to carry on the family fortune. Until the most immediate generation, when Irving Shapiro became chairman of the Du Pont Company, there had never been a chief executive who was not either born into the family or married into it. (Irenée du Pont, Jr., broke the string, retiring as a senior vice-president and saying, "I as a stockholder would have objected to me as president.") To take one branch of the family: Margaretta Lammot du Pont married Crawford H. Greenewalt, who became president of the Du Pont Company from 1948 to 1962; her sister Marianna's husband, Henry H. Silliman, was vice-president of the family-owned brokerage house that handled their mutual funds; another sister, Octavia, is married to a director of the family bank, Wilmington Trust. The daughters of that particular branch of the family—seven of them altogether—were so famous for their dynastic impulses that the familiar saying in Delaware was, "All Irenée's daughters ever did was marry." The family continues in its centuries-old tradition of bearing large broods—so much so that on New Year's Day, known as Calling Day in du Pont circles, everyone now has to wear name tags to ensure recognition when the male cousins greet the women with candy and flowers.

An interesting variation on the marrying-for-managers theme has occurred among the current du Ponts, with Elise R. W. du Pont. She was married for quite a while to Pierre S. du Pont IV, who became governor of Delaware for two terms, before anybody realized she was going to break out of the mold of du Pont wives. When she finished bearing four children, she raced through law school at the University of Pennsylvania, then dashed off to Washington—aided, no doubt, by her close working relationship with one of the nation's most respected Republican governors—to take a job as assistant administrator of the Agency for International Development. This involved being chief of the Bureau of Private Enterprise. Appropriately, that bureau works to promote capitalism in Third World countries. After three years of exporting capitalism, Mrs. du Pont resigned to run for Delaware's seat in Congress, which her husband held from 1971 to 1977. In the mold of Pierre, who asked to be called Six-Pack Pete, Elise announced she was running a "people's campaign." But not enough of the people were interested, and she lost a narrow decision in 1984.

Anyone with the remotest sense of the workings of the modern world can recite the names of the great dynasties in the United States: the Vanderbilts, the Whitneys, the Rockefellers, the Mellons, the Astors. And in the rest of the world: the Rothschilds, the Guinesses, the Thyssens, the Agnellis, the Matarazzos. In many of those families, the critical link in creating a dynasty is the women; they are the bearers of the family tradition and the immediate cause of there being any heirs. Perhaps the richest of all the heiresses of great dynastic fortunes is Cordelia Scaife May, the granddaughter of Richard Beatty Mellon, who inherited more than $200 million from her mother in 1965, which has since grown to more than $400 million. She is also one of the most horrific examples of the disintegration of a dynasty. "Cordie" May now lives in a house called Cold Comfort outside Pittsburgh, a reflection on her brief marriage to socialite Herbert A. May, Jr., and her later one to Robert W. Duggan, one of the strangest men ever to be district attorney of a large city.

Mrs. May had a conventional upbringing, within the context of Pittsburgh society, where, needless to say, her family background guaranteed her a major role. Educated at Foxcroft, then Carnegie Tech and the University of Pittsburgh, she married May when she was twenty-one. Workmen spent two weeks putting the Scaifes' Penguin Court into shape for a wedding that the *Pittsburgh Press* said "far outshone" a competing nuptial at the King Ranch in Texas. The marriage was dissolved within six months—without public notice; Cordie continued to use her married name whenever she did anything in public, which became increasingly rare. Her only significant public appearance in recent years was her wedding in Nevada in 1973 to "Dixie" Duggan. Duggan had grown up in the Mellons' Rolling Rock Hunt Club circle; his father ran a major ice dealership in Pittsburgh and built up a 240-acre estate in Ligonier, the tony exurb for Mellons and Heinzes.

Cordelia's brother Richard Mellon Scaife was Duggan's treasurer in his successful reelection campaign for district attorney of Allegheny County. When Duggan's chief detective, Sam Ferraro, was jailed for contempt of court in an investigation into protection rackets, Richard requested that Duggan supply him with a list of the people who had contributed the $10,000 in cash that Duggan passed on to the campaign treasury. The names were phony. Shortly after federal investigators subpoenaed Cordie's financial records, she married Duggan; a wife cannot be forced to testify against her husband. Seven months later, as Ferraro began talking to a grand jury, Duggan put a double-barreled shotgun to his chest and pulled the trigger. Since the tragedy, Cordelia May has lived quietly, putting her fortune to work through her Laurel Foundation, whose main interest is zero population growth. She works very hard at it, meanwhile maintaining a nearly phobic dislike of personal publicity. Her attorney's letter in response to a request for an interview stated: "Mrs. May is indeed committed, as you put it, to certain 'progressive social causes,' principally human overpopulation, and she is as willing as the next person to expound her views in any forum where their expression might be expected to do some good. I hope, however, that you will not be offended when I tell you that we have in the past had mixed success in dealing with reporters and writers of books, too many of whom turn out (despite many protestations to the contrary) to be more interested in gossip, scandal, net worth and lifestyle than in a serious discussion of viewpoints on important social issues." Mrs. May certainly does know her media. She did not agree to an interview.

Cordie's cousin, Cassandra Mellon Milbury, has a $100 million–plus share in family trusts, which she puts to work in philanthropy and civic affairs. Another cousin, Catherine Mellon Conover, has half a share in an estimated $250 million trust fund. She is an active environmentalist, but her chief claim to fame is as a former wife of John Warner, the senator from Virginia who later married Elizabeth Taylor.

There are always the Rockefellers. Eight Rockefeller women are among the top four hundred on the *Forbes* list: three daughters of John D. Rockefeller III; two daughters of Nelson Rockefeller's first marriage; the daughter of Nelson and John D. Rockefeller III's sister; and two sisters who are great-great-granddaughters of the first and most infamous John D. Rockefeller. They are a strange bunch. John D. III's daughter, Sandra Ferry, dropped her last name in 1959; once she tried to give away her entire inheritance, but discovered she couldn't; since then she has lived as a recluse in Cambridge, Massachusetts, her only regular visitors being a psychiatrist and a music therapist. Family lore has it that she once spent five years recovering from a broken toe. Her sister Hope lives quietly in Woodstock, Vermont, after a career as a feminist writer in New York. Alida, much the youngest and possibly the most sensitive of the three sisters, went from a standard rich girl's career as a charity worker and producer of television documentaries in California to a marriage to the rich (though not as rich as she) and ambitious Mark Dayton, who spent the most money ever on a senatorial campaign—more than $5 million—but still lost his bid to be elected from Minnesota in 1982. Alida lives quietly with their children, answers her own phone, and has resisted personal publicity except when her husband's campaign advisers demanded she submit to an interview.

Their two female cousins in Nelson's family have reacted sharply against their father's exuberance. Ann, the eldest daughter, was the quietest child; she spent time as a social worker in the East

End of London, then the Bronx, later bore four children and married a husband with four more. Mary married Thomas B. Morgan, once an aide to New York City mayor John V. Lindsay and later, writing in *Esquire*, an inexhaustible opponent of her father, then governor of New York. Each of them is worth something in the range of $150 million in intertwined trusts set up by their grandfather and controlled by the family office in Rockefeller Center. Like all the cousins—the children of the brothers, the male grandchildren of John D. Rockefeller—they have spent much of their conscious lives struggling with the problems of the rich. In the case of the Rockefellers, those problems are compounded by the family's nearly insane insistence on public service to overcome the stigma of the gains ill gotten a hundred years ago. Less directly burdened by those concerns, no doubt due in part to the fact that they do not bear the Rockefeller name, are Laura Simpson O'Neill and Abby Rockefeller Simpson, the two daughters of Marilyn Milton Simpson and great-great-grandchildren of the first John D. Rockefeller, who also are worth $150 million apiece in family trusts. Both around thirty, they have not yet gotten their names in the papers. Apparently not troubled at all—she lives a classic big-house, big-family, big-charity life in Oyster Bay, Long Island—is Abby Milton O'Neill, who appears to be doing all those proper things in reaction to her mother, Abby Rockefeller Mauzé, who *was* strange.

Scattered among the richest people are other heiresses to great American fortunes. Doris Duke is quietly and rather strangely living out the life of a poor little rich girl on her estate in Somerville, New Jersey, still worth some $250 million. Not far away, in Far Hills, is Jane Engelhard, widow of Charles Engelhard, the "Platinum King" who had the dubious distinction of having the Ian Fleming villain Goldfinger modeled after him, and who left her some $250 million upon his death in 1971. Josephine C. Ford lives as a suburban housewife in Grosse Pointe, Michigan. As one of the three surviving grandchildren of *the* Henry Ford, she has something like $150 million worth of stock in the family business. Even more determinedly housewifely are the two granddaughters and heiresses of John Thompson Dorrance, who founded the Campbell Soup Company: Marie Hill Hamilton, known as Dodo, stoically graces stodgy Main Line parties and benefits and runs a little shop near her home selling house furnishings. Her sister Hope Hill van Beuren also ran her own shop until recently, selling dresses near her home in Middletown, Rhode Island, and has said, "I'm just a regular American housewife; I raised my children." Each of them is worth at least $130 million.

Similarly wealthy is Anne Phipps Sidamon-Eristoff, who also inherited the substantial remainders of a nineteenth-century fortune, this one created by her grandfather Henry Phipps, a steel baron. Helen Clay Frick, the daughter and sole heir of "Coke King" Henry Clay Frick, was ninety-six at her death in 1984; she made most of her public appearances in "Letters to the Editor" columns, defending her father against slurs on his sainthood. Phoebe Hearst Cooke was the force behind her family's successful struggle to regain control of father William Randolph Hearst's publishing empire from the hired hands who wanted to hang onto it after his death. Each of the five Annenberg sisters owns 9 percent of *their* father's publishing conglomerate (*TV Guide, Seventeen, Daily Racing Form*), worth about $125 million each, which they have managed to hold onto through waves of unsuccessful marriages. Suzanne Searle Dixon is the inactive owner of something over $300 million worth of stock in G. D. Searle & Company, the drug manufacturers, founded by her great-grandfather. Four women who were the illegitimate children of H. L. Hunt until he married their mother have successfully grabbed a total of about $700 million worth of the incredibly fecund oil-based estate.

Jane Cox MacElree is rich from Dow Jones & Co.—not *as* rich as Jane Bancroft Cook, but rich. So are Bettina Bancroft and Kathryn Bancroft Kavadas, each with a one-fourth share in trusts worth $600 million. Dominique de Menil inherited some $200 million from her father, who founded the oil-supplies company Schlumberger Ltd., and has used it to buy a $75 million collection of modern art in Houston. Dolly Green, Liliore Green Rains, and Burton Green Bettingen are three quiet Los Angeles sisters who came out of obscurity with a vengeance when in 1979 Shell Oil bought their late father's company, Belridge Oil, for $3.65 billion. Burton celebrated by paying $5 million for the recently deceased John Wayne's house on the water in Newport Beach. Anne Windfohr Sowell is unusual among heiresses in that she got it from her *mother*, Anne Burnett Tandy, who had accumulated her pile by judicious marriages (four altogether) into ranching, oil, and banking fortunes in Texas. Marion MacMillan Pictet and Margaret Cargill are both flush with the substantial remnants of the Cargill

Inc. grain-trading operation. Ruth Chandler von Platen and Alice May Chandler Goodan are both ancient children of Harry Chandler, who built the Times Mirror Company in Los Angeles. Virginia McKnight Binger got her $125 million grubstake from her father, William McKnight, who founded the 3M Company in Minneapolis. So that's how you do it the easy way: just pick your parents right.

Inheriting It from Your Husband

Somewhat more difficult, but the only way to fly for those who have already failed to be born properly, is to marry money and then inherit it. This is by no means an automatic proposition, of course. Prenuptial agreements have come out of the closet even for those without much to disagree over, and many rich men's lawyers are strong advocates of the practice. For reasons of both taxes and prudence, trust funds are a great favorite among this sector of the economy; when they are in effect, of course, the widow of a rich man has nothing to say about the disposition of the money and may not even see any income. For an object lesson, simply examine how hard Jacqueline Kennedy had to struggle to ensure herself an adequate living after she was widowed. Thus, there are far fewer women among the very rich who have married their way into wealth than have been born into it. But when it is done right, it is a thing of beauty ranking somewhere up there with a well-turned pivot on a double play.

"You don't get dumber by learning something," observed Janni Spies, who in 1984, at the age of twenty-one, headed back to tenth grade—an easily digestible provision of the will that left her more than $110 million, quickly making her one of the richest women in Europe, and, by acclamation, the second lady of Denmark after Queen Margrethe. In two years, she will come into full possession of the charter-travel empire built by her husband, Simon Spies, who pawned a ring in 1955 to take his first group of twenty-five people to Mallorca. Janni, an elegant Dane—aren't they all?—left high school when she was sixteen to become a message girl in Spies's company for $200 a month. Her ultimate employer was a one-time hippie who, before he found joy and stability with Janni, was known for his entourage of secretaries and his predilection for short marriages. Luckily for Janni, he died after one year of their marriage, at the age of sixty-two, before she became another statistic.

Betsey Cushing Whitney has turned the marrying-right trick to perfection and is now reaping her reward. She and her two sisters were legendary beauties who came storming out of Boston—they were the daughters of the noted brain surgeon Harvey Cushing—to put together the greatest marrying act of the twentieth century. One sister, the late Babe, married William Paley, the founder and still grey eminence of CBS.[7] Betsey married John Hay "Jock" Whitney, the remarkable rich boy, sportsman, diplomat, movie producer, newspaper owner (*New York* and *International Herald Tribune*), and general all-around important person. A third sister, Mary ("Minnie"), was married in 1940 to Vincent Astor, then publisher of *Newsweek* and heir to his family's fur, then real estate, fortune. (Vincent could not believe it when she asked for a divorce in 1952, convinced as he was that anyone would always want to be Mrs. Astor; "she must be mad," he told a friend. He gave her the divorce anyway.) Betsey married Jock on his rebound from Liz Altemus, the deb of her era, one of the outstanding horsewomen of the twentieth century and still a fixture on the Palm Beach circuit. Betsey had already given indications of her social and financial ambition through her brief first marriage, which was to James Roosevelt, eldest son of President Franklin D. When Jock died in 1982, Betsey inherited virtually all of his side of the family fortune. The Whitneys built subways in New York when such things actually made money; they also put money into oil, tobacco, real estate, and lumber, and more recently into movies, newspapers, and art. Mrs. Whitney lives now on their estate, Greentree, in Manhasset, Long Island, a five-hundred-acre spread. *Forbes* says she is worth at least $275 million.

It is in the nature of inheritances that heiresses are constantly waiting in the wings. For example, Jock Whitney's brother, Cornelius Vanderbilt "Sonny" Whitney, is still alive and hearty—in fact, he goes to work most days in his Whitney Industries office on Fifth Avenue—but he is well into his eighties, and even Whitneys do not last forever. His wife, Marylou, whom Whitney met

7. Paley's first wife was Dorothy Hart, who before him was married to Jack Hearst, one of the wastrel sons of William Randolph Hearst.

while he was producing a movie called *Missouri Traveler* in 1959 and she was playing in it opposite Lee Marvin, will no doubt be a capable successor, for Marylou Whitney is nearly as remarkable a person as her celebrated husband. (Sonny Whitney has been an internationally known polo player; a major breeder of thoroughbreds; a pilot in World War I, officer in World War II, assistant secretary of the air force and under secretary of commerce; a producer of *Gone with the Wind* and *Rebecca*; the founder of Pan American Airways and a participant in its first flights to South America and the Pacific; a founder also of Marineland, in Florida, and of Hudson Bay Mining and Smelting.) When Marylou was eighteen, she started her own show for servicemen, "Private Smiles," on a radio station in her native Kansas City. She toured Army and Navy camps with plays, then after the war wrote radio serials in New York. In 1948, Marylou Schroeder married Frank Hobbs Hosford, an heir to the John Deere tractor fortune, and quickly had four children. When that marriage broke up, she moved to Arizona, where she hosted a five-days-a-week television interview show and sold real estate. She also kept her social credentials alive and growing in the unlikely environs of Phoenix: at one point she helped Zsa Zsa Gabor to stash away Porfirio Rubirosa, "the prince of playboys," while he was running around with Zsa Zsa on the side during his short-term marriage to Barbara Hutton.

Approaching sixty, Marylou Whitney remains a dervish of activity. As her personal press package puts it, "Keeping one household together is more than enough work for most women, but watching over seven houses scattered around the world [in Manhattan, Saratoga, the Adirondacks, Lake Placid, Florida, Kentucky, and Mallorca] is but one part of the busy life of Mrs. Cornelius Vanderbilt Whitney. In addition to her considerable housekeeping abilities, Mrs. Whitney has managed to find time during a remarkable career to excel in radio and television, motion pictures, writing, and painting. This is not to mention her service for numerous organizations." Nor her widely known talents for cooking, flower-arranging, house decorating, party-giving, hosting presidents and royalty, and lunching with the ladies who lunch. When she first saw the then run-down house that Sonny owned in bluegrass country, she said they could fix it up "with my imagination and your money," a one-two punch that has gotten the Whitneys through many a challenge. By all indications, such as Sonny's lavish praise for Marylou in his writing, she stands to inherit control of his side of the family fortune when he dies. Then she can buy herself her own houses, instead of relying on Sonny to give her one for her birthday, as he once did. (On other occasions, he has also given her, a $50,000 bathroom and $100,000 to redistribute to charity.)

Vivian L. Smith is a good example of the problems inheritances can run into. Her husband R. E. "Bob" Smith used profits from his oil business to buy up land in Harris County, Texas; at one point before Houston boomed he owned seventeen square miles inside the city limits, including the land under the Astrodome. He was supposed to have been worth half a billion dollars when he died in 1973. He intended to leave it all to his wife in various trusts, but the tax man intervened, and before he was through the pile was pared in half, which is how it stands today.

Jules Stein did it a little better. The founder of MCA, he gave his wife shares of stock amounting to about 7 percent of the company while he was still alive. When he died in 1981, therefore, it hardly mattered that he left only half his estate to Doris Jones Stein. (The rest went to charity and children.) She spent her time and her $135 million on English antiques for her Beverly Hills house and support for the Jules Stein Eye Institute at UCLA before her own death at eighty-two in 1984.

In many cases, the death of a wealthy husband—especially the domineering types who have created their own wealth—allows a woman to come out of the shadows and establish her own presence. This is a common, and generally accurate, perception, and it frequently manifests itself in the lucky widow becoming suddenly active in charitable affairs. There is an intriguing subset here, however: the women who marry wealthy men once they have already become wealthy themselves tend to be strong-willed, organized types who know what they want and go out to get it. "It" is frequently a rich and powerful husband. That is approximately what Marylou Whitney did; similarly, Caroline Leonetti.

One of the most influential women on the West Coast was born into a family of Italian immigrants in San Francisco, "though they became very comfortable in time with a great deal of hard work," she has conceded. Caroline went to the University of California at Berkeley, where she supported herself by becoming the campus representative for a department store. At the age of twenty-two, she started Caroline Leonetti Ltd., a school for the improvement of young women that still exists under the leadership of Caroline's daughter, Margo. Born during a brief post-collegiate marriage, Margo turned into a controlling factor in her mother's remarkable career. Caroline did not remarry for seventeen years, she told an interviewer, because "I was fearful that my new husband would not feel the same way I did about children. I knew precisely what I wanted for my daughter, and I was not willing to compromise. . . . I had a three-year-old daughter and I had plans for her, a whole sixteen-year plan that included college, graduate school, and travel." She dedicated herself to the self-improvement school on the one hand, the daughter on the other, and when they both grew up she married them off to one another. Caroline Leonetti has been at great pains to insist that when she *did* remarry it was because of who her intended was (Howard Ahmanson), and not, not, *not* because of what he was, which was, reportedly, California's first billionaire. "The assumption is that when a woman meets a wealthy man, she is attracted primarily if not solely by his money. But I had been divorced for seventeen years and never intended to remarry. I had raised my daughter and educated her well, and I had a flourishing business. I had a life of my own choosing. I could take time off when I wished, and I traveled a great deal. I had a position in the community which I enjoyed. I felt that my life was as I wanted it. So meeting Mr. Ahmanson at that point in life was right for me. It was one of those happy things that were right for both of us. Naturally, I was impressed by his enormous wealth and success—who wouldn't be?—but I was financially independent and I married him because he was a remarkable man."[8]

Much more typical of what rich women do with the money they inherit from their husbands are the philanthropic careers of two well-known New York socialites, Mary Lasker and Brooke Astor. They are part of the well-born, monied circle of ladies who lunch in New York—some of whom, for no very obvious reasons, turn into titanic forces for good works once they get the opportunity, in the form of the inheritance. Mary Lasker has been widowed for more than thirty years; her husband was Albert D. Lasker, advertising pioneer and philanthropist. His will

---

8. A cogent expression of the common explanation by women that it was not *quite* the money that impelled them towards their rich husbands; the money was merely a sort of numerical expression of greatness of character. Much more on the intricacies of the meaning of sex and marriage amidst plenty is found in Part Five.

set up the Lasker awards for medical research. Thirty-six of the recipients of the annual prizes have gone on to win Nobel Prizes; among them, the honorees have developed polio vaccines, antihypertensive drugs, and the heart-lung machine. The annual awards luncheon at the St. Regis Hotel attracts the predictable crowd of glitterati, as well as a healthy admixture of medical barons. All of her parties are *for* something or someone—never just fun, although that happens to be a consistent byproduct. Society columnist Suzy (Aileen Mehle) writes:

> One of the most beloved and admired women in New York is Mary Lasker, a charming, brilliant person who really cares about the city. As administrator of her late husband Albert Lasker's tremendous foundation, Mary has made possible great strides in medical research. She is also a social creature who entertains with style, and her annual Christmas party is the one everyone wants to be invited to.
>
> For the past several years, since she sold her Beekman Place townhouse, Mary Lasker has been giving her annual party at La Grenouille, which she takes over for the night. She orders a superb meal for the 90 or so guests and calls in Lester Lanin and his players to handle the music. This year [1983], Mary wore a beautiful dress especially designed for her for the party by Philippe Venet— black velvet with black organza dotted with crystal dewdrops. It was the perfect thing to wear at a dinner party honoring Baron Guy de Rothschild, which is what the evening was all about. Guy de Rothschild seemed very happy to be there and made an amusing speech saying so. White-haired and distinguished, he was certainly eyed by the women in the room. They didn't miss another white-haired and distinguished man in the room either, Gianni Agnelli, the Fiat tycoon and perennial Italian idol whose mystique is legend. But you knew that. . . . The place for Mary Lasker is the top of the Christmas tree.

Among the other ornaments on that particular Christmas tree were Eppie Lederer—Ann Landers, who is, surprisingly, a fixture on the rich girls circuit—Enid Annenberg Haupt, the Duke and Duchess of Bedford, Marietta Tree, Mary Wells Lawrence, Angier Biddle Duke, the omnipresent Jerry Zipkin, and Drue and Jack (John H., Jr.) Heinz. Suzy did not get where she is by biting hands that feed her well for free, but devoting almost an entire column of adulation to a single party is reserved for those at the zenith of the social constellation.[9]

9. See Chapter 24 on social climbing.

As one has always imagined, women who have had the good fortune and skill to marry extremely well are delighted with themselves and their perquisites. "Just think of the fun it is to give money away—wouldn't you like to do it?" Brooke Astor said to an interviewer from *Vogue* in 1982. Brooke Astor is out of the mold of southerners and terrific flirts, and was an obvious candidate to capture a rich man. "We were in the same group—Herman and 'Dumpie' Oelrichs, the Vanderbilts, Elsie Woodward, all that," her friend Lillian Gish has recalled. "Brooke was very sought after—everyone always wanted her *there*. She hasn't changed. She's full of laughter. She has a pixieish quality—that humor is in her eyes, it's in her face. . . . And always, she's been very popular with men. She'd never tell you, but oh, I'd love to know how many people have wanted to marry her."

"I learned a thing or two from [my mother]," Brooke said. "I still like to go out, I still like to talk to men—why not?" She married Vincent Astor on his rebound from Minnie Cushing. In addition to his other attributes, Vincent Astor was the great-great-grandson of John Jacob Astor, who, through fur-trading, became by far the richest man in the United States. When he died in 1846, "he was the richest man, colossally rich," Brooke Astor noted. "Twenty million in 1846—and the closest to him were people with two million." The family put that money into land in Manhattan, and before long were the biggest landowners there—with consequent implications for their wealth. She was married to Vincent Astor for five years; since he died in 1959, she has been the chief executive, main reason, heart, and soul of the Vincent Astor Foundation, which contained about $60 million when she inherited it and is down to about $31 million, as Brooke plows ahead with her plan to get rid of it all before somebody else inherits it. Vincent Astor also left his widow $2 million outright and the interest on $60 million for her lifetime, as well as the ability to leave it to whomever she wants: *that* particular provision must have relatives and needy philanthropies scurrying.

All of that was not a bad haul for five years of marriage. But Brooke did earn it in a way, since Vincent Astor in his last years was a moody and suspicious man who made her spend most of her time alone with him and even forbade her to talk to her friends on the telephone. So his death gave her not only the means to make everybody love her but the occasion to release her pent-up sociability. Her segue into philanthropy was, then, a natural transition from smart marrying. "I don't mind being a monument, even though it sounds stuffy," she has said. "I have seen too much and done too much not to be contented with my lot. 'Don't die guessing,' cautioned Mother, and I hearkened to her words. I am not guessing. I have led a full life. Now at my age I want to enhance the lives of others by good humor and understanding. I want people to know that I really care for them." Now she spends her days giving away money—to neighborhood-redevelopment projects in Bedford-Stuyvesant, the Lower East Side, and Harlem, then to the Metropolitan Museum of Art, the New York Public Library, the Bronx Zoo, Rockefeller University, and other major institutions of the New York Capital-of-the-Universe complex. In the past twenty-five years this Lady Bountiful has dished out approximately $130 million, which will buy a lot of love. In her seventies, Brooke Astor continues to bear witness to the seldom-acknowledged fact that being a rich woman is a full-time job and more.

Everybody thinks that Yoko Ono lucked into John Lennon's money, one of the great entertainment fortunes of all time. (Those of Elvis, Sinatra, and Bob Hope come close, all in the range of $150 million, while Paul McCartney has easily bypassed his old colleague and rival, Lennon, with an estimated $400 million.) This is slander. The only reason that Yoko was pursuing a career as a sort of free-lance free spirit when she met John in London was that she is the daughter of an heiress to a Japanese banking fortune, and she had gone to Sarah Lawrence. Her mother advised her never to smile in public, saying that "smiles are for shopkeepers"—that is, for people who need to work for money. So it was not really a surprise that, once she and John had overcome their penchant for lying in bed for peace, she would take over the management of the family fortune. Even before his murder, Yoko was the chief executive officer of the diverse group of investments into which John had put the earnings from his Beatles music copyrights. Besides the management of Lennon-McCartney copyrights and a variety of music companies, Yoko diversified into real estate, farms, cows, and other valuable life-affirming things. The investments apparently have been made with the help of various seers, which may be as good a way as any to pick them; it certainly worked for Yoko. How she won John's affection, what she did with his money once she was there, whether he actually wanted to be the world's richest househusband—all these are mysteries made no clearer by the spate of books by various hangers-on who claim to have been present when rock history was being made. What seems most likely is that, even before John's tragic death, the couple had settled down very happily to the enjoyment of their huge income. These days, Yoko is much like any other wealthy matron in her early fifties; she spends her time managing the money and giving it to charity from her bases in New York, San Francisco, and Palm Beach.

Georgia Rosenbloom Frontiere, a blonde bombshell singer, struck it rich on her sixth marriage. It was to Carroll Rosenbloom, the domineering owner of the Los Angeles Rams—domineering, that is, toward everybody but Georgia, who was perhaps the only person he ever really fell for in his life. In 1966, with time's winged chariot hurrying near, Rosenbloom divorced his wife of twenty-five years to marry Georgia, who was not a star, but not far from it, and who was by all accounts an incredibly attractive woman. In 1979, Rosenbloom, a strong swimmer, drifted out into the Gulf of Mexico off their Florida home. Georgia was an hour late for the funeral. She inherited majority ownership in the Rams, and her first move was to fire Rosenbloom's son, Steve, the executive vice president, and a dozen other top executives. As the first and only female owner of an NFL team, Georgia has received mixed reviews. Some players admire her delight in the team, which extends to rambling onto the practice field to hug them, pads, sweat, and all. Others were appalled when she made them stand for hours in the hot sun so she could film a commercial for American Express. Love her or hate her, she has proven herself wonderfully adept at the difficult art of marrying a fortune and capturing it for herself.

The most recent entrant into the small circle of female professional sports club owners from southern California is another blonde musician who managed to capture a married, immensely rich tycoon. And when Ray Kroc died early in 1984, Joan Kroc inherited the San Diego Padres along with her late husband's $500 million empire based on McDonald's. She also inherited a predilection for spending the money for fun—like producing movies—and good works, like dozens of charities. "When I was a little girl," said Joan Kroc, "I wanted to be rich so that I could help people. I really did." Besides, the gigantic fortune enables her to act the nothing-can-stop-this-woman role to the hilt. She says she enjoys twitting the other owners of baseball teams, who don't quite know what to make of her. ("They're so cute. They tickle me to death.") And she is looking for ways to back up her words combating Jerry Falwell and promoting a nuclear freeze. Above all, she is just planning to spend as much as she can on fun and worthwhile projects while she can (she is in her middle fifties). Toward that end, she has tried to separate her public image as a crusader against drug and alcohol abuse from her private desire to be accepted by the boys. So she overcame her scruples and went to the Padres's National League pennant-clinching party and told pitcher Rich Gossage, "Goose, get the champagne." The boys threw her in the pool and "I took it as a compliment."

3 | WHERE THERE'S A WILL

LILLIE, THE ELDEST DAUGHTER of Hugh Roy Cullen, who made nearly $1 billion by continuing to drill Texas wells that everyone else thought were dry, was a strange woman. She ran off to Los Angeles and married a bit actor named Paolo di Portanova, a man who made the usual unlikely claim to being a baron. After her divorce, Lillie holed up in a hotel in Times Square, emerging occasionally to wander the streets, buy coats whose buttons she replaced with safety pins, and take home enough Coke and sweet cream to build herself up to nearly four hundred pounds. But she had already given birth to two sons: one was declared mentally incompetent; the other started a court fight that aptly illustrates the bottomless difficulties that can confront women with money to leave to their heirs.

The current "Baron" di Portanova, Ricky, actually acts more like a baron than many more pedigreed aristocrats. He lives profoundly well in his twenty-four-room palace in Acapulco (where the likes of the Henry Kissingers visit him), his vineyard–cattle farm outside of Rome, and his mansion in Houston's hard-to-believe River Oaks section. But Ricky would like to live even better than that. He claims that his mother's three younger sisters deviously deprived him of a proper share in her estate when, in 1964, they sold a controlling interest in Hugh Cullen's Quintana Petroleum Inc. to their husbands and two nephews for about $18,000. Ricky (Enrico) and his mentally incompetent brother, Ugo, already receive more than $25 million a year from the Cullen estate—but they want more, and they want control. Indeed, they are asking for more than $500 million in punitive damages, and Roy Cohn, the onetime lawyer for Joseph McCarthy's infamous House Un-American Activities Committee who has transmogrified himself into a more-than-socially-acceptable attorney for the wealthy, projects that client di Portanova's winnings could go as high as $2 billion.

As in many of the cases of disputed wills, the question turns on what Daddy really meant. Hugh Roy gave Lillie a trust equal to those of her sisters—but he made them executrices and left her out of the control panel. Did that mean that he allowed them leeway to take her sons for a ride? To what extent was it an attempt to force his heirs to "find some legitimate business in which Enrico can become active," as he wrote in a 1956 letter introduced into the voluminous court record? After endless convoluted court proceedings, the world will someday, perhaps decades from now, know the answers to these burning questions. In the meantime, Ricky di Portanova is doing his best to keep his spirits up.

Constance Francesca Hilton had a different, and a more common, problem. The case of the Cullen will was one in which the benefactor's intentions were not clear; Constance, however, was merely acting out of the normal human feeling that what her father left her was too little. The 1979 will of hotelier Conrad Hilton was depressingly clear: he left Constance $100,000 from an estate presumed to be worth more than $100 million at the time. (More recently, the inheritance that went to Francesca's half-brother William Barron Hilton was worth more than $300 million.) As it came out in court, it was not entirely certain that the plaintiff was in fact Miss Hilton: she was born, in 1947, more than two years after Conrad separated from her mother, Zsa Zsa Gabor. Conrad Hilton mentioned a "daughter" in some biographies and not in others. Constance Hilton argued that the inconsistency arose from an "insane delusion" that he was not the father. "He was so tormented and so tortured by the fact that he had fathered [Constance Hilton] while unmarried in the eyes of his beloved [Catholic] church, which he believed to be a cardinal sin, he could not live with that fact just as he could not live with [her] mother," her attorney wrote in the 1979 lawsuit, in the overcooked diction of a pessimistic lawyer.[10] Constance Hilton's pleading claimed that Conrad Hilton's advisers "should have known that the change in 1971 from a caring and loving father to a fear-ridden old man who renounced his daughter was the result of the ravages of old age, illnesses, cerebral accidents, and his extreme obsession with his religious beliefs." It did not take a Superior Court judge in Los Angeles long to throw the case out of court. He simply ruled that under the circumstances, Conrad Hilton needed no "insane delusions" to question his paternity of Constance. "This case is an attack on the moral values and work ethic of Conrad Hilton," an attorney for the estate argued. "He believed that his children and grandchildren should work for a living, and that was a virtue, hardly an insane delusion." There was no reason to think, the judge ruled, that granting Constance what she wanted from the estate—$50 million—would be treating her "in the fashion a daughter ought to be treated."

In death, as in her storied life, Rebekah Harkness, the Standard Oil heiress and eccentric patron of the arts, was a controversial figure. True, much of her fortune, generally estimated to have been $75 million at one point (she had inherited it herself on her second husband's death in 1954), had been dissipated in her quixotic drive—in which she largely succeeded—to influence the world of ballet. However, she did leave a fortune worth some $15 million (mainly in the lavish homes she collected like jewelry, including ones on the Hudson River, in Tucson, in the Carlyle Hotel, in Palm Beach, in Gstaad, Switzerland, and in Nassau, the Bahamas), which got everyone's attention when Mrs. Harkness died of cancer in 1982. Edith, her youngest daughter, re-

10. Not to mention a lawyer unfamiliar with the dogma of the Catholic Church: Conrad Hilton might have considered himself guilty of a *mortal* sin for marrying in a civil ceremony Zsa Zsa Gabor without having first gotten an annulment of his first marriage in the Church, but cardinal sins are entirely different things.

sponded first: the troubled heiress who as a teenager had tried to kill herself by flinging herself out a penthouse window (she was saved by the heavy snow on an awning below) finally succeeded shortly after her mother's death, this time with the aid of a fifth of vodka and a bottleful of barbiturates.

Under circumstances still waiting to be hashed out in court, Rebekah, beginning in the middle of 1981, signed a series of wills and documents that very firmly indicated the disdain in which the dying woman held Allen Pierce and Terry McBride, the two children of her first marriage. Pierce, who is in jail for manslaughter, was to have a one-seventh share of a $1 million trust; Terry got only a Dali painting and a family ring. By contrast, two members of the last inner circle of Rebekah's life made out like bandits. In the first will, Bobby Scevers was to have $1,500 a month for life and Nikita Talin was to get $50,000. A year later, as Rebekah began to fail more rapidly, she signed a revised version in which the Palm Beach house—a spread she had just bought for $800,000 and never lived in—was to be sold and the proceeds split between Scevers and Talin. Another character made her way into later versions: Maria New, the dying Rebekah's physician in New York Hospital; she was to get half the proceeds from the sale of Harkness House (the East Side town house that served as the site of Rebekah's ballet school) for her research, and a few other baubles, such as an ermine coat, a sable coat, and a string of pearls.

The beneficiaries quickly realized, however, that Rebekah personally owned neither Harkness House nor the Palm Beach estate; they were owned by a foundation and a trust respectively. In the new document, drawn up three days later, Rebekah left her last retainers $250,000 in cash each in lieu of their shares of real estate. Her attorney tried to have the heiress's signature witnessed by the employee from the Kenneth Salon who had arrived with a load of wigs for Rebekah to try on; but finally an associate of Dr. New's was brought down to make it official.

When Rebekah finally died, her children were not about to take their disinheritance lightly, even though they each had trust funds of several million dollars from William Hale Harkness, who was not even their father. Terry McBride immediately went to court, hiring the ever-popular counselor to the rich, Roy Cohn. Her argument is that her mother was being heavily medicated by a doctor at the same time that she was leaving the doctor her money, furs, and jewelry. Terry also insists that if she and her brother succeed in upsetting the will, they will keep nothing for themselves but make sure most of it goes to Harkness House.

Marion du Pont Scott was a prophet when she wrote of her farflung, immensely wealthy family, "I can't see sixty or seventy of them agreeing on anything."

They proceeded to disagree at length when she died in 1983, at the age of eighty-nine, leaving an estate estimated at $80 million. The focus of the dispute was her Virginia mansion called Montpelier, about 100 miles southwest of Washington—a former home of James and Dolley Madison—on 2,677 acres, attached to a trust fund that generated $3 million a year. "Counsel . . . who have dealt with people of substance know they have peculiarities about money," said one of the twenty-five lawyers who participated in the case. Although it lasted only nine months, it pitted dozens of family members against each other—in some cases minor children against their parents, and including representation of unborn children. The pith of the disagreement was Mrs. Scott's determination to turn the historic landmark into a museum. That upset Henry du Pont, her nephew, who had visions of living there himself in baronial splendor. Finally convinced that even a du Pont could hardly afford to maintain an estate whose upkeep costs $30,000 a month, Henry agreed to give up his one-fifth interest in the home—for $2 million. The public should be seeing regular tours of Montpelier by 1986.

It is no revelation, of course, that the proximity of unearned wealth can get the feral juices flowing where there ought only to be the warm milk of familial affection. And circling around the feuding heirs are always those who seek to take advantage of the situation, which frequently involves stoking the bitterness. Such was the case with the two Bonfils daughters who inherited parts of the *Denver Post*.

It began early when, in 1904, May, the eldest, finally decided she could no longer stand her tyrannical father, Frederick Bonfils, and eloped with a piano salesman. Like many self-made men, Bonfils had demanded obedience in return for his largesse; in his rage at her flight, he refused to send May her belongings, and warned that unless she got a divorce her inheritance would be cut in half. She did not, and it was. The younger daughter, Helen Bonfils, was happy to exploit the unexpected opening to gain a permanent advantage in the headstrong sisters' long-standing struggle for their father's affection. When Frederick died, May started a long, bitter legal battle to overturn the will; but in the end it was to no avail, and she was forced to settle for 15.67 percent of the Denver Post Company stock versus Helen's 34.33 percent plus the rest of their parents' estate. This was not a financial disaster for May; her shares churned out an average annual return of $212,000 in the years before World War II, which she used to build herself an eight-hundred-acre retreat just outside of Denver and to surround herself with the materials of wealth, including a world-famous collection of jewelry. But it was not enough to salve the bitterness between the sisters. Fuel was added to the fire when, after the war, Helen embarked on an ambitious scheme to build the *Post* into a monument to her beloved father's memory. The new plant was so expensive that, after 1948, May's dividends dropped to $80,000 a year. But worse was the psychic punishment that the majority owner of a newspaper could inflict. Helen instructed her editor, E. Palmer "Ep" Hoyt, that May's name was never to appear in print unless in an unflattering context. May suffered in silence for years, but in 1959, when she was in her mid-seventies, the *Post* failed to mention her livestock's victory in an important show. For the first time in Hoyt's thirteen-year tenure, she called to complain. Then on July 30 that year, the piano salesman, Clyde Berryman, died. May had divorced him more than ten years before—far too late, of course, to do herself any good in her father's eyes. His obituary in the *Post* contained several references to the still-grating subject of the elopement. That tore it for May. She shouted at Hoyt over the telephone, "This is the last straw. You are going to regret this." She was right.

May's idea of revenge was to find somebody who would buy her stock in the paper—somebody who would not only pay her handsomely but would be a thorn in her sister's side. She found such a person in S. I. Newhouse, the great newspaper conglomerateur. In 1960, May sold him her stock for about $3.5 million, on two conditions: that he never sell it to Helen, and that May become honorary chairman of the board if Newhouse succeeded in his takeover attempt. Newhouse was happy enough to agree to those terms, and for the moment his prospects appeared bright. Helen was giving signs of not being much of an opponent; at the age of sixty-nine, she had recently shocked everyone in Denver society by marrying her forty-year-old chauffeur, Edward

Michael "Tiger Mike" Davis, who was known to the couple's acquaintances as "the foulest-mouthed man alive." As it turned out, though, Helen was just crazy enough to put all her energies into fighting Newhouse's takeover try—especially after May, in announcing the sale of her stock, insisted publicly and gracelessly that she and not Helen had always been their father's favorite. Helen maneuvered adroitly to keep the remaining stock out of her pursuer's hands, until, in 1968, Newhouse was forced to go to court as a last resort. With former Supreme Court Justice Arthur Goldberg arguing the Post Company's case, Helen finally carried the day in 1973. It was a Pyrrhic victory, for the feud between the sisters had forced the postponement of any planning for the future. As a result, profits dropped drastically, and the paper had to be sold in 1980 to the Times Mirror Company.

Much the same sort of dispute recently rocked Superior Oil Company, the largest independent oil and gas producer in the United States. In 1983, Willametta Keck Day, daughter of the company's founder, decided that her brother, retired chairman Howard B. Keck, was using his 11.5 percent of the firm's stock to throw around his own weight and not necessarily to provide large dividends for her 3.5 percent share. The feud between the siblings dates to the death of their father, William M. Keck, in 1964. Mrs. Day, who lives on a ranch in Nevada, has said that she always has wanted her brother, who is chairman of the W. M. Keck Foundation, to use foundation money to build a mausoleum for their late parents in southern California.

The dispute got worse in 1980 and 1981 when Mrs. Day learned that Howard and the late William M. Keck, Jr., were both paid more than $400,000 in each of those years to administer the trust that finances the foundation. This was a trust whose main function, according to the terms of the will, was simply to go out of business when its 10.9 million shares of Superior Oil stock are distributed to the foundation. Howard somehow had not managed the seemingly easy task of making that distribution in the twenty years or so since his father's death. In the meantime, of course, he had been able to vote the shares and thus to maintain his stranglehold on company policy. Late in 1982, Mrs. Day began to complain publicly that she and other stockholders were getting shortchanged.

In 1982, she noted later, the company earned $1.75 a share on total revenues of $2.04 billion, but paid out only twenty cents per share in dividends. Fortunately for Mrs. Day, that parsimonious approach made the company cash-rich and therefore an attractive candidate for a takeover. Mesa Petroleum Company, run by T. Boone Pickens, Jr., who is generally referred to as a "maverick oilman," was long rumored to have a hungry eye on Superior, and by the middle of 1983 had bought 3.2 million shares. In defense, Howard Keck pushed a bylaw change through the board of directors that allowed directors to remain on the board indefinitely, instead of being forced to retire at seventy as they had been.

That had immediate repercussions not only for Keck himself, who was sixty-nine in 1983, but for two of his allies on the nine-member board who had turned seventy in the preceding year. In April 1983, Mrs. Day sued her brother and his director cronies in an attempt to force them to change the retirement age back to seventy. The feisty founder's daughter also sponsored a stockholders' initiative that would force the board of directors to accept any "fair" offer to buy out the company. She wrote to stockholders, "I have always felt a responsibility to all other owners of Superior stock who have placed their faith in my father's company. Those of you who know me also know that if I believe something is wrong, I won't keep quiet about it." She told a reporter, "I don't think my father built Superior to benefit the individuals who are paid to run it. I believe he built it for the stockholders who were willing to risk their money along with his."

Mesa, while denying it had been in contact with Mrs. Day, naturally expressed satisfaction with her approach. The Keck-controlled company, though, wrote back to shareholders that Mrs. Day's ideas were "poorly conceived and contrary to your best interests," adding, "You can be assured that if an acquisition proposal were to be received—and none has been—the board would give it full consideration." Mrs. Day won after a bitter proxy battle, which in the event proved the end of the line for her brother as well. He resigned bitterly after the stockholders' initiative won, and then—a final concession—he turned against his previous allies in management and announced that he favored a buyout. It was the sale of his shares, Mrs. Day's, a nephew's, and those of six charitable trusts that in March 1984 accounted for Mobil Corporation's first step in a successful effort to take over Daddy's company. Mrs. Day made slightly more than $200 million in cash in return for the rights to her patrimony.

Death of parents is not always necessary before heirs go to court. For example, John Dodge, grandson of the automaker Horace Dodge, had to sue his mother, Gregg Dodge Moran, in 1983 to get back some of the $4 million of his inheritance that he alleges she spent during an $11 million worldwide shopping spree. Dodge, apparently not suspecting his mother would try to pillage his wealth, had signed papers allowing her access to his bank accounts. He finally had to settle for $500,000 at most—and the depressing knowledge that money can be thicker than blood.

The difficulties of being an heir are nothing, of course, compared to the difficulties of *not* being an heir when one knows one actually is. The most famous recent struggle for such recognition was waged by Terry Moore, the flaky aging ingenue who was finally judged in 1983 to be the widow of Howard Hughes, after a legal odyssey that had lasted since his death in 1976. Indeed, it turned out that she was actually a multiple bigamist, since their marriage—in 1949, on Hughes's yacht off the West Coast—was never legally dissolved, while she went on to marry football star Glenn Davis, entrepreneur Eugene McGrath, businessman Stuart Cramer (whose ex, Jean Peters, had already married Hughes, making that an undetermined additional degree of bigamy), and Richard Carey, who was later indicted for grand theft and forgery.[11]

Hughes, Miss Moore says, was a megalomaniac made predictably strange, like so many other men, by their wealth and power. Women in particular seem to feel the wrath of these powerhouses; the frustrations of having a fabulous woman, life's best ornament, and yet not being able to control it absolutely produces a distinct pathology. Thus, even though Hughes owned RKO Pictures, says Miss Moore, "He hated me being in the movies. He was jealous of all my leading men, and he tried to wreck my career." He had her followed from the first moment they met, and ordered her to wear a constrictive brassiere even while sleeping to defeat the effects of gravity on her breasts. He

---

11. Terry says that Carey took her for $200,000 by having her sign a file of legal documents when she did not have her reading glasses on.

ran around with other women, and they fought constantly. Despite the humiliations and his insistence on keeping the marriage secret, Hughes was, naturally, "the love of my life," Miss Moore says now. In return for adulation and her charms, he gave her baubles like a ten-carat diamond—and eventually, through no particular desire of his own, a settlement estimated at up to $20 million from his half-billion-dollar estate.

Nor is that all, for the fascination with the reclusive, paranoid, drug-riddled Hughes is such that his wife is in a position to market tape recordings she has of his telephone calls to her, her own autobiography, product endorsements, posters, and television projects for a Hollywood long uninterested in this particular starlet *manqué*. Miss Moore, by all accounts, already has enough money from her own earnings and her marriages and is not particularly interested in her windfall—just the acknowledgement that she is in fact Mrs. Hughes. A person who *is* interested in her money is Jerry Rivers, the fast-talking personal manager in his mid-thirties (twenty years younger than Terry) who serves as confidant and boyfriend. "Money doesn't mean anything to her," Rivers told *People* magazine in 1983. "She gives it away. She's a darling girl who is fifty-one years old [actually fifty-four at the time, according to her birth certificate] with the attitude of someone nineteen." Luckily for the wrinkling naïf, her windfall will continue to attract managers like Rivers to take care of her.

An even more extravagant illustration of the fact that rich men—especially self-made men—are extraordinarily rough on their families is the Texas-size saga of the three families of H. L. Hunt. Like many other men who create business empires, Hunt felt quite simply that the normal rules did not apply to him. In his case, however, this was a far more profound and wide-reaching sentiment than the one acquired by most powerful men. It was not limited to the usual succession of casual affairs with "secretaries" scattered across the landscape. While it was true that H. L. was congenitally unfaithful, he also saw in his philandering an opportunity and a need to create a family as big as a sheikh's. (His daughter Caroline once compared him to King ibn-Saud of Saudi Arabia, supposedly the father of three hundred. "He just likes children, until they get to be about six or seven years old," she said. "Then he isn't interested anymore.") Hunt once confided to a business associate that he thought he carried a "genius gene"—that he was actually creating a master race for the future by breeding as rapidly as possible.

This predilection of the tycoon's produced more than the problem that besets all widely known wealth—strangers popping up from nowhere claiming to be illegitimate children and thus heirs to the fabulous fortune. For H. L. Hunt kept, as it turned out, three distinct families even while he was making his Dad Joiner deal in the East Texas oilfields and laying the foundations for his descendants' unfathomable riches. He married his first wife, Lyda Bunker, in a standard enough way: she was a schoolteacher whom he wooed, apparently for a certain amount of social cachet, when he was a gambler just starting to get into the oil business in Lake Village, Arkansas.

Life was for a time normal, if gritty, in the Arkansas oil boom during World War I. But H. L. grew restless, sold out his respectable but increasingly humdrum holdings, and headed for the booming west coast of Florida to put his fortune into real estate. In Tampa, he met Frania Tye, a strikingly good-looking Polish-born young woman who showed him a piece of property. As "Major Franklin Hunt,"he married her in 1925, despite the fact that he had a wife and several young children back home in Arkansas. Traveling businessmen suddenly becoming an acceptable commodity, H. L. Hunt being a charming and fascinating and well-heeled husband and father, neither Frania nor Lyda was aware of the other's existence, even after H. L. moved his second wife and her children—four of them, eventually—to Dallas, where he had already set up his first wife and *her* children (six of them). Finally, in 1934, the evidence of Hunt's duplicity became undeniable, and Frania broke up the household. She did continue to see Hunt, but she turned down his entreaties to move to Utah and become an acceptably bigamistic couple. Turning to greener pastures, Hunt at this point started going with a twenty-one-year-old secretary (Frania's age when he met her) at Hunt Oil named Ruth Ray. She had four children by him and was rewarded by being installed in yet another large Dallas home, where they lived under the name of Wright. Lyda died of a stroke in 1955, and Hunt married Ruth Ray two years later.

It all came out in the wash after Hunt himself died in 1974. (He achieved the entirely respectable age of eighty-five but fell well short of his goal of becoming the world's oldest human.) Conceding that over the years she had received almost $1 million in cash and trust funds for her children from the oilman, Frania sued to be named his putative, or commonly accepted, wife, with the consequent legitimization of her children. It is the classic recent example of the complexities of wills among the richest— a matter not only of the truly staggering sums being bandied about,[12] but of the underlying tenderness of feelings in which each dollar represents a drop of affection. Testimony in a Shreveport, Louisiana, courtroom in 1978 strung out the seamy details for the world: the bizarre double and triple lives of H. L., the bovine acquiescence of the wives and children, the 1942 meeting in a Dallas hotel in which Frania signed away her claim to be Hunt's wife in return for a monthly payment of $2,000. Frania's testimony turned out to be enough to crowbar a settlement from the other relatives before all the details of their familial lives were dragged into court. The first and "second" families agreed to pay Frania, her lawyers, and her descendants an additional $7.5 million as a final settlement of her claim to be H. L.'s wife.

Meanwhile, the other two branches reached their own settlement in the related matter of Hassie. The first son, though institutionalized after mental illness and a frontal lobotomy, was still the titular heir to half a billion dollars, and the first family was worried that the Ruth Ray children as well as the Frania branch would have standing to challenge his will. In the negotiations over the exit of Frania and her children, both other branches agreed to keep their hands off Hassie's portion.

The magnetic association between the financial and psychic rewards to be had from wills has been even more publicly paraded by Joan Irvine Smith, a woman whose professed need for privacy has been trampled by her own insatiable need to reclaim what she perceives as her grandfather's legacy. Simply put, Mrs. Smith has spent her entire life in the thrall of her grandfather, James Irvine II, and the immensely valuable remnant (if eighty thousand acres can be called a remnant) of the one hundred forty

12. In the case of the Hunts, by the estimate of Harry Hurt III in *Texas Rich*, the total fortune of the family is something between $6 billion and $8 billion. The only contenders for richest family in the United States, and possibly in the world, are the Rockefellers and Mellons, with about $5 billion apiece, and the du Ponts, who with up to $20 billion are the runaway winners. However, in the other three family groups—especially the du Ponts, who have been rich for two hundred years and more—the money has flowed into numerous branches and tributaries. With the exception of the Rockefeller "Brothers," the European royal families, and more recently the Arab groups that are related to the royal families of the Persian Gulf, there has perhaps never been such a concentration of wealth within a tight family group.

square miles of southern California's Orange County that he partly inherited and partly acquired as grazing land for sheep and cattle. Exactly what Joan wanted has never been very clear, especially to the beleaguered trustees of the Irvine Company— a group of her father's old cronies who were given majority control over the estate in Irvine's will.

The root of Joan's strange behavior, friends have said, lies in her "poor little rich girl" upbringing. Her father died when she was two, and the future heiress was raised by a succession of governesses, who reportedly bossed her around in the family's elegant houses in San Marino and Pasadena. She grew up beautiful—with a resemblance to Marilyn Monroe—and wild. She is remembered at her Pasadena school mainly for liking low-cut dresses; later she turned into a manic outdoorswoman. As a young adult she flew over the Andes in a small plane, hunted on the plains of Argentina, and fished for marlin off the coast of Mexico. She had two divorces and two children by the age of twenty-four, which was when, in 1957, she inherited a 22 percent interest in the Irvine Company. At that point, the firm owned the eighty thousand acres in soon-to-boom Orange County, as well as portions of California's Imperial Valley and Montana. In between a continuously stormy personal life—two more failed marriages and another son; the 1959 death of her uncle, Myford Irvine, then the company president, in a much-questioned "suicide" on a camping trip; a break-in at her house in Laguna Beach, which she believes was related to her struggles with the Irvine Company, and which has persuaded her to conduct a peripatetic life that is an attempt to dodge future would-be kidnappers— Joan embarked on a career, possibly unprecedented in business annals, as the largest single stockholder constantly battling her own company.

Her central motivation has apparently been to preserve the Irvine Ranch in the fashion that she believes her grandfather would have wanted; her secondary struggle, to maintain what she believes the value of her holdings should be. Frequently, her moves have attracted wide popular support. She fought to sell sixteen hundred acres of the Ranch's three and a half miles of Pacific oceanfront for a state park when the trustees wanted it developed commercially. She battled a plan to import water from the north, contending that the land should develop only as far as its own groundwater would take it. She forced her board to donate one thousand acres to the University of California for the

Irvine campus. Overall, her impulse appears to have been to create an ecologically sound planned community, with land reserved for agriculture, in an area that has not been known for undue attention to the planet underneath. Frequently her business acumen has surfaced in the midst of seemingly mindless activity: in 1977, she sparked a bidding war that not only prevented Mobil Oil from buying the company from the directors but left her $70 million richer when the acquisitors she brought in for the battle bought up half her stock. (Her partners were among the biggest names in business: Henry Ford II, A. Alfred Taubman [the Michigan shopping-center developer who recently bought Sotheby Parke Bernet], retailer Milton Petrie, and New York financier Herbert Allen, Sr.)

But Joan's style has been peculiar to say the least, and her immediate intention never very clear. She has filed something like twenty lawsuits in her battles with the board of the company, generally after she is the sole dissenter on whatever question is before it. She has apparently spent most of her waking hours either attending meetings of governmental boards that impinge on the Irvine Ranch, reading reports from lawyers she sent to other meetings, or writing letters to all concerned. In 1979, Peter Kremer, then president of the Irvine Company, was so exasperated with Mrs. Smith that he called in reporters to show them eleven hundred letters that he had received in the previous eighteen months—all of them from her, on topics covering every conceivable aspect of the development of the ranch. At the time, Kremer said, Mrs. Smith had stepped up her output to ten letters a day; he said he read them all and answered those that called for it, "but sometimes I let them pile up for a day." Once, former board member Max Fisher got so annoyed at her points of order that he snapped at her, "Why don't you go get married?" Through it all, Mrs. Smith, while becoming more and more a recluse, has made herself frequently available to reporters who contact her through her Los Angeles lawyer. By all accounts she delights in her orneriness ("I love being called the Dragon Lady," she told a reporter) and is happy to put on display her upper-class disdain for those who try to thwart her will; she regularly referred to her latest and most effective antagonist, Donald Bren, as Dawnald in a drawling rich girl's tone of scorn. The *Los Angeles Times* quoted a former company official as saying, "She's like a little child who waggles her spoon in a jar and demands that her mother give her all the bananas."

Donald L. Bren, the son of actress Claire Trevor and one of the largest real-estate developers in the United States, finally proved Mrs. Smith's match. In 1983, he made the second half of his purchase of 86 percent of the company's stock, which by now is estimated to be worth more than $1 billion altogether. Her last lawsuit failed in November 1983, when a Superior Court judge in Orange County refused to stop a merger between the Irvine Company and Bren's holding company, Newco I Corporation; the ruling meant that the Irvine Company would assume the debts that Bren had incurred in purchasing it, effectively giving him overwhelming control. Spurning an offer of $115 million for her remaining 11 percent share—which, as usual, she considered grossly undervalued—Mrs. Smith exercised her "dissenter's rights" and has left it up to a court to decide how much her holdings are worth. Her grandfather, she said, "would have thought it was a smart move. He was a very thrifty fellow who didn't like taking risks." With the consolation prize of $200 million or so as her takings from her long battle, Mrs. Smith will have to take very few risks herself.

As Joan Irvine Smith found, and as Dickens reminded his readers in *Bleak House*, inherited money can easily be a lifelong weight. While most people without money assume that it is a freeing influence, those who have been left it frequently find that they can't live with it and can't live without it. Sandra Ferry Rockefeller, for example, found in the midst of a violent rebellion against the powerful family tradition that she literally could not alienate her share of her generation's trusts. (She settled for dropping her last name instead and now lives as a recluse.) There are, indeed, few stronger examples of how the desires of previous generations can be imposed through wills.[13] In the case of the Rockefellers at least, the physical existence of a trust fund that each member of the current generation (the cousins) came into upon their majority, of between $5 million and $9 million, firmly expressed the meaning of their belonging to the aristocracy of wealth. Michael Rockefeller, who not long afterward was to disappear off New Guinea, wrote in 1959 to John D. Rockefeller II:

---

13. We also happen to know a lot more of the details of the Rockefellers' legal arrangements than most families', thanks to Peter Collier and David Horowitz's remarkably detailed book *The Rockefellers: A Family Dynasty* (N.Y.: Holt, Rinehart and Winston, 1976).

Dear Grandfather:

On my twenty-first birthday, my father made known to me the trust which you have established out of consideration for me and my future. For this I am deeply grateful. It is unique and extraordinary that the third generation after Great Grandfather will be able to share in the privilege and wonderful opportunities coincident with taking responsibility over a trust which he made possible.

The distribution of John D. Rockefeller II's money—the Fidelity Trust, set up in 1952 with one hundred twenty thousand shares of Standard Oil stock—can be taken as an illustration of the way in which a typical scion of fabulous wealth (if a typical such person can be imagined) comes into his inheritance. The children of Laurance Rockefeller were allowed $5,000 a year from the trust when they turned twenty-one, then gradually increasing annual amounts to twenty-four, after which the disbursement continued to increase in annual increments of $5,000 until it jumped to $65,000 at age thirty, and then to the full amount of income afterward or upon marriage—$200,000 to $300,000 a year. The obvious intention to wean the recipient away from financial immaturity is even more striking in the machinery needed to touch the principal of the trusts. There are stipulations about what purposes are legitimate; and even when they are, a formal application is necessary to the trustees, who have included the likes of William McChesney Martin, former chairman of the Federal Reserve Bank, and Nathan Pusey, the former president of Harvard. Abby Rockefeller, who turned out to be a sort of Marxist mirror image of her father, David, recalled that she once went to Room 5600 in Rockefeller Center—the Rockefeller family office—in an attempt to determine exactly what her holdings were. At a "surreal" meeting, she told writers Peter Collier and David Horowitz, "They handed out a little red portfolio with all 'my' investments in it. Everything was so altogether done that I could hardly feel like a participant. [J. R.] Dilworth [chief operating officer of the Office] suggested to Lee [an accountant] that he run through my investments. He did, giving me a little synopsis of what each one was doing. He got to Exxon and said, 'Well, here's an old friend.' Then came Mobil, and he says, 'Now Mobil is a kind of little sister of Exxon.' That kind of stuff. Good-humored, but clearly meant to put distance between me and the money and to leave in question the degree to which it is *mine*. It worked. I felt like I had a mask over my face and was being laid out ready for an operation. Room 5600 is an institutional replica of my father's manner; it prevents one from asking questions that might explain its inner logic." Indeed, it took several group meetings of most of the cousins before they could even force the disclosure of the outlines of how the Rockefeller family office worked. (It turned out to have more than two hundred employees and a budget of $6 million.) Nor could individual cousins, when they tried, vote their relatively minor shares of companies to support stockholder resolutions such as withdrawal from South Africa.

Not all trusts, needless to say, are so formidably restrictive, and very few are as large as the Rockefellers'. But all heiresses of substantial fortunes face, in the concrete form of the executors of their forebears' wills, physical representations of the problems that spending that wealth can bring upon them.

It would be remiss to leave the subject of heiresses without mentioning one who, it is already clear, will definitely be among the richest of her on-charging generation. That would be Lisa Marie Presley, the namesake of her wild father's ninety-six-seat private jet. Lisa Marie is the major beneficiary of Elvis's untimely death. She was also very lucky that her father died before her mother, since child-bride Priscilla Presley had signed a prenuptial agreement that would have left the daughter's future to the mercurial whims of her father.

When Elvis died in 1977, his tangled affairs eventually yielded an approximate worth of $30 million. However, Lisa Marie's court-appointed attorney had a struggle of several years before Colonel Tom Parker, the late singer's Svengali manager, could be dislodged from his boa-constrictor hold on half the revenues from the estate. In 1983, Parker was bought out for some $2 million more in an out-of-court settlement. Priscilla Presley got $2 million. Lisa Marie is sole heir to the rest, which is now valued conservatively at $25 million. But the estate also includes all the rights to Elvis music, movies, and memorabilia. Given the seemingly bottomless fascination with the pioneer rocker, *Forbes* has calculated that Lisa Marie will automatically join the ranks of the four hundred richest Americans when she comes to collect her trust fund, in 1994, at the age of twenty-five. And the incredible unending stream of Elvis's royalties from records and movies could well end up making her into the richest woman in the world before she is through.

No one knows much about this one-woman economic superpower, because her mother, Priscilla Presley, has assiduously cultivated privacy for her. If she were more visible, Lisa Marie would surely be one of the most celebrated children in the world—not for her wealth alone, but as the flesh of the King. "I've gone to every length to protect her, traveled under different names at all hours and to places where I knew photographers couldn't possibly guess," Priscilla told an interviewer. "Most of all, I've had to protect her against Elvis-adoration. Everyone would idolize, give in to her because of her father, never stop her doing anything she wanted because of him. The kid hasn't a chance to find out what she wants to do for herself." That fascinating, overwhelming prospect of unlimited possibilities is, in somewhat diluted form, faced by all the centimillionaire children in the world.[14]

Priscilla is also practically manic on the subject of keeping Lisa Marie from turning into another Beverly Hills princess; she may be the least spoiled kid in that spoiled-rotten paradise. Elvis had wanted to buy her furs and diamonds when she was five years old, but Priscilla put her foot down. It's still down. Lisa even tried to work in a delicatessen to earn extra money, but she had to quit when everybody found out she was there. She has to get by on an allowance of $10 a week.

14. See Part Five for the problems of the rich.

4 | Making the Most of Your Inheritance

One important point to keep in mind about women's inheritances is that, much more than for men, they are bound up in trusts. Until very recently, women were not liable to be the natural heiresses to the family business. Indeed, there are many women on the boards of their fathers' or grandfathers' companies, and in some cases they actually wield some influence; but for the most part women are passive possessors of wealth created in the previous generations. As a result, heiresses have traditionally been concerned with philanthropies of various kinds, with horses and dogs, with flowers, with parties—and very seldom with the businesses that have created the family wealth in the first place.

This is changing to a certain extent in the current generation. Businessmen such as John H. Johnson (publishing), Dr. Jerry Buss (sports ownership), Meshulam Riklis (Rapid American), and Hugh Hefner have announced their intention to groom their daughters to take over the business. More and more young women find themselves able to appreciate the experience of Linda Johnson, who, in her mid-twenties, is vice-president and heiress apparent to Johnson Publishing Company, which puts out *Ebony* and *Jet* magazines. "I was exposed at a very young age to the working arena," she has said. "After school, kids would go out to play and I would come to my dad's office." Leon A. Danco, president of the Cleveland-based Center for Family Business and the man generally considered the guru of the family-owned company in the United States, says, "Increasingly, daughters by choice are entering family businesses and wrestling with their brothers for control and a place at the top." If that trend continues, it will radically alter the percentage of rich women with actual control over their wealth and over segments of the economy, for 99 percent of all the corporations in the United States are privately held, and altogether they account for half the gross national product. Moreover, the concentration of wealth in the hands of a few family members means that when private businesses take off—as they tend to do, since they are generally smaller than public corporations—the owners can acquire immense chunks of personal wealth overnight.

Perhaps the most glamorous and amazing heiress-apparent in the world today is Nabila Khashoggi, who in her early twenties has already been made president of the Triad Commercial Corporation, the conglomerate created by her father, the Saudi businessman of uncounted wealth (some estimates say $6 billion), Adnan Khashoggi. Seemingly little daunted by the traditional restrictions on women of the Arab world, Nabila was educated in England and Switzerland, privately tutored in business administration and marketing, then worked for a while at an advertising agency in London and a bank in Beirut. Now, from headquarters aboard the state-of-the-art 270-foot yacht named for her, she stays in touch not only with her duties with Triad, whatever they might be exactly, but as a partner in Infolex, a new computerized advertising medium, and the director of the family's Khashoggi Foundation. She also takes time off to show it isn't all hard work, posing for *Town & Country* recently in a set of jewelry her father gave her for her twenty-second birthday, in which each eye-popping emerald stands for one of her immediate relatives.

But it is for the next generation to witness the flowering of the heiresses who have specifically been reared as royalty in the business world. Among the present-day crop of women who run their own businesses, most have inherited their titles and power only after the logical male successors have been accounted for. In some cases it takes tragedy, such as that of Katharine Meyer Graham. Before Katie Graham attained fame with Attorney General John Mitchell and Watergate, she was little more than a bright and rather troubled Washington matron whose life revolved around society functions, snobbish Georgetown gossip, and her four children. Indeed, her rich girl's outlook would remain as obvious as her Main Line Lockjaw voice, even as she moved on to her career as a dominant political and literary figure. She appeared to be relaxed only with those who came from backgrounds such as her Madeira School education, and even after she became publisher of the *Washington Post*, she allowed herself to be feted at Truman Capote's stunning and bizarre masquerade at the Plaza Hotel, with five hundred forty guests from politics and the glitterati, four hundred bottles of Taittinger champagne, and $12,000 worth of food.[15]

It remained for her husband, the brilliant but erratic Philip Graham, to force her out of that comfortable niche in his backhanded way. It is difficult to tell how much Phil's obvious ability to take over the *Post* from Eugene Meyer, Katharine's banker father, contributed to her decision to marry him; one telling point may be that among the men she was previously expected to marry was John Oakes, of the family that publishes the *New York Times*. At any rate, Katharine was clearly dazzled by Phil when she married him, and content to remain in his shadow. But there soon came signs that the shadow was more a threatening than a protective one. Finally, in 1963, after years of openly running around Washington with his girl friend Robin Webb ("the Popsie," Katharine called her bitterly) and displaying an increasingly quirky hand on the tiller at the paper, Phil Graham killed himself with a shotgun in the first-floor bathroom of his estate in Middleburg, Virginia, while Katharine slept upstairs.

At least Phil's death brought an end to the enervating scenes, to his incessant threats not only to subject her to a divorce but to take the paper away from her as well. (It is hard to imagine that he could have.) It was, however, not at all obvious what the widow would do next. She had been a reporter for the *San*

15. Mrs. Graham did say later that the affair seemed like "an odd, overaged and gray coming-out party" and she drifted away from those particular New York circles after that.

Francisco Examiner as a young adult, her father had considered her, of all his children, most like himself in intellectual toughness, and she had maintained an interest in the *Post*'s finances. But she was painfully ignorant of most phases of the operation, and her self-confidence had been badly eroded by most circumstances of her life extending back to her mother—"a Viking," Katharine now calls her—who had denigrated her daughter's abilities from the time she described the just-born Kay as a "hideous little object."

As a consequence of such emotional maltreatment, Kay Graham was miserably shy. (When in 1965 she took Benjamin C. Bradlee out to lunch at the F Street Club—the luncheonette for movers and shakers in Washington—she was so overwhelmed at paying for a man's lunch that she vowed never to do it again.) But so strong was the upper-class urge of duty to family that she seems never to have doubted that, whether by inertia or some yet unknown force, she would take over her beloved father's newspaper. On the day of Phil Graham's funeral she gathered the board of directors and told them, "This has been, this is, and this will continue to be a family operation. There is another generation coming, and we intend to turn the paper over to them." She apparently meant it literally about the next generation taking over at that time; her oldest son Donald was still at Harvard, but she talked constantly about him coming down to assume the mantle. Then she stopped talking about it, and more than twenty years later Donald is still only heir apparent.

The startling change into a commanding businesswoman came gradually. Inevitably, Mrs. Graham faced the problem of being a woman in what was, at that time and that level, entirely a male universe. She found herself not especially sure of what she wanted, while at the same time she held potentially enormous power. Clare Boothe Luce, who had gone through similar things in publishing and government, told her, according to David Halberstam in *The Powers That Be*, "You're a woman in a world of men and you're not really prepared. So every time men come to your office to talk, try and move away from your desk to the sofa. Try not to be intimidating. You're going to need all the help you can get."

However much she needed, she got. Kate Graham turned out to be not merely a competent caretaker, but a publisher and businesswoman of rare ability. Hiring Ben Bradlee to run the editorial side was a stroke of legend, leading directly to the *Post*'s present stature as an exciting, necessary-to-read and beautifully written paper. By 1966, only three years after Mrs. Graham took over, the *Post* had moved into third place in the United States in advertising linage (to the *Times*es of Los Angeles and New York). She pumped the additional revenue into the paper, rapidly doubling the editorial staff and sinking $25 million into a new plant, eventually increasing the *Post*'s journalistic prestige and financial solidity (the two *sometimes* go hand in glove) to the point where its Washington competitors, the *Daily News* and then the *Star*, were driven out of business. In 1971 she took the company public, greatly increasing her economic leverage. The meek widow turned into a tornado in the executive suite, canning her top lieutenants with such abandon that the *Post* itself reported that fear and loathing of her tactics had caused half a dozen top candidates for the job of vice-president in charge of production to refuse the position at any salary. Although Mrs. Graham eventually realized that not all problems were soluble by decapitation, her perfectionism did result in the assembling of a top-drawer management. She might well have been a student of Dr. Johnson: when a man knows he is to be hanged in a fortnight, it concentrates his mind wonderfully.

But the self-doubt suggested by the sudden, unnerving dismissals of top executives was nowhere in evidence by the time she got around to dealing with the paper's printers and craft unions. Her attitude could be fairly summarized by her criticism of a reporter who wrote a sympathetic story about the beleaguered printers; she bluntly accused him of "romanticizing those bastards." The printers were soon bought out, and then there remained only the pressmen. Having won virtually all her journalistic battles, Katharine Graham was ready to throw all her firepower into destroying the union, whose archaic contract terms seriously eroded the paper's profitability.

On October 1, 1975, she was awakened at 5:00 A.M. with the intelligence that the pressmen had begun their strike by beating up their foreman and damaging all nine of the *Post*'s presses. She drove to the paper herself, not wanting to awaken her chauffeur, and walked through the lines of angry strikers, telling herself (so she said later), "They're not going to hurt me. I'm sure they're not." They didn't. It turned out that they had only hurt themselves with their old-time union destructive tactics.[16] The Newspaper Guild, the union that includes reporters, consistently voted to cross the picket lines. Many management employees had already been sent to the Newspaper Production and Research Center in Oklahoma City—essentially, a school for management to learn to put out papers while their workers are on strike; and between computerized printing and a sort of Berlin-airlift operation in which finished pages were flown by helicopter to nonunion printing plants, the *Post* had no major difficulties in publishing through the strike. It ended a few months later with the hiring of an entirely new, much smaller, and nonunion press crew. Katharine Graham had not only destroyed the *Post*'s union and thus vastly enhanced profits; she had kept the paper on the cutting edge of journalism by showing management, for the first time, that unions could be demolished with impunity. Wall Street loved it.

In 1979, Katharine Graham stepped aside as publisher of the *Post*, and her son Donnie took over. She remains chief executive officer of the corporation and owner of the bulk of the voting stock. *Forbes* estimates that she is worth easily $125 million.

Rich women have a particular affinity for newspapers. Being a reporter, of course, was one of the earliest ways in which a woman could go to work as a relatively serious person; witness *His Girl Friday*, Lois Lane, and a host of spiritual descendants, such as Mrs. Pynchon on "Lou Grant." Mrs. Pynchon is not a bad approximation of Katharine Graham, as a matter of fact. Publishing is perfect as a business for rich women: it is immensely profitable because it lends itself to consolidation and monopoly; it demands a vast array of skills from its management but not specific expertise from the top bosses; and it rewards creativity and intuition. Thus, it has been by far the business in which women have excelled. They have especially excelled not in starting newspapers themselves but in taking them over from deceased fathers and husbands and then—as in the case of Ka-

16. The famous placard on the picket line read: "Phil Shot the Wrong Graham." As usual, the unions were not getting tremendous public-relations advice. The *Post*, on the other hand, hired J. Walter Thompson to publicize the damage to its presses. The advertising agency distributed glossy photos of the damaged presses and estimated the damage at between $1 million and $2 million—an outrageously high figure.

tharine Graham—building them into something far greater. Partly this has been the luck of the draw and the fruit of longevity: the twentieth century has seen the progressive growth in the profitability of the media for a variety of reasons. But it goes beyond luck. Women have never been great entrepreneurs, with the few exceptions we will see later; but they have always been strong infighters in inheritance situations. That is a skill that has not only tended to give them control over newspapers, but also gives them excellent skills with which to run them, for newspapers are unique among businesses in giving leeway for instinct.

The history of newspapers is rife with strong and rather amazing women. Indeed, when Eugene Meyer, Katharine Graham's father, bought the *Washington Post,* one of its chief competitors was the *Washington Herald*—later the *Times-Herald*—a sassy paper owned by William Randolph Hearst but published by Cissy (Eleanor) Patterson, of the family (including the McCormicks) that still owns the *Chicago Tribune* and the *New York Daily News,* as well as a group of television stations.

Cissy Patterson was a jazzy, twenties sort of redhead who was notorious for her early life beauty, her huge personal fortune, her love affairs amidst a wild life, and her dangerously strange but profitable management of the newspaper. When Meyer bought the *Post* in 1929, Cissy Patterson immediately picked a fight over the rights to a number of comic strips, which were then, as now, among the best-read and most important features in a newspaper. Meyer won in a case that went to the Supreme Court. Cissy then called to ask him to let her run the disputed comic strips one last time, because they were already printed; he agreed she could if she ran a front-page box saying that from then on the strips would appear only in the *Post.* She ran the comics but not the box. Then she sent Meyer a box of flowers with the Shakespearean gift of a pound of raw meat and a note: "So as not to disappoint you."

At about the same time, Oveta Culp was performing the rather amazing act, for a twenty-five-year-old Texas woman, of running for the state legislature. She lost, of course; but the next year she married William Hobby, the governor of Texas from 1917 to 1921. In 1930, he bought the *Houston Post.* In the course of a remarkable career, Oveta was head of the Women's Army Corps in World War II, was appointed the first secretary of health, education and welfare by President Eisenhower, mothered the current longtime lieutenant governor of Texas, William Hobby, Jr., and in 1952 became coeditor and publisher of the *Houston Post*. While no one would ever accuse the *Houston Post* of being one of the world's great newspapers, it is the second-largest paper in Texas and an influential voice in that city of many influential voices. Now the family wealth, diversified into radio and television at her behest, is in the hands of family members for estate reasons, but Oveta Culp Hobby still controls most of it—at least $350 million worth, by *Forbes*'s estimate. And "control" is the precise word for this formidable yet insistently ladylike woman. In 1982, when she was honored for being one of the Associated Press's four most powerful women in Texas, James Crowther, the executive vice president and general counsel of the *Post* and so, admittedly, not a person to render biting judgments of the owner, said, "She is the chief executive in every sense of the word. . . . She has great warmth, concern for people and a fine mind. Maybe more important, she has a sense of justice of what's right. She asserts herself and makes intelligent decisions." In 1956, when she was collecting an honorary degree from her alma mater, Mary Hardin–Baylor College, its president, Arthur Tyson, called her "the number one woman of the world." Quite an achievement.

Even more remarkable, because more unexpected, has been the career of Helen Kinney Copley, who runs and owns 90 percent of Copley Press, publisher of the *San Diego Union and Tribune* and a batch of smaller and even less journalistically impressive— but highly profitable—newspapers. That they are highly profitable is Mrs. Copley's doing.

Her late husband James built up the chain that his adoptive father, Colonel Ira Copley, had started in 1905 by purchasing the Aurora, Illinois, *Beacon* with the express purpose of battling a local politician. But James Copley was an unfortunate blend of political conservative and fiscal profligate. His closest associates realized that, in a changing world, Copley's intense Republican partisanship was making even the news columns of his newspapers ridiculous. When John F. Kennedy stumped in San Diego in 1960, he drew the largest crowd in the city's history; the *Union* put that at the bottom of page one, well below a banner headline about Richard Nixon's campaign appearance in Omaha. An employee softball team adopted the irreverent nickname The Sacred Cows. Moreover, Copley was widely known as a sentimentalist with a compulsive lack of interest in the bottom line. The combination of no news but mad spending was nowhere better illustrated than in Copley's 1965 purchase of the *Sacramento Union*: he spent an estimated $20 million modernizing the plant and turning the paper into a showcase of computerized graphics, but it never had anything worthwhile in its news columns, and it never made any money.

It took the irresistible forces of marriage and death to change the pattern. Helen Kinney had answered a classified ad in 1952 and become Copley's secretary. In 1964, Copley divorced his wife Jean after a seventeen-year marriage, and the next year he married Mrs. Kinney, who had also been divorced. When Copley was dying of cancer in 1973, Helen "assured him I would do the best I could" in keeping the chain alive, she has said in an interview. Her best was very good. Burdened, like Katharine Graham, with a nearly invincible shyness,[17] she took public-speaking lessons and forced herself into such situations as day-long question-and-answer periods with the company's employees.

Mrs. Copley's revivification of the company was a thing of corporate beauty. Within a year of her accession, the *Union* ran a roundup of the local clerics' views on abortion—a topic utterly taboo under her late husband. In 1984, the San Diego papers were the target of charges by the mayor of San Diego, Roger Hedgecock, that they were out to destroy him politically through their consistent reporting about his investments with J. David & Company, the foreign-currency investment firm that went belly-up earlier that year with investigators unable to find some $112 million in investors' funds. Hedgecock said Mrs. Copley's alleged animus against him stemmed from her close friendship with the defeated candidate in the last mayoral election, Maureen O'Connor, wife of Jack-in-the-Box multimillionaire Robert O. Peterson. The idea of a Copley paper kicking up a fuss with a local political figure was something utterly alien to the chain in the past. While it is still unlikely that any Copley newspaper will win a Pulitzer Prize in the foreseeable future, the overall content has been brought much more into the great blended mainstream of American journalism.

17. After much twisting and turning, which included a substantial discourse on her dislike of publicity ("I know it's a terrible thing for a newspaper publisher to say"), Mrs. Copley declined to be interviewed for this book.

Helen Copley's business achievements have been even more startling. Forced by the exigencies of Copley's will—estate taxes came to some $16 million—to confront the tough facts of financial life, Mrs. Copley also did away with many of the trappings of her husband's sentimental journey. She quickly sold the corporate plane, and even the Copley family mansion in Aurora, which James had maintained as a sort of shrine. She has also run roughshod over the network of old cronies that James Copley had allowed to take over the chain during his years of terminal cancer; she unceremoniously chopped away much of the bureaucracy, going so far as to hold small meetings with editorial employees to listen to their complaints—events still remembered with some amazement in the chain. And she has gotten the company into cable television. As a result, the chain is now immensely profitable; *Forbes* estimates Mrs. Copley's worth at a minimum of $200 million. She is grooming David, her son by a previous marriage, to take over eventually.

Enid Annenberg Haupt came to be a publisher in a somewhat indirect way. Not only did her father, Moses, the tough circulation director, publisher (*Philadelphia Inquirer*), and convicted tax evader, have to die, but her younger brother Walter, who inherited all the voting stock—though his sisters got enough of the dividend-earning stock to make them all centimillionaires in their own rights—had to ask her to join the business. She was rather surprised when he approached her in 1953 about taking over *Seventeen* magazine; but, sharing the profound arrogance abundant among the Annenberg children,[18] once she started as editor in chief she had no doubt she would do a good job.

Since she knew nothing about magazines except that she liked pretty ones—indeed, her entire experience in publishing had been writing features for the *Inquirer* during the war—the staff at *Seventeen* predictably resented a woman they considered a rich dilettante marking time at their place of work until something else struck her fancy. Enid quickly demonstrated that she was not to be slighted. An executive she had asked to show her around replied that she was "too busy," and the new editor in

18. Throughout the family it has led to an intense desire for privacy, even while the sisters give parties at their Palm Beach houses and Walter his world-class affairs in the Palm Springs showcase, Sunnylands. Charlotte Curtis wrote of Enid Haupt's philanthropies that "since she is not in the least gregarious, sharing is her way of participating while keeping the world at arm's length."

chief fired her on the spot. But it was also her eye—she was already a prize-winning flower arranger—and her capacity for work that won over the staff. She was driven not only by a knowledge that she *was* wonderful, but the corresponding fear that somebody might get the impression that she was *not*. She sought advice wherever she could find it and rapidly taught herself much of the magazine business. She worked such late hours that for her first two years as editor and publisher, she has said, she was too exhausted to dine out socially. She even wrote an advice column for teenagers, a rather humorous matter considering that she herself had eloped at the age of seventeen with a distinctly unsuitable man twenty-two years older. Enid quickly gained such confidence that she became one of the few people who dared to argue with Walter Annenberg, who was chairman of Triangle Publications to everybody else but only a fellow stockholder and little brother to her. In 1970, she consolidated her advice to teenagers into an etiquette book and retired from a thriving publication to indulge her green thumb and her reclusiveness.

Other women have contributed to the growth of newspapers quietly, as the late Jessie Bancroft Cox did to the *Wall Street Journal*, simply by backing editors among the major stockholders. When the *Journal*'s editors were trying, after World War II, to turn it from a financial sheet into its present-day incarnation as a general business and economic publication, Mrs. Cox supported them on the board of directors. (The formal vote was cast by her husband, William Cox, who needed her consent as holder of the stock.) When the company went public, she insisted that the heirs of founder Clarence Barron retain a controlling interest to ensure the paper's independence. (It also ensured the huge fortune of a number of descendants.) When Vermont Royster became editor of the paper in 1958, he was asked by Mrs. Cox how he was getting along in the new job. He mentioned that he felt that some outside directors were trying to push him to change the editorial direction. "Pay no attention to them," she said—a reply to which Royster attributes the independence of *Journal* editors ever since.

Even when they have no formal ownership stake in the family publishing enterprises, women have made significant marks on the institutions—largely because a newspaper can be changed and manipulated in ways that simply do not apply to, say, the production of petroleum. Dorothy Buffum Chandler, for example, was a key figure in the creation of the modern *Los Angeles Times*—and also, through the *Times*, in the creation of modern Los Angeles as well. The wife of the late heir and publisher Norman Chandler, Buff, as she was known, pushed him distinctly away from the staid, rather fearful world of old money centered in WASPy Pasadena. Her impact was felt in the newspaper directly. "Wounded and rejected by one social order, Buff Chandler set out to redefine the social order of the entire city," wrote David Halberstam. "The instrument of this change was the society section of the *Los Angeles Times*." By the 1950s, the women featured most prominently in the paper were not simply those who had organized DAR functions or their daughters' debuts; they were women who had accomplished something, gathered money for worthwhile causes, led the community in some way. The Woman of the Year, the epitome of the qualities Buff Chandler wanted to see in rich women, was always chosen largely by Buff Chandler herself. The older high society, with nothing to recommend it but its own undying sense of self-worth, would have to do without public recognition in the future.

At the tabloid *Los Angeles Mirror*, Buff created the Best Dressed for Your Life feature, which was to showcase women whose active, valuable lives were appropriately complemented by their wardrobes. The grandest of the circles she created was the infelicitously named but very influential Amazing Blue Ribbon Four Hundred, which was composed of people who had given at least one thousand dollars to the abuilding Chandler Music Center. Consistently well featured in the *Times*, the Amazings thus served not only to buttress Buff Chandler's formidable power to declare who was in and who was out, but also to fund that great monument to her personal generosity. She affected the newspaper's policies through her husband as well: at the 1952 Republican convention, for example, she warned Norman, according to Halberstam, that she would not have sex with him until he switched his allegiance from the archconservative Robert Taft to Eisenhower. Norman switched.

But Buff's most permanent legacy to what has become an enormously influential (as well as incredibly profitable) communications conglomerate was her coup, in 1959, in removing her husband as publisher of the *Times* and replacing him with their son Otis, who was only thirty-two at the time. Persuading Norman to move upstairs to chairman of the parent company, while leaving power over the newspaper in Otis's hands through the present time, was a smashing victory for Buff over her in-laws, the old and stodgy Chandler family, who had wanted instead the conservative Philip, Norman's younger brother. The well was slightly poisoned, however, by Otis's own wife, Missy, whom Buff, in classic smothering-mother style, naturally disliked. While Missy could never dominate Otis the way that Buff had Norman, she was frequently the source of what little information newspaper employees got about their secretive publisher, and she was considered a great influence in persuading Otis to endorse Nixon in 1968. The fluid nature of a publisher's product gives a wife unusual influence over the newspaper's content through the wife's influence over the publisher, even in cases where the women do not inherit papers themselves.

Publishing has been a universal avenue for women to exercise control over wealth. In Brazil, a Latin American country that fully lives up to the stereotype of Hispanic condescension to women, the late Countess Pereira Carneiro was perhaps the most powerful publisher of the twentieth century. Until her death in 1983 at the age of eighty-four, she was the owner, publisher, and *diretora-presidente* of *Jornal do Brasil*, one of the largest dailies in the country and the voice of its Catholic and conservative establishment. A young widow, she started her professional life as the secretary and collaborator of her father, Dunshee de Abranches, the author of more than a hundred very serious books. In 1942, she married Count Pereira Carneiro, an industrialist and politician. At the time, the *Jornal do Brasil* was a small advertising publication. When the countess, who had the toothy look of Eleanor Roosevelt, took over upon her husband's death in 1953, she turned the paper into a modern publication, brought in new talent, expanded the staff until it is now the largest in Brazil, and gradually turned it into one of the major forces in Brazilian life. "For the countess," reads the newspaper's publicity release, "journalism is more than the mere reporting of news; it is a weapon in the spearhead of the country's progress." It has also been enormously profitable. In 1982, the *Jornal do Brasil* companies earned over $92 million in gross revenue.

Gayatri Devi, the Rajmata (former maharani) of Jaipur, is the Indian subcontinent's sparkling example of a woman who has managed her inheritance into her own continuing wealth. Need-less to say, the future maharani was brought up grandly; as the daughter of the Princess Indira Gaekwar of Baroda ("the most beautiful and exciting woman any of us knew"), her childhood swung between the intricacies of noble behavior, dazzling opul-ence, the complexities of tutors and governesses, the greeting of distinguished international guests, and the aristocratic thrill of the hunt. During a period of thirty-seven years, she records in her memoirs, her grandfather listed his kills in the jungles of Cooch Behar and Assam as 365 tigers, 311 leopards, 207 rhinos, 438 buffaloes, 318 antelopes, 259 sambars, 133 bears, and 43 bison. She was twelve years old when she shot her first panther. Amidst the decaying splendor of international society between the wars, Gayatri Devi grew into a sultry, stylish young woman.

In 1941, she became the third wife of the Maharajah of Jaipur— "Jai," an international sportsman and socialite with his own polo stadium, a ski chalet in St. Moritz, and mansions in London, Paris, Cannes, and Nice, and a future ambassador to Spain. That event brought her such presents as a black Bentley from the Nawab of Bhopal, a Packard from one of the nobles in Jaipur, and a house in the Himalayan foothills from her Baroda grand-mother, as well as the standards such as a set of pearls, a set of rubies, and a diamond necklace. Ayisha, Jai's first (and consid-erably older) wife—"First Her Highness," as Gayatri Devi re-ferred to her—had managed to impress even the massively rich Barbara Hutton, when the latter visited India with her first hus-band in the 1930s, by showing her solid-gold trunks filled with uncut diamonds. Gayatri Devi had grown up with such luxury and was unfazed as she moved into the Jaipur palace and made her peace with four hundred servants. One of her first duties was to preside at the wedding of Jai's eldest daughter, Mickey, to the Maharaj Kumar of Baria, just before independence in 1948— "perhaps the final grand display of the pageantry of princely India," as she recorded it in her autobiography. Some eight hundred guests, mostly Indian nobles, attended the festivities, which lasted two weeks, with lavish banquets and parties every night. The book of instructions for all the functionaries putting on the show was two inches thick. Gayatri Devi, who was as-signed to collecting Mickey's trousseau, had representatives of the best shops in Delhi and Bombay come to the palace, and from them she selected two hundred saris, and equal numbers of Rajputani skirts, bodices, jackets, and veils. Henri Cartier-

Bresson was hired to make photographs. Until recently, the *Guiness Book of World Records* listed it as the most expensive wedding in history.[19]

But that was not the only record Gayatri Devi set. She has been listed in that same book for the largest margin of victory ever achieved in a democratic election, when she was elected to the Indian Parliament in 1962 in a great outpouring of popular affection for the former rulers of the Jaipur state. Her popularity was not hurt by the fact that she had the wherewithal and the inclination to provide help for her constituents out of her own purse; she also started her own girls' school, in which she retains an active involvement. When Gayatri Devi visited Washington with Jai later in 1962, President Kennedy said to her, "I hear you are the Barry Goldwater of India." Kennedy's wife returned the visit while she was still First Lady, and it was the beginning of a lifelong friendship with Jackie, who still stops by Jaipur to see Gayatri Devi when she visits India.

It has not, however, been all smooth sailing for her highness. Former royalty is a convenient whipping-boy for the leftist governments of newly freed colonies; and Indira Gandhi, who went so far as to declare the infamous "state of emergency" to guarantee herself power, was perfectly happy to take advantage of the situation. In 1980, a former justice of the Indian Supreme Court suggested in a report to the Parliament that Gayatri Devi, along with the wife of former Prime Minister Charan Singh and the son and daughter-in-law of Singh's predecessor, Morarji Desai, had improperly used political influence. Given that her fellow suspects were family members of Indira Gandhi's political rivals, it seems more than likely that partisan politics was involved. Gayatri Devi even spent a short time in prison on charges of hiding gold and jewelry.

19. The new world record was set on June 16, 1979, when twenty-year-old Maria Niarchos married Alix Chevassus, sixteen years her senior, at her father Stavros's estate in Normandy, France. Guests housed in four football-field-sized tents consumed some twelve thousand bottles of champagne and red wine. The cost was conservatively set at $500,000.

That is the Guiness record, at least. But in 1981, the royal family of Abu Dhabi spent an estimated $33 million on the festivities surrounding the nuptials of Princess Salama and the son of Sheikh Zayid ibn Said al-Makhtum. Of course, 20,000 people attended seven days of festivities.

Another interesting record set in 1929 is still standing, according to Guinness. The largest recorded dowry is said to have been settled then on Elena Patiño, daughter of the Bolivian tin emperor Simón Iturbi Patiño; it was more than $22 million. The family still has incredible wealth and makes the international social scene.

Despite the fickle political winds, though, she remains in active charge of a number of large businesses in Jaipur. She turned the Rambagh Palace, formerly a royal residence, into one of the most lavish and expensive hotels in the world, with her son Joey taking over day-to-day administration; she herself now lives in the Lilypool, a not especially grand house in the gardens of Rambagh. She started and continues as chairman of a business to weave and export dhurries, the locally produced cotton rugs. She started a school for arts and crafts to preserve local workmanship. And of course, as the widow of a famous polo player, she directs a stud farm in Jaipur as well. In short, Gayatri Devi appears well on her way to converting a semifeudal fortune of incalculable dimension into a modern service-economy empire to pass along to her heirs. If you can't be noble, you might as well be rich.

Arguably the greatest female enterpreneur in the world today is an enigmatic woman who runs the third-largest business conglomerate in the Republic of China (Taiwan), Vivian Wu Yen. "I am just forced to take action by opportunities," she has said in one of the obscure pronouncements that drive both competitors and employees crazy. In her case, the opportunities have included a marriage of forty-seven years to Dr. Yen Tjing-ling, who managed to spirit twenty thousand spindles out of Shanghai before the Communists got there in 1949 and established the Tai Yuan Textile Company on Taiwan, which has since grown into the largest cloth manufacturer in that bastion of free enterprise. In 1950, getting bored with the needle trades, he traveled to Detroit to learn about the auto business. He learned well enough to establish the Yue Loong Motor Company, which produced fifty-seven thousand cars in 1981. Since Dr. Yen's interest was in cars, he passed along the management of Tai Yuan Textile to Vivian Wu; she had studied for it, more or less, by getting a master's degree from Columbia University while he was in Detroit. The partnership enabled the couple to corner a noticeable portion of the gross national product of Taiwan.

In 1976, Yen suffered a brain injury in a fall, and began to transfer total responsibility for the conglomerate to Vivian Wu. When he died in the spring of 1981, she became the head of the entire conglomerate, including the Yue Loong Motor Company, Tai Yuan Textile Company, Diamond Hosiery & Thread Company, China Motor Company, Yue Sheng Industrial Company,

Yue Ki Industrial Company, and Union and NHK Auto Parts Corporation. Under her leadership, in 1981 the business organization employed thirteen thousand people and had revenues of about $667 million.

The widow has reportedly moved rather smoothly into the operation of a major conglomerate after an initial period of feeling overwhelmed by it. By all accounts she is profoundly dedicated to the business created by her late husband and is strongly identified with it. Despite a few attempts to humanize her—the official biographical line recalls a "naughty" schoolgirl who "liked to talk and snack in the classroom"—accounts suggest a demanding, rather gorgonic presence. Vivian Wu's great goal is to produce the first car designed entirely in Taiwan. She prides herself on strict treatment and close questioning of subordinates. She certainly has no interest in the lavish living of other rich women, no doubt at least partly because of her conservative Chinese upbringing. Her punctuality and lack of interest in social life are widely known. Like many with a great deal of money, in particular those who made it themselves, Vivian Wu has little time or sympathy for those who complain that their sex has held them back. If it was a handicap, she overcame it, and they damn well can too. She told the *Free China Review:*

> Although I am a female business leader, I still think most female managers are inferior in performance to male managers. Many female managers cannot concentrate their energies and their minds on their careers. They consider their home affairs as more important to them. Young managers often discuss their household affairs among themselves.
>
> Besides, female managers are easily contented, impeding their progress. They are also more jealous and are often antagonized by others' promotions. Male managers also phone their friends, but more often than not, they are inquiring about information related to their jobs. In comparison, they are more responsible.
>
> As a department chief, one must be responsible for one's work. A female department chief should never be perfunctory in her performance simply on grounds that she belongs to the fair and weak sex. She should know that others will not be less demanding of her simply because she is a woman. In communicating with such women department chiefs, many men will show outward respect for the woman, but inwardly will hold her in contempt. On the social circuit, women in management cannot totally mix with their male counterparts.
>
> Nevertheless, there is little difference in real ability between the

two sexes. But because women managers usually have less contact with the outside world, they are not as informed as their male counterparts.

The number of women managers is smaller, and it is easier for them to rise from the ranks if they are really excellent. I do not like to be referred to as the "only woman entrepreneur." I like to be introduced as "president of the Yue Loong Motor Co." People should recognize that I attained my present position in my own right, not because I am a woman.

When I became board chairperson of Tai Yuan, most people thought it was a result of my relationship with my husband, Dr. Yen Tjing-ling. Actually, I got the position in my own right. Under other conditions, I would have preferred teaching. I would rather be called Professor Wu. Fortunately, most people now recognize the criterion was ability.

Elsewhere in the Orient, women have, fortunately, not heard much of Vivian Wu's discouraging words. In Hong Kong, Marjorie Yang is heiress-apparent to her father's textile business, having prepared for the presumed accession by studying at M.I.T. and then acquiring an M.B.A. from Harvard. Decades ago, Sally Aw Sian set the precedent for women to go into business in Hong Kong when she made her mark in publishing, that useful field for female advancement in the Americas. While she inherited the *Hong Kong Standard* from her father, it has been at her hands that it turned into a dominant newspaper. Indeed, it has been Patricia Cloherty's experience with the Committee of Two Hundred, which includes businesswomen from outside the United States, that "women owning a business is more prevalent in some Asian countries, like the Philippines or Thailand, than it is in the United States."

No doubt to the surprise of the upholders of the tradition of Hispanic macho, South America has proved a fertile breeding ground for female entrepreneurship. However, it is an entrepreneurship founded entirely on inheritance; Hispanic women simply do not set up on their own. The current head of the Matarazzo industrial group, one of the largest conglomerates in Brazil and the owner of the largest industrial plant in the Third World, is María Pía Matarazzo. A woman whose sole contact with the general public comes through her company's myriad products and a formal business photograph projecting a look of chilling determination, Miss Matarazzo is currently presiding, unfortunately, over one of the most spectacular declines in the country's industrial history. She has been forced to sell off four textile plants, an instant coffee factory, a supermarket chain, a bank building, and a cement business—$160 million worth of her patrimony altogether. Despite the sell-offs, the conglomerate estimated in 1983, when it asked bankruptcy court protection for eleven of its forty-three businesses, that it was still $160 million in debt, a breathtaking amount even in Brazil's inflation-addled economy. The scope of the disaster is enough to spur knowing sighs from the male half of Brazil's population that is not used to a woman in control of anything, most especially not what Miss Matarazzo described as once "the greatest business in Brazil."

Even more delighted, perhaps, were the two older brothers who quit the family business in disgust when the 1977 will of their father, Count Francisco Matarazzo II, surprisingly named the youngest of his five children as head of the empire. Miss Matarazzo, who inhabits the ancestral palace on São Paulo's Avenida de Paulista—one of the few mansions remaining on a street that was comparable to Fifth Avenue in the prime of the great industrial fortunes—is showing no signs that she's sorry with the hand fate dealt her. "We will continue to fulfill my father's dream," she announced to a gathering at the mansion in 1982 to celebrate the company's centennial.

Next door in Argentina, María Amalía Lacroze de Fortabat is one of the most impressive business owners in a country where merely surviving the deadly political currents has been a full-time job. She is president of one of the biggest cement factories in the country, Loma Negra C.I.A.S.A., whose name is proudly borne by a prominent Buenos Aires soccer team. She owns a good deal of land and contributes prominently to charity, which is a peculiarly United States art that has translated badly in South America. She has also taken time out to collect art; her most famous acquisition is J. M. W. Turner's *Juliet and Her Nurse*, which at the time of its purchase for $6.4 million from Sotheby's New York gallery in 1980 was the most expensive work of art in history.

Three weeks after the death in 1960 of Salvatore Ferragamo, the man who had sheathed the feet of Mae West, Eva Perón, and Queen Elizabeth in a career as the world's greatest shoemaker, his widow Wanda and their two eldest daughters made their funereal way from their thirty-room villa in Fiesole down the Tuscan hills to Florence. There, in the thirteenth-century palazzo on the Arno from which Salvatore Ferragamo sold his world-famous shoes amidst frescoes of Boccetti and priceless Renaissance furniture, Wanda Ferragamo informed her husband's staff that henceforth, she and the daughters would take care of the business. It was no small move for a girl from a country village near Naples who had never spent a day at the office in her life to take over a business in a country that to the present day has little use for *femina economica*.

Wanda herself may have been the only one in the headquarters who had no doubt of her ability to continue the family empire. "I was not born for cards—I was born to achieve something," she reflects, seated in her queen-mother pose in one of the enormous echoing rooms of the palazzo, glinting with pavé-diamond rings and a triple-strand pearl necklace. "Even as a little girl I would always fill up my days. I must have something inside." What she had inside was the inspirational genius to turn what was essentially a one-man show, albeit a very successful one, into a huge fashion empire that now produces sixty thousand shoes a month in twelve factories and has annual revenues approaching $80 million.

But Ferragamo does not reign by shoes alone. Matriarch Wanda has brought each of her six children into the operation: eldest daughter Fiamma designs the women's shoes; Giovanna does the ready-to-wear; first son Ferruccio is general manager; Fulvia is head of the accessories division; Leonardo runs the ten-year-old menswear line; and Massimo is studying the family's United States operations in New York. Once Wanda decided to retain control of the firm, there was never any doubt that the children would go into the business. The family's entire identity was tied up in Salvatore's work; the celebrity was intoxicating. "He made us to love his work," Wanda says. Besides, they were able to pick the portion of the business they wanted to go into, allowing scope for artistic or business talents to flourish.

But there seems no doubt, according to both the family and outsiders, that it was Wanda's unstoppable devotion to the family, defined as both relatives and business partners, that made Ferragamo one of the major names in classical fashions. "Work is a drug," says Wanda. There is little else she wants to do. She owns four houses in Italy, including "a paradise" on Capri, and an apartment in the superopulent Olympic Tower on Fifth Avenue, but "I can enjoy them very little because I feel such responsibility. Personally, I could live like a queen without working. Sometimes I would like to slow down, to go to the country or to Capri. But I cannot. I must be here, because every day I am doing something useful—for the children, for the house. The house must progress."

The Partners: Inheriting While They're Still Alive

Like Napoleon, Leona Helmsley has crowned herself. By now, Leona's advertising of herself as the "queen" of the Palace Hotel in New York, the nerve center of the twenty-seven-hotel Helmsley Hotel chain, has become such a part of the culture, at least among readers of upscale magazines, that it has even been satirized in a *New Yorker* cartoon. In the panel, a crotchety old lady asks her crotchety old mate, "Why can't *you* buy some hotels and make *me* your queen?" (An enlarged version hangs in Leona's office suite on the fifth floor of the Helmsley Palace.) As the cartoon suggests, Leona Helmsley is not, strictly speaking, either the builder of an inherited business or the creator of her own. She is, rather, the most stunning example of a developing phenomenon—the woman who, as it were, inherits some of her husband's business while he is still alive. Becoming a business partner along with a life partner is an increasingly popular enterprise of women who marry wealth.

Leona's creator is Harry Helmsley, the largest landlord in New York City—the owner of an estimated $5 billion worth of real estate on that tall, expensive island. Actually, the suggestion that Harry played Professor Higgins to her Eliza is, to hear the universally opinionated Leona tell it, a base canard that has somehow gotten abroad.

It only *appears* to the benighted that Harry gave her something. In point of fact, when she first asked to do the decorating for the Helmsley Palace, which Harry was renovating behind and fifty-five stories above the landmark Villard Houses on Madison Avenue, he told her, "Don't be a rich man's wife, the answer is no." Clever Leona, who had managed very well on her own until she married Harry, thank you—doing such things as peddling the first condominium in New York—quietly decorated three rooms and had a professional do three more. Harry liked hers, of course. And that was that. Her compulsion for quality came out when one soon-to-be-gone decorator decided on relatively cheap carpeting for the restaurant in the Park Lane Hotel on Central Park South, which is not only one of the chain's showcases but one of the homes of Leona and Harry. (Other stomping grounds include a lavish estate in Greenwich, Connecticut, which was recently on the market for $12 million, and a penthouse overlooking Lake Worth in Palm Beach.) Leona was not amused. "It's one of the most beautiful rooms in the city," she recalls. "When I saw the carpet I said I wouldn't do it to save three thousand dollars or ten thousand dollars because now the silk on the wall won't match and it's going to be an olio, a hodgepodge."

Anyway, that was enough to drive the decorator away; Harry was left with a half-refinished hotel and nobody immediately in prospect to finish it. Except Leona, of course. She started finishing hotels, and she hasn't stopped since. There was, perhaps, some snickering at first about the boss's wife taking over the hotel side. There is no snickering now. Whether it is cause or effect of her success, Leona possesses an outsize egotism, not to mention great stores of temper and determination. One would not make book that Leona couldn't take over any business she decided to, Harry or no Harry beside her. Her employees are quite clearly fascinated by her and terrified of her. When she sits down for an interview, it is all her gentle public-relations counselor, Howard J. Rubenstein, can do to keep her on one line of thinking; and this powerful counselor to many of the richest and most influential of New York dons a look of apprehension when he interrupts to suggest a change. As her ads say, the queen really does pop up in the kitchen to sip the broth and scours hapless managers' rooms to make sure there are enough real removable hangers.[20] When a waiter brings her some lunch in a warmer, she cannot resist browbeating him—"this is such a foolish way to serve this, the flame is so high it's cooking"—and he apologizes with something close to awe in his voice. She claims that when she took over the chain, her security force would not let her enter the kitchens because the seething employees had access to knives.

Leona has palpable need for activity and attention. But much greater than that is her compulsion to be recognized as an achiever by herself. She is not, by the way, a feminist: like many of her peers who are either completely or partially self-made, she has

---

20. The commitment to quality is not utterly open-ended; there are no real books in the Palace's library, for example, because they had proved "too tempting" to the guests.

the attitude that if she made it herself, anybody can and should be able to do the same. While she thinks there are so few women at her level because "women have not been trained for executive positions," she does not seem to consider her own sex to have been any sort of obstacle; being a woman in a man's business, she says, is "great. Fun. They cater to you. You're outstanding all the time. Why would I want to be with a lot of women and get lost?" In fact, her first job was as a model, and she was a Chesterfield Girl. She is supposed to be somewhere within striking distance of sixty, but she is still quite attractive—even more in person than in her ads—although she has added some girth that makes her look even tougher. She has a star's disdain for the crowd: she does not think much of the National Organization for Women and laughed at their decision to endorse the Democrat in the 1984 presidential race long before he had been chosen. The idea of abrogating a chance for power or leverage drives self-made people crazy.

Like almost all people who have acquired or taken over great wealth, Leona has a well-polished story of her miraculous ascension, which she tells, with occasional variations, to everybody who writes about her. The key component of the saga is Leona's rise by her own bootstraps in the world of real estate. The first caption on her personal publicity release is "A Real Estate Success in Her Own Right." From the predictably humble beginnings as a young divorcée with a child to support, Leona came to realize that she could sell sand to Libya. Before long she was so titanically successful at peddling high-priced apartments as cooperatives and condominiums that Helmsley had no choice, so the story goes, but to hire her away from the competition. She went to work for the co-op management and sales division of Helmsley's empire as a senior vice-president at $500,000 a year. A few years later, in 1972, he told her he would marry her if she lost twenty pounds. It was a deal.[21]

As a result of that merger, Leona now has time for two people in her life, with Harry as much on her mind and tongue as she is herself. She tosses him lavish birthday parties every March 4, with attendance a mark of status in the Manhattan elite—Annenbergs, Rockefellers, Frank Sinatra, governors and mayors, the

21. At around the same time, uranium tycoon Joseph Hirshhorn was also telling one of his employees that he would trade marriage for dieting as well; but Olga had to lose only ten pounds before she became Mrs. Hirshhorn.

other real estate barons, and so on. At the parties atop the Park Lane, she wears a button that says, "I'm Just Wild About Harry," and he wears one reading, "I'm Harry." As if anybody didn't know. At his seventy-fifth, Leona sprang for a set of eighteen pairs of dolls with the bodies of Ken and Barbie, the heads of Harry and Leona, and the costumes of famous couples through-out history. (One need hardly mention that Napoleon and Josephine were among them.) The current rankings in Leona's system of value thus are now Harry, one; Leona, two; Everybody Else, off the charts. "I did not have any close friends," she says, with her trademark bulldozer directness.

> I did not have time for it. I had acquaintances—people that would invite me to their homes, people that I sold apartments to and I had to agree to go. In addition to that, well, after three years [following the divorce] I did start to date and I think I dated almost every eligible in New York City. Everybody has an uncle or a cousin, and if they like you they make the date for you. It got to the point where I didn't want to go to dinner anymore. I said we could have cocktails. But I didn't have close friends. The same thing goes for my living today with Harry. See now, I know Howard [Rubenstein] coming on fifteen years—good friends, but we're not that close. I don't have that kind of time and my closest friend in the whole world is Harry Helmsley. I don't have any other *friends*. I told Harry things that I wouldn't dream of telling anybody else and vice versa. . . . Firstly, I work because I definitely want Harry's approval. I want Harry to say I'm wonderful and he should get so involved with me he will never leave me.

Noticing Leona's patent pleasure in the swirl her wake kicks up, one is hard pressed to imagine she did it all for love. She does, however, seem an ideal companion for a billionaire. If she outlives Harry, she will no doubt make a fine billionaire herself. *Her* consort will have to be a paragon—the Prince Albert of the twentieth century.

It sounds silly to call Ivana Trump a more ordinary person than anyone, but compared with Leona Helmsley she is positively homey. She is also an example of the much more common type of rich man's wife: the one who takes (at least in the beginning) a small role in his enterprises, typically in interior design, who becomes a "rich man's wife," as Harry Helmsley warned Leona not to. Harry Helmsley is the richest real estate man in New York now, and Donald Trump, Ivana's husband, makes no secret of his lust for the title. Anyone who has seen the new sixty-eight-story Trump Tower on Fifth Avenue—the sort of unbridled display of gaudy riches that has made Rodeo Drive notorious—needs no further analysis of Donald Trump's vision. In sharp contrast to virtually any other multimillionaire, Trump actually overestimates his wealth, pegging it at half a billion dollars when most observers would set it several hundred million less.

In Ivana, appropriately, he found a gleaming prize as well: she is half Czech and half Austrian, skied in the 1972 Sapporo Olympics, then raced professionally until she settled into a modeling career in Montreal, quickly rising to the top of *that* profession, and then capped it by meeting the overwhelmingly eligible Donald and weaning him away from his man-about-town days. Naturally, two of her chief occupations are bearing Trump heirs—she had her third child in 1984—and maintaining the rigorous regimen of exercise, massage, hair, and facial treatments that are necessary additions to the ornamentation of Trump. She also maintains a substantial social schedule and does most of the cooking for the family. But she has become heavily involved, much like the consorts of many other important builders, in selecting the color schemes and furnishings for Trump projects. *Only* for Trump projects: "Donald's afraid that if I go back [to outside work] now I'll get so involved that I won't have another child," she told the *Times* in 1979. So she works in the family business. She spent a week in Italy selecting the precise shade of peach-rose-and-salmon Breccia Perniche marble that makes the atrium of the Trump Tower so memorable. One of her most visible contributions to the Trump Tower experience are the uniforms of the guards, who look to have stepped directly out a forgotten Gilbert and Sullivan operetta with their gold-buttoned crimson tunics, epaulets, and towering black busbies. She claims she was just having some fun. To others, it might well look as though Ivana Trump has designed the uniforms for the personal royal guard of the burgeoning Empire of Trump.

Mrs. Trump now spends ten-hour days working on her husband's projects, and it is a trend that seems to be spreading wildly among the wives of rich and powerful men. Construction is an especially good field, since it affords so many detailed specialties that a woman can easily carve out a niche in. Among those who have recently followed this promising path are Mrs. Howard P. Ronson, the secretive wife of a secretive developer, who recently moved into Manhattan from England; and Gabriele Murdock, the artist wife of the centimillionaire California builder-financier David H. Murdock, who came into prominence recently when she took an active role in restoring Washington's Hay Adams Hotel to its former elegance and social prominence. The attraction for the women in these situations is obvious: it gives them something to do beyond bearing children and running the household. For the men, their value is in what has always been the attraction of working with family members: you have a much better hold over them than over mere employees. If you married a particular woman from among all those attracted to your wealth, you ought to have enough appreciation for her style to allow her to impose it on your buildings. These days, when a millionaire offers a woman anything she wants, what she generally takes is a chance to design his buildings.

5 | WOMEN WHO MADE IT THEMSELVES

THERE ARE THREE THINGS that are more important than sex or money, says Mary Kay Ash: praise, recognition, and applause. To the extent that that insight is shrewd, it has made its inventor something over $100 million. To the extent that it is true, it goes far to explain why so few other women in the history of the world have done so. There are perhaps a dozen women in the world today who have made the sort of money that Mary Kay, the cosmetics lady, has. There are several dozen more who control fortune-generating enterprises that they inherited from fathers or husbands. And that is the extent of active female involvement in the manipulation of large blocks of capital.

Women's role in huge business enterprises is even more restricted than that makes it sound, however. They run active fortunes almost exclusively within two business fields: cosmetics, like Mary Kay; and publishing, which as we noted proved extremely hospitable (at least comparatively) to female Citizen Kanes. Those who have succeeded to excess in traditionally male fields, who have made a fortune for themselves in manufacturing or retailing, stand out like redwoods.

Probably the greatest American example is Mary Hudson, the reclusive woman who, as a young widow in Dust Bowl Kansas, made herself one of the greatest fortunes a woman has ever created—well over $100 million—by starting a chain of gas stations that has since grown into the Hudson Oil Co.

Or did she? There is no doubt that Mrs. Hudson created a remarkable business empire, but in recent years there *have* been suggestions that she proved herself as adept as her male counterparts not only in the creation of wealth but in the fabrication of how it came to be. Even more sadly, the widow-with-the-will-of-iron myth was apparently backed up, as again frequently are her opposite numbers' across the sex chasm, by a willingness to grind minimum-wage work or less from her employees and to put her corporate thumb on the gas-pump register. To round out the satisfying parallel with male entrepreneurial comets, Mrs. Hudson is suffering now, in her old age, on the twin horns of public disapproval and financial setbacks.

But it started out so grandly. Mrs. Hudson's first husband was killed by an automobile accident in Kansas in the depression nadir year of 1933, leaving the twenty-year-old housewife with only a six-month-old daughter and her wits—neither of which appeared a good source of support at the moment. With her back against the wall, she has always told the curious, she borrowed $200 from her father and opened a gasoline station at the corner of Twenty-fifth Street and Broadway in Kansas City. To do so, she said, she had to leave her daughter to her mother's care. The young Mrs. Hudson was soon consumed with her entrepreneurial activities. She had a natural bent for the business and rapidly leveraged herself into a sprouting chain of gas stations. "Even though I loved beautiful clothes," she wrote in a twelve-page autobiographical sketch she sent to newspapers in 1966, "I could not forget the recession—with no money in the bank—so I preferred to save money to build stations." Nor was it merely a struggle to accumulate, Mrs. Hudson related. She had the usual difficulties of a woman trying to make it in a man's business, and she recalled acts of God that she had triumphed over as well: a serious boating accident, a cyclone, and an earthquake. She decided, prematurely, that she had "just about experienced everything to be encountered in life." She looked back on the struggle with some regret but an air of resignation at what she had sacrificed: "I would be away from Kansas City and my daughter, Joyce, for thirty days at a time," she wrote. "No trips for pleasure or vacation could be made—only business trips to protect and keep all the stations going. Knowing [that Joyce] was deprived of her mother really bothered me. However, remembering the lean years of the depression . . . no funds in the bank . . . perhaps molded my way of life."

There are those who say that Mary Hudson had neither the tenderheartedness to feel the missed joys of those years nor the honesty to admit what actually happened then. Three of the naysayers are in her own family: her nephews Mike and Tommy, and her sister-in-law Evelyn. According to those three in interviews with the *Kansas City Times,* Mrs. Hudson used her creativity in the 1930s mainly to invent the story of the widow with $200. Instead, they say, the Hudson Oil Company was actually started by her three brothers, the delphicly designated M. R., A. B., and T. J. They kindly took her in after the death of her first husband, according to this version—much to their later regret. For their dear widowed sister proved unsuspectedly adept at business manipulations. While working with her brothers, Mary Hudson began quietly acquiring her private chain of stations.

Somehow—this is a privately held company and details are hearsay—there developed at least two different Hudson Oils, Mary holding one and her brothers another, but the different companies also owning many stations jointly. It did not take a sybil to envision the approaching split. The brothers grew increasingly annoyed that Mary insisted she had started Hudson Oil (though it may have been true in the technical sense that she started the second company of that name); they were astonished to find that their sister was apparently getting their mail in her office through the similarity of the companies' names, then quickly buying up stations they had in mind; they were distressed when she insisted on cutting wages and benefits to the quick, thereby getting the kind of help she was paying for. By 1966 the two surviving brothers had had enough. They sold whatever Hudson Oil they might have owned to Mary; A. B. started the Highway Oil Company in Topeka and began referring to his "ex-sister"; M. R. founded the Fisca Oil Company but remained, for the time being, in half the same building as his sister. They soon began talking about "the Berlin Wall" that existed between the two halves of the headquarters.

Seemingly undaunted by family squabbles, Mrs. Hudson continued to roll up a fortune at a breathtaking pace. By 1981, she owned more than 270 gas stations in thirty-five states across the United States and had added her own twenty-thousand-barrel-per-day refinery in Cushing, Oklahoma. Sales hit $500 million a year. It was the largest privately owned petroleum company in the country, creating a fortune that climbed to well over $100 million and earning Mary Hudson a spot on the *Forbes* list of the four hundred richest Americans. She was a Mardi Gras Queen in 1965 and received a Horatio Alger Award in 1981. Conquering earlier qualms about lavish spending, Mrs. Hudson treated herself to ranchland in Texas, a new art collection, and a grandiose mansion in the Mission Hills section on the Kansas side of the Mississippi River.

Which was fine for Mary Hudson. But according to testimony in federal court, work at the mansion was sometimes done by Hudson Oil workers who put in seventy or eighty hours a week without being paid for it. It was not an oversight or an isolated occurrence. A federal judge ruled in October 1983 that several Hudson Oil–affiliated companies and Mrs. Hudson personally had violated federal wage-and-hour laws. (She had already been personally enjoined twice, in 1969 and 1972, to stop violating the Fair Labor Standards Act.) A woman named Paige Wiscombe testified that when she was pumping gas at a Hudson station, she was ordered to repay the company $300 that an armed robber had stolen from her; she quit instead. Early in 1984, the United States Labor Department was still trying to calculate how much money Mrs. Hudson and her businesses owe thirty thousand to forty thousand current and former employees who were cheated: it could be up to $10 million.

In July 1983, Mrs. Hudson was convicted of conspiracy to commit felony theft; she had personally ordered an area marketing manager to break state seals on gasoline pumps at Hudson stations to provide about eight cubic inches of gasoline less than they registered on a five-gallon purchase. Court papers alleged that the tampering stole $100 from customers at twelve pumps. It is true that the company needed the money. It was doing even worse than most oil companies after the late seventies oil glut, and had lost money for three consecutive years. Simply, it had no cash to pay its bills, and early in 1984 eight companies controlled by Mary Hudson filed for protection from their creditors under Chapter 11 of the Bankruptcy Act. That protects the companies, but it may not help Mrs. Hudson. She is the target of a number of class-action lawsuits to recover the money that customers lost in the pump-rigging scheme, and owes part of the $10,500 fine levied by the judge in that case. She was also ordered to perform two hundred hours of community service work at the Johnson County Mental Retardation Center. It may be a particularly onerous penalty for Mrs. Hudson. When she was twelve years old, she recalled in her autobiography, she was kissed by "a retarded boy, from a peasant family. This was the most embarrassing thing that could have happened."

Just as determined and crafty—though never as devious or reviled, and on the other hand never nearly as rich—was a southern neighbor of Mrs. Hudson's in a much more traditional "women's work" field. But there was nothing traditional about the ambition of Ebby Halliday, who used the well-worn entrepreneur's tools of brains, guts, and luck to become the most famous name in Texas real estate. "Ebby is your *friend*," proclaim billboards lining the freeways that lead to Ebby's headquarters in one of North Dallas's office parks. (Everybody calls her Ebby. This is not merely a saleswoman's affectation, although that is part of it. Rich women in general want people to call them by their first names; it is a sort of reverse snobbery, indicating that the first-namee has other valuable resources besides a title.) Ebby's firm did a friendly business of "a little over $1 billion" in the fiscal year ending September 30, 1983, making it the largest real estate firm in a large-scale town and one of the largest independent real estate companies in the United States. They don't reveal profits, but one of the financial officers once described them as "definitely large potatoes, and that's by Texas standards, mind you." The firm has twenty-three offices in Dallas–Fort Worth, about 140 employees in the headquarters, and 750 sales associates. Ebby herself is a rotund woman of something over seventy years who manages to be both perky and commanding at the same time, leaving no doubt upon first meeting that she has accumulated all this wealth and influence herself.

Indeed, her success has come not just through the bulldog determination and imperviousness to outside pleasures that most self-made people subscribe to; she has created a number of important real estate phenomena herself. She was one of the first in the country, for example, to use display homes: they were necessary to sell an early lot of practically indestructible but unattractive concrete houses. She was also one of the founders of

Inter-City Relocation Service, known as Relo, the first service to handle all aspects of a corporation's transfer of one or all of its employees. It has since been widely copied but remains one of the largest such operations in the country.

Ebby Halliday had a childhood that is far too tritely grass roots to make a respectable potboiler. She was born Vera Lucille Koch in Leslie, Arkansas, and until the age of seven was raised by her grandfather, a circuit-riding Baptist preacher. When she was eight her mother remarried and moved Vera Lucille and her siblings to Kansas. The new stepfather turned out to be a sort of prairie version of Joseph Kennedy, with a demented insistence on victory at all costs. "We were expected to get up at six in the morning, do the chores, go to school and do more chores," she told an interviewer from the *Dallas Morning News*. "He also expected us all to compete. He was obsessed with that. We were expected to win all the races at school and at the fairs. We were also expected to be Number One in our school work. More athletic pressure was put on the girls because my brother had had polio. He couldn't run fast. He had to excel in things like shot put." Once, her stepfather caught the future Ebby with a book in her hands and threw it into the fire. Unable to relax at home, she began her selling career by ordering a big supply of Cloverine Salve from a Kansas City mail-order house, paying for it with her egg money at thirteen cents a tube, and selling it door-to-door for fifteen cents. In high school, she began selling corsets and later millinery in a department store. She was transferred to Dallas in 1938, changed her name to Ebby ("that sounded like it had a lot of class") and met fate on an operating table.

Like most doctors, Ebby's tonsil surgeon was an expert on investments; but when she asked what she should do with the thousand dollars she had saved, he said he didn't advise women because they cried when they lost money. Convincing him that she didn't cry, Ebby received the sterling advice to invest in cotton futures and made $12,000 by the end of World War II. She put that into a hat business of her own, but a year later fate intervened again, this time in the person of a customer whose husband had built the famous insulated cement houses. And the legend was born.

Like her neighbor Mary Kay Ash, who was planting the seeds of her cosmetics empire at about the same time, Ebby is indefatigable in her praise for the men in her life, without whom she couldn't have done what she did. Maurice Acers is chairman of the board and husband of Ebby Halliday, in that order; knowing the type of woman Ebby is, one is not hard pressed to credit it when she says, "That wasn't a marriage, it was a merger." A lawyer and former personnel director of the FBI, Acers was a commissioner of the Texas Employment Commission when he met Ebby in an airport limousine in Beaumont, Texas. It was love at first client contact. When they married in 1965, they took an accountant and secretaries from both parties to the merger on their honeymoon to Mexico—twelve people in all. Ebby credits Acers with incorporating the firm and paving the way for its growth from its $12-million-a-year size of the time. In both her words and his, she has evolved into the "icon" of the company. She has aged gracefully from the dominating presence of the days when her billboards welcomed visitors to "Ebby Halliday Country" to the grandmotherly figure in the company literature who beams at a young girl's recital while the print underneath proclaims, "A friend is one who stands close by to ease those nervous moments. Like a teacher. Like a proud parent. Like Ebby."

Which is not to say that she has relaxed her hold over the firm utterly. Indeed, former associates say nobody has any decisive say in company operations *except* Ebby. (Ebby's paeans to the man in her life put one in mind of a fundamentalist hard-driver's jolly assertion that he couldn't have got nearly as far as he did without the little woman minding the store.) She interrupted a recent interview several times to take calls from the lawyer of a man who had agreed, apparently rashly, to buy a property for $2.5 million. The company is stamped firmly in her image: prospective sales associates are sieved through a battery of psychological tests to eliminate those who show signs of naiveté, tender-mindedness, or other traits inconducive to the bitter task of selling real estate. No one is allowed to smoke on duty—which, to Ebby's mind, incorporates virtually the entire waking day. Women wear skirts when selling; "the Ebby Halliday woman works like a man but dresses like a lady."

But her influence and reputation extend beyond her own company into the far reaches of the Dallas business community. Unabashedly self-promoting in her choices of civic duty, Ebby is chairman of Clean Dallas Inc., a director of the State Fair of Texas, the Bank of Dallas, and the Better Business Bureau, and a past president of the North Dallas Chamber of Commerce and the Greater Dallas Planning Council. On those boards, as in company business, the grandmotherly Ebby vanishes and the Napoleonic one appears in its place. She has been known to summarily quit boards and committees when she disagrees with a single vote. It is not an image she minds at all. "If I think I'm right, I try to change others' minds, and if they, in turn, believe they're right, then comes the clash," she says. "I don't like to compromise principle nor compromise an idea that I know very well is the right thing. So maybe I am stubborn. Perhaps that's one of the privileges of being a hundred years old. Maybe we do tend to get a little more autocratic, but age should have a few privileges. We certainly lose a lot."

For someone who had her eightieth birthday party in May of 1983, Ruth Springer Wedgworth has lost very little—a name here, an exact mileage there, but basically she has in her head and in her four thousand acres of fields the entire history of the sugarcane industry in central Florida. Mrs. Wedgworth had no particular intention of becoming a sugar baroness when she moved to Florida in 1932 with her husband Herman. They came down from Michigan State so he, an agronomist, could work in the Everglades agricultural experimental station. There was nothing then of the massive growth of sugar and vegetables through the fields, the elaborate pumping systems to keep the water level, the yellow buses of migrant laborers and slatted trucks to transport the cane to the refinery, or the black columns of smoke from the fields burning on the horizon. There were not even trees— they had all been blown down in the great hurricane of 1928, which killed two thousand people in the Everglades—only the vast expanse of utterly flat land, generally covered by the waters from Lake Okeechobee. Herman Wedgworth saw possibilities— for a farmer, all that land sitting idle must have been maddening—so he bought cheap land back from the road near the experimental station and began planting celery. The first year, they went to sleep to a light rain one night and awoke the next morning to find ten inches of water on the ground. That was the end of that crop. From then on, the Wedgworths realized that they would survive only as long as their ability to pump off the water did. So they put in pumps and became among the premier farmers of the Okeechobee area.

In 1938, Herman Wedgworth was killed in an accident in a packing plant, leaving Ruth with three young children and a fledgling farming business in an area that showed no lasting promise but plenty of problems. Even before the funeral, a neighboring grower approached with an offer to buy her out. She knew, however, that it would be difficult to sell for any money at all; it was depression time, and her husband had just signed a $90,000 mortgage to buy diesel engines. Fortunately, Ruth had already been keeping the farm's books, and she had spent a good deal of time in the fields beside her husband—remaining a lady by wearing a skirt over her boots. "So the employees knew me real well," she recalls, "so when the time came I told them I was willing to go ahead and carry the business on if they were willing to take the chance and stick with it. And the men stayed."

She managed the family, on top of the farm, with the help of a cook, members of her own and her husband's family, and summer camps; but it was so difficult that she is happy to see her own daughters now are able to stay home with their children. As Mrs. Wedgworth is sharp to note, she is no feminist. She has found no discrimination whatsoever in the muck lands. Well, there's no time for discrimination on the frontier. Women are respected as much for their work as for their childbearing and cooking abilities. "The men couldn't have treated me better," says Ruth Wedgworth. She is proud of remaining a lady—there is a note of regret, though, that "it was before the days of slacks"— but basically it doesn't seem to matter to her much at all, this remote suggestion of some sex discrimination. Ruth Wedgworth is really a sort of Auntie Em type, with the deep stillness of those who spend their days in the open flat lands, saying nothing, thinking only of the next task.

Only she was shrewder than Auntie Em. She continued to buy up more of the cheap land, getting along as well as she could with celery, beans, and virtually any other vegetable she could think of. She became president of the Florida State Horticultural Society, and was offered the presidency of the state Fruit and Vegetable Growers Association, but turned it down because she still had a child at home. As the crops came up only modestly year after year, it became clear that the muck around Lake Okeechobee—thousands of years of decayed, waterlogged growth, the largest muck land in the world—was basically too wet for any of those crops to grow very well. Sugar, or possibly rice, were the only logical crops. But it was not until after World War II that the sugarcane variety was developed that would make the fortunes of the growers who had stuck through the tough years. With the land increasing in value daily, Mrs. Wedgworth thought again of selling out. By that time, she had developed an acute sense of devotion to her land—it was finally out of debt and all hers—but she raised the question with her daughters just to test their reaction. The eldest said, "Well, mother, you're home as much as a lot of my friends' mothers that play bridge all the time." That was enough to put a decidedly unfrivolous person like Ruth Wedgworth back in the saddle.

Like other entrepreneurs, she was lucky as well as dedicated. Just as her sons were growing up to take over the operation, the most wonderful thing in the world happened: Castro conquered Cuba. The United States State Department, feeling under no obligation to Battista's successor, lifted the domestic production quotas that were intended to keep the Caribbean happy. Production in Florida, just over one hundred thousand tons in 1961, nearly doubled the following year, then doubled again in 1963. (It now goes well over a million tons annually.) With the disappearance of the Cuban sugar competition, and the old we'll-show-the-Commies determination, eight new mills were built in the Everglades in those two years; the acreage under sugar cultivation quadrupled by 1965. Ruth's son, George Wedgworth, took over operation of the family sugar interests as the land was rapidly turned to cane; he has also been president of the local cooperative since it was begun. The booming market in sugar, always a volatile commodity, attracted the attention of Wall Street by the middle 1970s, and there were several rough years when the value of sugarcane dropped drastically. By then, fortunately, all the bigger farmers were millionaires and able to survive.

Ruth Wedgworth is the grandest of the survivors. She is still there, in the office every day, though her involvement is decreasing and now is mainly dedicated to the fertilizer plant, with the sons taking over the farming operations. She has the great satisfaction of being well honored, of seeing the field tall with cane, the business employing two hundred workers, and her family thriving. She also has to suffer through the opprobrium of outsiders who, she is convinced, know nothing of Florida farming and so insist on producing television documentaries like *Harvest of Shame*, the famous indictment of the conditions under which migrant workers live and work. "A horrible picture," she says, suddenly looking older and tired. That people would actually believe her family's fortune was ever built on maltreatment of others! Sugarcane is a hard master—she will concede that. There is as yet no practical mechanical harvester, nor planter either; so those tasks must all be done by hand, frequently by workers imported for the season from the Caribbean. The growers say simply that no Americans will work in the hot sun for more than a few days. There are quibbles about the environment too, what with the constant burning of the fields to prepare them for harvesting. To all of that Mrs. Wedgworth gives one of her farmer's shrugs and a quiet smile. What it comes down to is that sugar is an immensely valuable crop. In the late 1970s, Florida passed Hawaii as the biggest sugar state in the Union. Palm Beach County's sugar crop sold for $447 million in 1983. Mrs. Wedgworth, who has been gazing over these fields since the time when its total value was zero, points outside her small, modern office in the town of Belle Glade, indicating the fields of cane, half a billion dollars a year, stretching away in all directions. "None of this would be here," says the proud entrepreneur, "if we hadn't started it all fifty years ago."

In sharp contrast to the old-fashioned entrepreneurship of Ruth Springer Wedgworth is the very modern story of Sandra Kurtzig, who is busily proving that women are perfectly capable of turning silicon chips into gold. Her tale is an inspiration to any women trying to Have It All, especially because she did it by ignoring the money part of the all until it chased her into a corner of her apartment and practically forced her to accept it. Mrs. Kurtzig started the process by quitting her marketing job at General Electric in 1972 in order to—don't gag—*start a family*. Fortunately for that family, she decided they weren't enough and invested $2,000 in a contract programming business that she was running out of a spare bedroom in her California apartment. She did have degrees in mathematics, chemistry, and engineering to help her along. In no time, she said when she was profiled in *Forbes* in the fall of 1983, "my part-time job was taking up twenty hours a day. I had the other four to start my family."

The rest is history, or would be if they believed in history around San Francisco. Eleven years later, Sandra Kurtzig was chief executive officer and owner of slightly more than one-fourth of all outstanding stock in ASK Computer Systems, Inc., which sells turnkey computer systems to manufacturing companies— making her worth $65 million, give or take a small fortune, by the end of 1983. It's a long way from the time when she was starting her part-time business and people would think, when she mentioned software, that she was holding home parties for women's underwear.

Even in an age of increased female participation in the traditionally all-male business schools and boardrooms, however, entrepreneurial success stories such as Kurtzig's remain extremely rare. Women simply do not, in general, look to create great wealth for themselves; the old saying is that women work for income and men for capital. Patricia Cloherty, who as a woman and a Manhattan venture capitalist naturally takes a strong interest in the topic, did a study of one recent year's public issues of stock and found that seven hundred businesspeople had become millionaires through that magical route. An even dozen of them were women—which is probably a good deal more than during the average year in the 1950s, but still, needless to say, far out of proportion to women's share of the population or the workforce.

Women are vastly underrepresented in the ranks of entrepreneurs partly because they have, as a group, seldom thought of setting out on their own; and that reluctance, in turn, can be and has been attributed to a slew of factors from general pressure on young girls to be submissive, through banks' refusal to lend women money. Things are changing, to be sure. Recent statistics show that women now own nearly one-quarter of the thirteen million small businesses in the United States, and are adding more at a rate at least three times as fast as men. True, all those businesses add up to only 3 percent of the United States economy. And 45 percent of those businesses are in the services, so one could conclude that women are merely moving out into the business world in the sort of home-economics roles that they have always filled, and aren't necessarily making more at it than they would if they depended on wealthy husbands and just took care of the house.

On the other hand, the service sector is easily the most buoyant in the American economy, so it is obviously a good one to be in. Moreover, even manufacturing has become "softer"; the hottest maker of new fortunes is no longer oil, much less the heavy industries of the turn of the century, but electronics—which, with its emphasis on marketing and white-collar innovation, will presumably be more hospitable to women than more roughneck businesses. "Among women now, there is an increased awareness of expanding capital," says Cloherty. It is an awareness she is encouraging, for she is also president of the Committee of Two Hundred, an organization of female owners or important executives of substantial businesses. So in the near future there will doubtless be more tales like that of Kurtzig; or like Debrah Charatan-Berger, who started her commercial real estate company in New York in 1980, when she was twenty-three years old, and in 1982 sold $50 million worth of the stuff. And in ten years a few of those fledgling female pioneers might be taking the places of the Mary Kays who made a fortune by assuming that their mothers would always have the time and interest to attend cosmetics parties in their homes.

Africa is no more likely than the Orient to spawn great business ventures headed by women—but, like the Orient, it has been done there occasionally. Indeed, there is a story from West Africa that would be immediately rejected by the crassest producer in Los Angeles as too unlikely. In 1919, to no great portents, there was born, in the small town of Dzake-Peki in the Volta region of Ghana, then a West African possession of Britain's, one Esther Ocloo, the future founder of the first food factory in Ghana. Her parents were both illiterate. At the age of six, however, little Esther went to live with her grandmother, obviously an ambitious type, who had the girl baptized into Presbyterianism and then enrolled her in a boarding school. At school, Esther's inoculation with Western ways began in earnest. "The four years spent at the school were the first trying and challenging times in my life," she relates.[22] "Apart from feeding myself and doing other assigned chores before the beginning of classes, I occasionally got beaten up by some of the boys, out of jealousy for being the best student." Perhaps they had a premonition they would be working for the future capitalist some day.

Surviving her elementary education, Esther attended Achimota College in Accra, the capital, on a Cadbury Scholarship. By the time she graduated in 1941, World War II had broken out, stranding her parents in French Togoland and leaving Esther alone and penniless. "These experiences, rather than discouraging me, made me a more confident, industrious, and disciplined young lady," she relates. The next step was going into business, which she did with an initial capitalization of six shillings. On the old theory

22. Typewritten letter to the author.

that you might as well do what you can, Esther began bottling and selling marmalade. Six years later, she had made enough money to send herself to England to study large-scale cooking and canning. After a hiatus of two years working at her fledgling business back in Ghana, she began more advanced studies in London, working at a canning company while studying the microbiology of canned foods and developing recipes for canning soups and tropical vegetables. When she returned to Ghana this time, in 1961—"armed with a strong sense of commitment and purpose, sacrifice, hard work, and God's help"—she founded her factory.

Nkulenu Industries Ltd., Esther Ocloo managing director, is now one of the larger African-owned enterprises in Ghana, producing fruit juices, jams, marmalades, and *dzomi* (red palm oil) for the domestic market, and cream of palm fruit for export. Esther Ocloo has managed to collect a trunkful of honors and appointments and an honorary doctorate along the way: she is past president of both the Federation of Ghana Industries and the Ghana Manufacturers Association, and has been a member of the Council of State and executive chairman of the National Food and Nutrition Board, as well as a major figure in church groups, women's business organizations, and village development projects. Not bad for a tough little girl from up the river.

None of the female Third World entrepreneurs we have met so far remotely approach the unique financial success of Imelda Marcos, the iron butterfly of the Philippines. The wife and possible successor of the strongman of that troubled island nation, she is known throughout the world of international trade as Miss Ten Percent for her acclaimed ability to siphon off a portion of every major development project in the country. (Her own awareness of her reputation lends her an air of frightening ingenuousness. When Mrs. Marcos was accused in a stockholders' suit of paying Henry Ford II $2 million to build a stamping plant in the Philippines, she responded, "Can you imagine I would bribe Henry Ford? Usually it's the other way around. They call me 'Miss Ten Percent.' ") Although the clandestine nature of her "investments" makes an accurate assessment of her wealth even more difficult than in most foreign countries, she has consistently made everyone's list of the richest women in the world. While she has clearly achieved the foundation of her fortune through her marriage to Ferdinand Marcos, "president" of the Philippines, she has pursued it so singlemindedly and so successfully that she rates consideration as an entrepreneur in her own right.

In Center Moriches, a settlement on the southern shore of Long Island sixty miles east of New York City, an old resort hotel called the Lindenmere fell further into desuetude every year, awaiting the renovation efforts of the sort of tycoon who has long since fallen out of fashion in the United States. The Marcoses, however, filled in admirably. They bought the eight-acre estate in 1980 for a reported $1 million and then spared no expense to make it over into a private retreat for Imelda, who vacations frequently in the United States and other wealthy countries less offended than her own by conspicuous consumption. The entire upper floor is reserved for the Marcos security staff, a necessity for the controversial couple; housing for the permanent household entourage of twenty is provided on the grounds; the old swimming pool was turned into a reflecting pond, a new one dug and set off with a gazebo. When the couple arrived for President Marcos's 1982 state visit to the United States, they rented the Presidential Suite in New York's Waldorf Towers for him, the Royal Suite for her, and for their entourage, twenty one-bedroom suites and two two-bedrooms in the Towers and an additional thirty rooms in the Waldorf-Astoria next door. Total cost for lodging: $109,500 for six nights, not counting food, taxes, or tips for the bellhops who carried their eight hundred pieces of luggage.

Imelda is not retiring about the need for such luxury. "It's a hypocrite who says, 'I don't like pretty things, I don't want to be beautiful,' " she once told an interviewer. "When I travel around the world they know I am Miss Philippines. They say, 'Imelda's our representative, our mama. She cannot dress like a hobo.' . . . The important thing is to go as someone who has made a little success of life. You must serve as a symbol of prosperity." Nor is Imelda, to her own mind, a symbol of wealth alone. During the state visit, she said, "My role is to be 'S and S'—star and slave. To star so the people have some standard to reach for, and to slave so everybody becomes a star. Before you can intervene with information, education, and training programs, you've got to motivate people, and you can only inspire people with what is beautiful. . . . I will continue to be a soldier for beauty."

Miss Ten Percent's ambition to make each of her people a star is a perfect echo of another first lady of a developing nation with a Spanish cultural background, the notorious Eva Perón. Like Evita, Imelda started out as a destitute provincial girl who had nothing but beauty and an unslakable ambition to drive her to glory and riches. Like Evita, she seized immediately on her military-hero patron once she found him. (It took Imelda only eleven days upon first meeting Ferdinand to marry him; Eva took Perón away from a rival actress at a party and never left his side. But the comparison is odious to Imelda, who was never a prostitute like Evita.) Both women managed to parlay their contradictory mystique as a soft-but-strong woman in a man's world into a unique hold on their country's popular imagination. Imelda does not bother with the leftist cant that Evita, surrounded by powerful unions, employed to co-opt populist sentiment; but she, like her predecessor, has dragooned the country's largest enterprises into "donations" for massive public projects and other, vaguer purposes. Both women have conducted lives of blinding splendor above the bitter poverty of their countrysides, preaching to their adoring believers that all that and more besides would one day be theirs.

Both, meanwhile, enriched at least that part of their society that belonged to their immediate family. One of Imelda's brothers, for example, is generally thought to control the Bataan Shipyard & Engineering Company, as well as Manila Bay Enterprises, the gambling monopoly; a second brother, "Kokoy," once ambassador to Peking and later governor of an island, owns the *Times Journal* newspaper and a number of important industrial enterprises. Imelda's sister, Alita, is married to Rudolfo Martel, whose family owns a majority interest in Manila's swank Century Park Sheraton and the block-square Harrison Shopping Plaza, built on city property once intended for a zoo. The First Lady's first cousin and personal physician, Dr. Inday Escolin, has expanded his business interests from a small cigarette-filter company into a holding company that controls $200 million worth of various enterprises; he has also received millions in commissions for having a nuclear-power plant construction contract switched from General Electric to Westinghouse. "Sometimes you have smart relatives who can make it," says the star and slave.

Sometimes it seems that even their deadly enemies are related to the Marcoses. In 1984, for example, another former beauty queen, a woman named Au-Au Manotoc, became one of the more celebrated candidates for the Philippine parliament on an anti-Marcos ticket. It was not merely her glamorous background—much like Imelda's, of course—that brought such celebrity upon her, nor just the feral personal attacks that Imelda made, nor only her periodic mysterious disappearances, nor even her outfits of black leather pants and see-through tops. Even more intriguing than all of that, Au-Au (a cutism for Aurora) was the first wife of Tommy Manotoc, who got a scandalous quickie Dominican Republic divorce from her in 1981 in order to marry Imee, the Marcoses' eldest daughter. Imee Marcos ran for parliament herself in 1984. It ought to be quite a legislature.

The Sukarno family of Indonesia is no longer in power, but its women remain in the public eye, and in their bankers' ledgers. Like Evita and Imelda, Dewi Sukarno was already a noted teenaged beauty (in her case, in Japan) when she met the dictator of her dreams (in her case, Achmed Sukarno of Indonesia). In 1959, when they met, he was fifty-eight years old and had been ruler of Indonesia since he helped free it from the Dutch in 1945. Dewi became his third, and favored, wife. The idyll ended in 1967, when Sukarno's generals unceremoniously removed him from power, shipped Dewi home to Japan, and allowed her back into the country where she had been First Lady only to see her husband on his deathbed. Any questions about the Sukarnos' financial achievements were settled by Dewi's new life as an international butterfly, creating a stir with her Oriental decorations and her amours that were noticed even in jaded Paris. Eventually, she got a little tired of the whole routine: "Can you imagine getting old and having nothing to do but go to stupid parties?" she asked. Instead, in 1982, she returned for a visit to Bali to introduce her teenaged daughter Karina to the ancestral land she had never known. The government was so anxious to make peace that it gave her back one of the three factories that was formerly registered in Dewi's name.

Another of the women of Sukarno's family appears to have learned much about the subtle appropriation of major sums of money. Some of the facts remain sunk amidst intractable lawsuits, but there is no question that at one point Rukmini Sukarno Kline, daughter of Sukarno by a previous wife, was president of Frankenburg Import-Export Ltd., a firm incorporated in Wichita, Kansas. She served as an agent for the sale of ninety-three thousand meters of carbon-steel pipe by Nissho-Iwai American Corporation, the distribution arm of a Japanese manufacturer, to

Petroleos Mexicanos (Pemex), the Mexican national oil company. The total price to Pemex was $5,584,392, and Mrs. Kline's firm was supposed to get a commission of $177,860 from Nissho-Iwai. After a series of letters between Mrs. Kline and Pemex, she somehow managed to persuade them to give her a check for the full amount of payment when she appeared in person at their Houston office in August 1980. Nissho-Iwai contends that check was supposed to end up in a post-office box under their control in New York. Instead, it was deposited in a Frankenburg account in the Chase Manhattan Bank. Shortly afterward, all the funds were withdrawn, the account was closed, and Mrs. Kline disappeared, never to be heard from since, except through her lawyer, who says she is "somewhat disillusioned with the American system of justice." In 1983, Mrs. Kline was indicted by a Harris County (Houston) grand jury on charges of stealing the $5.6 million.

An intriguing contrast to Imelda Marcos is the even more powerful but apparently much less rich Indira Gandhi, who was prime minister and occasional dictator of the second most populous country on earth. As the daughter of Nehru and would-be spiritual heir to Mahatma Gandhi—she was no relation to Gandhi—Mrs. Gandhi made a great show of humility and poverty; she had, for example, been seen shopping in Woolworth's during visits to the United States. But like Imelda and Evita she craved power and used it to the benefit of her family. Her son Sanjay, who did not have his mother's compunction regarding lavish display, used his consanguinity to indulge his taste for fast planes, for government power, and for the accumulation of a great deal of money; in one deal, he set up a sports-car plant that he owned personally. Even while he was in his twenties, he became his mother's most trusted adviser and heir-apparent, and much to the distress of the bulk of the Indian population he used his power to conduct a notorious campaign that forced the sterilization of thousands of men.

When Indira was routed in the elections of 1977, largely over public distress at the powers she had vested in her son, she was jailed for blocking a 1975 investigation into his business deals, and Sanjay was imprisoned for destroying a film about political corruption. In January 1980, however, their Congress party won a smashing electoral victory. But the triumphant return was shattered six months later when Sanjay crashed a high-performance plane he was poorly qualified to fly. Deprived of her heir-apparent, Indira quickly turned to another son, Rajiv, and had him elected to a seat in Parliament. Meanwhile, India was amazed and titillated to find Mrs. Gandhi kicking Sanjay's widow, Maneka, out of the prime minister's house, and Maneka responding by trying, not very successfully, to establish a new political party to challenge her mother-in-law. Maneka owns a trucking company for consolation, however. It is an apt illustration of how to make a success of oneself in a Third World country where the line between public and private property of the leaders is thin or nonexistent. Women have proven themselves adept novices at the fine art of making the public private.

An intriguing business area that has only been invaded recently by women—one woman, it should be said—is winemaking. In 1976, Laura Mentzelopoulos became the proud owner of Château Margaux, one of the most illustrious vineyards in France. It cost something in the range of $17 million, and the tight circles of wine-loving snobs muttered that it was just something to amuse a rich man's wife. When she dismissed substantial numbers of employees, began replanting the vineyards, and began getting publicity for the normally arcane and secretive world of French winemaking, it was enough to cause coronaries among the all-male councils of the proud old vintners. Mrs. Mentzelopoulos is the first to admit that she knows nothing in particular about the finer points of wine. She was a law student from Toulouse who happened to marry a Greek-born financier, through the circumstances that they were both skiing in Switzerland and she was stunning. Although he put up the money for the vineyard—corporately, through Félix Potin, the best-known grocery chain in France, of which he owned two-thirds—it was clear from the first that it would remain in the family and that she would run it. When Mentzelopoulos died suddenly in 1980, he left it to Laura for the eventual transmission to their children. Meanwhile, she has continued her weekly plane trips to the château from her homes in New York and Paris. Although she knows little technically about wine, she has discovered what generations of male entrepreneurs already knew: all you have to know is how to find the experts who do. She has pumped in nearly as much in reconstruction as her husband spent for the vineyard in the first place—an approach made easier by her marriage in 1983 to K. Alexis Mersentes, another golden Greek, this one a shipping tycoon. The result has been general acclamation that Château Margaux has returned to the first rank of Bordeaux, which in turn makes Laura Mentzelopoulos one of the premier, as well as one of the richest, vintners in the world.

Mary Kay Ash is, of course, one of the most outrageous people to have lived in the twentieth century. Late every year, she holds a "Seminar" in the Dallas Convention Center, which is like no tutorial your average student has ever attended. To the strains of *Also Sprach Zarathustra*, the small, round great-grandmother steps through a swirl of chemically induced clouds on the stage to give away pink Cadillacs and hug her people. Then she gives away (as she did in 1983) eighty-seven fur coats, seventy diamond necklaces and five hundred other prizes, hugging all the while.

It was Mary Kay's peculiar genius to perceive that a great mass of American housewives would do virtually anything to get out of the house, to feel productive, to feel feminine and romantic—to feel, above all, *appreciated*. The amount by which the actual value of those women's work can be paid in the currency of appreciation rather than cash has built Mary Kay, since she started the business in 1963, a gilded ten-story office building in North Dallas with a move pending to a self-contained company campus on 177 acres nearby; a wardrobe containing seventy-nine of the evening gowns she favors; nearly five million shares of stock—which she has mostly transferred to the name of her son Richard Rogers, the president of Mary Kay Cosmetics—worth about $200 million until recently; two best-selling books (*Mary Kay* and *Mary Kay's Guide to Beauty*); her own golf tournament; near sainthood in her Baptist church; and the adulation of the two hundred thousand beauty consultants who form her in-the-home sales force.

Given those facts, a visitor can easily suspect that he is being at least partly misled by the trappings of the empress's office. A large doll of Lambchop, the Shari Lewis puppet, is propped up dopily on the pink sofa (pink being Mary Kay's trademark color). The entire office is awash in what one's mother-in-law always called *chatchkas*: a cabinet full of china figurines of Minervas and ballerinas; ferns and pussy willows in vases; on her desk a fluffy pink quill, a candle in a bed of plastic petals and roses, a southern belle figurine, a little golden set of Greek urns, and a tidy stack of correspondence on a tray with a letter opener. A telephone console is the only sign of business in the entire sanctuary. Mary

Kay herself participates in the riot of cute detail: a wooden giraffe, zebra, rhino, and lion march across her necklace. As one might expect, she is also the most carefully made-up person in the state of Texas. The care given to the makeup is something that extends throughout Mary Kay's life and career; and the frothiness of her office and her Seminar performances are frivolous only in a way carefully calculated to appeal to her audience. It is quickly apparent that Mary Kay did not luck into this fortune.

Unlike, say, hotel queen Leona Helmsley—who believes that women who complain about discrimination are only rationalizing their inability to compete in a Darwinian world—Mary Kay Ash has a genuine, if rather obsolete, sense of the burden that women have labored under when they labored. Indeed, the official reason for the start of the company was a desire to help other women. When she retired after twenty-five years of a direct-sales career, Mary Kay relates in her autobiography-cum-peptalk, she thought to write a book: "In the years that I had worked, I had encountered many problems. I thought my experience could perhaps help other women over these same hurdles. To organize my thoughts, I began by writing down all the good things the companies I had worked for had done. I hoped doing that would clear my heart of the bitterness I felt just then, and it did. After writing for two weeks, I didn't feel nearly so bad about the opportunities that had been denied me just because I was a woman. The next two weeks I spent writing down all the problems I had encountered during those years. It was a long list, and I began to think about a 'dream company' that would be based on the golden rule and offer women unlimited opportunities." Rightly perceiving that books don't make the kind of money that companies do, Mary Kay put aside her manuscript and gathered up her experience, her family, her few dollars, and the formula that she allegedly bought from the granddaughter of a tanner who noticed that his foul-smelling leather salve softened his hands. Five years later Mary Kay Cosmetics went public and turned her into a millionaire. Good-bye bitterness, hello Wall Street.

The future popularizer of the pink Cadillac grew up in Houston, the daughter of a tubercular, invalid father and a mother who worked fourteen hours a day managing a restaurant to support the family ("undoubtedly she was paid less because she was a woman"). Much like Ebby Halliday's background—much like, some would say, the entire ethos of Texas—Mary Kay's upbringing instilled in her a bedrock belief in the efficacy of hard work, unshakable self-confidence, and a competitive spirit. Her mother provided the self-confidence, her financial hardships the need for hard work, and her friend Dorothy Zapp supplied the competitive spirit. Mary Kay tells Dorothy Zapp stories to explain her success—complete with imitations of little Dorothy's voice. "Dorothy had everything I didn't have," says Mary Kay. (This is as real to her today as it was fifty years ago.) "She had doting parents. It wasn't that I didn't have doting parents, but they weren't available. My mother worked from five o'clock in the morning until nine o'clock at night. My father was an invalid. It wasn't that they didn't love me. It was just that I could not have the same kind of attention that Dorothy got."

To judge by the stories, Mary Kay appears to feel that the central purpose of the friendship was competition. Dorothy was a relatively wealthy kid while Mary Kay was the achiever, and Dorothy's parents were willing to trade their approval and treats for Mary Kay's good influence on their daughter. When Dorothy's father got a promotion and moved the family to the right side of town, Mary Kay was so struck by their social success that she committed the address to memory. (Four thousand twenty-four Woodleigh.) The future cosmetics empress got so competitive, unfortunately, that when she could not afford to go off to Rice Institute as Dorothy did, she contracted an unhappy marriage instead, quickly had three kids, then suffered through a divorce.

As with most things in the lives of those who make themselves a fortune, it seemed in retrospect to be fated. The need to support her family turned Mary Kay to direct sales for the Stanley Home Products Company. Stanley was the granddaddy of the direct-sales approach that uses a "party" in a home to peddle its products to those attending; a number of other entrepreneurial firms, most notably Tupperware, have adapted the idea to their products with a great deal of success. Many more, on the other hand, have failed, and it is Mary Kay's extraordinary—blinding—success that invites admiration and analysis.

The key to making a fortune through product parties—as it is throughout direct sales—is not in the selling itself, but in taking percentages of new recruits' sales. Mary Kay works like this: new "beauty consultants" are generally persuaded to spend between $500 and $3,000 on their start-up inventories. The beauty-care kits cost them $20.75 each, and they sell them for $41.50. This is a tidy 100 percent markup; but common sense reveals that after a few hundred dollars in such profits, all but the most gregarious saleswomen will start to run short of potential customers to invite to parties. The road to riches for the ambitious beauty consultant in Mary Kay Cosmetics, therefore, is to recruit other consultants: after you have eight recruits, you get 8 percent of their sales; when you hit twelve, you get even higher commissions and you become a "director." That in turn makes you eligible for the big prizes, including the pink Cadillac (sales by you and your recruits must exceed $72,000 for a six-month period). There are even higher poobahs in the empire, "national sales directors," who get percentages of percentages of percentages—such as the Mary Kay legend Helen McVoy, who has been with the company since the beginning and made $375,000 in commissions one recent year. At headquarters, of course, Mary Kay and her son's accountants are calculating their percentages on the sales of the beauty products they manufacture; they sell about 4 percent of all cosmetics in the United States. (The consultants have also invaded Canada, Guam, Puerto Rico, Australia, and Argentina.)

But many others have seen the irresistible logic of such pyramid retailing and gone broke while seeing it. Mary Kay's genius was in adding more than financial incentives to the idea. As she says, almost certainly correctly, no man could have created the company. Her crucial insight was that women—at least the ones she had in mind—will not work as hard for money as they will for recognition, admiration, love.

It is a wonderful paradox that one of the most successful women capitalists in the United States created her fortune by trading on the anticapitalist instincts of her fellow women. Mary Kay's first nonmonetary reward was the Golden Goblet Club. "I think you've lost your mind," son Richard told her when she broached the idea. "And looking at it from a man's standpoint," she writes, "you might also wonder who in the world would knock herself out to win a goblet—even if it was gold-plated! But a lot of women did! They competed with themselves to win those goblets." The concept has blossomed into a sort of neofeudal ranking system; the women who attend seminars can be assessed by their grey sales directors suits, adorned with Ladders of Success—sapphire stars, sashes, ribbons, golden bumblebees, clusters of gold stars, "warm fuzzies," and of course some drive the ultimate pink Cadillacs. This is competitiveness, of course, but it is meant to be a warm, nonbusinesslike competitiveness, designed especially for women. Mary Kay notes, "Andrew Carnegie, the great industrialist, once said, 'The first man gets the oyster, the second man gets the shell.' That kind of competitiveness, where there's only *one* winner, may motivate some men, but I think it often has an adverse effect on others—and particularly on women. At Mary Kay Cosmetics, everyone has an opportunity to get the oyster, the shell, *and the pearl*. But we go a step further: instead of pearls, we award sapphires, rubies, and diamonds!"

But Mary Kay's genius went beyond the reward system to appeal to what she would call the entire woman. God and family are invoked frequently at Seminars and in the autobiography. The entire Mary Kay pyramid is built on the concept of a stay-at-home, insecure, man-dominated wife who must overcome those obstacles in order to succeed for herself and all her supporters at Mary Kay. Every tyro consultant is told that the purpose of sales directors is to "believe in you until you believe in yourself." "Even in this enlightened age," Mary Kay writes, "relatively few women are zeroing in on professional careers. Many of them are just dreaming about that 'fellow on a white horse.' We *know* women have as much ability as men. The problem is that *women* don't know it." Mary Kay herself never had that particular confidence problem; her mother, a powerful proto-feminist, had been a nurse and insisted that Mary Kay become a doctor, which she tried until the premed classes became too great a burden for a working mother of three children. Nor, after her early mistake, did she have unsupportive husbands of the type she anticipates among her recruits. The recruits are advised that their first "sale" is their husband, and that they should avoid mentioning "petty annoyances" at home—and especially that they must keep in mind that "men can't take criticism."

Much like a Japanese company (a topic on which she has just written a third book), Mary Kay is an extended family. She sends out two hundred thousand birthday cards and condolences a year, and hands out turkeys on Thanksgiving. At seminars, the twenty-three thousand or so who attend each year not only admire one another's awards, they sing songs like "That Mary Kay Enthusiasm" and "If You Want to Be a Director, Clap Your Hands." As might be expected from the intersection of southern fundamentalism and cosmetics, it is considered a point of profound importance that sales consultants behave like ladies—they do not smoke in public, they do not curse, many do not drink at all, and they do not wear pants. "Everything a woman touches should be ennobled," says the book.

It is a matter of wonder that such a gospel of self-conscious femininity should have been worth hundreds of millions of dollars during the past twenty years, a period of some of the most striking social changes in American history. There are indications, however, that the larger world may finally be catching up to Mary Kay. Profits and stock values have dropped sharply during the past few years; the family's share of the stock, worth something like $200 million in 1983, has dropped to a mere $50 million a year later. (It is pleasant, of course, to be able to describe your $50 million fortune as "mere.") The reasons are obvious: recruiting is off sharply, and with it the pyramid effect that has supported the sales directors and stockholders at the acme. The pool of shrinking-violet housewives who need to be liberated by cosmetic-sales parties is being drained by the increasing desire of women to get full-time jobs. Regular work not only eliminates potential sales consultants; it cuts sharply into the time when customers might attend parties. Moreover, trends like higher divorce rates, later marriages, and more frequent moves ruin the "old girls network" of close neighborhood and family ties that Mary Kay has always counted on for recruitment.

There are too many women who want to be like Mary Kay Ash, not like a Mary Kay saleswoman. As a result, there may never be another entrepreneur quite like Mary Kay. But if the Dallas dynamo's perceptions of American femininity are no longer convertible into massive cash, her enormous energy and aggressively positive thinking remain qualities that hungry young women and men alike can use in their anticipated conquest of the capitalist world.

It is logical, though it has not always been the case, that women would be leaders at selling women's things, like cosmetics and fashion. Indeed, cosmetics has been one of the few fields in which women were important pioneers and have continued to make names and fortunes for themselves. In 1886, Harriet Hubbard Ayer became one of the first women to found a substantial company of any kind in the United States when she packaged a concoction she claimed had been used by Madame Récamier, a famous Parisian beauty of Napoleon's time, and began selling it through extensive newspaper advertising. It was Ayer's innovative merchandising that was largely responsible for creating the cosmetics market among the moneyed classes; it had previously been considered rather "fallen" to paint one's face.

Her successors in entrepreneurial cosmetics included Elizabeth Arden (born Florence Nightingale Graham), who not only built a chain of more than a hundred salons throughout the world, but started Maine Chance, the oldest of the health spas that have recently become a crucial part of the rich woman's itinerary; then Helena Rubinstein, and most recently Estée Lauder, who has made a huge fortune with her unique combination of drive and eccentricity. But the greatest of these—the first woman in history to make a million dollars herself—was the spectacular Madame C. J. Walker.

The creator of the earliest giant direct-sales empire was born Sarah Breedlove, with the twin handicaps of being female and black. She did it, moreover, during the period of lynchings and deprivations of civil rights that came in the wake of Reconstruction and is known historically as The Nadir. In fact, her story is so outlandishly Horatio Alger that one is tempted to dismiss it as apocryphal. Born in Delta, Louisiana, in 1867, she married at fourteen, but was left alone six years later with a small daughter when her husband was killed by a lynch mob. Traveling aimlessly up the Mississippi River, she eventually settled in St. Louis and began working fourteen hours a day as a laundress. The work gave her considerable cosmetic problems—her skin dried out, of course, and her hair began falling out—but it also gave her a view of the dressing table of the white middle class, which were beginning to be cluttered with Madame Récamiers and its cousins. "One night," Madame Walker told a writer years later, "I had a dream; a big black man appeared to me and told me what to mix up for my hair. Some of the remedy was grown in Africa, but I sent for it, mixed it, put it on my scalp, and in a few weeks my hair was coming in faster than it had ever fallen out. I tried it on my friends; it helped them. I made up my mind that I would begin to sell it."

One recognizes the black counterpart of Mary Kay's more secularized myth of the creation of her beauty preparations; in both cases—in any advertising for cosmetics—the founding geniuses are aware that they are selling not a jar of paste but the idea of Romance. And like Mary Kay's tanner, Sarah Breedlove's demiurge, once he had served his purpose of delivering the product, was supplemented by old-fashioned hard work and innovative packaging and marketing techniques. The young laundress whipped up an initial batch of $1.50 worth of remedy into "Hair Grower" and sold it to her friends and neighbors. It was the first time that anyone had tapped a specifically black market, and it proved to be golden. Obsessively devoted to her work, Breedlove exploited her minor initial success by moving rapidly into other products that became standards in black households through the present day. The great breakthrough became "the Walker method," the hair-straightening process that featured the first hot comb distributed on a large scale in the United States. (It was manufactured to Walker's specifications in France.)

Madame Walker started the tradition that female entrepreneurs recruit business allies through marriage or other family ties; her husband, Charles Joseph Walker, remained with her only a short time, but his experience as a newspaperman in Denver was instrumental in developing the advertising techniques that soon made the Walker method and products known throughout the black universe. Madame also set up one of the earliest and for a long time the largest direct-sales force that the United States had seen. By 1910, she had a network of five thousand black women "Walker agents," who held local distributorships not only in black communities around the United States, but in the Caribbean and occasionally on circuits of London, Paris, Rome, Palestine, and West Africa. Associates from the early days make Madame Walker sound even more like a forebear of Mary Kay. "People would want to become agents and learn the trade so they could travel," one early colleague told an interviewer. "They found out that they could make money plus have a new way of getting away from home." Another longtime employee said, "All of the Madame C. J. Walker agents had a great love for Madame. They felt she had given them an opportunity to make a living for themselves, which was different from the living that most colored women were able to make at that time." For a black woman to have any independent source of income was, at the time, a much more radical idea than for a Mary Kay consultant to earn commissions in her spare time. To be a Walker agent was to be a figure in the community.

The profits (revenues eventually hit a thousand dollars a day) and prestige from her enterprise catapulted Madame Walker into the top ranks of black leaders in the early twentieth century: she was close to Booker T. Washington, who tutored her after she moved her headquarters to Indianapolis in 1911, and a friend of Mary McLeod Bethune and benefactor of her Bethune-Cookman

Carolyn Farb with some of her wardrobe.
(Shelly Katz/People Weekly © 1983 Time Inc.)

Marylou Whitney poses with the
miniature reproduction of her Lexington,
Kentucky, house, "Maple Hill."
(UPI/Bettmann Archive)

Marylou and Cornelius Vanderbilt Whitney (left) greet John and
Irene Roosevelt at one of Marylou's legendary parties.
(Bill Aller/NYT Pictures)

Lynn Wyatt at the door of her
Texas home.
(UPI/Bettmann Archive)

Water aerobics at the Greenhouse, one of the most popular and
exclusive luxury spas.
(UPI/Bettmann Archive)

Ethel DuPont and Franklin
Delano Roosevelt, Jr., at their
wedding.
(UPI/Bettmann Archive)

Liz Whitney with her prize horse, Nobody's
Fool, at the National Horse Show of 1938.
(UPI/Bettmann Archive)

Olga Hirshhorn.
Marjorie Lenk

Josephine Abercrombie works on the giant
gold and diamond star of Texas that was
exhibited at the 1954 Texas State Fair.
(AP/Wide World Photos)

Pamela and W. Averell Harriman at the
annual Democratic Congressional Dinner in
Washington, D.C.
(*AP/Wide World Photos*)

Jacqueline Kennedy Onassis speaks with the Duchess of
Alba at a charity ball in Seville.
(*AP/Wide World Photos*)

Dewi Sukarno speaks with fashion designer
Marc Bohan in Paris.
(UPI/Bettmann Archive)

Imelda Marcos and Andy Warhol at a Metropolitan
Museum of Art opening.
(UPI/Bettmann Archive)

Electra Waggoner Biggs in her wedding dress, July 1933.
(Edward Steichen. Courtesy Vogue © *1933 [renewed 1961] by the Condé Nast Publications, Inc.)*

College. She also became perhaps the highest liver of any black person of the time. She rode in an electric automobile and a private railway car, spent lavishly on jewelry and clothes, ate prodigiously, and bought property in the South and Midwest, two town houses in Harlem, and her most prized possession, the huge Italianate Villa Lewaro in Irvington-on-the-Hudson, above New York City. In a sort of foreshadowing of seminars, prize-winning Walker agents from around the country used to gather at the mansion to celebrate their success.

The Walker Company still operates out of its own building, which went up in Indianapolis eight years after Madame died in 1919, although the firm no longer has a major share of the black beauty market. By the terms of her will, the company must always be headed by a woman. Her daughter A'Lelia succeeded Walker, but A'Lelia was much too interested in being the consummate hostess of the Harlem Renaissance to pay much attention to business affairs. The company president is now A'Lelia Ransom Nelson, granddaughter of Madame Walker's attorney and general manager.

Estée Lauder is the reigning empress of the world of cosmetics, the only current figure who remotely approaches the legendary status of her two great feuding predecessors, Elizabeth Arden and Helena Rubinstein. She is a glorious example of the trend noted by Charlotte Curtis, in which the wealthy of today associate with—indeed, pursue—those who in an earlier generation would have been thought merely servants. Estée Lauder is also a prime example of the creation of a fortune from myth in the fashion world. She is, finally, one of the richest women in the world; Estée Lauder, Inc., the third-largest cosmetics-and-perfume company in the United States, with revenues around $1 billion annually, is owned completely and equally by her and her two sons, slices worth at least $200 million apiece.

It is difficult to write the history of Estée Lauder because she, in the manner of cosmetics queens, is in the constant process of rewriting history herself. There is a tradition in the beauty business that Hungarians have more beauty secrets in their closets than any other people in the world. (One cornerstone is the story of the Hapsburg princess who was executed for bathing her skin in the blood of human infants.) Thus Estée Lauder's mother, in the official biography, is a famous beauty from Budapest who met her father in Vienna. (Even her son's wife is described in *her* official biography as "from a family noted for generations of Viennese beauties.") Then, the official line goes, "she dreamed of becoming a skin doctor . . .but fate stepped in with marriage. . . . So a next-best career for Estée was developing beauty treatments for women." Famous for her scattered remarks, she alternately left people with the impression that she was from Milwaukee, Scranton, or (most likely) Long Island, and was an heiress to some vast though vague fortune ("In Milwaukee a woman used to come to our house every day just to brush my mother's hair"). Wherever she started, by the 1930s she was peddling concoctions developed by her uncle, John Michael Schatz, a cosmetics chemist who arrived in New York from Vienna. Already in those days on the Upper West Side, Mrs. Lauder was an accomplished beauty maven with a sure instinct for how cosmetics looked on women, and how women could be made to want them. "Beauty is my life," she said. "I used to stop women on the street and on trains and give them tips." Even in the later years of dizzying social ambition, Mrs.Lauder never lost her Jewish-mother's this-is-what-you-ought-to-do-dear style.

The Estée Lauder story began another chapter in 1946, when she and husband Joseph, who had bounced around several small business ventures in New York, realized that she would end up as no more than one of hundreds of thousands of Avon or Mary Kay saleswomen if she did not move into a larger-scale operation. After peddling the stuff for two years through the mail and in a few beauty salons, the Lauders achieved their major breakthrough when Saks Fifth Avenue gave them counter space. Since then the Estée Lauder approach has varied only by size. She and her sons insist on appealing solely to the high-bracket department store trade; they price their creams and perfumes higher than any other mass brand, on the theory that if it costs more it looks higher-class; and their advertising has retained the same coolly lavish tone since it began. But it was actually the scarcity of advertising dollars that led to the promotional technique that not only endowed Estée Lauder but conquered the entire industry. They gave their products away free at fashion shows and through mailers; the gift-with-purchase technique has now been adopted by virtually all cosmetics manufacturers. With the sort of divine-right reasoning that seems extant only among women cosmetics entrepreneurs, Estée Lauder has recalled, "I gave my stock out of charity, and God has been good to me because of that."

Both the giveaways and the class-above-all attitude are deeply part of the personality of the founder. She bought constant attention from the beauty press with fancy lunches and gifts for favorable stories (a practice widespread in the industry), and she bought herself acceptance in the highest social circles in the world. When Estée Lauder set about conquering Palm Beach, the whispering had it that she lured the Duchess of Windsor, no naïf in contracting out her quasiroyal presence, with a constant shower of lipstick. She bought the spectacular Villa Abri in the Riviera's glittery Cap Ferrat, and then used that prize to attract the widowed Begum Aga Khan, herself easily one of the richest women in the world. All the personal publicity in the society columns, in turn, helped establish the image of Estée Lauder as the wealthy woman's perfume—and thus continually replenished the treasury that was being endlessly drained in the quest for the trappings of the imagined aristocrat. With the fortune made, however, Mrs. Lauder abruptly absorbed the paranoia of the rich and began pleading with puzzled reporters to stop publishing details of her wealth and the locations of her mansions. She has been in near seclusion since the death of her husband in January 1983. But the Estée Lauder achievement remains: she was not only one of the first "tradespeople" to gain social status equal to that of the people she catered to; she was also one of the most accomplished social climbers in recent history, using personal generosity and judicious charitable contributions in a textbook campaign to achieve the position that her wealth craved.

No one has made the kind of individual wealth in the fragmented fashion market that is possible in a mass-consumption field like cosmetics, but it is worth a look because women have invaded the production end heavily in the last decade or two. The first and originally the most successful—certainly the most famous—of the new wave of rich women designers is, of course, Gloria Vanderbilt. "Little Gloria" suffered through one of the most lugubrious custody trials ever to be celebrated by the legal profession, and spent the remainder of her life aggressively worrying about one field of endeavor after the next "seemingly desperate to earn her celebrity," in the words of her recent biographer, Barbara Goldsmith. As fast as she ran through husbands she shuffled from one pursuit to the next. She achieved some measure of acclaim as a painter, then an actress, then a poet and writer. Through it all she was, first and last, a socialite of rare celebrity. Though no one knew it at the time, that agglomeration of publicity and caste was the perfect background for success in the world of fashion. Designers had naturally always been celebrities, at least among the *haut monde*, but Gloria Vanderbilt was the first person to do it in reverse—to convert celebrity into a fashion fortune. There was something odd and yet appropriate about that name, already dragged through the messiest custody battle of the century, suddenly blossoming on the derrières of the aspiring fashion world. In commercials for the jeans, she has appeared after an introduction of the world of the previous Vanderbilts to adulate "my new status jeans." Gloria is not, however, a princess merely selling her kingdom's name. She gets up at five-thirty and starts work at eight, driven still, presumably, by a need to prove herself as something other than a cartoon socialite; she still throws lavish parties occasionally, but does not let it interfere with the serious business of selling jeans.

Possibly as rich as Gloria Vanderbilt and very nearly as famous, but coming to her position from a different country, is Diane von Fürstenberg. In the fashion galaxy, von Fürstenberg was a comet somewhere between Estée Lauder, who first sold her cosmetics and then used the profits to purchase a niche in society, and the rich girl dressmakers like Miss Vanderbilt, Carolina Herrera, and Jacqueline de Ribes, who used their social currency to purchase immediate cachet as designers. Diane von Fürstenberg was born Diane Halfin in Brussels—her mother was a concentration camp survivor and her father an electronics distributor—and she met Egon von Fürstenberg, an heir to the Fiat fortune and a genuine title, while they were both students at the University of Geneva. When they arrived in New York in 1969, Egon's princedom opened doors to the rich, the partying, the fashionable. They went to more parties than the actresses arriving that year from Fort Wayne. However, his connections do not seem to have been critical to her success, at least not compared to her own determination, fashion sense, and some crucial financial backing from her father.

She worked hard to convince the moneymen to back her, although the time was blessedly short before it was obvious that she was a fashion Midas. "In the beginning, I had such a hard time," she said in a 1974 interview. "People weren't taking me seriously; they thought I was another of those social girls who pretends she wants to work." That did not last long, as the Diane von Fürstenberg drive became the stuff of legend. Indeed, she

was one of the socialites who convinced the world to take socialites seriously as businesswomen. She broke up with her husband in 1975 in what appeared to be a fundamental conflict
between the worlds of society and work, those twin pillars of
the garment trade. "When we first came here [to New York], it
was all very glamorous," she recalled at about that time. "We
were invited to everything and we went to everything. We would
go to an opening for new toothpaste. My husband was much
more social than me, I think. My philosophy is to simplify everything. I mean, I want to be a good mother, and to work and yet
remain a woman." She has ordered her life strictly between her
work and her houses—one on Park Avenue and the other a farm
in Connecticut—and does not pop up frequently in the gossip
columns. On the other hand, she maintains an old-fashioned
attitude that helps her support the weight of a multimillion-dollar
enterprise on her fine-boned shoulders. "It is helpful being a
woman," she remarked. "If a man fails, then his whole life is a
disaster. For a woman, a career is still an accessory."

That sentiment would certainly be disputed by two other rich
women of the fashion world, Carolina Herrera and Jacqueline de
Ribes. Both these precious international socialites have lately taken
up fashion design with a vengeance. Both insist that there is
nothing frivolous or ironic in their sudden dedication to the world
of hard work. Indeed, there is some truth to the notion that no
one works as hard as a rich woman, whether she is making
money at it or not. But more on that later.

Herrera and de Ribes share a lot, including the admiration and
envy of the circle of a few thousand who wish they had such
ease of access to Le Cirque and the pages of *Interview* magazine.
Herrera is a little over forty, de Ribes somewhat older; both
maintain the classically handsome face and aura that looks dread-
fully uncomfortable to be married to, but does set off expensive
clothes well and is the indisputable cynosure of the self-consciously rich. The "exquisite taste" of both is widely acknowledged, and has landed them both a niche in the International
Fashion Hall of Fame. Both are foreigners (Herrera, Venezuelan;
de Ribes, French) who have been plying the international social
circuit for an eternity of Suzy columns, and both have more
recently—like virtually all the richest people in the world—set
up semipermanent bases in New York. Both married young and
very well, in financial and social terms. Both have devoted them-

selves to the creation of a life as seamless as the lines of one of their gowns. And both have suddenly decided to become world-famous fashion designers.

Historically, that had considerable precedent, although much more in the years before World War II than afterward. It is true that modern high fashion was largely a creation of a man, Charles Frederick Worth, who set up shop in Paris in the middle of the nineteenth century. For the first time, an accepted style dominated the sensibilities of rich women all over the world. Worth himself was the first to perceive that his entire livelihood depended on the *invention* of new fashions; in other words, style was now to be something handed down from authorities, not created by the noblewoman herself with the help of her in-house *couturière*.

Still, there were plenty of women of the bourgeoisie who were quick to poach on the territory Worth had carved out for himself and his heirs. Worth's main competitor at the turn of the century was Mme. Paquin, who foreshadowed the advent of today's working rich girl designers by borrowing her banker husband's money and business skills to set up her shop. Like Worth, her clientele was made up of not only the predictable European noblewomen and American millionairesses, but the high-priced courtesans who revolved around the courts of Europe, such as the famous Cora Pearl. Mme. Paquin was followed before long by a string of well-known women, including Elsa Schiaparelli, Coco Chanel, Jeanne Lanvin, Madeleine Vionnet, and Mme. Grès. During the years between the wars, the spice of the spring and fall showings came to be movie stars rather than the royal hookers of yore. Most of these female-headed houses have not survived in much prominence. They have been replaced by men, including Yves St. Laurent, Karl Lagerfeld, and among the new crop of Americans, Oscar de la Renta and Bill Blass. Why this should have happened is not entirely clear; there have been some theories that women simply don't trust other women as much as they do men, but that would seem to have been disproved by the great French women designers. But it may not remain the case for much longer, if the torrent of socialite-designers of the 1980s has anything to say about it.

It is clear upon first meeting that Carolina Herrera has been a member of the international cash-and-fashion elite since birth. Her father was a military man of means, a pioneer of aviation, and later governor of Caracas. Carolina grew up the predictably stylish daughter in a family of the sort of cultural importance and dignity that can only be found among the Latin American elite. The family inhabited your basic movie-set tile-roofed villa amidst tropical gardens. Carolina learned English and other finishing-school necessities from her strict Hungarian governess, which has left her with an incredible accent. Descended from a grandmother and mother who made yearly pilgrimages to Paris, she has been fascinated by fashion since she cut her own clothes for dolls, and she has not stopped making clothes for herself since. A trip to Paris and a meeting with the *couturière* Balenciaga when she was a teenager was the equivalent of a Tibetan visiting the Dalai Lama. She was married at eighteen; the feeling in that circle was, of course, why wait around? It didn't work. In 1969, she ran across Reinaldo Herrera, a childhood friend, and married him.

Now, Herrera is *real* Spanish gold. His family owns half of Venezuela, a publishing house, banking interests, and God knows what else. His mother, Mimi Herrera, is a well-known patron of the arts. *Her* mother was an even better-known socialite of excess. The grandmother used to cross the Atlantic, Reinaldo says, with 140 pieces of luggage. (By contrast, Carolina uses only twelve or fifteen suitcases.) From Mimi Herrera, the Herreras have taken over La Vega, a mansion of sixty-five rooms that was built in 1590 and has remained one of the grandest houses in Latin America. They "are one of those charming-and-amusing South American couples who give a certain tone to Le Cirque," wrote Julie Baumgold in *New York* magazine. "A suggestion of low-slung cars, falling out of Club A at 3 A.M., white silk shirts open to the waist, and men with glasses perched on their heads on the terraces of the Hacienda de la Vega. Tinkly laughs! Blue moons. They give Le Cirque this relaxed lovely-to-look-at air compared with which restaurants like Le Cygne, the Four Seasons—even sometimes La Côte Basque and La Grenouille at lunch—look like hotbeds of serious purpose and tax-deductible work." A petite spitfire, rather less formidable than one might imagine from her reputation for exquisite perfection, Mrs. Herrera does her Lupe Velez impression when *that article* is mentioned. It is difficult to credit how perfidious Julie Baumgold was, she avers: she sat right at the next table, unannounced as journalist, and actually ran a tape recorder under her table! Carolina Herrera came out of it relatively unscathed—just a neutral comment about having dinner with Betsy Pickering Kasper Theodoracopoulos Kaiser, the famous model and marrier, in one of her previous incarnations. Herrera has the haughty disdain of a Marie Antoinette for the "person" who wrote that piece, and thinks "absolutely nothing" about the whole thing.

The magazine description is accurate enough. Carolina and Reinaldo live golden, seamless lives. For years and years, Carolina has made the rounds: having lunch with Jerry Zipkin and dinner in the Rose Garden, palling around with Princess Margaret in Mustique, getting her portrait presented to her by Andy Warhol, charmingly doing all the charming things—and doing them fairly frequently with her husband, not necessarily the escort of choice in such circles. Many of the events were, of course, for charity, and Carolina tested her wings the way many potential rich-but-getting-richer women do—by throwing an event herself. In her case, it was a 1982 party at the Dairy in Central Park for the Children's International Summer Villages, of which she was international chairman. She has to lead this public life because their Manhattan apartment is not that grand, and also because, shameful as it might be for a supersocialite to mention, she doesn't like to cook.

So what happened? Does anybody really believe her days of frivolity are over?

Carolina Herrera leans forward in that *entre nous* attitude that has captured hearts on three continents and confides that yes, of course, everybody started off with the predictable jabs to the effect that this was going to be quite an expensive hobby for Reinaldo. First of all, while Carolina had no formal training in either business or fashion, she had designed dresses for herself and friends, and she had also run the family, which rich women love to suggest is tantamount to being chief executive officer of a small corporation. "I had been in the business of my home, you know?" says Mrs. Herrera. "That's a real business, to run a house with children and servants and all that." Underneath it all, however, there lurked the incipient specter of *upper-class discontent*. Running a family, she says—"It's not enough. Not at all. It's good for the organization, though. I suppose you have to run a business like a large family—you learn discipline and organization from a family." Well, over the years, while the four daughters were growing—one has just made her a grandmother—there was sprouting in that well-coiffed head the idea that she just might get into the business. Count Rudi Crespi, who is a sort of midwife for fashionables getting into fashion, provided the immediate encouragement. "So I went back to Caracas and I put a collection together with my seamstress. Then I came to New York with my collection of my twenty dresses. A little collection, but it had everything—daytime, evening, evening-evening. I called the buyers just to see what their reaction would be. Saks, Martha. They always wanted to buy the collection from the first moment they saw it. I had no production! So the next step was to look for a backer, a partner." At a party, she ran into Armando de Armas, the biggest publisher in Latin America. As it happened, Carolina's auspicious little debut had just been covered in the Spanish *Harper's Bazaar*, which de Armas owns. She thanked him for the coverage, they began chatting, and three days later de Armas was bankrolling the newest fashion designer in Manhattan.

Not one to skimp, Herrera set up shop in two floors of a building on Fifty-seventh Street just east of Fifth Avenue, which happens to be one of the most expensive ribbons of real estate in the world. In 1981, she invited all her hundreds of good friends to a showing at the Metropolitan Club. An aggressively optimistic woman, Herrera remembers immediate unqualified success.

Not quite. *Women's Wear Daily* waspishly dubbed her "Our Lady of the Sleeves" for the butterfly-wings effect she lavished on everything. Carolina admits a preference for dramatic arm coverings, on the theory that it's easier to spot them than skirt details in a crowded room. She is not ashamed, either, of the stratospheric prices ($3,000 is usual, and $800 is bottom drawer) or her preference for materials of breathtaking rarity and cost. The Herrera confections, in the beginning, were elaborate even by the Versailles standards of her friends.

What with the raised eyebrows after the first collection, it was time for a girl's friends to help out. Diana Vreeland said she was "a blonde bombshell," not to mention "remarkable." Princess Elizabeth of Yugoslavia, the Duchess of Feria (Spain), and Rudi Crespi's American-born wife, Consuelo, all appeared bearing Carolina's aggressively swank clothes in Latin-hot colors. Cornelia Guest wore a taffeta Herrera to her debut. Nancy Reagan appeared at a Beverly Hills party in the same one-shoulder coupe de velours item with a matching maribou cape that Carolina wore herself to illustrate her *Interview* piece. By 1983, people were noticing the resemblance of her designs to the *soignée* mode of Bill Blass. Her showings at the Pierre were filled with her stellar acquaintances and customers: C. Z. Guest and her last-of-the-debutantes daughter Cornelia, Pat Buckley (Bill's wife), Nan Kempner, Dina Merrill, Diana Vreeland, Bianca Jagger—the heavyweights. The Countess Donina Cicogna was so impressed by the entire fashion-design scene that she let it slip, late in 1983, that *she* was about to share her designing gift with the world. Pilar Crespi, the Crespis' daughter, is doing the same thing. Sometimes it seems that everybody is doing the same thing. That's okay with Carolina; the way she sees it, she started the whole thing, although perhaps Jacqueline de Ribes would get annoyed at that pride of place. At any rate, Carolina likes to act the elder stateswoman: "Everytime I see them I say, 'welcome to the club.' . . . I always tell them that you have to have discipline—you may want to do some amusing things but you cannot, because you have to stay working, no?"

Yes. Another area that requires an adjustment is social butterflying. When she is working on her collection, Carolina rarely goes out at all. When she is not designing, she is on the road, making personal appearances (during one recent month) in Shreveport, Louisiana, in Japan, and at the Miss Universe contest in Miami, where she served as a judge. She does not miss the social circuit, she claims. In three years, the company has grown from six employees to forty, but that is nowhere near enough for Herrera. *This is not a hobby.* She is looking to make it big on her own. This would be through licensing agreements: Mrs. Herrera positively glows with her desire to put her name on just about anything anyone would care to offer—though she does draw the line at chocolates.

If she manages to consummate the discussions she says are occurring now, she will have a share of a market which, while now showing some signs of saturation, still creates for the fashion kings incomes that compare favorably to those of the rich women they once designed for. In one recent count, there were no fewer than forty-seven designer scents on the market. Between them, Calvin Klein and Ralph Lauren account for approximately $1.5 billion in sales yearly. Klein received $7 million in 1981 as his personal share of the licensing cornucopia. And so Carolina Herrera, who once dreamed of the most refined of Parisian fashions, of parties on gardenia-scented terraces that never ended, of the family's wonderful history and name, now says that she shares the dream of every designer: franchising. Getting that name, when it becomes "strong," on every derrière in America.

If Carolina Herrera had the world of fashion handed to her on a silver platter, Vicomtesse Jacqueline de Ribes was born in the pantry. No less an authority than *Town & Country*, the Koran of the socially elect, proclaimed her "the world's most stylish woman" in an issue that featured her staggeringly handsome profile on its cover. Daughter of the Comte de Beaumont, she married Edouard de Ribes when she was seventeen, and at nineteen was named to the international best-dressed list. That was no particular problem, for this girl's adolescent rebellion consisted of sneaking into her grandmother's wardrobe and appropriating a few items. Said the vicomtesse when she was launching her career, "My grandmother was a very elegant woman. [This is not hard to believe.] She never went to a *maison de couture* for fittings—everyone would come to the house. I would find out when she would be fitting a dress and I would be around to watch." When Jacqueline was sixteen, she cut her first ball gown. Her pal Betsy Bloomingdale, a fixture in the Nancy Reagan circle, noticed once she met her that the vicomtesse would never wear a ready-to-wear dress as was, but always added some feature herself. She just "picked up" designing, Jacqueline de Ribes allowed. "I never went to design school. I'm very—how can you say—*sensuelle*. I have to work with the material. I have to have it in my hand before I decide what to do with it. I'm not going to draw something and decide right away whether it's going to be in crepe or wool."

The teenaged vicomtesse was as precociously social as she was fashionable. In 1951, she was noted to be the youngest woman at the "party of the century"—an eighteenth-century-theme masked ball thrown in the Palazzo Labia overlooking Venice's Grand Canal by the playboy Don Carlos de Bestegui, to which fifteen hundred of the most dazzling of the international set floated in fleets of gondolas, to the cheers of thousands of Venetians on grandstands erected for the occasion in the next-door piazza. By that time, Jacqueline had already married Edouard de Ribes, who like her was not only social and beautiful but also very rich. Between them, it goes without saying, they have had a blessed life; rather like the Herreras, in fact. They are good friends of the Rothschilds and all those folks who follow one another around the globe by season, from Manhattan to Cap Ferrat to St. Moritz to Mustique and around again. Chez de Ribes is an overwhelming mansion on Paris's haughty rue de la Bienfaisance, clotted with tapestries, fauteuils, marble floors, papered walls, tasseled curtains, crystal, silver, ormolu, velvet, mahogany, silk, antiques, antiques, antiques—whew.

The Rothschilds and the rest began asking the vicomtesse's advice and referring to her as "every inch a clothes horse," "a fashion goddess," "the epitome of the *soignée* Parisian," and other such nicknames. It is the attitude many rich women aspire to but few can achieve to perfection: the carriage of a cobra, the bones of an Erector Set, the superior air of a waterfall. "Whenever I wore something I had designed to the States," she said, "these wonderful, marvelous, positive friends of mine would say, 'But, Jacqueline, why can't we wear something you've designed? Why don't you take yourself more seriously?' " Overcoming whatever insecurities she may have had—the vicomtesse does not seem one for quavering introspection—she decided to get to work. We will leave untouched the nagging question of just how much Jacqueline de Ribes was tracking along behind Carolina Herrera; perhaps it was just the *Zeitgeist* of the eighties that pampered rich women would all suddenly feel the need to make a fashion statement on a commercial scale. At any rate, swinging into the world of work was not the hardship some outsiders might have predicted, for de Ribes maintains, like virtually every other rich woman in the world, that she has actually been crushingly busy for her entire adult life. "The people who are close to me and who know me, know I have always been involved in serious things," she assured an interviewer. "I have been involved in producing television shows, administrating a ballet company, and doing things on a large scale for UNICEF. It is not my nature to sit at home and lunch with my girlfriends. I've always been busy." Indeed, the vicomtesse looks as though a spoonful of lunchtime cholesterol has never passed her rubied lips.

Fortunately, Edouard was most supportive, allowing the "family house" to be emptied of all its precious contents for the showing of her first collection. Yves St. Laurent, her favorite designer—he returns the favor: unlikely as it sounds, he has written that "she radiates the brilliance of a thousand lights"—popped in for the showing in March 1983, dragging along design colleagues Valentino and Emanuel Ungaro, as well as Olimpia de Rothschild, Marisa Berenson, and the rest of the *crème* of Parisian society. Jacqueline de Ribes designs turned out to have the flying-nun sleeves too, along with bubbling, flowing collars atop a slinky stem, so that the finished woman looks more than ever like a rare orchid. The whole effect is said to be reminiscent of great influence from St. Laurent. And all for only $2,000 to $7,500 at your nearest Saks, I. Magnin, or Neiman-Marcus! Everybody loved it, and it was off to the races—almost literally. De Ribes has spent much of the rest of her life making personal appearances across the United States. She reportedly is heavily involved in her shows, personally cuing them, selecting music and lighting, and cutting and pinning up to the last minute. It has worked. Saks reported toward the end of 1983 that the line was selling "extremely well." Of course, with prices like those, half a dozen sales adds up to extremes of revenue. As with many of those who have more than enough of it, Jacqueline de Ribes does not discuss money; but she seems assured of a plenitude even if somehow the inherited wealth vanished, say into the maw of socialism.

But one of the great advantages of this sudden profusion of social designers is that, even if their husbands should lose their money in a coup tomorrow, at least their Fashion Hall of Fame sensibility could still sail around a hundred Billy Baldwin dining rooms on the backs of the remaining rich.

PART 2
GROWING UP RICH

6 | Mothers and Daughters

Marylou Whitney! She has a lunch within two hours with Charlotte Curtis, the *New York Times* writer about the rich, the famous, and the famously rich, at Le Cirque. She is dressed appropriately, in a pea-green shift with a matching scarf (and matching eyes), as well as a set of yellow, white, and grey pearls of formidable presence that encircle her ears, her fingers on both hands, and leap forth from a brooch. "A million-dollar view" is the sort of cliché that comes from somewhere, and where it comes from is Sonny and Marylou's porch. It features the unspeakably grand sweep of the gaudy autumnal trees in Central Park, the proud solidity of Central Park West, the glitter of midtown to the left. Her next-door neighbors are the Laurance Rockefellers, and other residents of the building, 834 Fifth Avenue, have included the first Mrs. Henry Ford II and Elizabeth Arden. Indeed, the Whitneys' is the same apartment in which Elizabeth Arden hung her Georgia O'Keeffes. The butler, Peter, brings tea on a silver heirloom set. Mrs. Whitney is polite and unhurried until she really

[131]

must leave for lunch—but that is something of an illusion, for she is in the midst of packing for the next day's trip to the camp in the Adirondacks, where the house is nine miles from the nearest public road. Mrs. Whitney realizes that the kind of wealth represented by her extravagant duplex on Fifth Avenue above Central Park is something that is not automatic even to her children—inheritance laws being the sticky way they are, and the truth about inheritance being that sometimes people who are potentially very rich cannot live the way they want.

"My daughter," says Marylou Whitney, "when she was working came here and it was impossible for her to make enough money to live and so she said, 'I don't want to live in Manhattan.' " Nevertheless, Whitney children realize early on that they are heirs to one of the classic—and still one of the huge—American fortunes, made originally in oil, tobacco, "traction" (trolleys), and land. Mrs. Whitney does not tell them how much they are worth, of course. "I told them that . . . busy people are happy people and you must not be lazy—and they are all very energetic." Her children have all worked and, as people used to insist upon, they know the value of a dollar, or even of a million dollars. One of Mrs. Whitney's sons, who went to Tulane, worked summers on a Mississippi riverboat and started a fabric shop on the side. This habit of working-as-if-you-need-it has carried over into investment bankerhood, for the son still gets up to play tennis or polo before he goes to the office at nine. The other son, who went to Georgia Tech, outdid all that: he worked at *three* different jobs one summer in Atlanta, among them collecting garbage and tarring roofs. Marylou Whitney believes strongly in the family and the Episcopal Church for imbuing children with the virtues of energy, of busyness. Like Renaissance nobility, the Whitneys have private chapels spread over the world—at the Adirondack camp, in Kentucky, in Saratoga, and used to have one in Mallorca. Religion and family worked like a German camera; the children are self-sufficient, accomplished, family-oriented—very much like their parents. About all they drink, it appears, is fresh-squeezed orange juice. One of the Whitney daughters just had her first art show, on Nantucket, in the summer of 1983. (This too is like the parents; both Sonny and Marylou have had shows of their paintings—in such haunts of the avant-garde as 57th Street, Saratoga, and Palm Beach). Afterward, the fledgling artist told Marylou, "Mommy, I didn't make enough money." Employing the Whitney creed, the young woman decided that she would conquer that problem by reducing her overhead, so she went to work in a framing shop. Such a gesture makes Marylou Whitney very proud; it is the self-assertion in a quiet way, the unpampered air of it, that makes her glow.

"Well, you see, my children always come up with ideas like that," she explains. "And it's really unfair what they say about children of the rich. I think there's a difference between children of the—and I really don't like to use the word nouveau riche because it really is a naughty word, because I have nothing against nouveaux riches—but my husband believes the children should do things on their own, you know, and not hand out a lot to them. Give them an education, but then they had to work for a living."

Here we have an enormous bulk of the mores of wealth dissipated into typically roundabout society talk. Although far too polite to talk about it using anybody's name, Marylou Whitney looks askance at some of the luncheon society she of necessity bumps into by dining at places like Le Cirque. ("So many of them are frivolous, don't you think?") This feeling is rooted in the historical necessity of behaving like a Whitney—which is to say like an outdoorswoman, a Christian gentlewoman, a non-complainer, a generous person, a happy person, and an un-snobbish person. Such families have seen far too many of their financial peers' children disappear into an abyss of self-indulgence, rootlessness, and the sort of money-can-fix-anything attitude crystallized by F. Scott Fitzgerald's Daisy and Tom Buchanan. Neatest of all, it is part of this philosophy of muscular Christianity that one not explicitly acknowledge the superiority of it—that one concede the nouveau can indeed act well, which is to say, act like the longtime gentry. And for one final paradox: "I think the children that grew up with names [that is, precisely the ones with a tradition of sturdy achievement inherited from noble families], it's really harder for them, they have to work harder. I know it sounds funny, but they do."

As Marylou Whitney mentions, "Laurance [Rockefeller] does the same thing with his children." Indeed, the Rockefellers, with their literal isolation from the common herd on the vast Pocantico reserve, their unsubtle lectures about the responsibilities that come with their trust funds, their insistence on public service, their protection of the capital, and the privacy, the arcana of the family office—in all these structures, the Rockefellers have made themselves synonymous with raising children into old-family wealth. But throughout the United States, and to some extent around the world—especially in countries where the aristocracy retains some importance, like segments of the British or German nobility—there are families raising their children in the style of the Rockefellers and the Whitneys. It is a style that exalts, at the same time, family ties and individual sturdiness.

With this emphasis on family, women are of crucial importance: they do most of the child-rearing, and before that they are responsible for selecting the proper male appendages to the family. This is a specific type of woman—an athletic woman, an energetic and entertaining woman, a woman able to manage the multiple details of living rich and yet still take the time to *look* rich; and yet with all of this competence, the requirement (at least until this generation) that the husband be acknowledged as head of the family.[23] The exigencies of wealth create the stereotype of the Rich Woman.

The fact of money is something ever-present in the way a child is raised, even outside the circles of standard-bred eastern gentility. Lynn Sakowitz, for example, was born in Houston sometime around 1930, the great-granddaughter of a Russian Jewish immigrant. By that time, the family was doing quite well. Louis Sakowitz, the immigrant, was convinced by a member of the Galveston Chamber of Commerce that the Texas Gulf city was going places. Louis, consequently, went to Galveston and established a ship's chandlery, which prospered in the shipping boom brought on by the oil rush. His sons Tobias and Simon opened haberdashery stores first in Galveston and later in Houston, which was then a miserable mosquito-ridden settlement that fully deserved the scorn of cultured easterners. During the prosperity of the 1920s Sakowitz started growing into the retailing giant that stands for swankness throughout the South. Bernard Sakowitz, Tobias's son and Lynn's father, joined the business in 1929 and further expanded it through the depression. Lynn's brother Robert is the current president and chief executive officer of the chain,

---

23. This applies almost as thoroughly when the woman is rich as it does when the husband bears the inherited wealth. However, the strain is much greater when the woman is rich. The marriages have traditionally lasted longest when the woman is submissive and the husband active, as in the du Pont family, and crumbled more easily when the women are as active and strong-minded as the Rockefellers. See Part Five for the intricacies of sex, love and marriage among the rich.

which is still closely held by the family and worth many millions. Lynn—"nobody's fool," as she describes herself—is acutely aware of the presence of a great deal of money and has thought about it considerably.

The fact that we had department stores—my peers in high school always thought that I could just walk into a store and get any amount of dresses that I wanted, and therefore I could wear a different dress to school every single solitary day. Of course it would cause a lot of enviousness and jealousy, etcetera. Number one, I couldn't do that, because it's not made right there at the store; someone has to pay the manufacturer, someone has to pay the material people. I mean—it has to start from scratch somewhere, and something has to cost money. My mother would take me to the store, and say I would choose five dresses, in the fitting room, and she would say, "Hey darling, have one." And I would say, "Oh, but I love this one so much, oh, but I can't make up my mind." "Well, make up your mind, because you cannot have the five." So I was brought up that way, and that kind of thing stayed with me, that I *couldn't* have everything I wanted. And even though when one is a teenager, it's expected that one will be more spoiled at times than an adult, I was told that I couldn't have—I had to make my choice. And so I had to make my choice in a way that, number one, I loved the dress; number two, that it wasn't something completely faddish, it was something that was going to last, it was something that was of good quality, it was something that I could wear more than once and people wouldn't say, "Oh yes, I remember that dress." And that taught me good fashion sense at the same time.

Lynn Sakowitz was taught a great many things very well. After college at Bennington—a rather unusual choice for a rich girl from Texas, with its reputation for freethinking and artiness at a time when those qualities were not synonymous with college life, setting it even more apart from the norm than it is now— she grew up to marry Oscar S. Wyatt, Jr., the mercurial founder and chairman of the Coastal Corporation, a large integrated oil company that he created in 1955, at the age of thirty. In a recent takeover offer, the value of his shares was pegged at something around $65 million.

Their combined fortunes are evident in the incredible mansion they own on River Oaks Boulevard, set on four acres just outside of downtown Houston. The River Oaks section is entered off a busy artery between Houston's two major business centers. It is a phantasmagoric square mile or so of massy homes in every conceivable style, with a severe overgrown Tudor next to a Mexican fantasy on top of a Plantation Big House with the requisite dripping Spanish moss. Built in the early 1930s, in the first flush of the city's great wealth, the Wyatt house is a sprawling six-bedroom dwelling that one enters through the traditional checkerboard marble foyer with a traditional shuffling southern butler. Lynn Wyatt descends the spiral staircase, imperially graceful in her just-sitting-around-in-the-afternoon knit pantsuit in key-lime green. It is part of the wardrobe that has won her a place in the International Fashion Hall of Fame. Her vaunted graciousness is just as evident: she inquires anxiously into the question of how well her cinnamon tea is appreciated. And the Bennington training, combined with the typical rich girl attention to taste, has brought the standard collections to her living room—Ming dynasty vases, little clocks, and so on in the sideboards. Over the fireplace in the sweeping living room are twin portraits of the lady of the house by Andy Warhol. She looks very good in the pictures—almost as good as she does in person, with her lambent blue eyes and golden mane. She has four sons, describes herself as "very family-oriented," and has spent much time considering what the money does, or could do, to her family.

As far as raising our boys: my husband and I have very much the same theory on that. Since they were very small and we started spending most of the summers in Europe, our theory was, the older they got, the less amount of time they had there. So when they were young, they would play in the sand, they would be in the south of France, it was wonderful. When they got a little bit older, they either had to go to summer school, or camp. When they were past the camp age, they either had to go to summer school or they had to work. They could spend a *little* bit of time in the south of France with me. My husband wouldn't normally spend the whole summer there, ever. He was always commuting back and forth, back and forth and here and there. But the children—the older they got, the less amount of time they spent there. In fact, there were times when they were old enough that they were working—one of them worked in Paris, the one that speaks good French, and the other one worked in London—and I would say every weekend, "Oh, can't you come this weekend?" and it ended up that they both came for only *one weekend* out of the entire summer, because they were inundated with their work or they had their own life or something. But it also gave them the sense that—

you know, they could very easily have turned into *playboys*, where they just spent the whole two months staying at nightclubs all night long, and playing tennis all day long. And it's very *easy* to fall into that kind of life.

And so they were brought up that the older they got the less amount of time they spent there. And then, not this summer but the summer before last [1982], my son who's the lawyer graduated from law school, and then he had a vacation in the summertime before he started work, and his father said, "Take as long as you want, because after you start working at your law firm, God only knows when you're gonna get another vacation." So I think he spent a month with me in the south of France. And so he had all these friends that he grew up with there, and so he was delighted. But it was the first time, really, that he had this holiday. But it was a *deserving* holiday, because it was after his law graduate school and it was before his work—the kind of thing that it was deserved, and he *played it to the hilt*. I mean I said, "You're wonderful except I never get to see you." He'd come in at six in the morning and go out at night.

But this was the kind of upbringing they had, that they couldn't sit and stare at the stars and play tennis all day long. I mean they had to be doing something constructive, and if they weren't in summer school then they had to be working. And then if they weren't working, then they could come over for maybe just a week or so. And they would look forward to it with such glee, of course. It was never that they could just spend the summer there—they had this inbred into them. I think that's something that has to be taught early, because I think if you give children everything when they're growing up, and all of a sudden when they're in their teenage years and they say, "I want something," and you say, "No you can't have it," they say, "Well, what's the matter, you don't love me anymore?" So it has to be inbred early that there are things that are important in life other than playing—that playing is the reward that you get after you've done your work.

Needless to say, families for whom money *is* a consideration have a much simpler time with the practical details of informing their children that playing is the reward of work. Perhaps the most crucial danger, Mrs. Wyatt thinks, comes among families in which the entrepreneurial parent believes that his own work ought to be rewarded by a life of play for his children. The dreaded nouveaux riches again rear their overstyled heads. "The parent that's grown up and he hasn't had those things," Mrs. Wyatt says, "he loves his children, and his first impression is to give his children things that he didn't have. That's the easiest thing to do. . . . The child himself wants that, so the easiest thing is to shower the children and to give them things. . . . It's very difficult to say, 'No, you can't come over now, you're going to have to find a job,' or, 'No, you can't have this car,' etcetera. It's much more difficult to say that—and for them to understand why. And if they've grown up with that inbred in them from an early age, they sort of know that without your having to tell them.''

Not all families with the values and styles of the Rockefellers and the Whitneys and the Sakowitzes, of course, are like them in the centimillionaire class. But that gracious upper-class attitude is most frequently found among families that have at least been in that major income bracket in a previous generation. They never lose the attitude. Sarah Pillsbury, for example, is an early thirties heiress of perhaps a few million dollars—or perhaps much more— from the flour company, which has long been prominent in Minnesota business and civic affairs. Miss Pillsbury had the classic rich girl's WASPy upbringing, full of tumbling competition in the outdoors, but a very socially active environment as well, plus a sense of the need to do things for others, of noblesse oblige. That impulse translated itself into the creation, with some of her wealth and that of other young rich folks around Los Angeles, of the Liberty Hill Foundation of Santa Monica, one of numerous such "alternative" philanthropies established recently by wealthy children of the sixties. Such organizations presumably fight people such as their parents, who own a great deal of property and generally see that it is managed to the maximization of their profit. But Miss Pillsbury sees her interest in the lower classes' freedom as the logical outgrowth of a family ethic of universal concern and pragmatic activity. There was "no rebellion," she says; "I'm almost my mother's clone." The attitude was nowhere better expressed, perhaps, than in the telegram Sarah Pillsbury received from her ninety-six-year-old grandmother as she was matriculating at Yale in 1969. It read, "Keep up the reputation!"

That is the ideal, but it is frequently failed by the children of the very wealthy. Indeed, it is a matter of common agreement among the Rockefeller cousins and the rich kids that Sarah Pillsbury knows that the children of old, immensely monied families growing up in present-day America face self-created craggy values of questioning their right to their inheritances. Sometimes the protective veneer—the implied trust that involvement in an active and concerned life justifies immense possessions—founders on unconvincing explanations. For example, one might think from Marylou Whitney's approving nod toward the Laurance Rockefellers' childrearing practices that their children were as well-adjusted as hers. They are, in fact, decidedly peculiar. Laurance's daughter Marion, for example, is attempting to live a life utterly devoid of money, growing her own food and raising her children in the isolated highlands well above San Francisco. "The fortune should be made extinct," she has said. "I don't want it passed on to my children. I don't want them to have to deal with what I've had to deal with. I hope the social revolution will come soon and take away from us the necessity of having to deal with it."

Marion and her sisters traced their questioning adulthoods directly to the upper-class way in which their father raised them. "My struggle is for recognition," Laura Rockefeller Chasin told Peter Collier and David Horowitz."I was never recognized for myself by my parents. The servants gave us individual presents. Our parents gave us tons of presents, but never any that were for *me*. I became fond of the maids and the servants, and then when I heard my parents talk to them as though they were nonpeople, I vowed I would never treat anyone like that." A third sister, Lucy Rockefeller Waletzky, became a psychiatrist largely out of her need to examine her own psyche (like most psychiatrists, of course), and is active in organizations promoting the importance of involved parents, such as La Leche League. "We were not so much isolated as children as we were encased in a vacuum," she recalled. "Nobody wanted to communicate. Nobody bothered to orient us to the world. Nothing was really talked about at home. They operated on the theory that you don't talk about important things to your animals, or servants, and you don't tell them to your children."

Nor can rich parents isolate their children from the implications of their wealth merely by trying to bring them up like everybody else. Inevitably, their young playmates find out that their little pals will some day have vast economic power over them; the annals of rich families are full of stories of the kids coming home and asking how rich the family actually is, because little Susie was saying her parents had said we were filthy rich. Lisa Marie Presley was confronted by charming little playmates who filled her in on the details of a best-selling book that described her father Elvis's sexual peccadilloes. It took her mother several years to persuade Lisa Marie that her father was not *all* bad. "Now, I think she's pretty proud of her dad," says Priscilla Presley, sounding rather wistful. Electra Waggoner Biggs tried to rear her two daughters like normal people, sending them to the local elementary school in Vernon, Texas, with the other children, whose parents for the most part worked for her directly or indirectly. The children were brutalized. Electra Waggoner Biggs's older daughter, another Electra, felt the scorn of her peers incessantly. "It did something to her," Mrs. Biggs recalls. "It made her very timid—very withdrawn, very shy. Because they want to meet friends. All children need friends at their age."

The early wounds have perhaps, although Mrs. Biggs does not mention it, contributed to Electra's decision to stay in Texas—in Houston—being simply a housewife. She does none of the social sorts of things her mother so obviously enjoys. Second daughter Helen has gone even further, living on the Waggoner Ranch itself, only a mile from her mother, and sending her children to the local schools. The decision to remain in Vernon has, of course, transferred the same problem to the next generation. Mrs. Biggs has ready at hand a Polaroid snapshot of a willowy twelve-year-old, Helen's daughter Jennifer, in a full-length quilted dress that won her a prize at school. "She made that dress by hand," Grandmother remarks with pride. "They told me at school that if she did something wrong she'd go to school, take all the stitches out and redo it. So she deserved to win. But the children come up and say, 'Well, the only reason she won is she bought it.' Which is cruel. It hurts their feelings."

Mrs. Biggs knows that the playmates get their antiwealth bias from their parents, but that is no comfort to the children. Meeting Mrs. Biggs, it is difficult to believe that she could have produced withdrawn children. In fact, *she* did not: it was the rest of society. Eventually, the local schools turned out to be too poor academically, and the children were packed off to the exclusive Hockaday School in Dallas. But the school, and the Biggs's obviously close and rather down-home family, did not counteract the larger world the children grew up in. At bottom, it is the money itself—not the ability of the parents or the time they spend with the children—that is the most important factor in a rich childhood.

From the outside, consider the recollections of a woman named

Peggy Mackenzie, who was a classmate of the Bronfman girls at a rarefied girls' school called the Study in Westmount, the most exclusive suburb of Montreal. By virtue of attending the school and living in Westmount, Peggy was a fairly sophisticated upper-middle-class child, but she remembers with awe a visit to the Bronfman mansion, Belvedere Palace, for Minda Bronfman's tenth birthday party. "We were seated in a great, long dining room and while there may not have been a butler or footman behind every chair, there certainly were an awful lot of them," she recalled later for author Peter C. Newman. "We were all spread out in these big, high-backed oak chairs and every child was given a present. I got a hard-cover Conan Doyle classic, enormously expensive-looking, particularly in the middle of the depression, and the other gifts were of comparable splendor. The entertainment was a movie in the downstairs recreation room, the first film most of us had ever watched because in Quebec you weren't allowed to see movies until you were sixteen in those days. The whole thing was quite extraordinary." So obvious was the gulf between the Bronfman children and even their fairly wealthy neighbors that their mother frequently reminded the girls that since other children might feel uncomfortable around them, they must take the initiative themselves in forming friendships.

In these situations, difficult as they can be for the children, at least the love and occasional attention of the parent provides a support when the adolescent or young adult needs to grapple with her heritage. It is much worse when money is used by the parents specifically as a means of distancing themselves from their children and permitting themselves their freedom from parenthood. The "poor little rich girls" of the 1930s—Barbara Hutton, Doris Duke, and Gloria Vanderbilt—are the classic examples. In one way or another without parents, they were forced to grow up with little emotional stability but the rapidly growing awareness that they could buy anything they wanted, including love. In the first two cases they learned very badly and grew into peculiar, seeking, rather pitiful adults. Gloria Vanderbilt turned her soap-opera beginnings as the object of the famous custody battle into a quest to prove herself in multiple artistic fields and numerous marriages, and seems to have finally settled down rather happily. The burdens of wealth have not dissipated for the current generation. One need only look at the notorious examples of Patty Hearst, Edie Sedgwick, and Sasha Bruce—respectively, a gun-toting revolutionary, a drug suicide, and an apparent murder victim of her boyfriend—to realize that growing up rich without proper parents can induce massively self-destuctive behavior.[24]

24. See Chapter 27.

7 | WHAT A Rich Kid SEES FIRST

WHATEVER THE INNER STRENGTHS or torments of growing up, most rich children outwardly lead the lives of their upper-middle-class neighbors. They live pretty much as rich people live in the movies: in huge duplexes towering above Fifth Avenue; in stately mansions on grand boulevards in the sixteenth *arrondissement*; in chalets in St. Moritz or Vail; on yachts in the Mediterranean; on a few remaining English country estates; in the candyland of Palm Beach; on ranches in the American West; on grand estates— not infrequently in family compounds—in suburban, or more likely exurban, communities. The great common denominator of growing up rich is the endless variety of *things* available, and generally available for the asking, even in relatively strict families like the Whitneys or Rockefellers. So many things are available, in fact, that it is frequently difficult for the rich child to assimilate them all. "These are children, after all," writes Robert Coles in *Privileged Ones,* who have to contend with, as well as enjoy, enormous couches, pillows virtually as big as chairs, rugs that were once meant to be in palaces of the Middle East, dining room tables bigger than the rooms many American children share with brothers or sisters, and, always, the importance and fragility of objects: a vase, a dish, a tray, a painting or lithograph or pencil sketch, a lamp. A boy or girl who is just beginning to figure out a dependable rhythm of activity and restraint for himself or herself has to stop and wonder how much of a "comfortable, comfortable world" he or she dares include in various journey or forays through the house. And how much of that world can the young child even comprehend? Sometimes, in a brave, maybe desperate, attempt to bring everything around under control, a child will enumerate (for the benefit of a teacher or a friend) all that is his or hers, all that goes to make up what an observer might call the "setting," the background against which a life is carried on. Large trees get mixed up with globes built into tables; a pond is linked in sequence with a library of thousands of books; a Queen Anne desk shares company with a new motorboat that goes so fast the child's father, no stranger to speed, has begun to have second thoughts about the safety of those who go aboard with him.

Be It Ever So Humble

Most specifically, there is a rich way of interior decorating. Not all rich parents are interested in it—Electra Biggs, with her metal flowers and her bluebird decals, is decidedly out of it— and many children, like Electra's, care as little for their surroundings as middle-class children do. In many cases rejecting elaborate interior design is a way for the child to separate herself from the daunting complexity and power of her parents' lives. Many of this generation of Rockefellers live more or less simply, and some are downright Spartan. Similarly, Carolina Herrera's eldest daughter has no eye and no interest in fashion whatsoever. However, for those who do care, infinite money allows the enormous indulgence of surrounding oneself with the perfect environment. One Christmas, fresh out of philanthropic impulses, which she normally indulges with her husband's money, Marylou Whitney said the hell with it and spent $50,000 on a bathroom; "it's a lovely bathroom," she avers, without fear of contradiction.

There are, of course, differences in style and taste among the very wealthy, ranging from the austere statement of Dominique de Menil's house by Philip Johnson—*the* society architect of our day—to the tradition-soaked interiors that Mrs. Whitney creates wherever she goes. For the *dernier cri* in decorating, one must read *Architectural Digest* religiously. Paige Rense, the editor of that last word in design, makes and breaks careers of designers and the hostesses they work for through her ability to reject the thousands of surplus designs that are offered her each year. Decorating is, for those part of the social spin, similar to fashion in clothes in that it advertises not only the woman's taste but her ability to indulge it; and like clothes, it can be used as a weapon in the endless battle for social clout. In this world, having the latest in gowns or wallpaper advertises the ability to combat constant obsolescence. That is why masses of fresh and exotic flowers are the ultimate fashion statement: they are not only pretty, they last no time at all. Similarly, hiring premier decorators whose fees overwhelm hand-held calculators, like Billy Baldwin or Mario Buatta, advertises rich taste. The people one is seeking to impress with this display know precisely how much that velvet on the chairs costs, just as they know what a facelift costs, or a Carolina Herrera dress.

Still, the latest expensive look moves within a compass that those outside it would consider fairly narrow, so there exists what can be described as a distinctly rich look of some permanence. In single-family mansions, as opposed to Manhattan co-ops, it is extremely helpful to have *soigné* gardens outside, a grand staircase, a huge door attended by a footman, and a hall of marble. Marble may not be very cozy, but it is grand. Black-and-white checks are favorites, with a veined off-white also fine; there may be a vogue for pink marble in the wake of the Trump Tower success. Inside, the basics: walls of neutral colors, good Oriental rugs on polished wood floors, puffy sofas and chairs in bright colors or flowered prints, curtains of good chintz. The accent pieces frequently run to the invaluable, such as antique vases, important paintings, memorable furniture, and portraits of the owner or family. Fresh flowers are everywhere. Throughout the house there are dainty pillows good approximately for one elbow. Rich women are great collectors of small items— pillboxes, fire engines, owls, anything petite and cute—which are generally lined up in huge cabinets. The only really standard item in bedrooms are linen sheets by Porthault. Bathrooms are major barometers of taste, of course, since so much time is spent in them. The sophisticated, especially those of an older generation, do not go much for Jacuzzis and such. Olga Hirshhorn has an amusing collection of little *bibelots* in one of hers. Lynn Wyatt's has a sitting room outside the actual bathroom, with a puffy chair, a French Provincial telephone, a dressing table, small oils, and pearl hat pins, just in case. And all over the house are portraits, framed in gilt or silver, of ancestors and children, and, sometimes, celebrities the rich person hangs out with.

Everybody complains about the high cost and unreliability of help, but nothing changes: the rich keep right on hiring butlers, maids, and social secretaries. It is in the nature of being rich that one gets an enormous amount of mail, so virtually every rich woman worth her haughty tones has a private secretary of one kind or another. The massively wealthy ones, like Cordelia Scaife May, employ lawyers, stockbrokers, and other professionals full-time to look after their wide-ranging affairs; people of several hundred million dollars' net worth are small corporations. In England, a man named Ivor Spencer runs a school that, for $2,550, gives lessons to would-be butlers in classes of twelve once a week for six months, then ships them off around the world, to households from Hong Kong to Houston—especially Houston. Demand is so great that Spencer takes only one applicant out of twenty, and this for a job that pays $25,000 to $30,000 for sixteen-hour days. There is no such school for what used to be called social secretaries; they generally come out of more or less the same class as their employers, though without the money, and therefore do not have to be instructed in the details of protocol among the superrich. Marylou Whitney has had the same secretary, June Douglas, for nearly twenty years, or most of the time that she has been married to Sonny Whitney. From her office on Cape Cod, Mrs. Douglas performs for her employer much the same functions that an executive secretary does for a corporation chief executive officer—which indeed is not a bad analogy for the breadth and intensity of Mrs. Whitney's involvements. Mrs. Douglas not only arranges Mrs. Whitney's staggering schedule, she keeps tabs on expenditures in the New York household, which must be quite a giddy task. And she refers to her employer as "my best friend." In the case of Palm Beach, a woman named Janet Grant has parlayed her longtime employ by Mary Sanford, the redoubtable "queen of Palm Beach," into a thriving business organizing and staging both charity functions and private parties. Governesses, however, seem to be out of favor these days; people as disparate as a number of Rockefeller women and Patty Hearst have decided that they do not want to raise their children at a distance, as they were raised. Still, many of a rich child's earliest acquaintances and friends are with the service people who abound in rich households. It is precisely by growing into their superior position over these people that the rich acquire that air of easy command that marks so many of them.

Socializing

The children of the rich are the particular heirs of Western culture. This is true even in Asian or African countries, where the small upper crust generally emulates Europe and the United States. The stuffings of museums, of art galleries, of Neiman-Marcus, of Harry Winston, of Hermès, of Loewe, of Sotheby's—all these things are in transit from or to the homes of wealthy people. The parents of rich children are, for the most part, an extremely well-educated and well-socialized bunch, of course. They generally want their children to acquaint themselves with all that the world has to offer. Thus, rich kids are frequently deluged with shopping trips, visits to museums, music lessons, riding lessons, painting lessons, gardening lessons, French lessons, tutoring from parents or others in dressing, in manners, in learning to handle money, in discrimination in thousands of different categories. As Coles notes, travel is a crucial difference in the childhoods of rich kids. The typical heiress is, before her debut, closely familiar with New York's Upper East Side, with one or more Caribbean islands, with the Right Bank in Paris, with Bermuda, with the Italian hill towns, with St. Moritz or Vail, and frequently with more exotic locales like Nepal, the Nile, or the Andes. Many of the very wealthy grow up into an international elite, particularly those outside the United States. The richest families of the world—the Greek shipping tycoons, German industrialists, South American ranchers, French nobles, Arab sheikhs—almost unanimously buy outrageously priced *pieds-à-terre* in Manhattan. They vacation together too, on Florida's Gold Coast, in Marbella, in Cap Ferrat, on Sardinia's Costa Smeralda.

The result is a constant influx of social reinforcement in the enormously complex process of acting rich. It gives rich children that unmistakable air of owning all they survey. The rapid, full-time socialization, the emphasis on achieving and conversing and keeping active, also produces those marvelously poised eight-year-old adults that one can see wandering Park Avenue or the

Avenue Foch in their miniature blazers. A wealthy childhood is a fleeting phenomenon, since its entirely realizable goal is the achievement of mastery over the entire world. In a very real sense, being rich is not a matter to leave in a child's hands.

It's as Easy to Marry a Rich Boy

It is a truth universally acknowledged, that a single man in possession of a good fortune, must be in want of a wife.

—JANE AUSTEN

Rich families tend to be conservative, politically and socially—although in a grand and sometimes dissipated manner, as distinct from the pinched conservatism of, say, ethnic Catholics in the United States. The socialization of rich girls, therefore, tends to lag somewhat behind the times, or at least the times as dictated by the urban intelligentsia. The overwhelming importance of a correct marriage is, for many rich families, part of the air they breathe and the caviar they eat. Among most families, especially these days, the parents hardly take aside their daughters to give them a birds-and-bees lecture about the importance of correct marriages. This was a tradition a generation ago—a necessary one, for by virtue of being both female and privileged, these princesses tended to be brought up with little sense of the world. On Minda's twenty-first birthday, for example, Sam Bronfman called her in and, in his Moses-on-the-mountain voice, gave her the lecture on money. (She had expected it to be about sex.) After outlining the immense boundaries of the Seagram's fortune, Sam told her, "You are an heiress, and don't ever forget it. A lot of men may seem to be interested in you but in fact will be more interested in your money. If you fall in love, make sure the man is not just a fortune hunter." But most families, especially these days, are nowhere near as blunt in preparing their daughters for the rigors of courtship and marriage. Rather, it is an effect achieved by repetition, something like building up muscles on a Nautilus machine. The mother reminds her children how to behave—how to make it on their own and not act nouveau, as the Whitneys preach; the sorts of things to expect in people; how to dress, what to appreciate. By implication, all these things are expected of their mates as well. By osmosis, a rich girl who is also attractive rapidly becomes aware that she will be the object of pursuit by men whose money makes them noticeable and desirable, and whose forcefulness makes their attentions unmistakable and hard to resist.

One crucial ingredient in growing up a rich girl is to be entertaining. It is a matter of great pride and determination among the wealthy families of the world that their women be diverting. Among the upper classes of virtually all societies, with the possible exception of Arabs, women have it drilled into them from birth that they must be spirited conversationalists, charming hostesses, and intriguing companions. Barbara Hutton wrote in her diary when she was a teenager: "To be dull, says Aunt Jessie, is a cardinal sin. 'Be mean, be stupid, but don't be dull!' "

Many of the richest women of the world, especially those on the social circuit, have ready for public consumption some variation on this comment of Carolina Herrera's: "I have an interest in almost everything—and I'm never bored. I think to be bored is ridiculous. Life is too short to be bored." Much of this is for the edification of the men who also must be constantly amused and who are, of course, paying most of the freight. A good portion as well is attributable to the need to prove that being rich does not mean being idle and useless. It justifies one's wealth to be constantly busy and interested in the things of this great world.

A substantial component of the act is a subdued, elegant sexuality—nothing at all crude, naturally, but just the tiniest hint that the fascination of this person arises not only from her control of all that wealth, but that there is an actual *woman* underneath it all, who might at times have actually, physically—please, hints only. Anyway, it is part of being a rich, social woman that one develop a reputation as the greatest flirt in the world. The orthodoxy in this world, albeit with with a tinge of southern coquettishness that the more phlegmatic northerners might have frowned upon until recently, comes from Lynn Wyatt. She learned flirting with her father as object at the age of two and a half, she says. "I don't feel it's demeaning and I don't think it means the woman is lustful either. [Please!] I classify myself as a big flirt because I love to flirt. I think it's amusing. I think it's the kind of thing that has a lot of whimsy and fantasy in it." One has only to be escorted to the door once by the willowy Mrs. Wyatt, watch her flutter those feathery lashes and issue her wistful, honeysuckle " 'Bye"—as though the present departure is the one that has hurt the most in a lifetime of loneliness—to believe that she has indeed practiced flirting for her entire gilded life.

The women who have learned all these lessons well seem to have been raised specifically to marry rich: one thinks of the Cushing sisters with their strings of brilliant matches, or Leonore Annenberg, whose two husbands before Walter were Belden Kattleman, a casino owner and playboy, and Lewis Rosenstiel, the neurotic chairman of the Schenley Industries liquor giant. Or consider, for example, the ambition of that peculiar phenomenon Cornelia Guest, shortly after her debutante-of-the-year appearance in 1982: "When I do get serious I want the man to be ten to fifteen years older than me, tall, dark, handsome, and exotic—maybe a foreigner. It's possible, because my parents [the late Winston Guest, an internationally known polo player, and C. Z., socialite and gardening columnist] know a lot of Europeans." At last report, things were well on track: Cornelia's boyfriend of nearly a year was Roberto Riva, a forty-three-year-old Peruvian real estate dealer with an apartment on Beekman Place. In her predilection for older foreigners, Cornelia was reviving an American rich girl tradition that had gone into eclipse in recent decades, but had not perhaps ever died. At any rate, the selection of an appropriate marital alliance, as we shall see in part five, is probably the most crucial decision of a rich girl's young life, and all too often one that she botches badly. It is the one area in which the careful teachings of parents, schools, teachers, and peers seem not to help very much.

8 | Acting Rich

Much easier is behavior outside the specific context of attracting a mate. Old money or just made, European or American, jet-setting or traditionalist, religious or decadent, the world's families of great wealth expect their children to behave like little ladies and gentlemen. There is still a general consensus on what, in the United States at least, might be designated an upper-class norm of behavior. It calls for at least superficial politeness to everyone, including servants; vivaciousness and interest in others' conversation; honesty; at least a casual regard for appropriate dress; avoidance of utter drunkenness; generosity; "being a good sport"; athletic interests; love of animals; and interest in current affairs, artistic events, and fashion, but no overbearing intellectuality. In Europe and South America, the values are similar but are likely to be tinged with vestiges of truly "aristocratic" behavior, which allows more indulgence of snobbery among the wellborn wealthy and consequent defensiveness and isolation by those with newer money. If they are frequently honored in the breach, these are nevertheless values that most rich parents—plus their surrogates, governesses, and teachers at prestigious schools—at least nominally try to imbue their children with.

While self-consciously upper-class behavior went into a very distinct eclipse during the 1960s and early 1970s, driving the *soignée* mothers of the world to a few kirs at lunch, it never completely disappeared. All it took to reinforce it was the upper-class woman's usual diligence. When Marylou Whitney's boys visited her in Kentucky at Christmas after their first semester from college in Boston during the 1960s, she "couldn't believe it—they were not neat, their hair was scraggly." Well, she just sat them on a stool and chopped off that hair and said, "Now I want you to go and scrub yourselves down, and furthermore if you want to be in this house, you are going to be well-dressed, and you have clean clothes and nice clothes and if you want to be with us I want you to look nice." It worked! The sons have not only turned out well, they dress for dinner now.

The Whitney children are as much a metaphor for the reculturization of America as Nancy Reagan is. It is no secret that manners and style have rebounded strongly in recent years. With the likes of Cornelia Guest in the vanguard—her two most admired people are Nancy Reagan and Diana Ross—a good portion of rich youth is rediscovering the joys of polite behavior. In 1983, the Emily Post Summer Camp opened at the powerfully elegant Breakers Hotel in Palm Beach, providing twelve young men and eight would-be ladies with the elements of style, not to mention the relief of not having to go to the camps where the kids put living things in your bed. It was already the third summer for L'Ecole des Ingénues in Taos, New Mexico, a rigorous two-week, $1,385 apiece (air fare extra, of course) exercise in everything most young women once thought they'd never need to worry about again. Anne Oliver, the *diretrice* of the stylish mountain camp, takes her teenaged future Charity Ball fixtures through smatterings of French poetry, personal grooming, self-image training, pastry preparation, opera and art appreciation, conversation, flower arrangement, meditation, being photographed, and how to sit at *le pique-nique* (legs together and folded under, please). And, of course, the ever-popular Pelvic Tilt, a maneuver used to correct the tendency of some young women in a hurry to "stick their butt out," as one young woman at the Ecole explained it. Miss Oliver insists that this is not all empty snobbery; it's more like well-filled snobbery. "In the world as it is today," she said in one interview, "you've got to package yourself. But there's got to be something inside the package."

Party Girls

What is frequently inside the package is an aspiring entertainer. Giving a party at the highest level is a science that requires not only considerable money, not only a cast of dozens of cooks and servers and car-parkers, but an expertise that in almost all cases has been handed down from the hostess's mother. Marylou Whitney's experience is typical:

> I've always entertained since I was very small. I always liked to entertain. My mother did too. My mother would always have parties and she'd say, "Don't just have a dull party—think of a theme." It was very difficult for mother, but we had a cook that had a good sense of humor. I wanted to have twelve girls for lunch, and I wanted each one to have a different meal. One would have an Italian meal and one would have a Greek meal. It was very funny. My sisters and I used to draw; we studied art, so we really could draw. We did little pictures of each person and their place at the table in Italian, Greek, Spanish costumes. I mean we really had it all—we did it with crayolas, we had marvelous little pictures.
>
> I always entertained. I always entertained in strange ways. I mean my friends could never understand why I wanted to give them nasturtium sandwiches, but I read one time that it was very chic, so we had nasturtium sandwiches. We didn't like them. I had to do different things. Mother was marvelous. I said, "Oh, mother, look at that thing"—it was a gypsy thing with a wheel that went around and it had numbers on it with the fortune teller and cards. I said, "What can you do with that other than advertise toothpaste or something on it?" and she said, "Can I have it?" and they said "Certainly." So she took it home and we covered this ad up, and spin the wheel of fortune and you get a piece of gum or a lollypop or whatever it might be. It was really great fun. [That must be taken on faith.] So we're always looking for new things to do at a party. We used to have garden parties out around the fish pond, and everyone had their little baskets with all their little goodies. We had a lot of fun decorating baskets for the guests. We just always—so I guess I followed in my mother's footsteps.

Lynn Wyatt does not think there's a particularly Lynn Wyatt way of entertaining. In this, she is at odds with virtually anyone who's been to a Lynn Wyatt entertainment. She does admit to giving a great deal of thought to her parties. "In the south of

France," she reflects, "many times, I will serve chili, for example, and fried chicken, and other Texas dishes to the French and the Italians—only because they adore them so much and they don't get it over there. So naturally they're so thrilled to have it. And one year I gave a party and I decided that I was not going to have it, and *screams* came—'How can you think not to have it?' So every year when I have a birthday party—every year I give myself a birthday party—and I'll have this food, mixed in naturally with some French food. But they eat that fried chicken, and chili, and rice, and—I think I had a tamale pie this year, and that kind of thing. And pecan pie for dessert, you know, which is always a hit. But I mean, that is sort of a Texas way of entertaining, but it's certainly not a Lynn Wyatt way of entertaining. Any Texan can throw a barbecue. But it's not what I would serve here. Here [in Houston] I serve people, usually, French cuisine. I have a cook that's been with me for nineteen years, and we talk about it together, what to have for dinner, and she does *everything*. I've never had any catering. So, no, I wouldn't say that there's a Lynn Wyatt way of entertaining. . . . [But] I like to think, and I would like other people to think, that whatever I do, I do it well, but I do it with a certain elegance and a certain gaiety that is not flamboyant. Low-key, but yet fun. Not totally extravagant, but yet enough glamour that it's still different, it's still amusing. Well, people tell me all the time that 'when I come to the house, I know that's what I'm gonna get.' So this is apparently what I'm striving for, and this is the highest compliment I could get."

9 | Schools

WHEN ELECTRA WAGGONER BIGGS's children were being emotionally terrorized by their playmates at school in the Biggs's company town of Vernon, Texas, the solution was simple: pack them off to the Hockaday School in Dallas. The function of such a school has been standard for approximately a century, since the establishment in their present form of the English public schools (that is to say, what Americans would call private schools; they were public compared with being educated by a private tutor). Private schools not only provide some of the better educations around; by virtue of being private, they preselect the type of children who attend them. Within the private school system, of course, there are also gradations—by religion, by cost, by boarding versus day, and by degree of exclusivity. Typically, the young heiress will attend the most fashionable local "country day school." Many of these are affiliated with the Episcopal Church, the denomination of the bulk of the United States's most social old families and, hence, the keeper of values frequently aspired to among old money and new alike. Afterward, the young heiress is likely to be packed off to boarding school to acquire the graces that specifically mark the well-monied and well-finished woman worldwide.

Many young women, of course, attend coed schools. The trend has gotten stronger since the 1960s, when teenaged girls as well as boys began discovering that marriage was a legal technicality having nothing in particular to do with sexual activity. The resulting trend toward coeducation put severe pressure, of a recruiting and hence a financial nature, on many of the single-sex boarding schools in the United States and Europe. Many of the previously all-male schools sought to combat this trend by opening their nicely manicured campuses to girls, which produced another set of options for the future woman of wealth in the forms of education at, say, the Kent School in Connecticut, or Institut Le Rosey in Switzerland.

Le Rosey is the oldest, most prestigious private school in Switzerland and very likely the most expensive primary or secondary school in the world; a year there comes to at least $15,000 per student, which is considerably more than, for example, a year at Harvard. The daunting size of that contribution to a child's education naturally ensures that his classmates will be among the world's richest people. Well-known graduates include King Baudouin of Belgium ('45–'46), Prince Karim Aga Khan ('46–'54), Winston Churchill II ('49–'51), the Duke of Kent ('51–'63), the late Shah of Iran ('32–'36), Prince George Radziwill ('32–'38), and Prince Rainier of Monaco ('37–'40). This is no school for obscure, unintelligent money either. It is so superprestigious that there is a huge waiting list for the 180 places for boys and 110 for girls. Many of the applicants are from the Middle East, others from Greek shipping families, French and German nobility, South American manufacturers, Texas oil millionaires—in short, just the sort of agglomeration that an aspirant to international filthy-rich celebrity might as well get used to sooner rather than later. The girls are kept on a separate campus and strictly chaperoned.

Switzerland as a whole is a Xanadu for young girls with international connections on their minds. The schools are of such immense overall expense that the student body is very carefully culled from the upper classes; one's classmates are liable to be not only wealthy but interesting exotics from around the world, providing lessons in catholic taste, as well as the convenience of plush accommodations in pleasant way-stations on the international circuit; second and third languages sprout like dandelions; Paris, London, and the Côte d'Azur are a quick plane ride away. Some of the Swiss schools remain for girls only, such as St. George's School in Montreux, which boasts the distinction of having educated Christina Onassis. "She seemed to be forever flying off for weekends in Paris, Athens, London, New York," a classmate once told a reporter. "It set her apart from the rest."

Swiss schools, moreover, tend to inculcate an attitude that goes well beyond mere parochial snobbery to a sort of ethereal superiority. The literature of the Institut Préalpina, in Chexbrès, whose cost is at the breathtaking level of Le Rosey's, asserts that "Mr. [Leonard] Bettex [the headmaster] only accepts pupils whose parents and background he knows. Mere rich showoffs cannot have their daughters accepted here, daughters who would be allowed to do anything by parents desirous of a quiet life. Préalpina is the wrong place for the three daughters of an oil tycoon who would like them to be treated like princesses." The school goes on to boast that only six Iranian girls were accepted out of thirty-five who applied one pre-ayatollah year. We are not, however, talking about Dickensian austerity here. The school has a staff of sixty-four for 115 girls—among them ten *gouvernantes* who awaken them individually while music plays, three laundry workers to provide linen changes daily and to wash everybody's wardrobe, two chauffeurs, and a travel agent. The school has not only the expected riding and skiing gear, but several sailboats, a motorboat for waterskiing on Lake Geneva, and a hairdressing salon.

American girls-only boarding schools have been hit hard by declining interest. Many have simply closed shop; others have merged, such as Rosemary Hall, which is now combined with Choate. However, the great names are still alive, with much of the United States's bluest blood, and a fair amount from foreign countries, flowing through their veins. These would be Foxcroft, St. Timothy's, and Miss Porter's School, conveniently strung along the eastern seaboard for easy access by the richest of the rapidly fading eastern establishment, as well as those with newer money looking to take their place. American girls' boarding schools are in a different tradition from the continental schools. The girls' schools in the United States were founded on principles quite similar to those of the boys' boarding schools that proliferated at the end of the nineteenth century. Both types of schools had heavily Episcopal influences, which at the time of the founding meant a great sense of self-confidence, insistence on physical activity, and a strong identification with British manners and mores. The girls' schools were also ardently feminist; they were all founded by strong-minded (and generally strong-limbed) women from the upper-class subset who believed that noblesse oblige demanded physical and intellectual activity from women on behalf not only of their rich husbands but of the society as a whole. For much of their history, however, that was a tradition honored in the breach by the great bulk of students, who promptly forgot whatever they might have learned about the social responsibilities of the upper class as soon as they had a chance to graduate into debutante parties and a correct marriage.

Indeed, the schools were widely seen as little more than expensive, distant cousins of the local dancing classes. That, at any rate, is how the girls' parents and frequently the girls themselves perceived them, to the dismay of the more serious among the teachers. Drugs and social turmoil in the 1960s had a drastic impact on the boarding schools, as they did throughout American society. While there will always be alumnae's daughters to fill some of the places, all the schools have long since recognized that snobbery, horsemanship, and a chance to dance at exclusive boys' schools are hardly sufficient reasons to persuade most parents nowadays to part with upward of $10,000 a year. Still, that figure naturally limits the clientele to the very well-to-do. And the boarding schools remain, for a significant portion of the extremely rich in the United States and abroad, important institutions for bringing their female offspring to adulthood in a physically and socially protected manner.

The most "serious" of the girls boarding schools is Miss Porter's School—or, to those on terms of breezy intimacy with the place, simply "Farmington," after its town near Hartford, Connecticut. Miss Porter's is also the oldest of the three (founded 1843 by the daughter of the town's Congregational minister) and the school most identified with the traditional eastern Establishment. Jacqueline Bouvier went to Farmington. So did Barbara Hutton, who was decidedly out of place. Barbara's lifelong obsessions with standing out and with wanting to escape were already apparent, as was her spoiled rich girl temperament, which prevented her from acquiring close friends. In those days in particular, Miss Porter's expected its young charges, all of whom were quite rich, to behave properly and modestly. Instead, Barbara wore masses of showy clothes (the school was fundamentally as preppy then as it is now), kept to herself, received visits from her gaudily dressed and chauffered aunts, and read popular novels; the latter habit brought her into constant conflict with the headmistress, Rose Day Keep.

A decade later, Gertrude Whitney, who wrested little Gloria Vanderbilt away from her mother in the spectacular custody case, eventually sent her charge off to Miss Porter's because Gloria needed "the whole influence and quality of the school." However, Mrs. Keep refused in the spring of 1939 to allow first-year student Gloria to return to the school because she had been spotted, at the age of fourteen, in the Stork Club with a boyfriend while she was supposed to be recuperating from an appendectomy. The Mellons, one of the half-dozen wealthiest families in the world, have been sending their daughters to Miss Porter's for generations—among them Constance B. Mellon, who was married for a time to J. Carter Brown, director of the National Gallery, and who has served on the board of Miss Porter's; and her distant relative from a "poorer" branch, Peggy Hitchcock, who is married to the former publisher of the *East Village Other*. Other graduates from among the wealthiest families in the country include Anne Cox Chambers, heiress to the huge Cox Communications fortune and former ambassador to Belgium, and Elise R. W. du Pont, wife of Delaware governor Pierre du Pont, and herself a former high official of the United States Agency for International Development and candidate for Congress. Today, Miss Porter's is widely considered one of the best schools of any kind in the United States, and its graduates have predictable success in getting accepted by the most important universities.

The outside world has, however, clearly worked major changes in what was once a well-sealed-off world useful for the passage of a rich girl from the cocoon of her father's house to the cocoon of her husband's. Much to the school's dismay, Miss Porter's achieved a vulgar renown in 1976 when a fifteen-year-old sophomore gave birth to a baby boy, who died shortly afterward. The school, quite in tradition, drew a curtain of silence over the entire distasteful matter. It was, of course, only a more egregious example, a particularly troubled case, of the general spread of relatively self-destructive behavior into the ranks of teenaged children of privilege—a class that until the sixties, say, had been quite sheltered from such influences. In short order in the spring of 1984, to take just two recent examples, six students were expelled from the Ethel Walker School, a Connecticut women's boarding school with its share of wealthy and well-known graduates, for using cocaine, while the same charges led to the expulsion of fourteen from Choate Rosemary Hall. The Choate students were found out after another student was arrested trying to smuggle $300,000 worth of cocaine back from Venezuela.

St. Timothy's School, in Stevenson, Maryland, seems swanker than Miss Porter's or Foxcroft—something like Princeton compared with Harvard and Yale. It remains a school where every new girl upon entering becomes a Brownie or a Spider, and is thereafter expected to practice the traditional cheers in preparation for the big basketball game between the two sides on Thanksgiving. St. Tim's development closely paralleled that of the great stylish boys' prep schools like Groton, Kent, and St. George's. It was founded in 1882—precisely the time of the great immigrations from southern and eastern Europe, when it was becoming apparent to the old families that had founded the United States that English stock no longer possessed the country by virtue of mere existence and would have to reinforce its strict standards with some new institutions. The creation of the prep schools coincided with a number of other important social developments—the movement to suburban estates to escape increasingly congested cities, the establishment of country clubs to ensure the quality of one's recreation companions, and the consolidation of the great manufacturing enterprises that made it all possible. The boarding schools gave concrete expression to the perception of the American upper classes that they had more in common with one another, and with important English families, than they did with the more questionable denizens of their own cities.

The fame of St. Timothy's spread like well-bred wildfire: by 1912 there were girls enrolled from Chicago, and there was a waiting list. In the 1930s, St. Timothy's, again like the great boys' schools, was of such crucial importance to one's social future that alumnae frequently put their daughters' names on the waiting list at birth. That phenomenon naturally produced an intensely inbred student body and, at least until the craziness of the sixties, a school whose highest value tended to be the exact reproduction of the mother in the student. Activities tended heavily toward aristocratic pastimes; many of the girls brought their own horses to school with them. The list of alumnae is predictably thick with the names of the old families—Auchinclosses, Peabodys, Choates, Crockers, Higginsons, Danforths, and the rest of the rock-ribbed old names that founded so many American institutions that eventually passed most of them by. Many of these people have a considerable amount of money, and some are from families that rank among the wealthiest in the world: such students as Holly Houghton ('63), daughter of Arthur A. Houghton, Jr., the richest member of the family that controls Corning Glass; and Joan Blaffer Johnson, an heiress to the Blaffer oil fortune in Texas. Claus von Bülow's wife Sunny Crawford and his mistress during the alleged murder attempts, Alexandra Isles, both attended the Chapin School in New York City and then went on to St. Tim's; Sunny's daughter by her first marriage, Princess Ala von Auersperg, went to St. Tim's too. Many of the students continue to fulfill the school's historical mission of providing intelligent, stylish women as wives to wealthy men. But St. Timothy's is destined to be remembered much more as the school that produced two of the most conspicuously self-destructive examples of the 1960s turmoil, Edie Sedgwick and Sasha Bruce.

At the time that the two old-family heiresses who would become so famous in such sad ways entered St. Tim's—Edie in the fall of 1958, Sasha in 1961—it was very recognizably a school for the privileged: there were girls in Sasha's class descended from Alexander Hamilton and John Aldrich; it was common for the students to fly off to Vail, say, during Christmas vacation; all but one of the thirty-six girls in Sasha's class later had formal coming-out parties. It was, however, hardly a "finishing school" in the pejorative sense. The sense of superiority that the girls absorbed was not an empty one: they were encouraged—pushed—to excel in academics, in sports, in conversation, in cheerfulness, in breadth of experience, in religious observance. The watchwords for the girls' destiny were "gracious leaders" and "Christian gentlewomen." At the end of the year there were two prizes given, one for the best student and the other for the best person.

Sasha and Edie exhibited similar reactions to St. Tim's and its ideals: they started by taking the place very seriously, while at the same time the serious depressions and sense of isolation that were to dominate their lives began in earnest. It would, of course, be foolish to blame the school for either Edie Sedgwick's or Sasha Bruce's unsettled life and early death. At school, they did nothing as scandalous as the later pregnancy at Miss Porter's, for example. Nevertheless, some distinctly upper-class aspects of the place clearly enhanced the disabilities that would later cripple the two girls. For Edie, St. Tim's represented an isolated setting like her childhood home on a California ranch, but a more public place, where she began her pattern of cultivating people with one hand and pushing them away unexpectedly with the other; a girls' boarding school, with its teenage crushes and hothouse sense of the importance of every movement, was a perfect setting for developing her intense self-preoccupation and her craving for adulation. Sasha was a very different girl, but she also found in St. Tim's a womb for her developing problems in fitting into the world. On the one hand, it was high-minded, sympathetic to the less fortunate, and yet striving for the skies. On the other, it represented the stiff-lipped established order that gave no indication that it cared, ultimately, how the rest of the world—Sasha included herself in that group—felt. Sasha's fate, in retrospect its shape becoming clear during her schooling, reflected her failure to resolve the conflict that rich children are born into. And her self-destructive (if not suicidal) behavior can be seen as an impossible wish to disown her patrimony by embracing the unknown subworld she had been taught to feel sorry for. For both Edie and Sasha, St. Tim's was a compression of the upper-class world in which they were expected to spend their lives; and as such it began the process of breaking down their confidence in their abilities to live in that world, or eventually in any other.

Foxcroft is the newest (founded 1914), the horsiest, and the least intellectual of the three major boarding schools. Situated on five hundred acres in Middleburg, Virginia, the heart of the horse country west of Washington, it is built around and largely preoccupied with riding. Nearly half the students, for example, take part in the riding program; the school itself owns forty horses, and a substantial number of girls bring their own mounts with them. Foxcroft's catalog is awash in pictures of the rolling countryside beloved of riders, of girls jumping in full regalia, of them gazing lovingly at their mounts, and leading around handicapped children in the Riding for the Handicapped program that the school sponsors. There is even a program for girls not currently enrolled at the school who want to take the horsemastership examinations; they board at the school and care for four or five horses in return for lessons in riding, teaching, stable management, and first aid.

Foxcroft was founded by Charlotte Haxall Noland, whose breeding in the Virginia society that still looked to the halcyon days of the antebellum was evident in the first catalog. It announced that the school would seek to combine "the best of the present with the best of the past. . . . Lessons and pleasures are guided by wise and judicious gentlewomen whose aim is by precept, training and the recounting of traditions to revive in its pupils the refined manners, cultivated minds and sympathetic personalities that have made the women of the South world-famous." As in many of the great private boarding schools, the personality of the founder made a profound impression on the malleable students; in the case of Foxcroft, she is remembered by more than half a century of classes, which she watched over through her death in 1969. Miss Noland was a paragon: a tough, sympathetic, hard-riding, gregarious woman, wildly ambitious for her girls. If the values inherent in the school later came to seem archaic, for their time they were decidedly progressive among the upper classes in the expectation that the blossoming young women would be athletic, self-composed and strong in character. (Scholastic standards interested Miss Noland somewhat less than did character—an attitude she held in common with many of the founders of the great boys' schools.) Indeed, the girls' boarding schools were largely responsible for creating at least the buddings of an awareness among rich women in the United States that they could be more than charming appendages to the friends of their brothers that they would inevitably marry (although they were eager to be that as well). Miss Charlotte was an ardent suffragette; she started social service and health programs in the county and urged the girls to participate; and she insisted on the value of fox-hunting because it requires quick decisions and, therefore, "it is the ideal training for the one thing lacking most in women—decision."

Miss Charlotte was extremely well-connected among the rich and wellborn—a matter of crucial importance in the success of any school intended for the production of "gentlewomen." One little boy who attended the day camp that accompanied the creation of the girls' school was Stuart Symington, the future senator from Missouri. Another petite camper, Wallis Warfield from Baltimore, would grow up to steal a king of England from his throne.

Later, Queen Elizabeth and Prince Philip would stop by the school. Meanwhile, Miss Charlotte cultivated the favor of the school's near neighbor, Paul Mellon, the fanastically wealthy scion of the great Pittsburgh family who lives in Upperville, Virginia; his wife was an alumna of 1947. Another student from the same clan was Cordelia Scaife May, herself now worth some $500 million. Du Ponts were well represented; the stables are named after Jean du Pont McConnell. C. Douglas Dillon, the New York investment banker-statesman, became an important benefactor. Probably the most famous recent student was the ubiquitous Cornelia Guest, who gilded the image most of the school's teachers would prefer to live down by dropping out at the age of fifteen to hit the riding circuit full time.

Today, Foxcroft remains the domain of wealthy and class-conscious Americans, with a smattering of girls from overseas. On the other hand, its very reputation as a school of refinement and wealth makes it a goal for those aspiring to the upper ranks. Girls from families secure in their wealth and status may well decide, unless they have a particular yen for horses or a single-sex boarding school, that they do as well or better at their local country day school or Quaker school; and there is considerably less pressure on rich girls today to act rich or to go to Mother's alma mater. As a result, all the private girls' schools have been forced to push vigorous recruitment drives and to modify the draconian rules in such matters as escaping on weekends. However, we are not talking about letting down the barriers completely. Since the boarding schools, while rich compared with most private secondary schools, have very small endowments by the standards of the wealthy colleges, scholarships, especially full ones, are rare. Naturally, this preselects the student body. Moreover, it is unlikely that someone from outside the circle of wealthy, English-stock families would have even general ideas of what a Foxcroft is like—much less the desire to go there. While the schools, these days, do not nominally discriminate in their admissions policies, there are very few names of Jewish or other ethnic backgrounds, and the black faces are much more likely to belong to girls from West Africa than from Watts.

For college, intelligent rich girls go on to Harvard, Stanford, the University of Chicago, Swarthmore, or the other big names like everybody else. However, there is a sort of Junior League circuit of less academically demanding but socially impeccable institutions that attract girls who have not seen the need to rely on anything more than background and looks for their suppers, but who on the other hand feel the general current upper-middle-class expectation that girls should go off to college as a bridge between adolescence and matrimony. These would include Finch (alma mater of Anne Cox Chambers, Mrs. Benson Ford, and Tricia Nixon), Mary Baldwin (Caroline Hunt Schoellkopf), Sophie Newcombe for southern belles, Pine Manor, Wheaton, and Sweet Briar. All of them are well represented in the wedding section of the *New York Times*.

10 | Debutantes

The whole point of being a deb is to have fun.
—CORNELIA GUEST

THE YEAR 1982 was the first in more than forty years to have the distinction of featuring a popularly acclaimed Deb of the Year. That would be, if it has slipped the mind, Cornelia Guest, whose favorite word was *wonderful*, favorite sport was riding and second favorite was spending her parents' share of the Phipps fortune, and whose favorite courtiers included such as Jerry Zipkin, Egon von Fürstenberg, and Truman Capote. It is difficult to say what made Cornelia the Deb of the Year, since she is, while pleasant and cutish, not ravishing and hardly brilliant by any definition. One reason, Truman Capote said, was that she is "from real patrician stock, unlike the Vanderbilts and Rockefellers, who are descended from crooks": her late father was a godson and second cousin of Winston Churchill and also a grandson of Pittsburgh steel magnate Henry Phipps; her mother, a Boston Brahmin. The mother, C. Z. Guest, once a showgirl in the Ziegfeld Follies and a famous debutante beauty, is now an extremely well-connected New York socialite, making it child's play for Cornelia to drift into the Doubles–Club A party circuit and garner herself some publicity.

At any rate, the exact dimensions of the Debutanteship of the Year are less important than the fact that such a title was actually bestowed, sometimes without quotes, by such mainstream (if not overly serious) media as *People* magazine and the *New York Post*. It has been a title without a pretender for several decades. The strange celebrity of Cornelia Guest has given a new legitimacy to those among the very rich who have, perhaps, had a secret craving all along not to bother sympathizing with the youthful social rebels they might run across at school. Cornelia was "presented," as they say in the coming-out biz, at the International Debutante Ball, an event that has appeared annually for the past thirty years just before New Year's Day in the Grand Ballroom in the Waldorf-Astoria in New York.

A woman named Beatrice Joyce founded the affair in 1954 and has presided over it ever since. There were some thin years for a while during the heyday of the counterculture in the 1960s and early 1970s, but now the dominant culture has reasserted itself. In December 1982, for example, there were no fewer than fifty-six blossoms of sturdy trees of wealth, each ready to spend what is generally estimated to be at least $10,000 of daddy's money on all the trappings—including not only the significant cost of the event itself, but the even more impressive expense of designer gowns for mother and daughter, plus ancillaries like grooming and limousines. The New York Debutante Cotillion and Christmas Ball is even bigger; within the past few years the numbers of its debutantes have crept well above the seventy that the organizers like to hold it to. Other organizations, such as the Junior Assembly and the Society of Mayflower Descendants, put on somewhat smaller but more exclusive affairs, where descent from certain families is a prerequisite for admission.

Even more exclusive are the only truly "society" affairs remaining in the United States, the gatherings of old families in Boston and Philadelphia. The Boston party is held each June in the Copley Plaza Hotel, but the traditional Boston Brahmin aversion to display combined with the erosion of "society" in the 1960s has reduced it to pretty small potatoes. It is not, at any rate, something that people are expected to spend lavish amounts of money on.

Even more thoroughly inbred is the Philadelphia Assembly (or, as it is put more regally sometimes, "the Assemblies"). Quite simply, you are born into the Assembly or you do not go. It is not strictly a debutante party, nor does it have the nominally charitable intentions of the splashier New York bashes; it is simply a gathering of old Philadelphia families with all their seventeenth cousins twice removed, and young women who are interested can of course use it to announce their availability to society. Many of those attending by now have no money to speak of, in New York or Texas terms. That does not adversely affect their vivid sense of their own worth.

It is not a matter of public record exactly how one *does* get invited to the big New York affairs. If a young woman's mother expresses interest to the organizers, she is delicately informed if their presence would not be appropriate. As with many matters among the very wealthy who are interested in the social aspect of their state, if you have to ask about it, you aren't liable to be involved in it. Almostly unanimously, that rules out Jews, blacks, and most other types of hyphenated Americans, if only because they tend not to run in the Anglo-Saxon circles that most deb ritual comes from. Clearly, attending a huge debut in a New York hotel would be a somewhat more depressing experience than an eighth-grade dance if neither the debutante nor her mother knew anybody else there. At any rate, following the shakeout of the 1960s, there remains very little insistence on family per se, provided one's father is not an utter recluse or a convicted felon. (Or perhaps even if he is: Cosima von Bülow could surely make a debut if she wanted to.) Hence, the recent phenomenon of the invasion of the Manhattan debutante circles by the young females of Texas. In 1982, the International Debutante Ball had eleven from the Lone Star State. Their principal contribution to the event is their ability to curtsey. "Those girls sink to the floor with such grace and assurance you think they're going right through it," observed society columnist Suzy.

They get a great deal of practice, for the Texas instinct that big is good and gargantuan is better extends to the debut. In Dallas—the most socially conscious and, by its own lights, the most socially valuable place in Texas—the real, real debutantes are the half-dozen or so selected each year by Idlewild, the men's club that embraces much of the older money in town. Some might think it a dubious honor, for it obliges the chosen few to participate in a round of ritual that sacrificial virgins might shrink from. For three months, October through the Terpsichorean Ball in December, the debutante attends two or three parties in her honor *each day*, six days a week, acquiring incipient varicose veins from standing for the fitting of so many different gowns and writer's cramp from the several thousand thank-you notes she must churn out. The cost is estimated at between $50,000 and $300,000. Alternatively, some girls have parties thrown for them by their parents, ideally at the behest of Idlewild; these have been calculated to run up to half a million dollars. Sistie Stollenwerck, the wife of a Dallas trial lawyer, received such a welcome summons in 1976, the year of her daughter Brooke's debut. She gave a circus at the Dallas Convention Center, complete with Brooke's name painted in the center star and on five thousand balloons, twenty-foot canvases of the family at the entrance to the sideshow, two bands, a lady with a bird act, dancing camels, and bears on unicycles. Brooke now owns a foreign-car dealership and still finds that people she doesn't know come in and ask, "Aren't you the girl with the circus?"

What can this be all about? The modern ceremony is a remote descendant of the French *jouer de but*, "to play for the goal." The goal, of course, was, and to a large extent still is, a husband. In the case of Dallas, which has the most ambition as well as the most excess for its coming-out rituals, the elaborate round of partying is specifically intended to reinforce the young lady's intimacy with those of her social class—and her parents' ties with those of their business, civic, and political caste. One recent debutante, Gwendolyn Kakaska, told a reporter that after she was presented at Idlewild, "All of a sudden, I was on a list. I was invited to every function that went on—symphonies, theater, music. They know a deb will spend that year, buy tickets and patronize new restaurants because they're supposed to. It's their season. The men who are the names here, they're out front, and we like it that way. We back them and help them do their business." An investment!—now that is reasoning that daddy the developer can understand.

Back in New York, where the more cosmopolitan economy is not quite as dependent on a tight, self-selected circle, the large debutante balls are tied to the major socially prominent charities. Thus they might be considered as a sort of practice for the round of politely useful things that rich women of a certain class expect from their daughters. Cornelia Guest herself has said, "I'm interested in some of the diseases—you know, like cancer and multiple sclerosis"; and she does things like assist in the organizing of the fall party of the New York affiliate of the National Council on Alcoholism.

Another of the major functions of debutantes is fashion. Here again Cornelia is a miraculous re-creation of the breezy young woman who populated the movies of the 1930s. Halston, who dressed Cornelia for one of the numerous parties she has starred at, had high praise for her. "She's a serious girl," he asserted. "She's a worker. It's so wonderful to have her carry on the great C. Z. Guest tradition of liking clothes and doing things. So many women don't seem to care about fashion any more." This occurred at a birthday party that C. Z. threw for her daughter in December of 1983 at Studio 54. (Yes, Studio 54 was already becoming a little passé at that point; thank God, the Guests' sensibilities extend to the feelings of disco owners.) C. Z. told Charlotte Curtis—the *Times* has apparently found it incumbent to increase its coverage of the glitterati or end up dowdy—that Cornelia had never really had a debut of her own, and so she deserved for her birthday "a big, bang-up Christmas-y thing with little villages, the Alps, and the press." (How Christmas-y can the press be?) Lest it seem that Texans are the only people who can spend five years of a middle-class family's income in a single night and then have it all swept away by morning, C. Z. did indeed hire the entire club for the evening and caused an Alpine village square to be erected inside, complete with darling storefronts and outdoor cafés, at which the two hundred guests (you know, Andy Warhol, Pat Lawford, Lester Persky, Polly Bergen, Carolina and Reinaldo Herrera, and all the little Phippses and Guests) were served masses of Italian tortellini, French pâté and cheeses, German wursts and sauerkraut, Austrian tortes, and fifteen cases of the standard-issue Dom Pérignon. At the end of the evening, fake snow wafted down on everyone. It had been a blast. And that, at bottom, is what at least New York debutantes expect from their time under the stars. "The whole point of being a deb," said Cornelia to a reporter once as a maid was serving her eggs Benedict for breakfast at 1:00 P.M. on the terrace of her parents' spread in Old Westbury, "is to have fun."

Like so much that has become part of the tissue of the public life of rich people in the United States, the coming-out ritual achieved its first flowering among the descendants of old American families who, rather suddenly, achieved tremendous wealth toward the end of the nineteenth century on the shoulders of the country's great industrialization. The debutante ceremony was one of the Victorian social trappings imported from England, the mother lode of proper behavior for those who might have found their money and their manners in somewhat cruder places. Wellborn English girls had at least since Regency times, at the beginning of the nineteenth century, been turned from birth into a narrow sluice designed to lead inexorably toward the expected husband. And the introduction of a teenaged girl at an adult party was, quite naturally, a sign that she was thereupon ready for marriage. So, the debut became a central part of the London season, and was adapted in whole cloth by the colonies when they found themselves with enough loose capital to be worth caring about. The debut, with its accompanying round of formal gatherings in honor of the newly eligible maidens, was a wonderfully apt idea for the times: not only could it be more or less assured that the blades dancing in attendance were of good family, manners, and fortune, but society as a whole was happy to stand chaperone over the strict virtue of the young women on the block. Like everything else of the period, it was done to excess. A man named James Paul, at the beginning of the century, decided that he would go all out in presenting his daughter, even though the audience was deeply conservative Philadelphia society. His inspiration was to import ten thousand Brazilian butterflies for the occasion and conceal them in nets near the ballroom ceiling. At the appointed hour they were released, with a ghastly shower of butterflies dead from the heat.

Such extremely poor public relations eventually led to a certain revulsion, not only among the immigrants huddled in the widely flung slums of the time, but in the tasteful drawing rooms of the more public-spirited and thoughtful rich. Hence, the beginning of a tendency toward balls that benefitted charities and the arts, which did not look quite as blissfully self-indulgent. Although few noticed it at the time, the hedonism of the twenties, with the birth of "café society," subtly changed the function of a debut. With most young people deserting their parents' grand ballrooms to experience the twin innovations of the age, highballs and jazz, the formal occasion of the debutante party was no longer any sort of link to an inevitable downward spiral into marriage with the proper acquaintance. It did, however, remain an important social function, a sort of bridge between the formalism of Old

Society and the confused mélange that was produced by the new wealth of the twenties, the demolition of old fortunes by the depression, and the emergence of movie stars and other performers as amusing (if still suspect in certain circles) functionaries in the grand round.

Combined with the well-known phenomenon in which the newly deprived turned to the frivolous rich for their entertainment during the depressing thirties, this new café society produced coming-out parties that were, if anything, more lavish than those of the Belle Epoque. In 1930, for example, the debuts of Ailsa Mellon, Doris Duke, and Barbara Hutton were all covered voluminously by the popular press with the sort of breathless sneering that their readers had come to expect as the proper attitude toward the undeservedly rich. Doris Duke's coming-out in the still important resort of Newport was peopled with the most fashionable of the New York old-line crowd, Astors prominent among them. Shortly afterward Louise Astor Van Alen, from a stylish Philadephia family, was also introduced to society in Newport in front of the same crowd. Barbara Hutton, who was present, did not think much of it. According to her recent biographer, C. David Heymann,[25] she found most of the men there "all pimply-faced and drunk, throwing up into their top hats. They threw up on the steps and every place else. It was appalling. . . . The girls didn't drink much. Mostly the boys drank and did a thorough job of it. They were all in college and not very eligible. Alexis [Mdivani, future husband of both Louise Van Alen and Barbara Hutton] very humorously compared the ritual of the debut to registering one's prize canary at the annual Madison Square Garden bird show. The reception line was miles long. On cue Louise did her court bow, a very low curtsy that made her look like a pup tent folding over in a high wind."

But it was Hutton's own debut that became the smash of the season. The tea party for five hundred in the Fifth Avenue triplex of her aunt and uncle, broker E. F. Hutton and his wife, Marjorie Merriweather Post, and the dinner-dance for five hundred additional guests at the Central Park Casinos were both merely

---

25. *Poor Little Rich Girl* (N.Y.: Random House, 1983). The publisher yanked the book from the bookstores after being threatened with a libel suit by a Beverly Hills doctor accused of prescribing large doses of tranquilizers for Hutton in the 1940s, when in fact the doctor was only a teenager. Still, there seems to be no serious challenge to Heymann's claim that he had access to the fascinating, sometimes outrageous notebooks that Hutton kept of her cloyingly opulent life.

warm-ups. The centerpiece was a formal ball at the Ritz-Carlton Hotel in Manhattan in December 1930, slightly more than a year since the stock-market crash had ushered in the Great Depression and the shantytowns along the Hudson River. It took hundreds of laborers two entire days and nights to metamorphose the whole first floor of the Ritz, strewing greenery and flowers—ten thousand roses, twenty thousand white violets, and tropical trees shipped in from Florida and California—throughout the main ballroom, the restaurant, the smaller ballroom, and the crystal room. The main ballroom was made over into the outdoors with dark blue gauze on the ceiling, lit by an electric moon and a firmament of electric stars. Artificial snow, which seems to be a favorite at these events, was piled everywhere. Maurice Chevalier dressed as Santa Claus to greet guests, who included Doris Duke, Louise Van Alen, Virginia Thaw, Gladys Rockefeller, Alice Belmont, the future Brooke Astor, and other representatives of the great fortunes, which appeared to be riding out the bad times nicely. Chevalier and his Santa's Helpers scattered gold jewelry cases containing unmounted diamonds, emeralds, rubies, and sapphires. (Giving away jewelry was to become a favorite Hutton pastime.) Two hundred waiters served two thousand bottles of champagne, one thousand seven-course midnight suppers, and another thousand breakfasts later. Four bands played. Lester Lanin, who was a drummer in his late brother Howard's band that night, has since said, "I've played for presidents, kings, queens, and maharajahs, but I've never seen a party like this one." The cost was estimated at $60,000 in deflated currency.

But in that era, at least, even the most lavish of American parties held no candle to being presented at Buckingham Palace. Barbara Hutton and other leading American and English debutantes bowed to Queen Mary and King George V in May 1931, amidst oppressive ceremony. Naturally, the unruly British press had a field day with the filthy rich American heiress; she was dubbed a "celebutante" and described in one account as "the prototypical American export, a heavily chaperoned eighteen-year-old heiress who has come here to steal the vaulted throne of the British Empire and return with it to the United States." The allusion was to Barbara's apparently innocent dance with Edward, Prince of Wales, at a garden party for the debs the day after the presentation at court. In fact, the future Duke of Windsor had recently met his future duchess, who was in the midst of disengaging herself from her second husband.

The public's fascination with rich debs continued through the glamor-starved thirties, and those in a position to do so were only too happy to oblige their fan's craving for outrageous display. In 1934, Ethel du Pont of the redoubtable Delaware clan came out in a much-publicized swirl of parties, including her parents' party for her that drew a thousand people to Wilmington, and was hailed as "the most beautiful and eligible wealthy bachelor girl in America." In 1938, an otherwise unremarkable girl named Brenda Frazier became a national obsession and ended up on the cover of *Life* magazine as the Deb of the Year. That same year, despite the gloomy prospects across the Channel on a continent already dominated by Hitler's aggression, the London social scene continued apace, with American girls vigorously striving to be among the thirty—from hundreds of applicants— selected for presentation to the king and queen. Indeed, with all the weighty problems of the world centered in London, it was a significant decision that year that Joseph Kennedy, ambassador to the Court of St. James, declared that American debutantes would no longer bow before the royals because the selection process was "undemocratic." (The ruling was in response to a plea on behalf of a Boston deb by Senator Henry Cabot Lodge. Debuts were no small matter.) Kennedy's own daughter Kathleen, however, was declared exempt from the new rule because she was associated with the diplomatic corps. She was one of the debs of the season at all the court balls. The looming war was so little thought of that, at Kathleen's own coming-out party at the embassy, one of her notable dance partners was Prince Frederick of Prussia. The following year, despite, or perhaps because of, the even thicker air of impending catastrophe— Chamberlain's folly in giving away the Sudetenland had been generally recognized—Kathleen and the smart circle pursued their well-worn rounds with determination. It was, in fact, the most brilliant season in many years. The Duke and Duchess of Marlborough purchased a London mansion as a base of operations for their debutante daughter, Lady Sarah Spencer-Churchill. Her own party was at the spectacular family seat, Blenheim Palace, where the gardens were floodlit and champagne flowed in the dozens of rooms.

World War II put an end to most self-consciously grand entertaining; or at least the war was more likely to make the cover of *Life* than was Brenda Frazier. The postwar period was a time of quiet devotion to duty, and what debutante parties there were tended to pass without much note. That is, until a *bon vivant* like Henry Ford II got into the act. The party of 1959 was the coming-out extravaganza he threw for his daughter Charlotte at the Country Club of Grosse Pointe. Ford imported Parisian interior designer Jacques Frank to turn the club into a Louis XV bower, complete with eighteenth-century tapestries, suits of armor, fake marble, and a corridor lined with two million magnolia leaves flown in from Mississippi. Among the twelve hundred guests who drank and danced nearly until dawn were the ubiquitous C. Z. Guest and envoys from such families as the du Ponts, the Roosevelts, and the Firestones. Henry had conveniently placed tanks of oxygen around the premises for the more disastrously drunk of the celebrants. The whole thing cost at least $150,000. "It's a good thing I don't have five daughters. I'd go broke," Henry II told his dancing partners. He did have one more, however, and to be unstinting he spent $250,000 on his bash for the debut of Anne Ford in 1961. The usual suspects were rounded up for the party. Bandleader Meyer Davis wrote a song called "Man, That's Anne" for the occasion, and Ella Fitzgerald sang "Night and Day." It took at least a hundred retainers to serve the midnight supper in the summerhouses that had been erected at each end of the garden in back of the Fords' Georgian mansion. "And it's well worth it," the proud father remarked as he watched his eighteen-year-old daughter drift down the curving staircase. Bunny Mellon is supposed to have spent a million dollars for the 1961 debut of her daughter Eliza, much of it to lay down roads on their Virginia estate, Rokeby, and then tear them up afterward so as not to detract from its rustic beauty. Jacqueline Kennedy was there.

There are less formal ways to be introduced to society. One recent one has been the growth of *Town & Country* as the semi-official journal of the world's rich. Occasionally it will run features such as one in 1979 introducing debutantes from around the world. On that particularly impressive list were Francesca von Thyssen, whose father, Baron Heinrich von Thyssen, is Europe's biggest steelmaker and the owner of probably the world's greatest private art collection; Antonia Mayrink-Veiga, daughter of a Brazilian industrialist father and an International Best-Dressed mother; and Princess Ala Auersperg.

Amidst all the fun of the lavish debuts of the world's richest teenagers there are, after all, only teenagers being strapped into a quasibusiness proposition. In retrospect, many of them could well have done without. "Actually, neither Charlotte nor I had any choice whatsoever about the debuts," Anne Ford said years later. "They aren't any fun at all. First you have to get ready. Then all you do is just stand in line and receive people. Do you mean would I want my daughter to have one? No." Barbara Hutton wrote a poem after her debut at Buckingham Palace that concluded:

> Well, the devil take them
> And their expectations,
> All they will get from me
> Is lamentations.

Looking back at her year in the limelight, Brenda Frazier also put her sentiments into verse: "I grit my teeth and smile at my enemies/ I sit at the Stork Club and talk to nonentities." In 1963, she published a memoir straightforwardly called *My Debut—A Horror*.

11 | FUN AND GAMES: THE GREAT RESORTS

ONE OF THE MOST CRUCIAL PROBLEMS of being rich is the obvious fact that rich people—rich women, primarily—do not *have* to do anything. This tends to leave great swatches of time to fill. Hence, much of what they do is nothing more nor less than play. Rich people having more resources than most other people, they tend not merely to go out of their ways to find pleasant and interesting surroundings for their vacations, but to create them.

The greatest single example is the peerless Palm Beach, a female-controlled fairyland of million-dollar pastel-colored houses, some of the world's most exclusive shopping on Worth Avenue, sex scandals, and a daily newspaper, the Palm Beach *Daily News*, that chronicles society's comings and goings on paper that is specially treated not to smudge (and is therefore known as the Shiny Sheet), and which may be the only newspaper in the world that has polo schedules posted on the secretaries' bulletin boards. The air of fantasy generated by the pale tints of the houses, the servile gardeners, the stately pace of the Mercedeses and Rollses, and the brilliant semitropical sun is heightened by a passing acquaintance with the astronomical prices that regulate commerce in the tiny island enclave. Mar-a-Lago ("sea to lake," i.e., the Atlantic to Lake Worth), the grandiose 118-room pink mansion on seventeen acres previously owned by the late Marjorie Merriweather Post, the longtime queen of PB society, was sold early in 1984 to two Boca Raton real estate developers (they plan to live there, not build on it) for more than $14.5 million. That made it the largest single residential sale in United States history at the time.[26] Forty-eight condominiums recently constructed near the landmark Breakers Hotel were priced from $810,000 to $1.9 million. The total value of the real estate on the island, which is fourteen miles long and half a mile wide, has been estimated at $12 billion. No one can calculate the combined worth of the island's residents, most of whom also maintain lavish homes elsewhere.

Transactions of hundreds of thousands of dollars are common in the Worth Avenue outposts of the world's great stores. Even your shopkeeper is liable to be a multimillionaire; Baby Jane Holzer, the Park Avenue heiress who became an Andy Warhol superstar during the 1960s, recently opened an ice-cream parlor on Worth Avenue (where her real estate broker grandfather planted the first palm tree), and Kimberly Farkas (heiress to the Alexander Stores fortune) runs a gourmet shop there. "Palm Beach is a funny place," says Baby Jane Holzer. "They ought to blow it up." The Breakers Hotel's Venetian and Mediterranean ballrooms are said to have generated more funds for charitable causes than any other pair of rooms in the world; in the 1982–83 winter season, some $27 million was ponied up by the few thousand intimates on the social circuit. The forty thousand people who in season (October to April) inhabit the town, which can be cut off from *déclassé* West Palm Beach by raising its three drawbridges, tax themselves to maintain the greatest police presence per capita of any place in the United States—one policeman for

---

26. Mrs. Post left Mar-a-Lago in her will to the federal government, but it was returned to the Post Foundation after even government bureaucrats were staggered by the maintenance costs of roughly $1 million a year. It remains an awesome sight: there is a nine-hole golf course on the grounds, immense stands of swaying palms, a $1 million dining table of inlaid marble and enough gold to prompt comparisons to Versailles. Supposedly Harry K. Thaw, the mad roué who assassinated the famous society architect Stanford White in a quarrel over the affections of chorus girl Evelyn Nesbit, gazed wonderingly on his first visit to Mar-a-Lago and muttered, "My God, I shot the wrong architect."

every hundred residents. Garbage is collected seven days a week. Small fortunes are routinely expended to maintain the lavish "nature" that gives the place its special appeal: huge coconut palms reign everywhere (they have been wiped out in much of the rest of Florida by lethal yellowing, a disease combatted in PB by expensive preventive measures); precious imports like tecoma, bougainvillea, and wild orchids flow over the loggias and poolside cabanas at the ocean-front homes. There are no hospital, no cemetery, no funeral parlor, no black taxpaying residents. There are, on the other hand, a constant round of semipublic and very private entertainments; the Palm Beach *Daily News*'s social calendar listed forty-one major events in the single month of February 1984, including twenty-five balls and big dinner parties. Palm Beach may be the last place in the world utterly devoted to the style of lavish living that seems to have gone out of style elsewhere with the demise of Sara and Gerald Murphy. "It is the United States in extension, in summit if you please, not a tangential spa," wrote John Ney in his book *Palm Beach*. "It is as much a part of the country's history as Gettysburg." Robert Frost wrote simply, "The shadows fall the way they fell."

Palm Beach was created out of a barren, sandy island by Henry Morrison Flagler, who was one of John D. Rockefeller's partners in the establishment of the Standard Oil trust. After earlier unsuccessful attempts to create grand resorts in Jacksonville and St. Augustine, Flagler finally seized on Palm Beach, some seventy miles north of what would become Miami. He declared his intention to build "a magnificent playground for the people of the nation." His workers pushed the first railroad through the swamps to West Palm Beach—the mainland town created as a campsite for PB workers—in 1894, and at the same time opened both the original Breakers Hotel (it was destroyed by a fire in 1926 and rebuilt) and the Royal Poinciana, which boasted accommodations for 1,750 guests and was the largest wooden structure in the world at the time. Flagler also threw up his own $2.5 million mansion, Whitehall, which, when it was finished in 1902, was described as "Taj Mahal in the land of flowers" and featured, among other extravagances, the largest pipe organ ever placed in a private home; it later became a hotel and is now the Henry Morrison Flagler Museum. It was the first of many huge, whimsical creations on the beach, for Palm Beach was a smash hit from the beginning. The first center of social life was the Beach Club, a lavish gambling hall that thrived until the death of the founder. Like the rest of Florida, PB really took off during the 1920s. That was the period when Vanderbilts, Phippses, and many other great names of American fortunes commissioned grand mansions by Addison Mizner, creator of the Spanish style that predominates in many of the estates from Mar-a-Lago on down.

Unlike Miami and Tampa, Palm Beach suffered no burst bubbles after the initial land boom, since there always seemed to be more than enough northern money pouring in to keep the economy percolating. PB almost immediately became the premier resort gathering place in the United States; before long it started to rival such established European resorts as St. Moritz and the Riviera. It was originally the home away from home for the classic eastern Establishment, which included not only those from the East but those who made their money elsewhere but partied in New York and sent their children to eastern boarding schools. It was the first, and remains the central, resort to attract distinguished names from throughout the country and even from Europe. As the magnet for such an impeccable group of people, PB became an important social force throughout the American aristocracy of money. Things that were said and done in Palm Beach were taken home to the corners of the globe by their well-tailored auditors.

The first of its great social arbiters was Isaac Singer, an illegitimate son of the sewing-machine inventor, who showed up rather suddenly with his longtime lover, Isadora Duncan, and proceeded to set social standards in league with Mizner. Their great creation was the Everglades Club, which quickly became the premier resort club in the United States after its opening in 1919. Soon afterward, "Queen Eva" Stotesbury, wife of a Philadelphian partner of J. P. Morgan, became the reigning hostess for the first two decades of PB's glory years, presiding from her Mizner-designed El Mirasol. She was in turn succeeded by Marjorie Merriweather Post, whose lavish parties at Mar-a-Lago became part of the legends of the very rich. It was not at all unusual for Mr. and Mrs. E. F. Hutton to import the entire cast of a Broadway play strictly for the one-night entertainment of a houseful of two hundred guests. The house, built in the middle 1920s for more than $8 million, had a staff that varied from sixty to eighty—not to mention its own nine-hole golf course.

Still keystones of the social structure of Palm Beach are the two ultra-exclusive clubs, the Everglades and the Bath and Tennis. The Bath and Tennis—B&T to insiders—has only 750 membership places and, consequently, an elephantine waiting list, which makes its allure all the greater. Built in 1926 as a reaction to the high-handed manner in which Singer ran the Everglades, the B&T was done in semi-Moorish extravagance by Joseph Urban, the architect responsible for Mar-a-Lago. Today it is the less flashy club, specializing in serious sports and allowing casual dress at lunch. The Everglades, on the other hand, is considerably more *soigné*, turning away women in pants even for lunch. But while it is better known for its exclusivity than the B&T, it is also about twice as large and consequently easier to get into.

Time, death, and inflation have taken their toll on the Palm Beach life-style. There is, for example, no obvious successor to Miss Post for the title of lavish party-giver. One thing that has not changed, however, is the presence of vast agglomerations of money. If the palaces along Ocean Boulevard had mailboxes, the road would read like an encyclopedia of American capitalism: Willis du Pont, Henry Ford, Ogden Phipps (the Phippses own more of Palm Beach than any other family), Estée Lauder, a number of Annenberg sisters, Mitzi Newhouse (widow of the publisher), Mrs. Caroline Hudson Lynch (Merrill Lynch money), Rose Kennedy, and, needless to mention, the never-misses-anything C. Z. Guest. The occasional visitors include practically everybody of any account who is not an actual homeowner: Mellons, von Krupps, the Helmsleys, various Whitneys, Rothschilds, Princess Lee Radziwill, Yoko Ono, and, reportedly, the entourage of the mysterious Arabian businessman Adnan Khashoggi, who is said to be planning to build condominiums on a tip of the island.

Palm Beach has two equally strong traditions: one for riotous excess, the other for rigid social stratification. Both have broken down somewhat, but not enough to remove PB from the list of the world's great pleasure-loving and society-conscious places. The Roxanne-and-Peter-Pulitzer show probably came as a shock to most outsiders unaware of the grand resort's tradition of wretched if discreet excess. It was not exactly a shock to longtime residents, but an annoyance; for the general feeling was that PB has become less outrageous and more serious-minded over the last decade or so. Even before World War I, Palm Beach had a reputation as the headquarters of the fastest segment of American society. The joke quickly spread that Palm Beachers believed that anything worth doing was worth doing to excess. That reputation wafted at least as far as the Groton School, perhaps the most socially correct of all the great New England schools, where the longtime headmaster, the Rev. Endicott Peabody, used to begin his Easter-vacation farewell to his boys by bidding them a good time but would then warn, *"Do not go to Palm Beach—that den of iniquity."* Extramarital attachments and rapid-fire divorces became common during the twenties. In 1936, as a sort of public service, *Fortune* magazine published a feature in which it listed some of the more prominent of PB's men and women about town followed by columns headed "Husbands I, II, III, and IV" and "Wives I, II, III, and IV." Delphine Dodge, the auto heiress, and Margaret Emerson, from the family that gave the world Bromo-Seltzer, turned out to have both been married, at different times, to the same director of the United States Mint. All that had somewhat faded from public memory as the carryings-on of society lost their fascination for the general public during the 1960s and 1970s—and perhaps, with the graying of Palm Beach (the median age of residents is fifty-seven), they lost their fascination for society people themselves.

L'affaire Pulitzer changed all that. Peter Pulitzer is the scion of the St. Louis publishing family, which had been one of the few clans of Jewish background that had been acceptable to PB society proper. His first marriage confirmed that pedigree; his ex-wife, Lilly Pulitzer, was not only the stepdaughter of Ogden Phipps, but the creator of the distinctive preppy-colored muu-muus that rapidly became a nearly universal badge of WASPy relaxation. (The company has since gone bankrupt.) In 1975, following their divorce, Peter met Roxanne Dixon, the young stepdaughter of a police chief in an upstate New York town who told the divorce court that she had come to Palm Beach to attend secretarial school. She did, at any rate, attend a party at the publishing heir's hunting ranch inland near Lake Okeechobee, shortly after which she dumped the real estate broker she had been living with and moved in with Pulitzer, marrying him a year later. There ensued a busy life-style, but not in the mode of what the PB Chamber of Commerce would like you to believe generally goes on there. Depending on whom you credited, Roxanne may or may not have ingested large quantities of cocaine, slept with Jacqueline Kimberly—wife of another much-respected Palm Beach socialite and sportsman, Kleenex heir James Kimberly—slept with her drug dealer, and tried to sleep with Pulitzer's teenage daughter, who also might have had sex with her father. The drug use, Roxanne testified, "was a peer-pressure type thing. . . . You get the feeling everybody on Palm Beach is doing it. Everybody talked about it. There were drugs at every party." The divorce court judge, a resident of the northern Florida Bible Belt, upheld the tradition that outsiders do not walk away with Palm Beach inheritances by granting Roxanne a meager $48,000 settlement, adding in his ruling that her "exorbitant demand shocks the conscience of this court, putting the court in mind of the hit record by country music singer Jerry Reed, which laments: 'She got the gold mine, I got the shaft.' " Pulitzer and Kimberly were no more ostracized by the A group in PB than Claus von Bülow was by Newport society when he was convicted of attempting to kill his wife.

While there has always been stray royalty stopping through—the Duke and Duchess of Windsor were big favorites, as they were among self-consciously select people everywhere—the foreign invasion has become more pronounced in PB over the past decade or so. It is fueled by the same craving for the classic combination of secure investments and social visibility that has bid up the market for Manhattan apartments to manic heights. Cubans are big; the rich ones had to go somewhere, and they certainly didn't want it to be wide-open Miami. José Pepe Fanjul, who managed to create an American agricultural empire before the deluge and has since branched out into money-market funds, is even something of a social arbiter: he has maintained the bizarre, quaint old society-resort practice of publishing a "list" of the two hundred or so home phone numbers you'll need most on the social circuit. His wife Emilia, who is from an American social background—a graduate of the Chapin School—runs the Junior Committee at the B&T and is engaged in a vigorous campaign to rescue the resort from its gerontocracy. "We wanted a dance for the young people," she explained to *Town & Country*. "How should I say this nicely? Without including the wheelchair set. This was an unheard-of idea at the B&T. In the old days everyone was invited to everything. But we did not want all those older people taking the best tables. It took a while to pass it by the club's high board and by Byron Ramsing, who's the president. But we are now finally able to make our own lists. You see, the Everglades doesn't like children. Nor does it cater to junior members. The party for young people we finally put on was, I think, one of the prettiest." The result is two big dances each year that attract hordes of socially correct students from the

Ivy League. Other recent arrivals include Annelise von Bohlen und Halbach, who advertises her ancestry by flying a flag with the Krupp coat of arms from the tiled roof of her mansion; Princess Maria Gabriella, the daughter of former King Umberto of Italy, who is married to giant European industrialist Robert de Balkany; and her sister, Princess Maria Pia di Savoia, who is living with Prince Michel de Bourbon-Parme. Former Queen Anne of Romania dropped by several seasons ago and is rumored to be looking for an American base as well.

Just as the pleasures of the rich run rampant in the greenhouse atmosphere of Palm Beach, so do their traditional weaknesses. The Pulitzer scandal, one can surmise, merely suggested what happens in many PB marriages. The resort has its share of suicides, which are not liable to appear in *Town & Country*; one 1983 victim of a cocaine overdose at his home on the grounds of the Palm Beach Polo and Country Club (PBPCC) was twenty-seven-year-old William T. Ylvisaker, Jr., whose father is chairman of Gould Inc. and the creator of the vast PBPCC complex, inland from the resort. But probably the most typical of the remnants of the dirty underside of high society that lingers—indeed, is preserved as part of history—is the great tradition of ethnic discrimination. Although the population of the town of Palm Beach as a whole is now something more than half Jewish, the B&T and Everglades both remain exclusively Anglo-Saxon. Jews belong to the Palm Beach Country Club, which is separated from the other two clubs by the entire length of the island. Nate Appleman, a partner in the Irvine Ranch and a sort of bridge between the two communities, forthrightly told *Town & Country*, "Yes, there's bigotry here. It's a holdover from fifty years ago. I just hope the younger generation isn't poisoned by it. Unfortunately, there are some people who encourage the bigotry by being too flamboyant, hiring PR agents, arriving from Chicago or Memphis and believing that they are making the social ladder. They make themselves ridiculous. Of course, I see this behavior on both sides."

The business of PR agents is another amusing aspect to life in the Queen of Resorts. There are no fewer than five active publications devoted to chronicling the doings of the select few thousand who whirl their way through life and charity, supplied by four full-time society photographers. Surely, PB is the only town its size with two daily newspapers. (Both, the Shiny Sheet and the *Palm Beacher*, are daily only from September to June, twice

weekly the rest of the year.) Then there are two weekly magazines and a monthly filled with more of the same pictures. One
of them, the *Palm Beach Chronicle*, runs a serialized tongue-in-
cheek soap opera, "Flagler's Legacy," which follows the doings
of a matron called Cynthia du Champ Livingston van der Schmidt
Wellson Carlston Neuhouse Townsend "Dee Dee" Beaumont,
presumably going to show that Palm Beachers actually can laugh
at themselves. For the most part, however, the business of social
one-upmanship is deadly serious. PB is one of the last places in
the world, therefore, utterly dominated by women. There is a
very good physical reason for it: many of the residents are widows with much money, much time, and little to do but be social.
The local social tigresses, all widowed or divorced, include such
prominent names as Carola Mandel (a Cuban who holds records
at shooting), Bunny du Pont, Mary Sanford, Mrs. Robert Young
(owner of an eighty-six-room house), Fernanda Wanamaker Munn
Kellogg, Jan Annenberg Hooker, Mary Donahue (a Woolworth
heiress), and hundreds more.

Mary Sanford, "the Queen of Palm Beach," is a crucial ally if
you want your affair to be covered by the local "journalists."
And, of course, coverage is a necessity for practically any affair.
It's like a tree falling in the woods with nobody to hear it: nobody
wants to spend $10,000 on tickets and clothes and then disappear
without a trace. Hence, the mad round of quests for invitations,
primping for photographers, then reading about oneself a few
days later in the Shiny Sheet. All that roundelay is presided over
by the few dozen hostesses who expend enormous reserves of
energy merely for the privilege of having themselves read about
by five thousand very wealthy subscribers. Still, because of the
huge amounts of money raised for charity and spent on luxurious
accoutrements—as well as the matched sets of ultraconservative
attitudes propagated at the constant affairs among some of the
world's richest people—Palm Beach hostesses could be seen in
some lights as among the most powerful women in the world.

Palm Beach is only the spiritual capital of a string of pleasure-
loving resorts facing the Atlantic Ocean that are collectively known
as the Gold Coast. Hobe Sound, north of PB, is a place of such
exclusivity and guarded WASPiness that its residents consider
their southern neighbor loud and *arriviste*. Among its longterm
residents have been the Averell Harrimans, the C. Douglas Dil-
lons, the H. J. Heinz IIs, Marshall Field IV, and Mrs. Prescott

Bush, and numerous Fords and duPonts. The late Joan Shipman Payson, a Whitney heiress and once owner of the New York Mets, was the social arbiter of the resort in her time. That position is now occupied by Permelia Prior Reed, known as the "czarina," whose late husband bought the island in 1934 and was chairman of the board of the Jupiter Island Club and president of the Hobe Sound Company, which owns everything in the resort except for the slightly more than two hundred private homes. Mrs. Reed is rumored to send unwanted new residents a black cashmere sweater, a white ski sweater, or a one-way ticket out of West Palm Beach Airport. ("Getting the sweater" is island slang for incurring her displeasure and being asked to leave.) This is not generally necessary, since even those few upstarts with an unshakable urge to get in where they don't belong will get tired of waiting for approval from all twenty-four members of the board of the Jupiter Island Club. And without the club, there is literally nothing to do on the island; the barber shop, the liquor store, the movie, and the library are all in the club, along with the usual golf and tennis. The only public things at all on the island are two roads, Gomez and Ocean; everything else is owned by the residents, either individually or collectively. Police follow unfamiliar cars through electric eyes tucked along the roadside. The ingrown nature of the place can be gauged from the way in which Mrs. Reed refers to Mrs. Bush's son, the vice president, as "Georgy-Porgy" when complaining about the security he brings in his wake. The list of people who couldn't get into Hobe Sound is quite an honor roll: Eisenhower *when he was president*, Jacqueline Onassis, and Perry Como.

Two other Gold Coast resorts are similar to Hobe Sound in exclusivity and shyness, but they are even smaller. Those are Manalapan, which was created as a rich people's resort when Consuelo Vanderbilt built a fabulous mansion called Casa Alva on this tiny strip a few towns south of Palm Beach; and Gulf Stream, slightly farther down the coast, which is probably the least known and most expensive section of real estate anywhere in Florida. Brasher and much bigger, but getting richer all the time, is Boca Raton, which Addison Mizner unsuccessfully attempted to make into a new and even grander Palm Beach (he was thwarted by the depression), but which now attracts enough fortune-laden immigrants, especially from the American Midwest, to give it a reported ratio of one millionaire for every forty residents. But rich people are spreading out all along southeastern Florida, including the "all-American city" Coral Gables, the good parts of Ford Lauderdale (which has probably the highest concentration of yachts in the world except for the French Riviera), and even near tacky old Miami, where the Palm Bay Club's condo owners and boaters include Liz Whitney Tippett, the horsewoman who was once married to the late Jock Whitney. One of the great debutantes of the thirties, Liz quickly gained a reputation for her outrageous behavior; Irene Mayer Selznick remembers her casually leading a horse into the living room of her Virginia manor house, Llangollen. Liz made a pattern of returning to Virginia for sustenance after her divorce from Whitney and again after the death of her second husband, Dr. Cooper Person; the second time she was rescued from her seclusion by Bing Crosby and the Aly Khan, upon which she spent two years chaperoning Aly and his myriad girl friends. These days, Liz continues her act in Florida now that she is married to a Kentucky colonel. She showed up in April 1984, for example, at a "Celebrity Croquet" gala to induce interest in the new St. Andrews Country Club in Boca Raton (prices for homes: $350,000 to $2.5 million), dressed in a fuschia pantsuit and driving a purple Rolls—those being her racing colors. Mrs. Tippett was the first to paint her helicopter in her racing colors, as well—an innovation that has since been adopted by horsemen and horsewomen the world over. She cruises to events via the Intracoastal Waterway on her yacht *Adventurer*, where some of the wine coolers are the gold cups her horses have won.

Making a bid in the perennial Florida competition for the wretched excess trophy is Turnberry Isle, in the Intracoastal Waterway behind Miami, which is strictly for people who admire Frank Sinatra and want to show how much money they have. The ambience is dominated by the presence of world-class tennis millionaires; Fred Stolle is the pro at the tennis club, which has twenty-four courts; Jimmy Connors, John McEnroe, and Billie Jean King live there, and Vitas Gerulaitis moved out in 1981 after selling his town house for more than a million. Thank God, there's room for nearly a hundred yachts in the marina.

The Mediterranean is the other, and the older, great warm-weather playground of the stylish rich. For a century and more, the Côte d'Azur in the south of France has been a Mecca for the people who can afford to go anywhere. The area was a distinct backwater during the centuries after the collapse of the Languedoc civilization, and it was only with the arrival of the railroad during the 1860s that the glorious climate and spectacular scenery started making it a popular wintertime resort. The first arrivals were Russians, Germans, and Britons, many of them from the gentility and nobility; and the stylized display of wealth they imported quickly made the resort area *the* place to be. People of a certain class and income backet meant only one destination when they talked of "going abroad for the winter." Queen Victoria's son Edward ("Bertie"), Prince of Wales, made it a regular port-of-call in the era named after him, joining the Vanderbilts, Astors, and other Americans who were rich beyond the dreams of anybody now except Arabian princes.

It was the site for his equally scandalous grandson, the brief King George VI, to pursue the woman he loved. King Leopold II of the Belgians, who made an immense personal fortune through the control of the Congo, bought up much of Cap Ferrat in the period before World War I, including a house that was later taken over by Somerset Maugham and, still later, by the Oscar Wyatts. Consuelo Vanderbilt, who had by then divorced the Duke of Marlborough and become Madame Balzan, lived out her life there in relative obscurity after the war.

The Riviera began achieving its current eminence right after World War I, when Scott and Zelda, Cole Porter, and the Murphys made it a household word for the twenties and thirties—especially with the publication of Fitzgerald's *Tender Is the Night*, set there. Indeed, it was this swank young crowd that started the idea of going there in the summer, which is now the season. "THE RIVIERA!" Fitzgerald wrote in 1924. "The names of its resorts, Cannes, Nice, Monte Carlo, call up the memory of a hundred kings and princes who have lost their thrones and come here to die, of mysterious rajahs and beys flinging blue diamonds to English dancing girls or Russian millionaires tossing away fortunes at roulette in the lost caviar days before the war." He described "the hot, sweet south of France" as "the most fascinating amalgamation of wealth, luxury and general uselessness in the world"—and while the area has been condominized thoroughly since then, the métier has changed very little.

Tennis came into vogue in the 1930s. Frank Jay Gould, son of the American robber baron—a man who traveled with his own ten-piece band so he would never be without the tunes he wanted to hear—created perhaps the most exclusive housing development in the world when he bought up Juan-les-Pins; he also contributed to building Cap d'Antibes. His widow, Florence, who was born to French parents in San Francisco and then, shortly after 1906, brought to France to be educated in preparation for the expected husband of position and property, carried on the traditions of the gracious living exemplified by her husband's first tenants through her own death in 1983; lunch and dinner at her house El Patio, near Cannes, starred such artists and writers as Jean Cocteau, André Gide, François Mauriac, Colette, Matisse, and Maurice Chevalier. Since she died without heirs, most of the incredible stuff she had stuffed into El Patio went at auction—including $8 million for jewelry at Sotheby's, a record for a jewelry auction; a projected $5 million for the books and antique furnishings, among which were a $250,000 pair of George III silver baskets that Mrs. Gould habitually used when she let her guests eat cake; and, still pending disposition, an art collection valued at more than $50 million. Much later, Aristotle Onassis would arrive in style on the fabulous yacht *Christina* with Maria Callas. Onassis liked the south of France so much that he not only moored there constantly, he finally bought a large chunk of Monaco. In American popular literature as well as social history, the Riviera has always been the site most immediately identified with wealth, from *The House of Mirth* and *Tender Is the Night* through the fairy tales of Rita Hayworth marrying Prince Aly Khan and Grace Kelly marrying Prince Rainier.

Anyone who imagines that such bottomless consumption is a relic of a happier or more private age need only cultivate a summertime friendship with Lynn Wyatt and angle for an invitation to Lynn's birthday party. This is an annual July 16 event on the Riviera circuit, in which the elite of elites—and Lynn does know her share of the elite—roll up to the Wyatts' incredible Villa Mauresque. The summer house was once owned by Somerset Maugham, an appropriately decadent heritage; it is situated in St.-Jean-Cap-Ferrat, a small, out-of-the-way promontory that shelters some of the greatest wealth of the United States and Europe at ease. Villa Mauresque is all white, so in 1982, for her birthday, as the night fell "like liquid dark coming down," it struck the lady's fancy to throw an all-red party. (As the careful reader may have noticed, theme parties are very much a rich-hostess thing to do.) Everyone did indeed wear red, including Prince Rainier (red-and-white polka-dot tie, red suspenders, and red socks) and Princess Grace, who matched the hostess's red Dior. Some of the big hits of the party were the Wyatts' houseguests: Liza Minnelli, Farrah Fawcett, and Ryan O'Neal. Mary Wells Lawrence, the world's leading advertising woman and no financial pipsqueak, dropped over with her husband from *their* house in the neighborhood, La Fiorentina, which in some circles is considered the most beautiful villa in the world. Other neighbors stopping in were Estée Lauder with her (now late) husband and Countess Donina Cicogna, so it is easy to see that the little community shelters its share of the world's billions. The international ownership set included São Schlumberger (of the world's most successful drilling-equipment company, a relative of Dominique de Menil), Brazilian industrialist Nelson Seabra, Sandra di Portanova, and Paola and Giuseppe Jermi (Italian silk money); and they were leavened with other members of the non-Belushi side of showbiz, including Christopher Reeve and Johnny Carson with then-wife Joanna. Plácido Domingo led a six-piece orchestra in "Happy Birthday to You." After dinner, the surprise visitor was Helmut Schmidt, the chancellor of West Germany. (The year before, Stavros Niarchos was the big hit, dinghying in from his yacht.) Just seventy of Lynn's closest friends.

The setting was appropriately dazzling. Cocktails were in the drawing room and out on the terrace in the soft, piney, romantic air, while dinner was served in the garden, where the galaxy of crystal and silver had been set up on black-and-white cloths. Naturally, the Wyatts offered chili and fried chicken along with the standard French menu. The year before, just to show that she doesn't entirely abandon her charitable aims in party-giving just because she's on vacation, Lynn had been chairman of a Yellow Rose of Texas Ball for the benefit of the American Hospital in Paris. You could—well, you had to—pay to get into this one, which was held at the Monte Carlo Sporting Club. Eight hundred people did, including a large contingent of Texans headed by Governor John B. Connally, who buzzed over for the weekend on a specially chartered plane at a package cost of $2,400. They not only got a lunch at La Fiorentina, they saw Princess Caroline, and they got to bask in the beauty of thousands of yellow roses, also flown over from Texas, sculpted into twelve-foot rose trees throughout the club. At the ball itself, the guests consumed two hundred pounds of caviar and a thousand bottles of champagne. *Someone* has to keep up the grand traditions.

Much of the world's great wealth follows the inland sea of the Mediterranean, as it did in earlier centuries at the hands of the

Phoenicians, the Greeks, the Romans, and the Venetians. Today, the greatest of the incredibly wealthy scattered along its shores are the Greek shipowning families—Onassis, Niarchos, Goulandris, Livanos, and lesser-known but still rich and cultured clans like Colocotronis, Georgiades, and Kulukundis—and the Arab possessors of the world's greatest supplies of black gold. The Greeks of course have their own end of the Mediterranean in which to play with their tankers and their private islands. Stavros Niarchos owns Spetzapoula, which features four houses, a platoon of servants, several helicopters, and masses of wild game for guests to shoot. Christina Onassis now owns her late father Ari's opulently outfitted Skorpios, and uses it several months a year to shield herself from the *paparazzi* and soothe her aching heart. Actually, Onassis was somewhat unusual among Greek shipowners in not having been born on an island at all. On Oinousa, near the coast of Turkey, for example, there are an estimated fifty families with fortunes of more than $2 million out of a total population of sixteen hundred—a windfall that has the effect of turning a longtime poor island into a sort of homegrown resort. Aside from being very lovely to sail around, select Greek islands can be considered the most exclusive resorts in the world, since a number of them are privately owned.

Owning a private island is not an exclusively Greek province, although they tend to be abler to afford it than most. Malcolm Forbes has one—Laucala, in the Fiji group in the South Pacific. The late William Wrigley, Jr., the chewing-gum heir, bought Santa Catalina Island off the coast of southern California, although he did not keep it for himself but built it up with the same sort of promotional activity Flagler had exercised on Palm Beach. Howard Coffin, heir to Curtiss-Wright, United Airlines, and Hudson Motor Car fortunes, did much the same thing with Sea Island, off Georgia; he commissioned the ever-popular resort architect Addison Mizner to build perhaps his grandest concoction, the lavish but not huge Cloister. Gardiners Island, off the eastern tip of Long Island, is perhaps the only island on earth that has been owned by the same family throughout the history of its deed; it was granted to Lion Gardiner in 1639 by King Charles I of England—one of the last grants that doomed monarch was to make—and is now ruled by Robert David Lion Gardiner, the sixteenth lord of the manor, who professes great pride that his family estate has outlasted those of the great patroon clans of New York, like the Morrises' ("that's the Bronx now") and the Livingstons' ("that's Grossinger's"). J. P. Morgan built a lavish country place on East Island, off the North Shore of Long Island. Naushon Island, near Martha's Vineyard, has since 1843 been the private retreat for the ancient Forbes family of Boston, who obviously decided that the Vineyard and Nantucket and the coast of Maine had started letting in just anybody.

Up in Maine, Mrs. David Rockefeller owns Bartlett's Island, near blue-blooded Northeast Harbor, where she runs a model farm. Mrs. Stuart Symington has rustic Dogfish Island, near Vinalhaven. Keewaydin Island, in the Gulf of Mexico off Naples, Florida, affords five miles of private beach to Mr. and Mrs. Lester Norris, she being the niece of "Bet-a-Million" Gates and a large stockholder in Texaco. Count Otto Stenbock of Sweden and his countess, Ebba, host hunting parties for guests like the royal families of Sweden and Monaco on their island Ornö, near Stockholm, where tea is served after the hunt and dinners are black tie. The Italilan Count Carlo Borromeo owns four islands in Lake Maggiore, and his German wife Marion zips over to Stresa in her speedboat to pick up guests for delivery to tiny Isolino. Benigno P. Toda, Jr., the owner of Philippines Airlines, runs a cattle ranch on his own Philippine, Hermana Mayor.

Considerably west of the great private preserves of the modern Greek gods are two resorts for the ultrawealthy that have each, in the great tradition, been created out of whole cloth by one wealthy builder who managed to lure the properly connected people always looking for the novel and the chic. Marbella is such a place. In 1953, the eye of the restless young Prince Alfonso zu Hohenlohe-Langenburg settled on a sleepy but sunny and scenic sector of Spain's Costa del Sol. The prince definitely needed something to do, for the war had appropriated the family's forty-five thousand acres of ancestral lands in Czechoslovakia and left them with something over thirty castles in Germany and Austria, all very expensive to care for, not to mention crumbling and drafty and cold. Marbella, fifty miles up the coast from Gibraltar, was a perfect marriage of sun and sea with a backdrop of mountains, with a climate that allowed semitropical plantings and a California life-style throughout the year. With $10,000 from his father and a great boost from his nearly infinite connections, Prince Alfonso instantly created the Marbella Club, which rapidly turned into one of the great resort magnets of the world. Thirty years later, the beautifully maintained club is still one of the most exclusive anywhere. Prince Alfonso and his cousin Count Rudolf von Schönburg, the hotel manager, personally screen all the guests, and for the peak periods of summer that means that about the only valid ticket for admission is the possession of a name like Princess Ira von Fürstenberg, Princess Marie Louise of Prussia, Prince Alfi Auersperg, or anything von Bismarck. Such a latter-day-aristocracy sort of place naturally attracts the mixture of old European blood and newer American money that, for example, Sunny Crawford found at the Austrian resort Schloss Mittersell. Indeed, Marbella turned out to be the bag-and-baggage southern extension of Mittersell. Baron Hubert von Pantz, who created Mittersell before the war, remains a fixture at Marbella. So does Princess Honeychile Hohenlohe, Prince Alfonso's sister-in-law, who as a glamorous Georgia-born comedienne (for a while she teamed with a young Bob Hope on radio) had followed the time-honored path of marrying European nobility; it was her inspiration and energy that rebuilt the postwar Mittersell into a meeting ground between the Communist-dispossessed nobility and American glamor and money. Joining that chummy group are, for example, representatives of the richest families in Spain, the Albas and Fierros, scattered relatives of the late shah of Iran, and showbiz folks from all over.

There is, however, another, darker presence on the glittering horizon: in a reprise from twelve hundred years ago, the Arabs have reinvaded Spain. The fabulous yacht harbor at Marbella, Puerto Banús, suddenly began filling up with boats named, if never sailed, in Saudi Arabia and nearby kingdoms; the basin was foresightedly designed with three-hundred-foot slips. Its creamy nightclub, the Menchu Bar (Menchu being considered "the Régine of Spain"), is filled with Arabs whose ethnic identification does not extend to the Koran's proscription of Scotch or unmarried (not to mention immodestly Western) women. The charter members of the Marbella Club are not at all pleased to walk outside their preserve and behold the gaudy, floodlit white cube of a mosque called Mezquita Del Rey Abdul Aziz Al Saud— the first mosque built in Spain in eight hundred years. It was constructed by Prince Salman, brother of King Fahd of Saudi Arabia. Above the mosque is Prince Salman's own Casa al Riyadh, and above that is King Fahd's Rose Palace, which is described as looking like an off-white White House. In their wake came an infusion of money of the size, if not the quality, that the founders of Marbella had dreamed of. Developers are throwing up Levittowns of garish houses on the hillsides that sell in the neighborhood of $2 million apiece. Drugs and prostitutes are said to flourish. The Marbella Club itself is now partly owned by Arabs. Not to worry, says Prince Alfonso. "The reason for my taking a partner into the business," he explained at a press conference necessitated by the panic in "society," "was to enlarge the capital of my company so as to be able to complete the dream of my life, to create something on this coast that does not exist anywhere else." In short, the international set retreated into the hills. Prince Ferdinand von Bismarck has created a nice, Christian enclave called the Marbella Hill Club a mile and a half inland. Now, scattered for miles and miles around, are the hillside villas of the people who finally found themselves unable to assimilate a new wave of wealth. Arabs do not send rich heiresses to marry handsome, blond, penniless resort owners.

A Moslem of a more congenial sort has created the other great big-money resort of the postwar Mediterranean. For centuries, Sardinia had been known as anything but an inhospitable, rocky refuge for some of the meanest bandits this side of Tamerlane. It took the brilliance and mosque-built wealth of the Aga Khan to make something of it, and what he made was the Costa Smeralda. When the Aga Khan got involved, in 1962, the Costa Smeralda was nothing but a rocky, piney, mosquito-infested piece of nowhere. Along thirty-five miles of the northeast coast of the island, the Aga Khan threw in some $600 million worth of development, including a new landscaping company, a ceramic-tile plant, and an airline. In an attempt to retain the scale of the peasants who have inhabited Sardinia for as long as anybody remembers, the Aga Khan decreed that the standard architectural expression would be the *stazzu*, the simple shepherd's house. Now he arrives in his grandiose yacht, the huge white *Kalamoun*, to enjoy the pleasures of an existence of stunning luxury in a land that was previously dedicated to the nurturing of the goat. Porto Cervo is the heart of the development, offering everything extremely expensive for the international yachting set.

Between Sardinia and the Costa del Sol is Mallorca, a large island with a heterogenous international set—no few drug dealers among them—but also a well-hidden circle of the social rich. The March family, which ranks with the Albas and Fierros for legendary wealth in Spain, is based on Mallorca. King Juan Carlos and Queen Sofia of Spain are regulars, as are the Greek royal family. Then there are Lady Astor, the Princess of Ligne, and

Adnan Khashoggi. When the Cornelius Vanderbilt Whitneys arrive at their Mallorcan hideaway, El Vila, they quickly gather their friends the Countess Ostrowska, Jinett Hennesy, and Jean de Quelar for the *intime* dinner parties that constitute the social life that matters on the island.

The fast lane is a little further south in the Balearics: on the island of Ibiza, to be exact—an adults-only scene if there ever was one, and very likely the druggiest of upper-crust resorts. The Marbella Club gang traditionally takes a boat or plane ride here sometime during the season to dine at Sausalito. Princess Ira von Fürstenberg is a regular. Arndt von Bohlen und Halbach jets in to his *finca* when Palm Beach gets too hot. The Duchess of Alba is one of the most important of the many important people who bask and party here. Princess Caroline sails in on her way to Africa. Jacqueline de Ribes flies in for long weekends. And so on.

Even when they are not private, islands make wonderful retreats for the wealthy: They are so *far* from everything. Scattered throughout the world are islands that, through particular beauty or just by accident, have become habitats of the very wealthy. Take Fishers Island, between Long Island and Connecticut. The saying is that strangers arrive at Fishers Island by yacht or by marriage. Social life on the island is run by Mrs. Sidney Legendre, who has been arriving on Memorial Day to take up residence since time immemorial. Her guests are likely to include such impressively pedigreed and endowed islanders as the Reynolds du Ponts (and others of that clan), the Arthur Houghtons (Corning Glass), and Mrs. Ogden Phipps.

Mackinac Island, in the Strait of Mackinaw in upper Michigan, has been a prominent resort since antebellum southern planters discovered it as a refuge from the brutal summers when only slaves would be foolish enough to go out in the sun. In fact, it had a foreshadowing of its future social acceptability and also of great riches when John Jacob Astor set up camp there in 1810 to trade for furs with the local Chippewa Indians. Among the early visitors were Susan B. Anthony, Mark Twain, and William Cullen Bryant. The automobile was banned on the island in 1904. The Grand Hotel there is one of the great hostelries of the world; Mrs. Potter Palmer, Chicago's reigning social arbiter in the late nineteenth century, used to hold forth on the world's longest porch (880 feet). Since then, the island's list of socially acceptable fortune-holders has included the Field, Armour, and Pullman families of Chicago; the Adolphus Busch family from St. Louis; and the Whitneys, Algers, and Newberrys from Detroit's old aristocracy.

In the middle of the Atlantic, of course, there is the nonpareil Bermuda. Its pink-tinted beaches, pastel-colored, lime-roofed houses (each of them with a name, no matter how small) and lanes planted serially with hibiscus, morning glory, and oleander have long since attracted the upper middle class from the eastern United States. Nevertheless, the more lavish mansions continue to house the descendants of the great American and English families who made Bermuda one of the more magical destinations of the age of ship travel.

Europe has several small islands catering to the needs and whims of the hereditary gentry and those who have bought their way into it. The unhappily named Sylt Island, an hour and a half out of Hamburg in the North Sea, is a resort dedicated to the worship of the body, which is done in the nude on many of the dozens of miles of beaches. The Gunther Sachses, Yasmin Khan (the model daughter of the late Aly Khan and Rita Hayworth), and the usual contingent of von Bismarcks are all part of the Jane Fondaesque crowd who take their exercise by striding vigorously through the wet sand, or *watt*, that extends out for miles when the tide is low.

Much less Maine-hardy are the islands off Naples in the Mediterranean. Capri is the better known, but the really slick and rich one is Ischia. Ischia is a largish spot and attracts several hundred thousand tourists during the season, but it is also a summer home to Rothschilds, Antonella Agnelli of the Fiat family, and a slew of international movie stars and producers. Like many other resorts, Ischia was developed after World War II; its angel was publisher Angelo Rizzoli.

Down in the Caribbean, just about any of the glorious sandy little islands is liable to house a dozen rich people. Among the most notable are Antigua, where the extremely tony Mill Reef Club houses such as the Paul Mellons, George du Ponts, and William E. Huttons; Mustique, made famous by Princess Margaret and later patronized by an interesting blend that includes Mick Jagger, Prince Andrew and Koo Stark, the Herreras and their crowd of Venezuelan industrialist families, and, recently, Dina Merrill, who sailed an entire party down on her mother Marjorie Merriweather Post's immense ship *Sea Cloud* just to throw a bash; and Barbados, which along with an increasing number of Europeans and South Americans has hosted, among others, Jackie Onassis and Jerome Zipkin, who attend parties thrown by, for example, Claudette Colbert. To the north, in the otherwise tacky Bahamas, lies the gem of Lyford Cay, yet another creation of the resort-building fifties. At the tip of New Providence Island, it has since attracted as many of the powerful rich as any other resort. Among the mere thousand homeowners or renters at any one time are thirty-five nationalities; owners and guests have included the Aga Khan, Lee Radziwill, the Henry Fords, the William Paleys, the Antonio Bragas from Brazil, Dolly Goulandris, and the H. J. Heinz IIs.

An odd and intriguing choice for the adventurous rich is Phuket, off Thailand, home of a pearl industry. Prince Rangsit and his princess, a Parisian, started a club here for their friends, who include a strong French contingent featuring Princess Napoleon and the Paul Louis Weillers, who are among the richest people in Europe.

The quintessential old-line summer resort of the United States eastern Establishment is Northeast Harbor on Mount Desert Island in Maine's Penobscot Bay. Mount Desert was established as a finely bred resting ground well back into the nineteenth century, when Bostonians, including the redoubtable Episcopal Bishop William Lawrence, started building on what had been an artists' colony. They were soon joined by Philadelphians, Baltimoreans, and scattered emissaries from the growing nation's local gentries. Bar Harbor, also on Mount Desert, soon became the breeding ground for some of the grandest summer "cottages" anywhere outside of Newport, but it was crippled by the depression and estate taxes and finally destroyed in the great fire of 1947. Since then, Northeast Harbor, which was always preferred by the more understated of the heirs to the industrial fortunes, has emerged—though not very far into the limelight—as *the* northern outpost of classy wealth. The Rockefellers have been coming here for generations; in fact, there are two Mrs. Nelson Rockefellers on the island, first wife Mary Todhunter in Northeast and her successor Happy in Seal Harbor nearby. Life revolves around sailing and huge cocktail parties afterward, known as "porch breakers." Among the famed hostesses are Mrs. August Belmont, Mabel Ingalls (a granddaughter of J. P. Morgan), and the ever-present Brooke Astor.

Prominent among the swanker and newer summer resorts is Southampton, the most social of the conglomeration of towns collectively called the Hamptons toward the eastern end of Long Island. Here many of the New York people on the constant social round keep, or less desirably rent, summer houses on estates of, say, five acres, lovely sweeps of expensive grass grown on imported soil and topped by solid, important-looking houses. The great axle of the social wheel is William Paley, the octogenarian mahatma of CBS, who can cause a dinner party to form on a moment's notice even in the height of the season, simply by agreeing to attend. (Paley, widowed from the formidable Babe, of the Cushing tribe, remains a fixture of the social and even romantic scene well into his ninth decade. He popped up in the gossip columns in April 1984, when he dropped into a party at the Acapulco spread of Baron Ricky di Portanova and his wife Sandra and met Veronica Uribe, described as a tall, dark, rich Colombian widow; they were said to be "necking" before the end of the night and jetting together back to New York before the end of the week.)

At parties in Southampton, Paley is liable to run across others who have been going there for dozens of summers—allegedly for the peace and the escape from the pressures of working and socializing—such as Felix Rohatyn, the investment banker and savior of New York, Gloria Vanderbilt, Lee Radziwill, Milton and Carroll Petrie of the department stores (she is the former Marquesa de Portago), investor supreme Herbert Allen, Charlotte Ford, and sister Anne Ford Scarborough. Ahmet and Mica Ertegun—he is the richest record producer in the world, she an interior designer of note—are known to import an entirely different house party each week. That is a clue to the inbred nature of Southampton. Despite the fact that anybody can drive there, anyone of any wealth can rent a house within the town limits, and there are a substantial number of restaurants, stores, and other public outlets, the resort maintains elaborate social codes, with very little mixing between different groups. Virtually all the vacationers are from New York, but it is still nevertheless quite rare for Jews to be accepted at either the Southampton Bathing Corporation or the Meadow Club, the two organizations that count. There are changes pulsing underneath the surface of the glittering life, though; some of the huger old estates are being broken up. "Summer people just aren't able to manage twenty acres," explained Madell Semerjian to a reporter. "Nobody can manage even a twelve-acre estate anymore. It's too difficult to get staff." The traditional whining about the servant shortage has a self-serving aspect on Mrs. Semerjian's part, since her husband George is trying to build as many houses as he can on the spare pieces of those crumbling old properties. The older set fights back the way it always has; it whispers about the Semerjians at the Bathing Corporation, even while it invites them for drinks.

Speaking of the di Portanovas' party, one should not slight Acapulco and nearby Puerto Vallarte as havens for the extremely rich from all over and during all seasons except the middle of summer. The di Portanovas take a lot of speaking. They have two houses in Acapulco; the newer one, Arabesque (is that a slur on all the Arabs who are poorer than this Italian Texan?), is the biggest of all the giant villas in Acapulco. It has twenty-eight bedrooms, twenty-six baths, five kitchens, four swimming pools, a dozen indoor waterfalls, a nightclub, a herd of plaster camels, a heliport on the roof and, guarding the whole, a tower manned by sentries with machine guns. Henry Kissinger, who can appreciate such armed vigilance, was the honoree at the first party given there. One of the neighbors is Loel Guinness, through whom the di Portanovas met Brooke Astor, who in turn threw a party for them when they got to New York in the spring of 1984. This is how the party keeps moving.

Mexico is also the site of another of the spectacular attempts to create a resort out of whole cloth through the importation of the rich, famous, and gossipy. Antenor Patiño, of the Bolivian tin fortune, did it in 1974 at Las Hadas, in Manzanillo. He and his wife Beatriz rounded up their friends and sent Air France jets for them: Jacqueline de Ribes from Paris, Mary Lasker, the Lauders, William Levitt of the Levittowns with his French wife Simone, the Bloomingdales, Lynn and Oscar Wyatt, Marylou and Sonny Whitney, and the rest of the gang. Beatriz Patiño flew in Monsieur Marc to take care of the hair; to his despair, the resort, meant to be the most luxurious in the world down to its marble floors for every room, had no hair dryers. The *problems!* Despite Patiño's pains, though, Las Hadas has become accessible to everyone with the steep price of admission; it was the setting for the Dudley Moore movie *10*.

Finally, among summer resorts, Newport has not utterly surrendered her old title as reigning dowager. One would never know it to visit tourist Newport, the rebuilt and repolished old colonial town on the harbor, to mingle with the serious and nonserious sailors in town for the America's Cup, or even to take a trip through the ghostly mansions on the tour circuit. Nonetheless, while Newport has indeed changed over the years, the monied summer colony lived on; it simply went underground. Newport was, with Cape May, New Jersey, the oldest actual summer resort in the United States and possibly in the world. By the 1830s it was visited in season by a constant stream of pleasure-seekers, particularly from Boston and from Charleston, South Carolina.

But the Newport of the popular imagination did not grow up until after the Civil War, when the country's new industrial wealth needed somewhere to put itself on display. Newport was chosen, and for the thirty years until the beginning of World War I became synonymous with all that was decadently excessive among the class with enough money to do anything it wanted. The legends grew thick and fast: the mock armada in front of a mansion, the fourteen-carat gold fruit on trees, dinners with dogs or monkeys as guests. World War I ended such mania, although the twenties saw plenty of Gatsbyesque parties in the still thriving mansions. After that, the old Newport mostly disappeared from the public consciousness; there were only occasional reminders that old money still dwelt there, such as the Grace Kelly vehicle *High Society* (1950) and the 1953 wedding of Senator John Kennedy to Jacqueline Bouvier at her mother Janet Auchincloss's home, Hammersmith Farm. Ostentatious display was out of fashion as the robber barons' families became more "aristocratic," and the fear of kidnappers and the taxman added to the reticence. The noisy activities surrounding not only the commercialization of the old port, but even such apparently upper-class events as the America's Cup, only prompted the Old Guard to retreat even further into their shells. Some of the retreat, of course, has been caused by the diminution of the great family fortunes; there are probably no Vanderbilts left who have enough to keep up their old palaces, Marble House or the colossal Breakers, even if they could have ponied up the enormous estate taxes to hang onto the latter when the last of the great dowagers, Countess Széchényi, died early in the 1970s. (As part of the deal leaving The Breakers to the public, her daughter, Countess Szápáry, continues to live in a fourteen-room flat on the palazzo's third floor.) But there were others who were moving in: Texans with money, and of course the von Bülows, who bought the imposing Paladian cottage Clarendon Court, which had been the setting for *High Society*.

Today, Newport remains an exclusive enclave, very difficult for anyone to penetrate without a combination of considerable wealth, personal charm, and at least remotely respectable family. As elsewhere, the Texans, who spend their money gaudily, have been partly accepted because they are—an all-important social concept—*amusing*. But the tone of the "important" people in the resort is still set by the descendants of the old families, many of whom retain a great deal of wealth while hiding it well. "Dodo" Hamilton, the Campbell's Soup centimillionaire, brings along her Philadelphia Main Line aversion to public display when she visits her flowery house perched above the ocean. "Most people here do their own marketing," she told a reporter for the *Philadelphia Inquirer*. "Whenever I go to the A&P or Crest Farms, I always see a pal pushing a cart." Entertaining centers around smallish private dinner parties and a couple of private clubs, including the ancient Reading Room, where men gather for drinks, and Bailey's Beach, the small, private strand where membership descends from generation to generation. Here, the pleasures are simple, the accommodations practically Spartan: a cafeteria that dispenses grilled cheese and clam chowder, plain cabanas. Nothing, in other words, like the aggressively stylish entertaining that goes on in Palm Beach or Marbella. But the money is just as old or older, and the social ranking perhaps more pervasive than in any of the other resorts. Like most resorts, Newport's society is dominated by formidable elderly women. Candace Van Alen, Noreen Drexel, and the crusty Mrs. John Nicholas Brown decide which newcomers will have a good time and who will not, a ruling for which money is a necessary but not a sufficient condition. Even when one is relaxing, being rich is serious business.

The Ski Resorts

At the Corviglia Restaurant, for lunch, it is not at all unusual for a group of people famished by mountain air to order one of the specialties of the house—slightly less than two ounces of the finest blue Iranian caviar piled onto either a baked potato or a blini, then blanketed in heavy cream. Those treats cost $45 each. Champagne is big also at Corviglia, and many customers who cannot get enough take away with them pots of *foie gras*, which cost $75, or black truffles, a relative bargain at $15 each. Not that the Corviglia is especially impressive-looking: the tables are plastic-laminated, plain linen placemats are their only decorations, and there is a cafeteria next door that serves the same food a day old for one-third the sit-down price. Also, the place is seventy-five hundred feet up in the Alps, and the cable-car trip alone costs $6. Despite the obstacles, or because of them, one needs a reservation days in advance, in season, to lunch at the preferred 2:00 P.M. seating. This is because the Corviglia Restaurant has become an important stopping place in the social minuet in one of the most socially important spots in the world, St. Moritz, the king of the winter resorts. Princess Caroline of Monaco stops by three times a week, and she is surrounded by the barons of German industry, Italian princesses, South American ranchers, and American oil heiresses. For St. Moritz exercises a magnetic attraction second to no other social gathering place. It is one of the few places left in the world where dressing, style, and social position are important day or night; and since it is a ski resort and reachable only by determination and considerable expenditure, it is that way all over.

Not far from the Corviglia Restaurant, also at the top of the famous Corviglia ski run, is an institution that makes the restaurant look like a hotbed of democratic socialism. This is the Corviglia Ski Club, generally considered the single most exclusive and important social club in Europe, where lunch is humbly offered to men of resounding value like Loel Guinness, Stavros Niarchos, Alfred Heineken, and Gianni Agnelli. The presence of such major businessmen is an indication of the weight of money in a resort that once prided itself on pure aristocracy; but of course these are men of considerable background themselves, their names hallowed by several generations of possession. Like any expensive European spa, St. Moritz will always have its share of major noble names, from the fabulously wealthy and established (the Aga Khan) to the international fast set (Prince Kiko Hohenlohe, Prince Manfred Windisch-Grätz), with enough assorted counts, marquesses, and baronesses to start a mountain kingdom. Which is, of course, what St. Moritz has been for all of the twentieth century. It was the first modern winter resort. St. Moritz was a sleepy summer spa, situated happily amidst the Alpine meadows, when an enterprising innkeeper bet his British customers their travel costs that they would enjoy the place even more in winter than in summer. Indeed they did, and by the 1870s proper Victorians—the British were really the only signif-

icant travelers at that time—were tobagganing, skating, and dancing throughout the winter. But the resort became a true social
destination only with the construction in 1896 of the Palace Hotel,
which was and remains the place to stay (there are suites at
$10,000 a week for those who demand them), to have a drink,
and to dance until dawn in the King's Club. The Dukes and
Duchesses of Windsor and Alba have been regulars in the tur-
reted, twisting hotel that looks like nothing so much as—well,
as a European palace. Outside there are sports for the rich: horse
races and ski-kjöring races at Lake St. Moritz, the latter a St.
Moritz specialty imported from Sweden, in which skiers are
towed by horses; hang-gliding over the Palace; or skiing after a
helicopter lift. Perched in the woods near the superchic Suvretta
House are fantastic chalets costing millions apiece, where the
Aga Khan and the Stavros Niarchoses live, and the late shah of
Iran had a notorious copper-domed growth built—all houses that
compensate for the cold, brisk sports outside with bowling alleys,
saunas, and swimming pools that are miracles of paint and mo-
saic.

Not nearly as historic but definitely in the same wealthy class
is Vail, Colorado, the unchallenged leader among American winter retreats. Created from scratch only slightly more than twenty
years ago, Vail from its beginnings attracted members of the oil
dynasties of Bass and Murchison from Texas, Olive and Thomas
Watson (IBM money), Leonard Firestone of the tire fortune, and
the Adams family, the biggest landowners in Oklahoma. Mixed
in with them have been upwardly mobile politicians (Gerald
Ford, Walter Mondale, John Glenn), athletes, and actors. Several
clans of rich Mexicans and Venezuelans have been regulars since
the creation; recently Dr. Friedrich Karl Flick, one of the richest
industrialists in Germany, set up shop, and members of the Saudi
royal family quietly moved in. George Caulkins, the Denver businessman who helped create the resort, is in the habit of saying
that he "couldn't afford to know any poor people." The town
has grown like a mushroom, but the perfect planning has led to
none of the crunches associated with Aspen or other western
United States resorts. In twenty years, Vail has gone from mere
wilderness to sixty miles of downhill trails, eighteen lifts, more
than four hundred instructors, sixteen miles of pipe for snow-
making, seventy-five restaurants and bars, a hospital, three theaters, and thousands of million-dollar homes. Cars are all kept
underground, so there is no traffic except for the twenty-four-

hour taxi service. Vail is an extremely American sort of place, not just in its damn-the-torpedoes ability to create an entire resort from scratch, or its nonimitative, pragmatically modern architecture, but in the absence of any particular social structure. There are "A" list hostesses, of course, but they are a diverse lot, from the best-dressed sophisticates like Lynn Wyatt and Nan Kempner to Fran Stark, wife of Hollywood mogul Ray Stark. The usual ankle-length furs and electric-colored skisuits and huge-but-cozy chalets, however, are much more important to visibility than any particular background or association with any group. *Vive* free enterprise.

Sun Valley, Idaho, the first American ski resort, remains an outdoorsy and unsnobbish retreat for a select group of summer and winter vacationers. W. Averell Harriman, then chairman of the Union Pacific Railroad, which had been founded by his father, commissioned the construction of the resort in 1935, and it succeeded immediately. Harriman and his current wife Pamela, the Washington politico-hostess, still spend summers here, frequently joined by her son from an earlier marriage, Winston Spencer-Churchill. But the affiliation with the railroad is gone, as is most of the proper eastern society crowd that were the only ones with the money or interest to attend the resort in its first thirty years. The railroad, in no need of another money-loser, sold the resort in 1965 to William Janss. Janss, a southern California real estate developer, did what the old-line crowd might have expected from a California developer: he threw up some shabby condos, and he lured what was then called the jet set. Bobby Kennedy danced barefoot in the Duchin Room in the original resort, where society bandleader Eddy Duchin once played; *paparazzi* flew helicopters after New York socialite Amanda Burden as she skied while waiting for her divorce to come through. In 1977, Janss sold the resort to Earl Holding, an oilman who spent large sums to restore the fading grandeur of the lodge and put the brakes on further development. Today, Sun Valley is a glorious retreat with some social life, a smattering of Hemingways, but very little concern for outward appearance. Somewhat typical is the attitude of Marion Butler Stuart, wife of E. Hadley Stuart, Jr.; he is one of two heirs to the immense Carnation Milk fortune, who quit the company as a vice-president in 1961 over the dictatorial practices of his father, the chief executive officer, and retired to the big Diamond Dragon ranch, outside nearby

Ketchum, where the two now raise corn and alfalfa. Mrs. Stuart is no stranger to the pleasures of money: the "ranch house" is an enormous, beautiful place with an impressive art collection. However, her energies are generally concentrated on her work in paleontology, in which she is internationally known. What money *has* helped Mrs. Stuart do is to build her own museum, housing what is known to be one of the finest collections of minerals in the world. She has a profound dislike of the social circuit so beloved of so many of the other women in her class of wealth. (Her husband is worth between $200 and $300 million.) "I don't like hangers-on, phonies or big cities," she has been quoted as saying.

The invaluable combination of vigorous exercise, potent scenery, social exclusivity, and geographical remoteness has made ski resorts such an important part of the rich-young-things circuit that they are now needed the entire year round. Fortunately, then, there is Portillo, nine thousand feet up in the Chilean Andes—hence offering reversed winters from European and North American skiing. The most famous ski resort in South America, Portillo offers a purer distillation of the sporting rich than probably any other place in the world, largely because of its remote and magnificent location. It is ninety-five miles of jagged road, ending in a dizzying corkscrew, from Santiago, which itself is thousands of miles from just about anywhere else. There is nothing anywhere near Portillo—no charming villages like the stately European resorts, none of the friendly, sunny, treelined valleys that the Rockies camps provide. The entire outpost is simply a huge, semicircular, yellow hotel in a volcanic moonscape far above the tree line and just below the famous statue of Christ of the Andes. The hotel took seven years to build in its inhospitable site, and when it opened in 1949 the Chilean government had to provide aid to keep it alive. It was put up for auction in 1960 and purchased by an upstate New York businessman, Robert Purcell, who was connected with the Rockefellers and so called on Richard Aldrich, a cousin of theirs, for part of the investment. The Americans still run the place, and as a result Rockefellers and Kennedys are among those who appear when all the old resorts begin to pall. You couldn't, of course, keep away some of the Hohenlohes. But the place is at least half South American in the composition of its guests, and probably has hosted close to half of South America's wealth. Roberta Matarazzo, one of the heiresses to the giant São Paulo–based family fortune, strolls around dripping in dead animals; a major hostess in the predinner cocktail hour is Marilú Pitanguy, wife of Dr. Ivo Pitanguy, the world's foremost plastic surgeon, from Rio de Janeiro; and the Mayrink-Veigas of Brazil add their dash of social and financial spice. The resort has the relaxed pace and giggling sensuality that distinguish South American social behavior.

Taking the Waters

There is a final category of resort, one that is every now and then scheduled for extinction but manages to survive all notice of its impending doom. These are the old-family "social springs," in particular the Greenbrier Hotel in White Sulphur Springs, West Virginia, and the Homestead just over the border in Virginia. Both are descended from the eighteenth-century tradition in which the great planting families of the Virginia Tidewater would take the Springs Tour, which included some 170 miles of travel in the Blue Ridge Mountains, with stops at springs called the Warm, the Healing, the Hot, the White, the Red, the Sweet, the Salt Sulphur, the Red Sulphur, the Gray Sulphur, the Yellow Sulphur, and the Montgomery White. Toward the end of the nineteenth century, fashion supplanted health as the springs' *raison d'être*, leading inevitably to the construction of ornate hotels and rows of semiprivate cottages that came to be occupied by contingents from the various cities. So at the White Sulphur Springs Hotel, the Old White, which became the most socially correct of the stops, there was a Baltimore Row. That was the first resort experience for the little girl Wallis Warfield, who would grow up to become Duchess of Windsor; she was taken to Old White by her grandmother, who had been going there for much of *her* life. The original Old White burned down in 1922, and its successor, the Greenbrier, has since been consistently kept in step with the progressively less Spartan tastes of the old-family rich and their tycoon pals. The Duke and Duchess of Windsor were largely responsible for the resort's preservation as a center of fashion after World War II, as they made it a regular stop on their endless caravan along with Palm Beach, Newport, New York, and their home base, Paris (with side trips to whatever lavishly appointed environs they could crowbar an invitation to). Their entourage included such stalwarts of the PB crowd as Mrs. Robert Young and her late railroad magnate husband (she is the sister of Georgia O'Keeffe and still a PB force), the Charles Wrightsmans, the C. Z. Guests, and the Woolworth Donahues.

Although the Greenbrier, like the Homestead and all of even the most exclusive resorts, now hosts business conferences and the like to keep baths and soul together during the long winter months, and there is a limit to how exclusive you can be with more than a thousand guests at any one time, its clientele still reflects the lavish and social bias of those years. Anyone making reservations is sent a dress code, which runs heavily toward the Izod–Lilly Pulitzer look; one does not wear shorts except to play golf or tennis. The prices are equally lofty, running up to $300 per person per day.

The Homestead, on the other hand, appeals to the sort of people who are proud to be going where grandmother did, even if it means a little dust in one's hair from the crumbling plaster— people who in fact rather look down on a place like the Greenbrier as too Worth Avenue. When the former Janet Auchincloss, now Mrs. Bingham W. Morris, spent one recent Christmas at the Homestead, she recalled that she used to bring her children Jacqueline Onassis and Lee Radziwill there for vacations decades ago, and added that the place now looked "just about the same" as it did then. In those days, the twenties and thirties, it was Mrs. Cornelius Vanderbilt's summer headquarters, and even in those times of the dominance of high society the publicity annoyed some of the more staid guests. There has been no successor to Mrs. Vanderbilt. Otherwise, things have indeed remained the same at the Homestead—except that everything is forty years older, and there has been little effort to renew it. Still, the glorious setting of the hotel's noble tower against the sixteen thousand acres of wilderness in the blue mountains has been enough to attract generations of various Vanderbilts, Phippses, Kennedys, Rockefellers, Mellons, and Fords. Today, it is a classically shabby-genteel place where nobody really knows how much money anybody has, except that everybody has some and some probably have quite a lot. Anyway, it still serves probably the most important purpose of any resort. Joan Tobin, who visited with her parents from Cincinnati and still does now that she lives in Washington, told *Town & Country*, "It was like going to your grandmother's house—or as close to it as you can get. It is a crazy and wonderful place, a nice safe place to get your children started socially."

PART 3
ACTING RICH

Mary Kay Ash with some of her favorite saleswomen.
*(Shelly Katz/*People *Weekly* © *1980 Time Inc.)*

Mary Kay Ash wins the key to the city of Houston, at a
presentation in the Astrodome.
(AP/Wide World Photos)

Babe Paley, one of the best dressed
women of 1949.
(*AP/Wide World Photos*)

Babe Paley with her husband, William Paley.
(*AP/Wide World Photos*)

Jacqueline De Ribes, one of the
members of the Best Dressed
Hall of Fame.
(AP/Wide World Photos)

Katharine Graham and Nancy Reagan at the 50th
anniversary celebration of *Newsweek* magazine.
(AP/Wide World Photos)

Rebekah Harkness.
(AP/Wide World Photos)

Dina Merrill and Cary Grant at a film premiere.
(UPI/Bettmann Archive)

Yoko Ono, with her son, Sean (left), and Julian (right), Lennon's
son from a previous marriage, breaking ground at Central Park
ceremonies honoring John Lennon.
(*UPI/Bettmann Archive*)

Wanda Ferragamo and the
Ferragamo clan.
*(David Lees/*People *Weekly © 1983
Time Inc.)*

Susanna Agnelli in her office.
(AP/Wide World Photos)

Carolina Herrera (in dark trousers) is congratulated after the
showing of her 1984 fall line.
(*AP/Wide World Photos*)

Leona and Harry Helmsley relaxing in their New York apartment.
*(Co Rentmeester/*People *Weekly © 1980 Time Inc.)*

12 | The Look

SINCE IT IS in the nature of being rich that one knows about it from first consciousness, every rich girl grows up "acting rich" one way or the other. Basically, there are two ways to go: to rebel, like the Edies and Sashas, or eventually to act out the lessons of rich behavior that have been ingrained from first light by parents, teachers, and peers. The great majority of rich women, of course, opt for the latter course (which allows a certain stylized wild period in the teens and twenties, bearing only a superficial resemblance to serious rebellion). And the first part of being rich is getting The Look.

The simplest way to acquire The Look is, naturally, through your genes, but just about anybody can have it with enough money—and nearly tireless devotion to it. The first thing about The Look is that it is meant to show that a great deal of work and money has gone into it. Forget your ideas of rich women as healthy, devil-may-care New Englanders utterly unconcerned with the size of the trust funds (as long as it has *some* size) or the latest current fashion, with their quaint notions that crow's feet and strong arms make women attractive. On the other hand, we are not talking about vulgar display, even in the case of the glitter set. We are talking about refined display. People who work on The Look know precisely how much they've spent on it, so naturally they know how much everybody else has. This is another area in which if you have to ask, you can't afford it. Having Way Bandy come to your house to put on makeup, or Monsieur Marc for your hair, or going to one of the Paris *maisons de couture* for your evening clothes, or toning your chassis at the Golden Door, or picking up a bauble at Harry Winston's—these are all activities that necessitate simply charging and waiting for your husband to pay. Advertisements for cosmetics, always implying an association with luxury, are becoming more explicit—in the case of the new and hyperexpensive La Prairie line, for example, Ann Getty and other socially significant women of a "certain age" will appear in ads in return for contributions to their choice of charities.

The single most important part of The Look is narrowness. One must try always to look like a destroyer about to slice through a submarine. It is hard to tell exactly where this manic preoccupation with thinness came from. From the 1920s on, however, the mood of world fashion has constantly been in favor of emaciation; indeed, the world of the very rich has been the cutting force in the drive toward ultimate thinness. At a time when the prevailing popular male fantasies were Rita Hayworth and Marilyn Monroe, for example, Barbara Hutton was being so browbeaten by her husbands about the untoward size of her breasts that she turned herself into one of the world's first known anorectics. (Since then, as usual, bourgeois taste has fallen into line behind the rich and elegant. Raquel Welch is perhaps the last movie star to have a body in the old style. Being outright flat-chested is not normally considered a bar to sexiness anymore, even in middlebrow culture. The very skin magazines, which pushed the whole bosom fantasy in the first place, have featured spreads of what used to be referred to as "boards"; and even the centerfolds have lost inches off their waists and hips over the past thirty years. Nobody wants to be 36–24–36 anymore.) The line, "You can't be too thin or too rich" can be taken as the anthem of the world's self-consciously upper-class women for the past half a century. The standards that have been held up as cynosures in this crowd have remained remarkably similar over the past few decades.

One of the acclaimed beauties of the twentieth century, Babe Cushing, was described this way in 1947, just before her marriage to William Paley, by *Vogue* photographer Erwin Blumenfeld: "The shape of her face is as attenuated as an El Greco. She has the most luminous skin imaginable and only Velázquez could paint her coloring on canvas. Her mouth is like that of the fascinating Madame Arnoux in Flaubert's novel *Education Sentimentale*. She has the gentleness, poise and the dignity of one of those grandes dames whom Balzac described in his *Comédie Humaine*. As for her clothes, instead of merely wearing them, she carries them." The idea, for those *Vogue* readers not thoroughly grounded in Western art and literature, seems to be that Mrs. Paley was very thin, long, and glowing. This pale, glowing look—it might also be termed porcelain—is one of the mountaintops every rich woman would like to scale. This look's present exponent nonpareil is Vicomtesse Jacqueline de Ribes, who is accorded the same sorts of accolades in the fashion press as Babe Paley and takes a backseat to nobody in attenuated and luminous. The goal of all these women seems to be to acquire skin so white that admirers can number the veins beneath. Hence, facials are of extreme importance. The Erno Laszlo approach, spurred by the Duchess of Windsor's patronage, started the trend; Georgette Klinger (stores in New York, Beverly Hills, Dallas, Chicago, Bal Harbour, and Palm Beach) and a host of imitators have followed. Bianca Jagger has a facial every day at noon at Janet Sartin in New York, no matter how late she has been out the night before.

Tan is still rich-looking and probably always will be, especially among the South Americans and some of the sun-starved northern European nobility; but now it is suffering under the disability of carcinogenic associations, added to what the resort-going rich already knew better than anyone—that it turns that lovely porcelain skin to leather.

Rich women share with many of their poorer sisters a craving for the new in cosmetics—a thirsting that the Estée Lauders, Adrienne Arpels, and Princess Marcella Borgheses ("once an honest-to-God resident of the Borghese Palace," reminds the princess's flack) of the world are happy to slake as part of their drive to join the rich in the drawing room as well as the beauty shop. The favored porcelain look dictates that heavy rouging is gauche. What makeup should do is highlight the much-desired high cheekbones, which are an important component of looking attenuated, and make the nose look good, which is to say Roman and distinguished, if that has not already been done by surgery. Jacqueline de Ribes is the *loca classica* of both those anatomical points; her cheekbones are the highest and roundest this side of Tibet, and her nose, which she delights in exhibiting in profile for the camera, is the sort of aristocratic protuberance that most American princesses would have had bobbed before they even thought of appearing in junior high school. A medium-red lipstick, worn religiously throughout the day, is *de rigueur*. The remainder of one's makeup is dedicated to enhancing the color of the eyes—dark blue is fine—and moving the eyebrows up for even more of that attenuated look. Some dedicated seekers after The Look have been known to trace the veins on their temples in blue eyeliner to make themselves appear even more like marble statues. And glasses are big; sunglasses can be glamorous, and even reading glasses are a useful prop for the rich woman's constant restlessness. Moreover, the recent fad for useful work among rich women has apotheosized the glasses-on-the-head bit. Jacqueline de Ribes has reportedly been seen in Le Cirque wearing glasses on both her skull and her nose at the same time.

Hair, of course, is one of the great preoccupations of the rich women of the world. There are two basic styles that qualify as The Look among the old-line, middle-aged rich. One is the tight chignon, which has always been fashionable and is given currency by the Vicomtesse de Ribes. This is an evening look of great severity; its problem is that it gives expensive hairdressers little room to show their creativity, and thus might not even show how expensive they are. The other old stand-by is the bouffant with a simple little flip, the whole held tightly in place by all sorts of modern chemicals. Gloria Vanderbilt is perhaps its best-known proponent now—before her it was the Duchess of Windsor and Jacqueline Kennedy—but it is pandemic among the old line such as Marylou Whitney or, for that matter, Nancy Reagan. Such hair does indeed appear ready to crack if the wearer were tipped over, as Joan Rivers always insists. The likes of Monsieur Marc are constantly trying to get their darlings to do a little something different, and in fact they have managed to add a little puffiness and looseness to the basic style. Another important trend in that direction has been the emergence of the Texas contingent; Lynn Wyatt, for example, wears her hair loose and flowing—blown-dry somewhat less stiffly than the average country club matron. So does Carolyn Farb, representative of the charming young things in Houston, who does it more wildly than her somewhat senior competitor on the Texas circuit. According to Monsieur Marc, who in 1983 felt compelled to record his observations on the society he so carefully embellishes,[27] this particular look was created in the middle of the 1960s as Baby Jane Holzer's lion's mane. It can still be seen in modified form on a good number of women, rich or not; those who are wealthy and working, such as Carolina Herrera, tend to appreciate its modified-trendy air, though Mrs. Herrera has also been known to appear in Le Cirque with something approaching a crewcut, the high-school-girl-who's-tough-but-doesn't-want-to-antagonize-everybody look. In Marc's assessment, for what it's worth, shorter hair is younger-looking at any age, and crucial for anyone over forty.

Dyeing—well, "highlighting"—is another important function, perhaps the most important, of the rich woman's hairdresser. One of the wonderful aspects of wealth is that it prevents the appearance of grey hair. It is simply a blank spot in the rich woman's ledger, just as there is no hospital in Palm Beach. (Babe Paley was an exception that proved the rule.) Blondes are the most desirable female animals among the rich as in other social groupings, but the natural ones nevertheless find it important to enhance things or to add some henna that helps tone down the ghostly effect of all that porcelain skin and light hair. Brunettes, of course, want to keep that dinginess away; they might also go for something along the lines of a "tortoiseshell" effect with some dark striations.

The Look, junior version, is a classic case of youth being wasted on the young. The women in their fifties working on The Look would *die* for naturally smooth skin, glowing hair, and those inimitably tight bodies. But those who possess them either do not care what happens to them, or actually do not know what to do about it. It is not as bad as the black days of the 1960s, when Marylou Whitney had to send the kids to the shower before they came to dinner. And in fact there are some young heiresses—European princesses, Texas belles, Cornelia Guest—who appear very interested in their mothers' concerns of what looks proper in every detail. But, between the freewheeling sex lives

27. *Nouveau is Better Than No Riche At All* (N.Y.: G. P. Putnam's Sons).

that the last two decades have brought into the open among the youthful rich, and the at least nominal commitment to "doing something" that has become all the rage, even the scionettes inclined to the intricacies of fashion hardly have the endless time needed to do it right. And, of course, they can—maddeningly— get away without all that much makeup at all. They tend to follow the trends in hair that start somewhere in the freaky middle class and then end up in the salons in SoHo; or else they simply let it grow long and stay there. Their clothes generally make them indistinguishable from the merely rich and spoiled kids from the suburbs, except perhaps for an extralavish lynx coat or some earrings that mother got from Harry Winston. But mostly they would rather hang around with the current celebrities: not Andy Warhol, who might be marginally acceptable to their mothers now at some event or other, but the present-day spiritual descendants of Edie. But even here it seems unfair to the middle-aged seekers of The Look. As Diana Vreeland noted with respect to Edie, "I've never seen anyone on drugs that didn't have wonderful skin." Or—the most unfair of all—those who look like rich women, because they are so beautiful and are hanging all over rich men, frequently turn out to be rich only with the money given them by the men—much closer spiritually to Vicki Morgan than to Mary Clark Rockefeller Morgan. So what that they will never be invited to Le Cirque or a party of Brooke Astor's, will have no occasion to wear Yves' latest. Furs and diamonds look even richer, to the outside world, than The Look alone. And the utterly galling part about it is that nobody under thirty-five really gives a damn about The Look at all.

There are more powerful aids than all the fuss of hairdressers and makeup artists. Cosmetic surgery is, of course, one of the things that was invented specifically for the rich, and it continues to be used by them liberally. It is a perfect thing for the wealthy: it not only costs a great deal of money for something essentially frivolous; it also requires that one have perhaps two months off to recover without looking hideous in public. Facelifts have always been and doubtless always will be the most important piece of cosmetic surgery: the fountain of lifelong youth. Women craving The Look know that, when they come out of their bruised seclusion, they will not actually appear miraculously younger; among the people they mix with, everyone can spot the signs, so they simply look like someone with a face job. But the great advantage not necessarily affecting the merely upper-middle class is that, as actresses have long since discovered, photographs don't show the scars. Among the wealthy celebrities who have benefitted are known to be Jacqueline Onassis, Betty Ford, and Queen Elizabeth; and it is a good bet that in any party full of the mature glitterati—"women of experience," as the euphemism has it—most of the faces have the telltale tugs and strains at the back of the temples and under the jaws.

New York or Beverly Hills hairdressers with that kind of clientele expend a good deal of their talent on cover-up work. And the prevalence of the facelift gives an added *frisson* of bravado to a woman's decision to wear her hair tightly pulled back to a formal occasion. There are other, semisurgical treatments as well, such as dermabrasions, which Manhattan celebrity doctor Norman Orentreich uses to remove wrinkles from the upper layer of skin; removing skin with acid via "chemosurgery"; or the nonsurgical lift that hairdresser George Masters achieves by simply pulling the hair back tightly, the skin with it, then popping on a wig.

Facelifts are by no means the entire repertoire, however, and the other choices are getting more popular every year. Less drastic facial alterations—nose jobs and eye tucks—are no longer rare, especially among the rich ladies who started out as actresses or models and are depending on their looks to carry them through a substantial marriage or a successful remarriage. Breast alterations seem to be confined to the movie community, silicon having gotten a bad press. But perhaps the most popular new frontier in plastic surgery is the great middle of the female body, with its depressing tendency to start off imperfect and then sag into shapelessness. "Tushy tucks" are the most important of the group. But probably the most eagerly awaited are various experimental and still questionable procedures that someday soon may be able to remove unsightly inches from the silhouette of thighs and stomach. It can't come soon enough for the women who have grown up believing that money should be able to buy anything, including themselves.

Many of the world's wealthy women can easily name a few of the best-known plastic surgeons—Thomas D. Rees, Vincent Michael Hogan, and John M. Converse in New York, and Robin L. Beare in London. But the one that most of them, and perhaps all with any international connections, would know is Dr. Ivo Pitanguy, who is not only the most famous doctor in Brazil, the world's capital of plastic surgery, but possibly the best-known socialite in Rio de Janeiro as well—no small achievement in a wide-open city whose daily excitement level is only slightly below the madness of Carnival. Pitanguy's specialty makes him a modern prince in Brazil, a culture whose preoccupation with youthful beauty makes the United States look like Vatican City by comparison. Vinícius de Morais, the country's best-known living poet, turned a widely quoted apostrophe that summarizes public sentiment; it reads in translation, "You homely people, I'm sorry to say it, but beauty is fundamental." Brazil is, of course, a heavily male-dominated society, so that women have barely thought of contesting their mates' preferences. Since Brazil is also such a young country—more than half the population of Rio is under eighteen—that preference is for tightly constructed, skinny, small-breasted, smooth-skinned women. And then Rio is beach country, so one's flaws all over the body are constantly subject to scrutiny. Hence, Pitanguy has had a wide-open field to create surgical procedures for improving virtually every part of the anatomy. He is credited with a number of important innovations. His most widely known is the thigh-and-buttock lift, which has removed "riding breeches" from the middles of much of Rio's *haut monde*; it is not widely used elsewhere, however, apparently because surgeons in Europe and the United States find that their patients are actually shaped differently from Brazilian women. But another Pitanguy technique *is* widely accepted now—the stomach-tightening incision at the bikini line that removes the bulge caused by bad genes or childbirth. Among Pitanguy's patients, numbering over twenty thousand, have been, he says, "lots of queens and princes," including Princess Farah Diba, Jacqueline Onassis, Brazil's First Lady Dulce Guimaraes de Figueiredo, and men of the same circuit, like the Italian publicist Count Rudi Crespi. The prices for his work, such as $10,000 for a facelift with eye tucks (comparable fees in New York are $4,000 to $6,000), enable Pitanguy to join his patients on equal terms in the social minuet. He frequently flies a few of his manufactured beauties in his private plane for weekends on his private island, Ilha dos Porcos, in the bay south of Rio. It was named Pigs' Island long before Pitanguy bought it.

13 | The Spas

IN THE SUMMER of 1982, a previously obscure New York stock-broker, Alexander Papamarkou, surfaced like a nuclear subma-rine in the rarefied air of the world's unforgettably rich. His vehicle, which may have surprised the uninitiated, was a week-long sort of house party at a spa in Escondido, California, called the Golden Door. Papamarkou invited thirty guests from the worlds of wealth and celebrity, or preferably both, including Ann Getty, the San Francisco hostess who is married to the reclusive billionaire Gordon P. Getty (he, emphatically, did not attend); Barbara Walters; Mrs. H. John Heinz III, wife of the senator from Pennsylvania, making a bid to match the social achievement of her mother-in-law Drue Heinz; Princess Pilar, the sister of King Juan Carlos of Spain; Dr. Jonas Salk, the polio vaccine man, and his wife, the artist Françoise Gilot, who is the mother of Paloma Picasso; together with a rich assortment of Greeks and Texans of renown. Even with the 15 percent discount the grateful health farm gave Papamarkou, his bill for the week ran to something over $50,000. Aside from its contribution to Papamarkou's social standing, the week's standing in the folklore of society was to fully expose the Golden Door, whose prime renown had until then been limited to those of the thin-and-avant-and-rich circuit. It gave fair notice that fitness had invaded the realm of the superwealthy: starvation alone was no longer a proper way for women to remain thin, and men too had to begin attending to their bodies.

Papamarkou himself had already introduced the Golden Door to society by writing an article for *Town & Country* earlier in 1982 about Men's Week. (There are nine men's weeks and seven for couples, the rest an entirely female experience.) In recent years, all the fashion and society publications, as well as most newspapers around the country, have taken note of the place, which was created by Deborah Szekely in 1958. (Cristina Ferrare did a big spread there for *Harper's Bazaar* in 1980, in preindictment days.) Its price, if nothing else, would make it worthy of contemplation: at $2,500 a week, it is apparently the most expensive spa in the world. In many ways, the Golden Door is the distillation of what rich women want when they go away for a week to pamper themselves. That is hardly a surprise, considering that it is one of the first such operations to shift from the traditional "fat farm" stereotype, prevalent in the forties, to a holistic approach that has since come to dominate the entire spa and health field. Mrs. Szekely, who grew up in what was once considered the oddball world of natural living, has come to be looked on as a minor guru in the world of fitness. With its combination of flagellant-level, twelve-hour workouts, and its shameless pampering of guests—gourmet if tiny meals, personal kimono-based wardrobes, 120 staff members for the maximum of thirty-four guests, the spa's own line of cosmetics in every room, Golden Door stationery with the guest's name embossed in gold—the Golden Door has achieved a remarkable dual reputation. It is known both as one of the haughty and exclusive places in the world, and as one of the most Spartan, serene, other-worldly, and effective of spas. In short, it perfectly serves the dual aim of high-minded great wealth: to preserve one's privacy but still to have it known how wonderful one is. "We don't get many nouveaux riches or second wives," Mrs. Szekely has noted, "because they don't want to work so hard." What they do get are the hardworking rich of the Hollywood world—Dyan Cannon, Leigh Taylor-Young, Piper Laurie, and Zsa Zsa Gabor have been regulars—along with the wives and daughters of great men of money, such as Bobo Rockefeller, Sophie Gimbel, Polly Guggenheim, and Karen Mellon.

Over on the coast, but not too far from the Golden Door, is a world of difference, and not only because La Costa is always coed. Since it was built in 1968 with money from the much-investigated Teamsters Central States Pension Fund, La Costa has stood for everything garish and overdone in California. Here one has an excellent chance of running into—and being snubbed by—a movie star or some of the rich people who like to hang around with them. Talking about nouveaux, this is where Mary Cunningham retreated during the unpleasantness about her alleged closeness with William Agee at the Bendix Corporation. The crowd runs heavily to the Frank Sinatra–Republican Mafia types that predominate also in the towns of surrounding Orange County. The place, which has a lot more rooms to fill than the Golden Door, sells itself as being "pleasantly affordable," and its press release adds that one of the reasons for going is that "guests can often mingle with celebrities on an equal basis." The health and exercise facilities are, it is true, among the most impressive in the world; there are fifty-five thousand square feet of the most modern facilities, a full regimen of strenuous workouts, and (of course) La Costa's own line of vitamin supplements and foods. However, the thousand-calorie gourmet dinners can be and frequently are replaced by the uncountable-calorie feasts in the complex's four other restaurants, while the siren call of unending shopping opportunities generally wipes out the good intentions of the first day or two in the gym. At $200 per person per day at the bottom—affordable for Golden Door regulars, perhaps—La Costa is a good place to be surrounded by the latest in all sorts of recreational facilities and to entertain the fantasy that everyone in the world is Californian and rich.

If the Golden Door is the queen of American spas, the Greenhouse, outside Dallas, is the crown princess. Indeed, much of the Greenhouse is patterned after the Golden Door, from its small size and lavish staffing levels (one hundred workers for thirty-four guests, always all women) to the cost ($2,450 a week, but who's counting?) to the delicately cooked low-calorie meals. But the Greenhouse has none of the Spartan dedication and Oriental simplicity that mark the Golden Door. Breakfast is served in bed so that milady should not feel *too* out of the womb. The exercises, while mandatory, are considerably less strenuous than those at the western cousin. Where the Golden Door would have a massage, the Greenhouse has a makeup session. Moreover, the Greenhouse's idea of inner peace is not an hour of quiet contemplation wrapped in a Japanese herbed sheet, but a lecture on fine jewelry or needlepoint, or the weekly fashion show by Neiman-Marcus, which comes accompanied by an opportunity to order from a catalog for delivery before departure, as well as a limousined trip to the store in Dallas one afternoon of the stay. Everyone wears indistinguishable leotards during the day, but for dinner the Halston dresses are pulled out like daggers. It is, in short, basically a place for latter-day southern belles, women who have not done a whole lot in their lives up to this point and hardly intend to start now. The Greenhouse does get its share of live wires: Liza Minnelli has been there, and the late Princess Grace, and Elizabeth Taylor, and Brooke Shields, and Estée Lauder, and the late Perle Mesta. But many of its clientele are from among the really social rich—Leonore Annenberg, Mary Lasker, the Duchess of Windsor. President Johnson sent the dumpy Lady Bird to the Greenhouse for a week and was so pleased with her discovery that there was such a thing as fashion that he quickly packed off his two roundish daughters, Luci Baines and Lynda Bird, for the same treatment.

There is really nothing in Europe quite like the modern American spas, since the European's watering-places traditionally grew up as resort towns alongside "the waters" and have mostly evolved into places much more like the Greenbrier than the Golden Door. Still, there are several that are known for their attractiveness to the *haut monde,* if not their ability to carve off poundage. Perhaps the simplest, and among the toniest, is Eugénie-les-Bains, which retains its exclusivity by being tucked into the southwestern corner of France far from the tourist hordes. About all there is to do in Eugénie-les-Bains is take a dip in the hot springs and then go to dinner at Les Prés et les Sources d'Eugénie, the famed restaurant where Michel Guérard developed the *nouvelle cuisine.* The swank island of Ischia is bubbling over with hot springs; the town of Lacco Ameno, with its Hotel Regina Isabella e Royal Sporting, features radioactive water used for mud baths and heated sand baths. Germany features the spas at Baden-Baden and Wiesbaden, both resort towns with illustrious histories and luxurious presents. Baden-Baden even has the Lancaster Beauty

Farm in the famous Brenner's Park Hotel, which includes a regimen of massages, skin conditioning sessions, gymnastics, and water-exercise classes, combined with a controlled-calorie diet from the fabulous menu at the hotel. For the most part, however, European spas are based much more on relaxation and skin preparation than any serious attempt at weight loss. They are good for the glowing, plump look, unless you go to St. Moritz and spend your nonbathing time on the slopes. All of them, however, are extremely pleasant places to be a rich woman.

14 | What Is Taffeta, Anyway?

Once one has achieved the face and body of a rich woman, of course, the necessary remaining part of The Look is one's clothing and jewelry. It is part of being rich that one *may* look any way one wants, and certainly many rich women could hardly be picked out of a crowd as anything special. Electra Waggoner Biggs, to take one, is perfectly capable of sitting around the ranch in a nondescript housedress of an unremarkable blue. It's hard to imagine paying little enough for that dress—though she is also known to don the de la Rentas when headed to a party. Women who work for their money, or for their husbands, do not normally dress very much differently from their more stylish saleswomen; Mary Kay Ash, who is notorious for her collection of outrageous evening dresses that are decidedly not close to The Look, wears an ordinary tan suit to the office, though she indulges her passion for the *outré* with some peculiar costume jewelry. Heiresses under forty, unless they happen to be Cornelia Guest, do not usually spend time on The Look; they dress, for the most part, like their upper-middle-class colleagues. No, you do not acquire The Look as a birthright, and there are women without fashion sense who persist in trying but fail miserably. But to achieve The Look you need the time to shop endlessly and, of course, the money to buy all those dresses at $5,000 a pop. Money is not a criterion of style, say Lynn Wyatt, Marylou Whitney, Jacqueline de Ribes, and the rest of the best-dressed list who have never had to worry about it.[28] ("I'm very down-to-earth," de Ribes the designer told the *New York Times*. "This craziness that my clothes are too expensive, for example. Everything I have is between $1,500 and $5,000. I know the price of every piece of fabric and I die when I can't use something because it's too expensive." Carolina Herrera is continually sunk in the swamp of disappointment over the precious fabrics she cannot use because they would price her things out of the market.) These fashionplates lie, of course, when they say the best-dressed list is not contingent on wealth. But this is not a vicious lie; it is not meant to be taken seriously. It is Rich Ladies Talk, which is used to communicate with each other when there are poorer people listening, something like spelling or speaking French around the children. Rich Ladies Talk usually involves a partial truth. In this case what they mean is that money is not *all* that one needs for The Look. The other things are inherent taste, time, stamina, and the ability to get along with couturiers.

There are actually two components to The Look: daytime and nighttime wear. For daytime, solid clothes in unexceptional colors and as many natural fabrics as possible are important. They are all, of course, done by the important designers—Marc Bohan for Dior, Yves St. Laurent, Oscar de la Renta, Bill Blass, Galanos, Adolfo—but there is no particular single style insisted upon. It can be relatively simple dresses, pants with jackets, skirts with jackets, pants-and-sweater combinations. The jackets are cut, recently, with fullish, butterfly sleeves that are generally difficult to keep out of one's lunch but do serve the purpose of making one's forearms and fingers look elegantly spare. The most important part of clothes' function in The Look for daytime is that they contribute to the long, lean lines that are so prized by the coddled rich. To this end, flowing scarves are important; this is

28. The remainder of recent best-dressed lists is a useful, though incomplete, list of the world's richest women. It includes Dewi Sukarno, the Begum Aga Khan, Baronne Olympia de Rothschild, Pamela Harriman and the Empress Farah Diba.

the look that Marylou Whitney affects one day when she is off to lunch at Le Cirque, the green woolen shift with matching scarf wrapped several times around the neck and tossed with painstaking carelessness over a shoulder.

For overclothes, of course, since furs tend to be so bulky and yet so rich-looking, it is important that they be long and, unless one is very thin and very young, dark; full-length sables will do nicely. Then, accessories are important; the nonmatching scarves should be Hermès, as should bags; shoes can be by Chanel, Delman, or Gucci; anything leather can be Loewe, which has arrived in force as the latest retailer shamelessly claiming to be the most expensive in the world at what it does. The more common initials all over something are generally looked down upon; the more rarified type, something like the Hermès H, are preferred to the interlocking LVs of Louis Vuitton or all those silly Gucci stripes, although everyone admits the Vuitton luggage does last forever.

Evening wear is something entirely different. While it is not impossible to have The Look in the forever-elegant black and pearls, most rich people have found, especially since the Reagans brought unabashed class back to the country, that less is less. Why have it if you can't show it off? So for the past five years it has been designer heaven. In this incarnation, The Look is unmistakable. Its first manifestation is that the dress says clearly that it could never be worn anywhere except to this particular event—that the wearer has $5,000 or $10,000 to spend just for tonight. The most extreme statements of this kind could be taken from the collections of Jacqueline de Ribes and Carolina Herrera, who both earned their spurs as designers by buying every other designer's clothes first. The vicomtesse, a disciple of Yves St. Laurent, believes in severe, starchy elegance. Her clothes flow to the floor, are meant to be worn by women who can walk like hangers all evening. Frequently they have dramatic cutouts in the back. The lines are of Greek austerity. Many of her gowns have great puffed shoulders, or perhaps a huge bow at the neckline, producing the effect of the face peeking out from an orchid on a satiny stem. Herrera has done the same sort of thing—to a fault, some would say, even in the overcooked-fashion circle. Her sleeves tend to be so outrageous that one is tempted to giggle. Carolina Herrera is known throughout her slice of the world as a woman whose back never touches her chair, and her dresses reflect the theory that style is discipline, not comfort.

This is obviously dressing to accentuate not merely the body, but the artist deep in these women's seeking souls.[29] They are rather equivalent to Mummers in the Philadelphia New Year's Day parade, marching in concoctions of feathers and bangles.

It is only by the general acquisition of a camp sensibility that the audience declines to laugh. The point, as it has been for hundreds of years in high fashion, is to celebrate the distance from the workaday world. Haute couture is the long fingernails of Western civilization. The determined pursuit of impracticality extends to the materials. Velvet, satin, chiffon, organza, and taffeta are preferred, with the much-remarked upshot that a fashionable dinner party sounds like a flock of doves when it enters the dining room, all rustling and cooing. Then there are the omnipresent gay touches like rows of beads—rhinestones, crystals, whatever—and metallic cloth. The daytime preference for simplicity and sparse ornamentation goes by the boards. It is one of the wonderful qualities of big money that it provides endless room for change, for inconsistency; and having radically different clothes for day and evening is as much a way of advertising that freedom as is travel. The trends of The Look for both daytime and evening—minus some of the European fashionable excess—are expressed for most rich "women of a certain age" by James Galanos. His collection never bothers with Japanese influences or Left Bank creations. He always has the flowing scarves, the puffy sleeves, the sweeping backs that flatter well-cared-for but nevertheless aging figures. Since the well-known patronage of Nancy Reagan, Galanos has pulled California couture level with whatever Paris can offer.

Partying with the Help

Nowhere is the peculiarly vacuous nature of high style more evident than in the composition of the parties that all these highly wrought creations are worn to. It was Charlotte Curtis who first

29. Since they have both entered the working world—with a vengeance, turning their previous hard-socializing existences into hard-working, world-touring events—both these women take great pains to insist that their designs are by no means all for frivolous socialites. "My clothes are, mainly, just very feminine," says Carolina Herrera. "Women who have pretty legs and tiny waists should take advantage of them. And my clothes always use the best materials. They are a little expensive [the cheapest is $800], but they are classics. They can always be worn." Jacqueline de Ribes says she tries to make clothes that the elegant woman can wear to work and then right out to her dinner-party.

noted that nowadays the high-society lady finds herself seated next to her hairdresser at dinner. When Cornelia Guest had her eighteenth birthday party at Mortimer's restaurant in Manhattan, her guests included Fabrice, who made her dress, Way Bandy, who did her makeup, and Francesco Scavullo, who took her birthday portrait. One of the gala evenings of the 1983 New York season was a twenty-five-year retrospective of Yves St. Laurent fashions organized by Diana Vreeland at the Metropolitan Museum. Monsieur Marc recently published an entire book explaining how he has "traveled far with his scissors, his gun, and his dinner jacket." Marc, Bill Blass, Oscar de la Renta, and Galanos attend state dinners at the White House. (Which can cause problems. At a dinner for the president of the Dominican Republic in the spring of 1984, Nancy Reagan's dinner partner was the Dominican Oscar de la Renta. Unfortunately, she wore a Bill Blass dress.)

This phenomenon of letting the servants eat upstairs is something that has happened as part of the general breakdown of society based on birth. As Estée Lauder got rich, it didn't matter that she was essentially a salesgirl; the wives of men who were out scrambling in the marketplace to keep them in their Palm Beach digs decided they could hardly object to her bourgeois interests. Designers like Givenchy, St. Laurent, Karl Lagerfeld, Valentino, Pierre Cardin, Halston, Oscar de la Renta, and Bill Blass, not to mention Ralph Lauren and Calvin Klein, all pull down huge incomes, many of them in seven figures, through the modern miracle of franchising agreements; those figures make them able to live as well as the richest of their customers, and certainly make them the envy of the members of the circle who are trying to live off the interest of an estate that has been partitioned for one generation too many. Of course, the designers generally had more taste than the people they were designing for; thus, for people whose central goal in life is looking right, it made sense to keep them around more and more, as advisers and especially as certifiers of one's correctness.

It was, then, only a small step from the fashion show for charity to dinner parties given by designers that attracted all the women of The Look. Bill Blass, for example, got much of his early patronage by meeting future customers at the Stork Club, El Morocco, and the other stomping grounds of fifties society. Then he turned into an invaluable "extra man" for women whose husbands had the annoying habit of tending to moneymaking when there were parties to attend. Finally, he graduated to his current status: Blass hosts a $30,000 party every year for the benefit of a music school, and donates $10,000 to run a fundraiser at the New York Public Library—both events of obvious high seriousness but which are happily leavened by dozens of Blass creations. (It is no longer a matter of shame to meet another woman in your dress; in fact, it has become something of a badge, like spotting another girl in a St. Tim's uniform on the Metroliner.)

Oscar de la Renta raised the social-climbing designer act to an art form. Born in Santo Domingo as Oscar Renta, he worked for a while for the House of Lanvin in Paris, then arrived in New York in 1963. He quickly hired himself a press agent and began escorting C. Z. Guest to parties. But his real success began with his marriage in 1967 to Françoise de Langlade, a former editor of French *Vogue* with a true passion for social manipulation. Until her death in 1983, Françoise de la Renta was one of the most important hostesses in New York. She was among those responsible for the careful blending of corporate chiefs, current or retired government officials, a few presentable journalists or intellectuals, some of the old-line rich, and a fashionable producer or actress to make the classic power dinner party. The wheel had turned: the designer, once no more than a lowly seamstress to be sent to the attic when the party started, was now actually giving parties himself. And people were flocking to them. There are few more reliable ways of drawing a crowd of extremely wealthy women than to invite Bill Blass. Clothes may make the man, but designers make the woman.

But clothes are not everything. Jewelry is everything.

15 | All That Glitters

ONE RECENT GORGEOUS WINTER DAY, Liz Whitney Tippett and Zsa Zsa Gabor were observed observing the Palm Beach Steeplechase at the Palm Beach Polo and Country Club, the outpost of the Gold Coast well upcountry in the unfashionable interior of Florida. Their entire interchange appeared to consist of a comparison of the diamonds they wore on their fingers, wrists, necks, and other exposed places.

Audemars Piguet, one of the lesser-known manufacturers of watches whose prices start in four figures, runs ads in *Town & Country* with headlines that read, "Adolfo knows. Peter Duchin knows. Douglas Fairbanks, Jr., knows. Ann Getty knows. Dina Merrill knows. Robert Mondavi knows. Franklin D. Roosevelt, Jr., knows. Arthur Schlesinger, Jr., knows. Geraldine Stutz knows."

As the copywriter knows, nothing separates the poor girls from the rich women faster than jewelry. With the possible exception of a few highly refined drugs, there is nothing like jewelry for being able to carry on one's person the lifetime earnings of the average middle-class worker. It has always been thus, and it always will be. There is something about jewelry so fine, so pure, so undisputed, so indestructible, so beautiful, that it is universally acknowledged as the badge of wealth and distinction. The impressiveness of a big diamond is beyond the power of cavil. Moreover, as a concession to the rich women's husbands, diamonds have in recent years been one of the best investments in the world, a reflection of the control exercised by the great De Beers monopoly.

The consumption of great jewelry is one of the most breathtaking exercises of the richest women in the world. Barbara Hutton's largesse was legendary: she would drop gems on husbands, relatives, and casual friends without a second thought. When she was in a Rome hospital suffering from a broken leg—she had, typically, tripped over a carpet in her hotel room—the jeweler Gianni Bulgari, knowing her reputation, pestered her unmercifully until she finally bought some sapphires to get rid of him. She offered them to her nurse, but they were turned down; she finally gave the woman a check for $5,000 to pay for an operation her husband needed. She gave the gems to Countess Consuelo Crespi instead.

In more recent times, that sort of excessive consumption has generally been inhibited by public outrage at the Hutton level of in-your-face spending, as well as an awareness that general knowledge of one's incredible wealth simply invites burglary attempts and other untoward intentions. Still, *somebody* is continuing to spend enormous sums on the estate jewelry that constitutes the bulk of the fabulous gems that come on the market. In April of 1984, for example, Christie's Gallery in New York set the record for the sale of a single collection of jewelry at auction, raking in a cool $8.1 million for the jewelry left by the late Florence J. Gould. Mrs. Gould, who had died in Cannes in the south of France in February 1983, at the age of eighty-seven, had managed to accumulate her pile by marrying the son of Jay Gould, one of the most notorious of the stock swindlers of the Gilded Age after the Civil War. The most expensive single piece was a ring from Van Cleef & Arpels set with a flawless diamond of 26.23 carats, which went for $1,375,000, while a sapphire-and-diamond necklace with a center sapphire of an enormous 114.30 carats was knocked down for $1,320,000, and a cultured pearl necklace with a diamond clasp fetched $990,000. Typically, the buyers' names were not disclosed, though it is hard to imagine what fun it could be to keep a million-dollar piece of jewelry private.

As in other areas of excess, Texans are among the star performers; at the 1983 Cattle Baron's Ball, a major charity event held every June in Dallas, an oil heiress named Kay Kirk came straight out and told a society writer that she "loves to spend her oil money on diamonds." But the champion current spenders must be Arab women, who seem to channel all their energies into the purchase of diamonds. In 1983, Sheikha Hesa Al-Khalifa, wife of the ruler of the oil-soaked little Persian Gulf community of Bahrain—and thus, obviously, one of the richest wives in the world—wandered into Laykin's, the jewelry shop in I. Magnin, San Francisco, and plunked down some $1.5 million for a pear-shaped diamond, a set of earrings, and a Burmese pearl necklace. According to a recent book (*Super-Wealth* by Linda Blandford), a London jeweler named Laurence Graff is among those catering to the booming trade with Arab women, who are among the few people keeping the carriage trade alive in England. One week Graff, whose Jewish background does not keep Arabs out of his shop—though it does keep him out of Arab countries—sold the wife of Prince Abdullah, brother of the king of Saudi Arabia, a $300,000 heart-shaped diamond pendant, then sold her a set of emeralds the next week. "Anyone who tells you the Arabs are stupid has never done business with them," Graff was quoted. "A fourteen-year-old boy from Bahrain spotted a flaw in a seemingly perfect stone last week quicker than most jewelers could. And if you try selling the Arabs gaudy, flashy settings, you might as well shut up shop. They look for value. The second they think you're driving too hard a bargain they lose trust in you; they don't say a word. They vanish. I'm more careful to be absolutely straight with an Arab than with the most experienced European dealer." Good advice for aspiring jewelers. The common wisdom is that there are at least six thousand Arabs who spend $500,000 or more per year on gems. It does not take much calculation to see that Arabs account for a major chunk of the entire world's trade in gemstones. It is a sort of common currency for them. When Mohammed Khashoggi, son of the billionaire Adnan Khashoggi, wanted to go out with the actress Heather Locklear, he simply sent around his man with a tray containing $2 million worth of jewelry. She picked a $100,000 set of diamond earrings and said yes. His sister Nabila's twenty-second birthday present from her father contains matching square-cut emeralds of dozens of carats apiece for each member of the family hanging from earrings and a huge swinging necklace composed entirely of a triple strand of diamonds.

In the twentieth century, the story of jewelry has been the story of a few great jewelers—Cartier, Bulgari, H. Stern in Brazil, Van Cleef & Arpels, and especially the incomparable Harry Winston. There really was a Harry Winston, as any rich woman of the past fifty years would know. Some of the richest people in the world stroll through the doors of the stately, imposing shop on New York's Fifth Avenue, the equally impressive store on the posh avenue Montaigne in Paris, and the shops in Monte Carlo and Geneva. Barbara Hutton was a regular visitor, constantly picking up, for example, a diamond-studded watch for a new husband. Before their marriage, Stavros Niarchos sent Charlotte Ford a pin from Harry Winston—and then, evidently reflecting that she had nearly as much money as he did, he sent her the bill. Winston was also happy to drop in on his customers, whose money made them used to that sort of service. He constantly shuttled out to Denver to see May Bonfils Stanton, the newspaper heiress who built an internationally known collection with Winston's loving attention, including the breathtaking seventy-two-carat Idol's Eye Diamond that he designed into a necklace for her in 1947. Irene Mayer Selznick related that when her husband, producer David O. Selznick, first struck gold in his movies, Winston zipped down to Atlantic City to sell him gems. From the estate of Evalyn Walsh McLean, Winston bought her entire collection for $1.5 million in 1949, including the forty-four carat Hope Diamond, the legendary jinxed blue stone that once belonged to Marie Antoinette, which Winston donated to the Smithsonian Institution in Washington, D.C., and the Star of the East Diamond, a 94.8-carat rock that he resold to King Farouk of Egypt for $1 million, but which was still not completely paid for when it vanished in the 1952 revolution. Other renowned jewels that have passed through his hands are virtually a who's who of jewelry connoisseurs throughout history: the *Titanic* pearls that Mrs. John Jacob Astor rescued from that disaster; the Empress Catherine the Great Emerald Clip; the Prince of Nepal Emerald Necklace, and the Mazarin Rubies, originally owned by the seventeenth-century French prime minister. At last accounting, Harry Winston Inc. had at one time or another owned 60 of the 303 major diamonds in the world. (Twenty-six others are among the Iranian crown jewels; five are British crown jewels;

five belong to Queen Elizabeth II personally, and one graces Elizabeth Taylor.)

Indeed, Winston was singlehandedly responsible for the now-widespread practice of buying jewels at auctions from the estates of the deceased. He began by putting together a mailing list from the *Social Register* and leading judges and attorneys, getting off to a great start by landing the estate of Arabella Huntington, widow of the California railroad robber-baron Collis P. Huntington. Winston was also the only diamond merchant in the world to process jewelry from the mine to the finished piece; workshops in the basement of the Fifth Avenue headquarters are still filled with gnomish figures going about the painstaking work of cutting, polishing, and setting stones. The charm that Winston showered on his pampered clientele was lost on his competitors, however, and he was sneeringly called "Napoleon" on Forty-seventh Street, the jewelry ghetto—a reference to his five-foot-four-inch height as well as his notoriously autocratic manner.

Upon Winston's death in 1978, his son Ronald took over and initiated some changes—particularly the pursuit of the booming market for "boutique" jewelry, or lesser-priced, more casual stuff with a much broader appeal than "fine" jewelry. But he continued the store's history of appealing to the world's richest women. A terrorist at the spectacular fiftieth-anniversary party Winston gave for itself in 1982 at the Metropolitan Museum of Art could have wiped out a significant portion of the world's female wealth; among the better-known guests were Gloria Vanderbilt, the Douglas Fairbanks, Jrs., Fran and Ray Stark, Nan Kempner, Carolina and Reinaldo Herrera, Elise and Basil Goulandris, Lynn Wyatt, Ivana and Donald Trump, Stavros Niarchos, Maria Niarchos, Charlotte Ford, Count and Countess Crespi, Mica and Ahmet Ertegun, Countess Donina Cicogna, Mary Lasker, Diana Vreeland, Mary Lasker, C. Z. and Cornelia Guest, Drue and H. J. Heinz, Jr., Betsy Bloomingdale, Patricia and William Buckley, and like that, as Suzy would say.

Nancy Reagan was not on the list, perhaps because she took several years to return the gems that Harry Winston lent her for her husband's inauguration. Winston has had a considerable tradition of lending jewelry not only for the inauguration of American presidents but elsewhere in the world as well; for example, the firm loaned Evita Perón $13 million worth of baubles for her general's installation. Winston is also widely known for its willingness to provide traveling exhibits of its spectacular gems for charitable events and for the home inspection of its privacy-seeking or distant clients. As can be imagined, this does not always work. In April 1982, Winston made the mistake of sending around a collection of jewelry on approval to the Miami bastion shared by Prince Turki bin Abdul Aziz, brother of King Saud, and Mohammed al-Fassi, a Moroccan who was an in-law of the Saudi royal family. Al-Fassi is the bizarre character who slapped red paint on the genitals of the statuary at his Sunset Boulevard mansion in Beverly Hills, then later offered to buy the town of Midland, Pennsylvania. There were estimated to be several hundred million dollars worth of gems in the collection. Unfortunately, it came back minus a $1.2 million ring that featured a 27.7-carat square-cut emerald with sixteen round diamonds surrounding it, plus five more diamonds on each side. On Christmas Eve that year, Allal, Mohammed's brother, was arrested trying to sell the ring to an FBI man working undercover. Allal was indicted by a grand jury but jumped his $25,000 bail and fled to Saudi Arabia. Like the rich people they cater to, international jewelers have their problems; but that's what insurance is for. And a jeweler who tried to ignore the patronage of rich Arabs, however outrageous, would quickly be out of business.

Harry Winston's New York store is a six-story architectural gem of classic Louis XIV design, as delicate and understated as the Trump Tower, across Fifth Avenue from it, is gaudy. The armed doorman, however, is not delicate. The main salon features what might be called power decorating: a towering chandelier dominates, gilded statues give it that formal feeling, while vases full of massed flowers and the wallpaper, white on grey, add to the air of great luxury. There is, however, a slightly surprising feeling of noisiness and energy; the salesmen, immaculately turned out, are evidently quite comfortable with their precious wares. The business portion of the room is behind several oval windows in the walls around the room, where cardboard necks are smothered in cascades of diamonds and pearls. Customers are led deferentially into the back portion of the building, where several closet-sized rooms are dominated by gilded desks with velvet tops for exhibiting gems. Norma Smith, the director of public relations who, predictably, has The Look of greyhound leanness and a slight nervous tension, sits in one of these rooms and remarks that business is not as good nowadays as it was, say, ten years ago. While it is true that there will always be *some* people with enough money to buy any of the baubles they want, there tend to be fewer of them nowadays, thanks to the recession of the late 1970s. While foreigners, including Arabs, Mexicans, Spaniards, Italians, and others, have helped maintain Winston in the style to which it is accustomed, American gaudiness has fallen off considerably. Still, things are not so bad at all with the boom in the stock market over the past few years; says Norma Smith, "there will always be a new crop of well-to-do people." In her opinion, the fine-jewelry market is, essentially, half of the human race, since she believes that women of all ages and stations in life love gemstones. "What we appeal to in particular," she says, "is the desire of women to have something of individual design, something that is almost as personal as a fine painting. I think women all over the world are a little competitive. They will always find themselves in a situation where they admire something that someone else is wearing and will want something like it. We have occasionally even had people come in who say they have seen such-and-such a piece and ask us to make them something like that, only bigger."

16 | The Act

WHAT GOOD DOES IT DO if a woman diets and purges herself into emaciation, drapes herself in chiffon and adorns her swanlike neck with the cold brilliance of Harry Winston's best, only to open her mouth and sound something like Judy Holliday in *Born Yesterday*? None. There can, indeed, be a certain acceptable daffy charm in an immigrant's florid behavior, such as Estée Lauder's; and manners among the rich have undoubtedly loosened up under the influence of the Texans, "jet-set society," and the general breakdown of social strictures. Sophisticated Europeans and South Americans of course have their own cachet. Nevertheless, the rich but unimproved *arriviste*, wherever she is from, is still much more likely to end up with the social clout of Pia Zadora rather than Lynn Wyatt. Hence, it is extremely important to acquire The Act to go with The Look.

The first and fundamental lesson is that *everything English is good*. This Anglophilia is not something new, of course; since any old American family can remember, its traditions have been taken as directly as possible from the English upper classes. But these people with real money are *serious* about it. We're not just talking about the Whitneys, who genuinely possess an aristocratic right to hang pictures of horses in their drawing rooms. Texans try to act British too, and so do Californians who become real estate millionaires overnight. Moreover, the mere fact that aping English manners is a retrograde impulse makes it appropriate. The manner of a rich woman is entirely and overtly directed, naturally, toward *appearing part of a rarer time and place.* And one of the more ideal places to hearken back to is the English town-and-country society of the nineteenth century—which is exactly what modern American "society" was modeled on.

There is, indeed, an alternate mode of The Act, entirely appropriate for women trying to be rich in aura: *the southern belle motif.* But southern belles, members of the first American millionaire class, came from a society even more heavily pro-English than the later industrialist class from the North; English sympathies were with the South in the Civil War, not with the egalitarian North. Moreover, the development of the national American elite in the later nineteenth century—it became, really, a trans-Atlantic elite—was greatly aided by the migration of poor but proud southern belles to the ballrooms of the crude new barons of machinery. They introduced the elaborate manners of the Belle Epoque, the utter dominance of women in "society" and powerlessness elsewhere, and the mania for marrying European titles. Their influence might be compared to the leavening effect of the dispossessed European nobility after World War II, which helped create the entire international-trash scene.

Genuine British aristocrats remain fashionable celebrities, whether they do anything or not, and are to be cultivated whenever possible. This applies in a more general way to any royalty, although if you want to be more circumspect and upstanding, it is best to confine yourself to those actively practicing either suzerainty or financial respectability, or ideally both. Thus, the Grimaldis of Monaco are wonderful, and even a touch of the exotic is fine—witness Marylou Whitney's palship with Queen Sirikit of Thailand and Jackie Onassis's with Gayatri Devi, the Rajmata of Jaipur—but it might be best to dodge involvement with the more dissolute of the international titled set, even if their titles really exist. The Duke and Duchess of Windsor carried royal sponging to an outrageous but inevitably accepted extreme. Scattered members of the British royal family, like Princess Margaret and John Bowes-Lyon, pop up interminably on the social circuit. Invitations to the wedding of Charles and Diana were, it goes without saying, better than a seat at a White House state dinner. Although Californians and Texans are not especially partial to the dismal weather, London itself remains an interesting place to go for the self-proclaimed elite; the influx of Arabian money has made it the fast-lane capital of Europe, with enough music, gambling, and artificial emotions to entertain the most jaded among the world's gilded youth. While the lavish English country weekend has long since fallen victim to socialism—it is now much easier to pay one's way into a grand country manor than to be invited—the style has been adapted by Americans and other sophisticates who *can* afford it. Dogs and horses are the animals above all others, while great attention ought to be paid to natural surroundings, especially *flowers*.[30]

Hunting, which is generally considered a blue-collar activity in the United States, retains its aristocratic connotations for significant portions of the rich. Carola Mandel, an upper-class Cuban by birth who married a Chicago department store heir and is still an important Palm Beach hostess, is the only woman ever to win an athletic title in national United States competition against men; she did it shooting. The Waggoner Ranch is a popular stopping place for the many people who seem to find themselves around Wichita Falls during the hunting season, and Electra Waggoner Biggs is a convivial hostess for the legions gunning for the dove, deer, geese, and wild turkey that frequent the ranch. Lynn Wyatt recalled her perfect weekend: "One night we were in Paris, my husband and I, having dinner with some business friends, and then we went to Régine's and met some of my social friends there. Left and came directly through the middle of the night, flew directly to Washington, went to a dinner at the White House that night, which was Saturday. Sunday, we stayed there until about noon, and Sunday night we were at our ranch, dove shooting in the field. It's in south Texas. . . . Three different places on three different nights, but that one element right there is what I love about my life: the variety."

But the most significant contribution the British upper crust has unwittingly made to the rich of today is nothing so concrete as horses or guns or tuxedos or gin. The Act is most apparent when a well-drilled rich woman simply sits around. First there

30. More in Part Four on the rich woman's pet mania.

is the *set of the jaw:* square, and it moves sideways when in the act of talking rather than up and down. Naturally, the words come out somewhat strained and drawled through such an apparatus. This is the famed Main Line (or North Shore) Lockjaw. It is always much in evidence, for another important concept in The Act is to *never shut up*. The well-bred rich girl should be able to converse about practically anything by the time she is of social age. This need not be a contribution to the sum of human knowledge—"that's fascinating; I have a cousin with a syndrome like that" is the sort of thing that covers multitudes—but the key ability is to talk constantly, brightly, and completely independently of what anyone else might actually be saying. This principle does not apply, however, at a dinner party where all one's good friends, and perhaps an acceptable society reporter, are in attendance. Under those circumstances, it is important to banter with as much brittle brilliance as one can muster. In the past, women did not have to tell the longish, wry, nonsequitur stories that the men did, but that has changed considerably since rich women have plunged so heartily into a few businesses and into running big-time charitable affairs.

As a matter of fact, talking is just the most important specific application of the overall principle that one should *never sit still*. Rich people play with things while they talk—glasses, pens, whatever comes into their hands. They should have slightly damp palms. They are always in a hurry, but ideally they are subtle about it, so that visitors feel it is something of a privilege to be allowed to depart from them and thus to contribute to their significant enterprises. If you are acting rich, it should be very difficult to get an appointment with you more than a few days in advance, because you never know when you'll be off to Cannes or Hong Kong. Name-dropping, especially as a way of showing wide experience, is fine, but it's important that you have actually met the people, because most of your audience probably has if you haven't. There is one important exception to the Rule of Constant Motion: one's legs must always be strictly together. It may seem difficult to achieve this, say, at the beach, but you can be reasonably sure that Betsy Bloomingdale can do it and that Vicki Morgan couldn't. The legs-together-and-slightly-slanted-when-seated look is part of the model's carriage, along with Pelvic Tilt and head afloat, that has marked serene upper-class confidence since the days when debutantes were supposed to practice walking with telephone books on their heads.

To return to speech. British locutions tend to make up a good portion of the verbiage: statements start with "of course" and drift off into "don't you agree?," while "terribly" and "rather" are so popular that one eventually wishes the speaker could find something, somewhere, that didn't need to be modified. But of course modification is an important part of The Act. The related principle of euphemism applies to vocabulary. One uses slightly girlish locutions; "naughty" might be the term applied, say, to a youngish man who appeared drunk at a party, or to a turn of phrase that sounds slightly too self-consciously aristocratic when there might be others present; Marylou Whitney uses it to soften her own usage of "nouveaux riche," for example. "Silly" is popular in the same way. Men who attempt The Act—this is a smaller group than the women—often toss in "bloody," and if women want to sound racy they might assay it as well. "Wonderful" and "marvelous" are heard constantly, though they do mark the speaker as something of a ninny, if there is no strong evidence to the contrary, such as her having shown the ability to marry somebody very wealthy. "Darling" and "my dear" are also much in currency, hard as that is to believe. But they must be said with just a tinge of wryness, indicating that one is *purposely* acting like a flighty rich person. Foreign phrases can be okay if they are thrown in aptly and archly: You might try calling your pregnant pal *enceinte*, but avoid the temptation to say things like *au fond* or *dernier cri* for no particular reason.

But the most important part of The Act is the quintessentially British Society trick of topping one's exquisite manners with *profound bitchiness*. You might, for example, observe, "Fernanda Fosdick's dress is fitting her much better than it has," implying that you've seen more of both the dress and the woman. This can take the form of cute little epigrams, taken from whatever variety of popular expression. When Hugh Carey, then governor of New York, married Evangeline Gouletas—whose family had just made some money in Chicago real estate (since mostly lost) and who was considered to act *déclassé*—and then had the effrontery to take her to Le Cirque for lunch, another diner was noted to glance significantly at the insular pair and remark, "What he did for love." References to Jackie as "the merry widow" were rampant. The great delight of this seemingly inane sport, of course, is that everyone within hearing knows, or is supposed to know, at least as many dirty details of the friend in question as the speaker of the moment does.

Which brings us to a final corollary of The Act. This is simply that *conversation ought to be about sex*. Other topics may contribute to the lingua franca: the charity being feted at a ball, houses, art, dresses, recent trips; like anyone else, the rich discuss at leisure what they do as a full-time job. But it is a given that, once all one's needs for comfort and celebrity are taken care of, the proper study of mankind is man and woman. If you can swing it, you might try to pull off the trick of the woman whom Monsieur Marc claims used to use sexual puns in French to describe how she wanted her hair done. There has been a long tradition of rich women, especially well-known hostesses, being associated with homosexual mentors, from Mrs. Stuyvesant Fish's Newport major domo Harry Lehr down through Truman Capote, who was the court jester for Babe Paley, the great doyenne of the sixties, and Andy Warhol, painter of the mundane, filmer of the bizarre, and publisher of a magazine, *Interview*, that celebrates the international glitterati that drifts through Manhattan. What these types add is the celebrated fag bitchiness and exaltation of the camp that so tickles rich women, plus the inestimable advantage of not bothering either one's husband or oneself with their advances. Capote's peculiar quasiautobiographical *Answered Prayers*—the part he finished and published as a magazine piece—sank like the *Hood* among the general readership, but it kept Fifth Avenue atwitter for years as the seeming ice maidens attempted to decipher which of their chums had taken which of their husbands or their other chums to bed. Indeed, *Answered Prayers* should be required reading for any new arrivals from Grand Rapids hoping to crack the A lists in Manhattan or Paris. Peter Pulitzer was hardly ostracized for his widely reported indiscretions; even Claus von Bülow has more invitations than he can fulfill. Aside from the fact that everybody knows these things are going on, and that publicity has not been a dirty word for decades, the Pulitzers and the von Bülows are far too naughty to discard when the prospect of boredom yawns behind every mound of caviar or specially printed menu.

PART 4
ACTING
Usefully Rich

17 | Horses

When my accountant raises her eyebrows over the vet's bills, I tell her they're better than bills from a psychoanalyst would be.

—Anne-Marie Rasmussen

Edith Eleanor Dixon, known as Ellin, is the only daughter of Fitz Eugene Dixon, Jr., the Philadelphia businessman, sportsman, horseman, heir to both the Widener and Elkins fortunes and philosopher of money. ("Sometimes, I wish I didn't have all this fucking money"—an estimated $150 million.) She is also an Olympic-level performer in the difficult and obscure sport of dressage. The aim of dressage is to make the horse and rider as much a single entity as possible—a goal that qualifies it as perhaps the quintessential rich-person's sport, given how much of the wealth of the world has long been devoted to making a rich person one with his or her horse. It is not very clear to anyone not born to riches why horses should be such a preoccupation of the wealthy. One reason, clearly, is that horses take a great deal of time and effort; thus, to ride is like wearing a large diamond or a lynx: it is a badge that practically no one else can wear. Then again, there is the historical association of horses with power and wealth. What distinguished a medieval knight

[245]

from a serf was his ownership of a horse. Horses made men faster, more enduring, taller, more powerful; they still do, which is why present-day police departments keep them for riding around in cities. Beyond all that, however, is the undeniable fact that horses have a sort of universal beauty and appeal that applies to, for example, diamonds and furs in equal measure. Horses simply *are* rich. They are part of the international vocabulary of wealth.

Even within the realm of horses and wealth, dressage horses are outstanding. Ellin Dixon's best horse, Jubilaeum, has been in training for more than five years specifically for dressage. This is not too difficult to accomplish in her case, since she lives with her father on an estate called Erdenheim Farms, a five-hundred-acre spread that would look more appropriate outside Dallas than Philadelphia. It has Black Angus cattle grazing in its fields, a stable for thirty horses that once housed Fitz Dixon's collection of race horses, grooms and trainers who do nothing but work on the Dixon horses, and of course its own training grounds. This would seem to make everything almost too easy for Ellin Dixon, but that has not been the case at all. In fact, she did the Cornelia-Guest-taking-off-from-school-to-go-on-the-riding-circuit routine, only to find out that she had nowhere near what it takes to be a good show jumper: she was never going to jump more than four feet and certainly never going to make the Olympic team. So she went off to college at the University of Vermont and forgot about the whole thing. But, one suspects, those superb training facilities waiting back at daddy's farm were too enticing to ignore.

Dressage is such a refined and obscure sport that the main criterion for becoming an American power is being able to afford the accoutrements—the several horses, the years of exquisite practice for both horse and rider, the private trainer such as the one Ellin imported from Denmark. But there is something precisely in the refinement, the obscure precision of the sport that has recommended it to an extremely rich young woman like Ellin Dixon. "There was a lot of time growing up when I was absolutely miserable," Miss Dixon told a writer for the *Philadelphia Inquirer* in 1983. "Around vacation times, you have lots and lots of friends because whoever was your best friend at that time would get to go on vacation with you. So you'd have friends for about a month before vacation and then they'd never talk to you again. That's probably part of the reason I learned not to trust people. You never know why people like you—if they really honest-to-goodness do, or if they do because they figure they can get something out of you." Horses, of course, like you even if you *are* rich; and your ability to control them depends only indirectly on the money you have inherited. Realizing the fantastic extent of her wealth, Miss Dixon reflected, "was the initial impetus to do something that . . . the only way to do it was if *I* did it well, because you couldn't buy into it. That's a little bit why I ended up going into horses . . . just to do something, to prove that I was capable. . . . If you have the advantages, there's nothing to blame it on. If you fail, you've failed. You can't say, 'Well, if I had a better horse, or if I had a better trainer. . . .' There's nothing to fall back on. If I mess up, then *I've* messed it up." As it turned out, she barely missed making the Olympics.

The cost of showing horses is fabulously high. A good show horse costs at least $75,000 to buy, and that is equivalent to purchasing a license to lose money. Feed, grooming, training, and transportation—not to mention the rider's inability to work for a living—can easily cost $100,000 for a year on the established American horse show circuit. In recent years, some of this cost has begun to be subsidized by prize money from corporate sponsors, including Moët & Chandon, Tiffany, and Saks Fifth Avenue.[31] The upscale nature of the corporate advertisers is, of course, a tribute to the blue-blooded history of horse shows. The National Horse Show, the most prestigious in the United States, was founded in 1883 by a group of well-to-do New Yorkers, including William K. Vanderbilt and F. A. Schermerhorn. The annual event, held in the various Madison Square Gardens, became a highlight of the social year, as resplendent with jewelry and condescending accents as openings at the Metropolitan Opera—but more accessible, because for the relatively small price of admission anyone could watch the goings-on. The combination of highly stylized sartorial splendor amidst the basic facts of horse life won the National's crowd the appellation "the mink and manure set." In 1887, the list of boxholders at the National was used as the basis

31. Similar arrangements have recently been made in regard to polo horses. Wealthy women have little to do with them, however, except in cases such as Barbara Hutton's, who used to give strings of polo ponies as wedding gifts whether her new husband needed them or not.

for the first edition of the *Social Register*, and in that same year the *New York Times* lauded the show as the most important social event in the United States.

The great Triple Crown events of the United States—the Kentucky Derby, the Preakness at Pimlico in Baltimore, and the Belmont Stakes in New York—have never been as exclusive as the National, but they have also drawn more than their share of Whitneys, Belmonts, Vanderbilts, Phippses, du Ponts, and Guggenheims, many of whom sat in owners' boxes and ended up in the winner's circle. Marylou and Sonny Whitney's two most famous parties each year mark race weekends at Churchill Downs and Saratoga; and much of the world's wealth gathers from Texas, New York, Palm Beach, and overseas for the racing scenes there, as well as at less well-known events at the Palm Beach Polo and Country Club, and at Dinwiddie Lamapton, Jr.'s, Hard Scuffle Farm in Kentucky for the most important and stylish steeplechase event in the United States. Those meets were modeled on the even more exclusive European events at, among others, the superaristocratic Ascot in England, Chantilly outside Paris, and the sort of steeplechasing events in czarist Russia in which Anna Karenina's Vronsky ran his horse to death.

In thoroughbred racing, and even in show jumping, one seldom any longer finds aristocratic dilettantes actually riding a horse; they simply pay the bills and accept the glory. And, more and more, they also accept incredible increases in the value of their investments. The best horses in the world have increasingly been costing huge sums, such as the $4.25 million that Robert Sangster paid in 1982 for a single untried colt by Nijinsky II, thus turning horse-breeding from a beautiful toy for spoiled rich women into a highly competitive and lucrative business. While there has always been an international horse-breeding elite, the key difference now is the sudden massive presence on the scene of Arab sheikhs, who have raced especially in Europe but are also coming now to Kentucky. This development has a historic circularity to it, since all of the approximately two hundred thousand thoroughbreds in the world today are descended from the famous triad of the Byerly Turk, Darley Arabian, and Godolphin Arabian, all bred in what became Saudi Arabia. One of the new Arab horsemen, Prince Mohammed bin Rashid al Maktoum, the defense minister of the United Arab Emirates, plunked down a cool $10 million for Jacqueline Getty Phillips's three-year-old bay

colt Dunbeath. Altogether, Mohammed and his three brothers, the sons of Sheikh Rashid bin Said, the ruler of Dubai, are
supposed to have bought more than $40 million worth of horse-
flesh in 1982 alone, giving them ownership of more than 250
flat racers with twelve trainers on at least four horse farms in
England.

In 1983, for the first time, women were admitted to the Jockey
Club. Those honored were notable examples of the old-money
heiresses of a roll-up-your-sleeves-and-get-into-the-stables type:

—Penny Chenery, the blonde Virginia heiress whose home-
bred horses, Riva Ridge and Secretariat, won the Kentucky Derby
in successive years, 1972 and 1973; she and her former husband
Jack Tweedy were among the founders of Vail.

—Allaire du Pont, a Philadelphia Main Liner who came home
from a Swiss finishing school before World War II to marry her
chemical heir, and has since gone on to horse-raising glory as a
syndicate shareholder in Northern Dancer, the most celebrated
stud in the horse world, and the owner in her own right of the
famous Kelso. She is in a great tradition of du Pont horsewomen,
including the late Marion du Pont Scott, the Virginian who was
married to the actor Randolph Scott and bred Battleship, the first
American horse to win the Grand National, and Alice Mills, who
owns Devil's Bag.

—Martha Farish Gerry, granddaughter of the cofounder of
Humble Oil, who with her mother inherited horses from her
father and then went on to acquire operating funds by marrying
the head of the investment firm Gerry Brothers.

Among the other important horsewomen of the present day
are Diana Firestone, herself a Johnson & Johnson heiress and
the wife of Bertram Firestone, whom she met at horse shows;
the irrepressible Liz Whitney Tippett, who finally found her true
destiny by marrying a Kentucky colonel; and Josephine Abercrombie, the reclusive five-time divorcée who left the isolated
three-thousand-acre Pin Oak Farm in Kentucky to make her home
in River Oaks. (With her change of scenery, Miss Abercrombie
has also added to her sports interests, trading up from strong
horses to strong men. In 1984, she started a pro boxing stable at
her seven-thousand-acre ranch, Cannonade, in south Texas. She
became the center of controversy when it was suggested that she
had been using the Olympic boxing coach to solicit the service

of boxers for her lineup. This came about through her donation of $150,000 to the Olympic boxing program, which also led to the selection of Cannonade as the final training site before the Games. Several of the boxers were angry about the choice, and the coach accused of steering boxers to Miss Abercrombie quit. As usual, Miss Abercrombie said nothing, letting her money do the talking.)

Entire areas of the country are organized around horses. Kentucky is one obvious example. Less well known but probably wealthier on average is the golden Santa Ynez Valley, up the treacherous Refugio Pass from Santa Barbara. Ronald Reagan is the area's best-known resident. But he may be one of the poorer. Ray and Fran Stark bought seven hundred acres of the Corral de Quati ranch, the haunted, beautiful land once owned by Francis Minturn Sedgwick, Edie's bizarre father. Brooks Firestone, the tire-company heir, and his Anglo-Indian wife, a former ballerina, have branched out into another rich-person's hobby, growing wine grapes on three hundred acres. As Josephine Abercrombie found to her dismay, it is a life made for the rich person who likes her own company.

18 | Dogs

In the same way that horses are less likely than people to make Ellin Dixon question whether she is really being liked for herself, so dogs have for ages been trusted friends of the most important women in the world. Dogs with highly decorated collars have been unearthed in graves from ancient Egypt. In imperial Rome, they were dressed in golden cloth and carried by slaves on walks with their mistresses. In the Middle Ages, some breeds were so precious that they could not be sold, only transferred as gifts to nobles. They were used as couriers of love, carrying messages to their mistresses' secret lovers in their bejeweled collars. The tendency of the rich and picky to surround themselves with canine affection was satirized as long ago as Alexander Pope's eighteenth-century *Rape of the Lock,* and preciously named and highly pampered dogs seem never to have gone out of fashion. Englishwomen of the eighteenth century were consistently painted with their lapdogs. When Anne-Marie Rasmussen was divorcing her Rockefeller and also suffering through the death of another member of the family, she related, "I took my Chinese Shih-Tzu along for company. The next morning I awoke to discover that the little dog had gone out on Mrs. Rockefeller's terrace and fallen through the balustrade, and lay dead on the pavement below. I got into my car and drove directly to a place where I knew Shih-Tzus were bred, and bought another. I couldn't stand having a third void in my heart to fill. . . . I have come, it seems, to share the possibly neurotic attachment of Americans to their dogs."[32] Queen Elizabeth feeds her Welsh corgis herself in special bowls she puts out on the priceless rugs of Buckingham Palace.

The notorious Mrs. Stuyvesant Fish gave a famous dog party one summer in Newport, to which a hundred of her favorite canine friends were invited and served a dinner of stewed liver, fricassee of bones, and shredded dog biscuits by their owners, who stood behind them at Mrs. Fish's grand banquet table. One of the dogs wore a $15,000 diamond collar. Another favorite trick along similar lines was to insert one's dog under one's own name as a child in the *Social Register*. Dog parties have survived well into present-day society. In 1971, one was given by Countess Margaret "Migi" Willaumetz, who invited twenty of Palm Beach's best-bred canines to a birthday party for her thirteen-year-old Yorkshire terrier, Mop. Their owners were people who spend a good deal of their time extolling their own serious good intentions beneath the froth, which is supposedly added to parties mainly to attract money to good causes. Mary Sanford, the queen of Palm Beach society, was among the chaperones.

In 1973, Michele Bertotti, a Manhattan art collector, gave a party for her schipperke because he had had two strokes and needed a little frivolity to cheer him up. The Animal Gourmet catered the affair and served pâté canapés, shrimp on rye bread, an entrée of beef ragout, steak tartare, and Swedish meatballs, and a birthday cake made from liver and dog meal with a yellow, green, and white frosting. Larry Apodaca, the owner of a bichon frisé, was later quoted as defending the party by saying, "This is a way of doing something nice for poor little animals, with no political implications one way or the other. After all, dogs are so

32. The best expression the author has heard of female attraction to their little uncritical friends came from a semi-drunken woman of a certain age one summer day in Cape May. "Men—who needs 'em?" she said, apropos of nothing. "All they do is call you 'son of a bitch.' Dogs don't call you 'son of a bitch.' They may think it, but they don't say it."

loyal, faithful and honest, and how often do you find that anymore?"

Eleanor Ritchey outdid them all. When she died in 1968, she left all her oil money, $4.3 million, to the 150 homeless dogs she had adopted. Under her will, they lived in style on her 180-acre ranch in Deerfield Beach, Florida, until they were adopted or died. When the last survivor, Musketeer, joined his benefactress in 1983, the estate—now nearly $12 million—passed to Auburn University's veterinary school, where it is used to fund what may well be the world's most lavish research clinic for small animals.

Though not nearly as big and prestigious a business as horses, dog breeding, care and showing has been an important function of upper-class life for as long as anyone cares to remember. Again, the historical association with England has helped. In the greatest of all aristocratic sports, fox-hunting, training both horses and dogs is of critical importance. It is a matter of pride when one is riding with the Essex Fox Hounds in central New Jersey—as Jacqueline Onassis has occasionally done—or perhaps as a Foxcroft student in the Virginia hunt country, that one is familiar with the training and breeding of all the animals. The entire business of dog shows has also been long associated with the leisured class. Like the owners of the Animal Gourmet, many people make money selling luxury goods to the owners of dogs who feel nothing is too good for their pet. Neiman-Marcus offers both jogging suits and dinner jackets for dogs.

19 | Horticulture

HERE ARE TWO EPIGRAMS from Enid Annenberg Haupt: "Books are the most important things in life besides nature," and "Nature is my religion." The type of rich princess who is spoiled for anyone else by a dominant father, in this case the publisher and convicted tax-evader Moses Annenberg, Mrs. Haupt is a perfect example of why flowers appeal so strongly to the rich: they are beautiful and they never, ever talk back; thus they are something like an especially good-looking young man who accompanies a wealthy woman utterly for her money, the type of character Barbara Hutton was given to hanging around with. Like horses and art collections, flowers are expensive to acquire, to put into order, and to evaluate, and they have qualities that are not even visible to someone outside the rarefied circle that knows them well. They also require considerable amounts of valuable maintenance and expert, full-time help. Gardening can be the object of philanthropy and hence public acclaim: Mrs. Haupt recently gave $10 million to the New York Botanical Garden. Finally, perhaps most important, flowers indulge the ultimate fantasy money allows—that enough of it gives its owner dominance not only over human society but over life itself. Thus Mrs. Haupt's fascinating withdrawal from anything that hints of a public posture, reminiscent of some Parisian esthete of the *fin de siècle*, with a paradoxical insistence on a love of nature from behind the carefully guarded doors of her Manhattan apartment and her Palm Beach mansion. She told Charlotte Curtis that she could not live without the *National Geographic*. "I adore programs on animals, insects and nature," Mrs. Haupt was quoted. "I love nature in all its forms, but I don't need to travel to see them. After almost thirty years of the *National Geographic*, I think I know. When friends go somewhere, I can usually tell them what to see. I've seen the best. When I was younger, my husband and I sailed every fall on the *United States* on the last sailing before Labor Day. What I haven't seen traveling I've seen here at home."

Mrs. Haupt was a member of the special organizing committee for the opening in May 1984, at the American Museum of Natural History, of an exhibit of peony paintings by Niki Goulandris, yet another member of yet another Greek shipping dynasty. (She not only married Angelos Goulandris, she herself was born a Kephala, another clan with shipping interests.) Other members of the organizing committee were Jacqueline Onassis and Rachel "Bunny" Mellon, wife of Paul, the richest of the Mellons, and herself a member of the Lambert family that made its fortune in Listerine and then became a sturdy timber in the structure of society in Palm Beach and elsewhere. Enid Haupt and Bunny Mellon have obviously been together a lot, for they say similar things: Bunny's remark is, "Gardens have always been my life." She has created them at the Paris apartment near the Bois de Boulogne; at Oak Spring, the four-hundred-acre estate in Upperville, Virginia, where groups such as the Herbs Society of America are occasionally welcomed for conventions; and especially on Antigua, where, Maxine Cheshire wrote in 1968, "the tropical horticultural Eden which she has created around her Antigua home reportedly requires a private water supply larger than the public reservoirs that service every other kitchen, bathroom, swimming pool and lawn-sprinkling system on the arid island." (The Mellons had a considerably different problem at their home in Osterville on Cape Cod. It had no dunes, so they trucked in some two thousand tons of sand from a site ten miles away.) Niki Goulandris met Jacqueline Onassis after she married

Aristotle; in the early 1970s, Mrs. Goulandris frequented Skorpios as part of her wide-ranging project to paint peonies around Greece.

It must be said that Mrs. Goulandris is hardly the stereotypical bored plutocrat who turns to flowers because she can think of nothing else. By her own description, she is the second best-known woman in Greece. (After Melina Mercouri; Christina Onassis hardly spends any time there.) She got that way by becoming, in 1954, the first woman ever to apply for admission to the Greek diplomatic service, and ending up, in the 1970s, as secretary of state for health and social services. But Niki Goulandris and her husband had already shown a keen interest in things of nature by founding the widely respected Goulandris Natural History Museum outside Athens in 1964. Mrs. Goulandris was by then well on her way to her career as a botanical painter, and in 1968 she published *Wild Flowers of Greece* with many of her paintings reproduced. In the way of Susanna Agnelli, Niki Goulandris is one of those European women of immense bourgeois wealth who combines charm with a profound seriousness of purpose. She travels a great deal, but, she says, always for research; she has no taste for idling in the flesh-and-money ports of the Mediterranean. When she talks about the importance of her work in what might be considered the dilettantish field of flower painting, it sounds much more convincing than the self-serving excuses that are used to explain away the internationalites' lavish display. "I must say that I miss [the political career]," she told Judy Klemesrud of the *New York Times* at the peony show opening. "When you serve in such a field, you feel you are an immediate help to people. But what we are doing now is not dull. We think we are making a very important investment in the souls of the young generation by showing them the importance of nature and natural resources."

Although Mrs. Haupt is something of an exception, her peers in the world of the unspeakably rich generally figure that the showier a blossom the better. Thus the preferred taste, both for growing oneself and for scattering around the drawing room, runs to flowers like lilies, freesia, anemones, peonies, orchids, snapdragon—things that bespeak great effort and money. Orchids in particular are prized not only for their aggressive beauty, but for the incredible pains they exact in growing. Mrs. Haupt remarked that one can start with thousands of orchid seeds and be lucky to come up with sixty healthy plants. These plants go well with the sort of overstuffed, vividly colored decor that so many rich women prefer. Keeping them looking fresh, especially where cut flowers are concerned, is an enormously and obviously expensive proposition. Moreover, they also go extremely well in the warm-weather resorts that the wealthy have staked out for themselves. Naturally, part of the attraction of California, Florida, the south of France, and other preferred vacation spots is that the climate is so blessed for growing things. Much of the miraculous fairy-tale feeling of Palm Beach, for example, is due to the heavy vegetation—not only the magnificent palms towering over everything, but the profusion of other plants flowering with all their strength even in the middle of winter. The mere presence of the plants bespeaks wealth, for there was no topsoil at all on that island, and certainly no palms in their elegant rows, before Flagler decided to create a paradise from sand.

Like horses and dogs, plants are big business. There is, of course, a great deal more to the business than a haven for the very wealthy. Nevertheless, flower shows have long had a considerable association with the suburban upper classes. The plants generally come attached with the name of a woman who goes by her husband's name with its beginning initial. One of the leading gardening columnists in the United States is the always popular C. Z. Guest.

20 | Art Collections

Olga Hirshhorn takes a seat on one of her simple Brown-Jordan chairs outside the house in Naples, Florida, and smiles cheerfully. And with good reason. The lawn slopes gently down to the creek where a forty-foot ketch is drifting lazily in from an afternoon's sail on the Gulf. The sun is glinting down on a seventy-degree February day. Mrs. Hirshhorn is a handsome, energetic, charming woman in her early sixties. She is recently engaged to be married. But that is not what makes her more significant than the hundreds of thousands of Mercedes owners scattered up and down both flanks of southern Florida. Her distinction is that she ended up becoming the fourth wife of the late Joseph Hirshhorn, the major collector of modern art and donor of the museum that bears his name on the Mall in Washington. She can hardly believe it herself. "If somebody had said to me twenty years ago, 'I predict that you will be in this situation today, the kind of person that you are today,' I would say that's impossible," she observes with patent sincerity. By the "situation," she means not only the glorious orange Florida warmth, the sailboat, the lazy voices drifting across the lapping water, the rocketing pelicans, the rustling palms, the gracious ranch house with its screened and bestatued pool, the big diamond engagement ring, and whatever of Hirshhorn's uranium money that she inherited—not much, she demurs—but the wonderfully accomplished rich woman she has become. She shows a visitor the orchids she is growing draped from a tree, blossoms of a startling magenta. She has recently learned to ski ("in two days—but it took me two weeks to learn to get off that damn lift") and to sail. She was selected an alternate Mondale delegate to the 1984 Democratic convention. Most of all, she is coexecutor of Hirshhorn's estate and thus suddenly, miraculously, one of the most important art connoisseurs in the world. "I have," she says with wonderful good humor, "discovered the whole new world of art."

And brought a good deal of it home. There is a massive Henry Moore sculpture out front, a Calder mobile in the back yard, an Eilshemius painting over the living-room mantelpiece, framed Saul Steinberg drawings on one of the walls, and hundreds of other pieces, big and small, scattered throughout the house and grounds, more than anyone without a few years' study of modern art could conceivably hope to identify. Olga Hirshhorn had the best kind of education of all, the kind that makes important collectors. She lived with a collection which, when its six thousand pieces were donated ten years ago to found the Joseph H. Hirshhorn Museum and Sculpture Garden, was valued at $50 million. (It would now easily bring more than $100 million.) And since then, Hirshhorn's widow has not only retained a seat on the museum board, she has been charged with the responsibility of disposing of the thousands of pieces her late husband left outside the museum. (She kept a few for herself.) Finally, she spends a noticeable portion of her time traveling with exhibits from the Hirshhorn and from her own much smaller collection, acting as a sort of living introduction to the show—and to the wonderful uranium king who made it all possible. "I guess what I'm doing is keeping my husband's memory alive," she remarks.

It has been a long and rather miraculous road for the woman who was born Olga Zatorsky to a gardener and a laundress who had immigrated from Greece to the velvety estate country of Greenwich, Connecticut. Off to a nice start as a popular student, newspaper editor, and tennis champion at Greenwich High, Olga at eighteen took the somewhat peculiar career course of marrying her high school English teacher, then quickly having three children. Before the marriage ended after twenty-three years, Olga, though without formal job training, had managed to turn one of her talents, swimming, into a profitable sideline by taking along the children of other Greenwich residents when she taught her own kids to swim. That turned into a day camp, then into a nursery school, and then, when her own youngest son had gone on to regular school, it blossomed into a baby-sitting service, and finally, in full flower, into Services Unlimited, a successful agency that offered chauffeurs, cooks, and other domestics to the rich and busy residents of Greenwich.

One of the busiest and richest was Joe Hirshhorn. Olga still remembers their first meeting: he was sitting in his garden having a bust made of himself. Before long Olga began working for Hirshhorn herself, first keeping track of correspondence and whatever else needed to be done, then escorting thousands of visitors through the house on charity tours and serving as driver when the pint-sized multimillionaire needed to drop in on galleries or artists' studios. After two years of this, according to the family mythology, Hirshhorn offered to marry her if she lost ten pounds. It seemed a small enough price to pay. She and Leona Helmsley should collaborate on the marry-a-rich-man diet book.

A resourceful and vigorous woman, the new Mrs. Hirshhorn found herself adapting rapidly and well to a manner of living that included, besides the Connecticut estate and the Washington town house, an apartment in New York and houses on the French Riviera and in the California desert. They bought houses the way other people pick up umbrellas, for the convenience of the moment; "we bought the Washington house in 1969 just to be near the museum and just to spend some odd moments there." (Making it far too easy for orthodox analysts, Hirshhorn told an interviewer before his death that they sold the Connecticut house and moved to Washington permanently "to be near the children [i.e., the donated art], like a good momma and poppa should." His relationships with his own five children were all notably embittered.) The neighbors marveled at the couple who blew in at all hours in evening dress and dashed off again just as mysteriously. Olga Hirshhorn, who had spent her entire life making the lives of the wealthy easy and efficient, was now in line for her *chef d'oeuvre*. The presence of a world-renowned art collection in her new life served to emphasize the extent to which a woman who marries a wealthy man does so, in almost all cases, as a business aide, a curator of his wealth.

As one can imagine, it was easier for a cultural nonentity to learn about art by living with Joe Hirshhorn than it would be taking art history at Bryn Mawr. "It was very easy," Olga recalls, "because our house was just like a museum. The mantles and tables were filled with art objects and the walls contained many, many paintings. We had sculpture in odd corners and on pedestals. And before the collection went to the Hirshhorn Museum we had about a hundred and fifty large pieces in the garden. But it was easy. Our friends were dealers and collectors and art historians and museum people and artists, of course. So it was a total immersion in art. It was by osmosis."

Mrs. Hirshhorn being the perfect rich man's wife—that is, a sort of domestic chameleon who adapts herself quickly to her husband's proclivities—she was soon visiting the galleries and Christie's and museums while Hirshhorn tended the fortune that supported this wonderful art. Never one to do things in small doses, Hirshhorn bought by the truckload. Soon he was thinking of a museum. He had no curator, but he had just married the perfect woman for it. Olga became the literal curator for the life and reputation of her great man. She nursed her elderly husband on into his fame. Her cataloguing was no dilettante's pastime: when the collection was moved to the Washington building in 1974, the two thousand sculptures and three thousand paintings had to be carried away by helicopters and fifty-five trucks.

Such was Hirshhorn's compulsion, however, that by the time of his death seven years later he had, somehow, managed to acquire another five thousand pieces with which to stock the Washington and Florida houses and his Park Avenue office. "After Joe died," says his widow, "I found myself coexecutor of the estate, which meant a lot of travel, which meant having to learn something about finances and investments and real estate. . . . I had no training at all [in business matters], because when I married Joe Hirshhorn I knew he was about two things—making money and art. And I just chose to learn about art, and nothing about making money. Fortunately it had all been made already. I'm still very much involved with helping to administer the estate. I have lawyers to guide me every step of the way." Early in 1984, she had to spend the entire month of January in Washington to dispose of the remaining pieces.

Olga Hirshhorn now had come upon a collection of her own. "I have a collection now that's traveling around the country for two years now," she relates. "It's a collection of paintings and sculptures—small in size, small sculptures, and rather smallish paintings. One-third were given to me by artists, one-third Joe Hirshhorn gave me, and one-third I purchased myself. . . . My collection kind of reflects Joe's taste, because we dealt with the same artists and dealers and went to the same galleries. So when he would buy a major work of art I would get a smaller piece from the artist or even from the dealer. My collection could be just a miniature Hirshhorn show." No terrible thing for a collection to be.

More than any other activity, collecting and sponsoring art has been *the* outlet of choice for the energies of women with time and large amounts of money on their hands. Throughout history, the crowned heads have been the sponsors of the greatest art of their time. One imagines some royal aboriginal pointing out to her tribe a well-built buffalo that needed to be limned on a cave wall. In Greek, Roman and medieval times, with the ability of women to control money for any reason not being highly thought of, they did not have much to say about what art got produced. That changed, naturally, when such powerful figures as Elizabeth I and Catherine the Great came to their respective thrones. In the United States, one of the first women of distinction for any reason at all besides her beauty was Isabella Stewart Gardner, who created a jewel of a museum in Boston at her home, Fenway Court, with the help of Bernard Berenson, whose first patron she was. (Although perhaps in her case "notoriety" would be better than "distinction," given the havoc wreaked by her rumored liaisons with her young male protégés and the scandalous amount of skin she showed in her famous portrait by John Singer Sargent.) After Mrs. Gardner, it became practically *de rigueur* for women of that social class to collect things—practically anything, but especially fine art. Indeed, the newly rich American women who, for one reason or another, decided against collecting a European title, were happy to settle for European masterpieces; the late nineteenth century was famous for the wholesale looting of entire churches and castles. While women aside from Mrs. Gardner were not among that first wave of American collectors, it was their standards of taste that frequently dictated what their husbands would spend their enormous fortunes on. Thus, art acquired a fresh association with great wealth. No longer was it simply produced by wholly patronized house artists (although there was at that time, as throughout European history, a great market for academic portraits and landscapes among the aristocracy). Now, the importation of the great works of Western culture lent immediate, if spurious, tradition to families whose founders had been clerks or common laborers two generations before. And with the acquisition of the works, it became a matter of gentrified taste to talk at least with some remote show of sophistication about them. The acquisition of "artistic taste" thus served as yet another of the signs of great and ongoing wealth. The more arcane the collection, the better. Barbara Hutton within a few years of attaining her majority had put together a peerless collection of Oriental artifacts, many of which she bought herself during her extensive tours of the East.

It has been a rare connoisseur who has been satisfied to collect in the dark. The most effective way to bring one's name to the attention of the public, as Isabella Stewart Gardner showed, was to create a museum. Thus, Gertrude Vanderbilt Whitney endowed the Whitney Museum of American Art. (Within a few years of its opening in 1931, however, she would be much more famous for her role in the Little Gloria custody battle than for her artistic interests.) Four years earlier, Abby Aldrich Rockefeller persuaded husband John D. Rockefeller, Jr., to give her $5 million so she could become one of the founders of the Museum of Modern Art—whose garden was built on property that the family donated—even though John D. Rockefeller, Jr., himself was on terms of mutual discomfort with the avant-garde characters like Matisse that his wife insisted on inviting to dinner. MOMA became known in the family as Mother's Museum, and outside the family as the Rockefeller museum, especially after Abby's son Nelson and her daughter-in-law Blanchette Hooker Rockefeller both became president. The board of MOMA, like many other great museums, especially in the United States, was also a vehicle for social achievement for others; William and Babe Paley were among its early stalwarts, and younger aspirants to social import, like the sons of Estée Lauder, recognized that path and followed it.

All over the world, the richest people quite naturally have always played the most significant role in creating, housing, and preserving the great art collections. In Europe and India, it has always been the preserve of the local nobility, which had a continuity never approached by American families and thus tended to inherit "collections" that were actually in many cases, heirlooms that had been commissioned by ancestors. By the most recent century, however, European collections have fallen victim to the pauperization of the upper classes through taxation, confiscation, and other assorted misadventures—not to mention the tax laws, which unlike those in the United States fail to allow the millionaire to make a business of giving. What great collections remain, at least those that escaped the plunder of the American Victorian industrialists, have by now acquired quasi-nationalized or actually nationalized status. Even the remaining private collections, like that of the Duchess of Alba, are frequently open to the public; in England especially, they are a means of living for the impoverished heiress to a white elephant.

But not to worry. What the French cannot care for themselves is now in the efficient hands of an American group called the Friends of French Art. This organization was founded by a wealthy California widow called Elin Vanderlip who, realizing the miserable shape of much of the omnipresent art of past centuries, especially the art of the châteaux, put together a deal in which those who make major contributions toward restoration get to spend several weeks partying *chez* the owners of the long-ignored old art. This is in the tradition of the Rockefellers and other Americans who also restored Versailles earlier in the century. Mrs. Vanderlip apparently has to be quite careful in choosing how to approach the haughty owners of decaying glories. Her friends like Cécile de Rothchild carefully steer her through the French social shoals—emphasizing the crucial part upperclass snobbery plays in international art circles.

Back in the United States, where the support of art has blessedly become a somewhat less Byzantine proceeding, cities and regions around the country have nevertheless also tended to structure their social hierarchy on support of art and cultural activities in general. In San Francisco, Ann Getty, wife of the richest man in the United States, serves on a number of arts boards and urges those less fortunate to do their part: "The arts need a wide base of support," she told Charlotte Curtis. "You have to create events to encourage giving. Those $100 gifts are so important." Who's to dispute that? Ramona Bass, married into the most powerful family in Fort Worth, not only collects seriously in her home town but drops in at the Whitney Museum for the thousand-dollar-a-plate benefits. Marie Gallo, wife of a son of Julio Gallo, the cofounder of the world's largest winemaker, is the queenpin of the surprisingly robust cultural life of the aptly named little town of Modesto in California's San Joaquin Valley.

But the social, almost political impact of art collecting can best be illustrated through the example of its birth, painful adolescence, and current shining maturity in raw, rich Texas. In the Lone Star State even more than in the established East, the women were the ones who led the way in the refinement of money through taste. The remarkable Ima Hogg had an easier time of it than most, for she never married and so never had to discuss the disposition of the fortune that suddenly sprouted in oil on lands acquired by her father, Texas Governor "Big Jim" Hogg. (Her bizarre name, from a character in an uncle's poem, helped develop an early toughness in her that may have contributed to her unmarried state. She herself used to explain, "I am fatally attracted to handsome men, and I know if I had married, I would have picked a handsome husband who was worthless." Good advice for any heiress. Alternatively, she would tell the story that when she was about thirteen, a meddling aunt took her aside and told her, "Ima, you may find boys who will come up to you and say you're pretty. But remember that you are *not* pretty. If a boy ever tells you you're pretty, he's lying." Whatever the psychological causes, if any, not having married made Miss Hogg extremely rare among rich women.) Before she died at the age of ninety-three in 1975, Ima Hogg tore through several different careers in philanthrophy, including mental-health research, support for families of servicemen during World War II, and finally the restoration of original Texas houses and the filling of them with paintings, American Indian artifacts, and especially American antiques, of which she was one of the first and most important collectors anywhere in the country. She took an energetic interest in all of them, traveling to house sales and auctions all over Texas with a small entourage, completely furnished down to her famous Fish House Cocktails in case the party was stranded in a dry small-town café. Miss Ima's celebrated River Oaks mansion, Bayou Bend—her father originally owned much of River Oaks, and she was an early resident—is now part of the Houston Museum of Fine Arts.

The definition of art having broadened considerably in the

twentieth century, such endeavors as the restoration of entire villages fit nicely into the good and much-respected work that rich women pour themselves into. For example, Jane Blaffer Owen has used much of her inherited oil money to restore New Harmony, Indiana, site of an early experiment in American utopianism, where she has also helped commission structures by modern masters like architect Philip Johnson and sculptor Jacques Lipschitz. (Her interest comes through her husband, Kenneth Dale Owen, a descendant of the Scots social visionary Robert Dale Owen, who was an early leader of the utopian community.) Meanwhile, Jane's sister, born Cecil Amelia Blaffer and now married to Prince Tassilo von Fürstenberg—and thus stepmother to Diane von Fürstenberg's ex-husband, Egon, as well as a successor to Tassilo's first wife Clara (sister of Gianni and Susanna Agnelli) and mistress of palatial lodgings in Monte Carlo, Paris, Salzburg, and New York—is the dominant force in the Sarah Campbell Blaffer Foundation, which sponsors a collection of Old Masters (Breughel, Rubens, Van Dyck) and abstract expressionists that travels the outback in Texas, bringing culture to the masses. (The Foundation provides $600,000 a year for purchases and more for exhibiting and publishing expenses.) The Blaffers are among the purest exponents of the theory that contributing to the redemption of the people by bringing art before them is the sign of the aristocrat.

A highly formal and stylized clan, they got a good portion of their fortune from Robert Lee Blaffer, father of Jane Owen and Titi von Fürstenberg, who was a founder of Humble Oil at the Spindletop strike of 1901 but gave the lie to the roughhewn H. L. Hunt stereotype of the Texas oil baron; he forbade his executives to gamble or patronize nightclubs because he did not think those proper activities for men responsible for the lives of others. He pithily summarized his attitude toward fraternization as, "Brotherhood, yes. Equality, no." His wife, Sarah Campbell Blaffer, had an oil fortune of her own, from her father, William Thomas Campbell, who signed the original charter of the Texas Company, the future Texaco. Their 1909 wedding in a little Episcopal church—even in Texas the Episcopal church was the denomination of choice for the gentry—was the Texas social event of the generation. Governor James Hogg, one of Campbell's partners, called it "the conglomerate of the century." His daughter Ima was the maid of honor. Called Sodie, Sarah Blaffer was another self-conscious aristocrat and a grande dame of Houston society until her death, at ninety-one, in 1975. She had visited Isabella Stewart Gardner's Fenway Court while at school in Boston, but it was on her honeymoon trip to Paris that she began collecting seriously, chiefly Impressionists and other then–avant-garde works. At that time she acquired the practically mystical belief in beauty and proportion that can pervade only very rich families, with their almost limitless ability to control their surroundings. Sarah Blaffer was among the important early patronesses of the Houston Museum of Fine Arts, giving works by Renoir, Cézanne, Franz Hals, Vlaminck, and Soutine, and it was her inspiration to create the traveling exhibit. "I believe that love of art is closely associated with love of God," she said in describing her vision. "It is an experience I want everyone to share: poor, rich, town folk and country folk alike.

Then there are those who have no desire whatsoever to share their accumulated riches—a sort of perverse reflection of the upper-class reluctance to demonstrate wealth, perverse because endowing art collections is such a universally recognized reason for praise. But as if to show her disdain for anyone outside her circle of interests, Barbara Piasecka Johnson has remained as mysterious a figure in widowhood as she was when, as a Polish immigrant art student working as a domestic for Band-Aid heir J. Seward Johnson, she became the third wife of the boss, who was forty years her senior. She not only threw herself into the immensely wealthy (last estimate $170 million) and peripatetic (Florida, Italy, the Bahamas) roundelay that Johnson led, she persuaded him to construct for her an entire fantasy palace, Jasna Polana, on a huge spread on the outskirts of Princeton. Built in utter privacy and thus the source of considerable speculation even in the extremely discreet university town, Jasna Polana was rumored to be intended as the final resting-place of the immense collection that Mrs. Johnson's husband's money and her predilection had enabled her to assemble. In July 1984, she outbid the J. Paul Getty Museum in an auction at Christie's in London to come home with a black chalk study of a man's head and hand by Raphael for $4.8 million—easily the highest price ever paid for a drawing in any medium by any artist. Even more incredible, it was apparently Mrs. Johnson's first foray into the purchase of drawings. Thomas Hoving believes her assemblage of old masters and modern paintings and antique furniture "may in time take its place among the best in the country." But there has been no recent word on the disposition of the art or, for that matter, of Johnson's other immense properties, which the widow might have to share with the six children from Johnson's first two marriages. (One, J. Seward, Jr., is a sculptor noted for his anachronistic lifelike pieces that hotels, municipalities, and other institutions love to display; they have become the war memorials of their era.)

Perhaps an even more transcendental vision of the need for art than Sarah Campbell Blaffer's belongs to Dominique de Menil, the heiress to $200 million worth of the Schlumberger oil-drilling equipment combine. A selection from her massive (more than ten thousand pieces) collection of modern art was unveiled to raves in 1984 in Paris's Grand Palais—not normally a locale associated with great appreciation for anything American. The baroness was born in France, where her father and uncle, members of the Protestant bourgeoisie, had created a company based on their discoveries about scientific measurements of the earth's substrata; the technology had no practical applications at first, but eventually proved to be perfect for charting likely locations of petroleum. Dominique was working for the family firm when she met her future husband, Jean de Menil, son of a French baron; he was attracted to her because he thought she was hardheaded, although she actually hated the routine, taking the earliest possible opportunity to escape her strict upbringing and engage the world of art. In 1934, for example, she had her portrait painted by a young, unknown Parisian surrealist named Max Ernst, although she didn't much like it and only found it much later tucked away in an armoire. Escaping before the Nazis came in 1941, they went to Houston so Jean could manage one branch of the suddenly booming family firm. The cultural itchiness the Blaffer women must have felt was nothing compared with the dislocation that settled on the profoundly sophisticated French couple in a malarial, animal- and gun-happy town that grew up as a hustling oil port.

But Dominique, bringing the strength of a cloistered, privileged, self-willed ego to a sudden discovery of surrealist art, was the sort of powerful woman who could as easily have established a world-class museum in Vladivostok. Even as her collection and influence in the art world were growing steadily in the fifties, she would show up at consecutive openings in the same strapless black gown with one green and one blue shoe, having left their mates in different cities. When people would arrive for dinner at her invitation, she would blankly ask what they wanted, then invite them back for another night instead. She wore mink coats inside out because they felt better that way.

This was not the sort of eccentricity that Houston appreciated. The de Menils' initial impulse to do something for the Museum of Fine Arts was rebuffed without ceremony. "Well," said Jane Blaffer Owen, "if they thought *they* were going to teach *us* about art . . ." "I would never have started collecting so much art if I had not moved to Houston," Mrs. de Menil has said. "When I arrived in Texas there was not much you could call art. Houston was a provincial, dormant place, much like Strasbourg, Basel, Alsace [the Rhineland industrial areas where the Schlumbergers came from]. There were no galleries to speak of, no dealers worth the name, and the museum—that is why I started buying; that is why I developed this physical need to acquire." Among her other remarks have been, "What I admire, I must possess. I call myself covetous. I have an enormous appetite for whatever turns me on." This is art appreciation with a vengeance, an incredible singlemindedness.

To indulge this passion where it was not wanted, the de Menils, who as good French Catholics (she had converted) had a priest as an adviser even in their art collecting, adopted an impecunious young college called the University of St. Thomas. Acting the overbearing role of the stereotypical convert to Catholicism, Mrs. de Menil virtually captured the tiny school, buying land, throwing up buildings, subsidizing professors, and spurring a growth from forty students to five hundred within a decade. It was a perfect outlet for the artists whom the de Menils would help make into the establishment: Philip Johnson, then a struggling young disciple of Mies van der Rohe and now one of the most respected and certainly the most fashionable architect in the world, designed the campus, as well as the de Menils' own home (it was his first private residence); they hung a Calder mobile in one of the new buildings and several of their huge paintings on the walls, and they talked of building a chapel to house even more of their art.

Their next venture was the Contemporary Arts Association (now Museum). The de Menils joined the fledgling institution started by others outside the pale of the Museum of Fine Arts and immediately made an impression by staging a showing of van Gogh—a first for Houston—and continued to bring in and show off modernist stars like Calder, Miró, Max Ernst, and Mark Rothko. Even at the much younger and experimental Contemporary Arts Museum, the de Menils' pushy generosity gradually irritated their new friends. The resistance struck back in 1959 by refusing to renew the contract of Jermayne MacAgy, a young, iconoclastic museum director whom the de Menils had imported from San Francisco to shake things up in their adopted city. With their power spreading like an oil slick, the de Menils were not especially concerned; they simply installed MacAgy as chairman of the art department at St. Thomas. At the same time, their obviously great, if difficult, generosity had finally won John (the Americanized baron) a seat on the board of the Museum of Fine Arts, where he quickly moved to bring his own director to *that* institution. He was James Johnson Sweeney, who had just resigned as director of New York's Guggenheim Museum. Sweeney was Manhattan all the way, which was fine with the de Menils and their allies; they supported his extravagant expenditures and frequent absences. But it was just too much when Sarah Campbell Blaffer, the grand old lady of Houston culture, offered Sweeney a "Fragonard" tapestry only to be unceremoniously refused on the grounds that it was a fake. Blaffer took her tapestry back in a huff and devoted her attention to *her* family school, the University of Houston. Sweeney was canned, and in retaliation the de Menils withdrew all but token support from the MFA, leaving themselves with only St. Thomas among their philanthropic children.

As if in compensation for a death in the family, they redoubled the intensity of their devotion, and increased it again when MacAgy died of a diabetic attack in 1964. Dominique de Menil for the first time became actively involved in the installation of art shows. It turned out that she had The Eye, the ineffable instinct for what goes with what. She also had the increasingly brute force of her generosity behind her. The de Menils wrote a check to cover the school's deficit at the end of every year, and they hired graduates to work at Schlumberger. Increasingly, they pushed the school in the direction of their sentiments, which tended strongly toward the chic ecumenism racing through the American Catholic church in the 1960s. They commissioned Philip Johnson to design and Mark Rothko to paint what would become a famous ecumenical chapel. They started a media department and screened Andy Warhol films. They pushed the priests to hire more professors in the social sciences. But with Mrs. de Menil herself at the helm, it was the art department that grew most unnaturally, out of all proportion to a school St. Thomas's size. Mrs. de Menil not only put on shows from the collection she donated, she wrote introductions to them in the catalogs she produced for them and finally ended up teaching an art history class, frequently punctuating her lectures by reaching into her handbag for some priceless artifact to show around the room. And when Jane Blaffer Owen, the daughter of Sarah Campbell Blaffer, tried to donate a tapestry to St. Thomas, Mrs. de Menil characteristically caused another scandal by snubbing this second Blaffer family gift on the grounds of low quality. Mrs. Owen wrote a rather remarkable letter of outrage that said things such as, "If a child brings a gutter flower to its mother, and tells her it is an orchid, should the mother throw the flower away because it isn't?" Mrs. de Menil apologized but still wouldn't take the offensive tapestry.

Eventually the de Menils' highhandedness became too much for the Basilian Fathers who had founded St. Thomas, only to find themselves made rich and famous by people who then came back like Rumpelstiltskin and demanded their offspring. The de Menils had the aristocratic insistence that everything they touched must be the best: the best house, the best artwork, the best university. They had created the conditions—the land, the money, the professors, the reputation—for St. Thomas to become a world-class institution, and now they demanded to see it happen. With their international background, the de Menils' ideas of making a Houston institution great included a strong dose of making it more eastern elite in its tone. They were part of a generation of wealthy, paternalistic supporters of black advancement: they put a statue dedicated to Martin Luther King, Jr., in front of their Rothko chapel when the city fathers refused it, and they went so far in boosting the career of Mickey Leland, who would eventually become a black Democratic leader and a congressman, that they donated $50,000 to Texas Southern University specifically so that Leland could study clinical pharmacy there. John de Menil urged St. Thomas's all-clerical board of directors to move toward cultural and religious diversity; a first step would be the introduction of laymen to the board, who would have the power to fill the president's chair, a position in which John de Menil was rumored to picture himself. The priests agreed to introduce laymen, but they decidedly did not agree with the de Menils' preferences for the new board positions, which included a predominance of what were rather accurately referred to as limousine liberals. A later president of St. Thomas was quoted as saying, "They wanted a bunch of northeasterners to come down and run the place—like Ted Sorensen [the classic Kennedy family camp follower and chronicler]. He didn't know St. Thomas from a hole in the ground."

In 1969, the conflict came to a head and the de Menils, rather quietly and shabbily, bade farewell to the college they had adopted. They had everything that they had ever donated reappraised, then bought back most of the art collection and library, and moved it over to Rice University, which had agreed after months of careful prenuptial negotiations to play the next host to the couple's traveling art circus. The de Menils kept the Rothko chapel, originally intended as the St. Thomas chapel, and turned it into a kind of nondenominational temple of the human spirit, where visiting Indian gurus could hold forth and marriages could be performed between Jews and Moslems—just the sort of place, in short, to stick in the craw of the traditionally conservative priests at St. Thomas. Worse, the de Menils took their pet art history teachers with them, and they kept for themselves most of the land that had been earmarked for the university's expansion, leaving it today as a cramped little place that has had to replace the Calder mobiles spinning in glorious space with a warren of cubicles in a lucrative but spiritless business school.

The de Menils grew increasingly cranky about what was done with their booming collection. Rice had the stature, and even the interest, to suit them; but perhaps it was too big, too much its own institution. They made it clear that they disdained the gallery Rice was building itself; the Rice administrators, in turn, were appalled when Mrs. de Menil proposed to throw up what was nothing more than a temporary metal shed as the Rice Museum she was to donate. (She was in a hurry because an important show was due from the Museum of Modern Art.) Rice stuck the building in an obscure corner of the campus, though not obscure enough for neighboring homeowners, who complained so heartily that the de Menils were forced to paint the structure a neutral color to cut down the glare. A few years later, the culture czarina brought in Louis Kahn to begin plans for a more permanent Rice Museum, which, it was rumored, would house her entire collection, by now becoming world-famous; but Kahn died after a few preliminary sketches and the project atrophied. She also turned down a proposal that she build a museum on city-owned land near the Museum of Fine Arts.

It was becoming increasingly clear that what Dominique de Menil needed was not a part of some greater institution to which she would make a wonderfully generous contribution, but a monument wholly to her—not just to her money and power but to her taste, something that would *be* Dominique de Menil.

The result of that dream is, typically, idiosyncratic: a four-hundred-foot-long building barely rising above the old Houston neighborhood called Montrose (known colloquially as Doville after its principal landowner's nickname). The museum is covered in wooden clapboard and painted an unassuming gray and is "in danger of looking a little like a lovable old beached whale," one observer remarked. The building under construction is quite like her home, as a matter of fact, which is surely no coincidence, for Mrs. de Menil obviously means to be the dominant force in her collection well beyond whatever years may be left to a woman in her middle seventies. And she got it all at a relative bargain: the Menil Foundation, created specifically to administer the collection, will give $6 million of the $30 million total projected for construction and endowment of the museum. Despite her minority role in funding the building, and the Menil Collection's nonprofit status, de Menil is all-powerful as president of the Menil Collection's board, which includes her son among other close associates. (All five of her children are art collectors, and her three daughters are active artists or patronesses in addition. Adelaide is a photographer and collector of Northwest Indian and Eskimo art; while Philippa de Menil Friedrich runs an art foundation in Manhattan that recently ran into legal problems after her Schlumberger stock plunged, forcing her to cut drastically into previously promised support for artists. Cristophe patronizes avant-garde composers.) Most of the superb collection's ten thousand pieces will remain in storage at any one time on the second floor of the structure, and Mrs. de Menil plans to take an active role in what is exhibited and who is permitted to view the works in storage.

Indeed, she has already given an indication, if one were still needed, of the proprietary role she takes in her collection. The first major exhibition of a large number of the Menil Collection works opened in April 1984 in the Grand Palais in Paris. It was an immediate sensation. The grand, fragile, eccentric, and very rich old woman was acclaimed by the land of her birth for the exhibit; The Eye had produced a show in which artworks from the earliest primitive cultures were placed next to artists of the future who had been discovered and legitimized by Dominique de Menil. Through her art, she had girdled the globe and time itself.

The social and recreational value of being an art patroness applies as well to music, of course, although music, being essentially a public commodity, does not attract the strictly self-aggrandizing rich as paintings, sculptures, and furniture do. Again, great ladies have been responsible for creating some of the most important of cultural institutions. We have seen how Dorothy Buffum Chandler almost singlehandedly forced Los Angeles to build the Chandler Pavilion. In New York, Alice Tully gave the hall that bears her name to the wonderful Lincoln Center. Ima Hogg was the founder of the Houston Symphony in her time off from her myriad other activities. The eccentric but unquestionably energetic Rebekah Harkness used up most of the $75 million Standard Oil fortune her husband left her by starting her own Harkness Ballet and buying the company its own East Side town house for a school, and then its own Broadway theater.

But perhaps the most lasting impact on the musical arts has been achieved by Catherine Filene Shouse. An heiress to the well-known Boston department store fortune, she grew up in a family that had already been present at the creation of the Boston Symphony and the Harvard Business School. With the rocky feistiness that marks the Boston upper crust, Kay Filene moved to Washington against her family's wishes to help with the war effort, became the first woman ever to gain a master's degree from Harvard (in education), wrote a seminal book called *Careers for Women*, which stayed in print for more than half a century, and divorced her first husband—because "I was bored"—to marry Jouett Shouse, who was then chairman of the Democratic National Committee. After decades of being a top hostess in a town filled with claimants to that distinction, as well as a classic country gentlewoman—her daughter has recalled seeing her with diamonds and a mink coat over old boots while she shoveled manure—Kay Shouse finally capped her career by donating 117 acres of her Wolf Trap Farm, in Virginia, as a site for a center for the performing arts, as well as $2.3 million to build a performance facility. When the place burned down twice, in 1971 and 1982, Mrs. Shouse gave money and her octogenar-

Candi and Stephen Wozniak with friend.
*(Roger Ressmeyer/*People *Weekly © 1983 Time Inc.)*

Cornelia Guest with Andy Warhol at
a party to celebrate the International
Jumping Derby in Portsmouth, Rhode
Island.
(*AP/Wide World Photos*)

Edie Sedgwick and friend at the filming of *Ciao,
Manhattan.*
(*UPI/Bettmann Archive*)

Patricia Hearst in front of the insignia for the Symbionese
Liberation Army.
(*AP/Wide World Photos*)

Mitzi Newhouse and sons, Samuel Newhouse, Jr. (left) and
Donald Newhouse, after attending funeral services for publisher
Samuel I. Newhouse.
(*AP/Wide World Photos*)

Sheikha Dena al-Fassi and her lawyer, Marvin Mitchelson, discuss the $3 billion divorce case against her husband, Sheikh Mohammed al-Fassi.
(AP/Wide World Photos)

Barbara Hutton poses for an admirer with her fifth husband,
playboy and diplomat Porfirio Rubirosa.
(*AP/Wide World Photos*)

Doris Duke, in one of the latest photographs
available, at the International Center for
Photography in New York.
(*AP/Wide World Photos*)

Doris Duke and her fiancé, Porfirio Rubirosa,
before their wedding.
(*AP/Wide World Photos*)

Rose Kennedy, after attending Thanksgiving Day services, in 1982.
(*AP/Wide World Photos*)

ian's energy to keep the music playing. "I never do anything out of a sense of doing good," the doughty philanthropist said briskly in explaining her role in rebuilding Wolf Trap after the second conflagration. "I do it because it needs to be done."

21 | Creating Art

In 1973, Rebekah Harkness, then fifty-eight years old, performed a six-minute flamenco dance with Roberto Lorca before an audience of celebrities in New York. The audience, always willing to politely appreciate the efforts of its own class, received it as something of a novelty, but an entertaining one. When Mrs. Harkness had recordings pressed from her own musical composition, however, the response from the general public was less supportive of what appeared to be her dilettantish dabbling; a writer for *Dance* magazine called her music "a compost heap of ideas." As always, it is the rich who appreciate the difficult struggles of a rich person. They understand; outside, the *sans-culottes* think it's all just a bed of roses. They don't understand that the rich, like everybody else—maybe more than everybody else—feel the need to leave something of themselves behind, some great work of art. The question has always been, Can the rich actually create art?

Some obviously can. Dina Merrill, the daughter of the unbelievably rich Marjorie Merriweather Post, raised amidst splendor on the *Sea Cloud*, nevertheless managed to achieve a highly successful acting career of her own. Grace Kelly was the daughter of a wealthy Philadelphia brickmaker. Edith Wharton was a child of privilege, and that was the constant topic of her novels. Amy Lowell, the poet, was from a family both moderately wealthy and highly talented. Jill Clayburgh's father is a prominent New York industrialist. Cindy Firestone, an heiress to the tire fortune and a graduate of Miss Porter's, made an auspicious debut with a film called *Attica*. Like many third-generation heiresses, Miss Firestone was biting the fortune that bred her: the movie, predictably leftist and antagonistic to that miserable representative of capitalist fascism, Nelson Rockefeller, was made on $40,000 borrowed from Cindy's mother, whom the filmmaker proceeded to describe as "slightly to the right of Louis XV." Phyllis Bronfman was the director of planning for the far-famed Seagram's Building, designed by Mies van der Rohe—an appointment that unquestionably owed a great deal to the fact that her father was the owner of Seagram's, but that was buttressed by her obvious possession of The Eye. She impressed Sam Bronfman into hiring her by critiquing the uninspiring drawings that he sent for her comments; she in turn was responsible for hiring van der Rohe, resulting in one of the happiest of modern buildings.

With the exception of a few examples such as these, the common assumption is that the rich are too sheltered or too comfortable, or both, to produce great art. This notion undoutedly owes a great deal to the popular Wagnerian image of the suffering artist, and also reflects the suspicion of dilettantes inherent in such reflections as Samuel Johnson's, "No man but a blockhead ever wrote except for money." Amy Lowell complained that her heaviest burden was being born into a class popularly assumed to be incapable of artistic creation. Cornelius Vanderbilt, Jr., found he was "trying forever to convince everybody that I am in earnest"—a cause not aided by his seven marriages or the sloppy, sometimes imaginary nature of his "journalism." Louis Auchincloss, himself a product of an ancient and honorable American fortune, as well as a lawyer and novelist, wrote in an introduction to a collection of a similarly privileged writer, Edith Wharton: "It is true, of course, that an upper class training may hamper an incipient artist by inhibiting his emotions, and in fields of direct personal exhibition, as the stage and the dance, it may well be fatal. But the novelist need expose no more of himself than he wishes." Geoffrey T. Hellman, in an entertaining 1963 article in the New Yorker called "Can the Rich Write?," named Wharton as one of the few "rich writers who could really write" and dismissed the rest of his fifty subjects as "crypto-novelists."

There are crypto-artists of all kinds. Electra Waggoner Biggs took up sculpting because, one gets the feeling, she didn't want to be a rich girl who did nothing at all. She found it easy. There are those who will say it *looks* as though her sculpture is easy. For them, Biggs has a quick answer: people pay good money for her stuff. "You know darn well, some person pays a thousand dollars to have me do a bust of them, you've got to be good or they wouldn't pay it—which is a satisfaction for the work you put in, for the study you've done, and the hours that I've spent, backbreaking hours in the studio, keeping my arms up in the air where I was practically going to fly." Biggs is as scornful of artistic snobs as social snobs; just as obviously, the self-proclaimed arbiters of art will have nothing to do with her works, which are all unfashionably representational and might simply be called Society Art. Biggs is laughing all the way to the bank.

As long as the rich are always with us, there will be rich little girls who decide that they want the glory of an artistic career and don't quite believe that all daddy's money can't buy that too. Most of them do indeed achieve the anonymity that the public expects of them. Many have no more desire for the hard work of real stardom than Cornelia Guest, who has been content to sing Elvis songs at society functions, at whose request it is hard to imagine. Much sadder are those who do work desperately hard at their art, and pour whatever resources they can command into it, only to find themselves reined in by a profound lack of talent. This practice of trying to buy stardom—a variation, if you will, on trying to buy love—has an ancient and dishonorable tradition. William Randolph Hearst and his Marion Davies were immortalized, even more than by his own and others' newspapers, in Orson Welles's Citizen Kane, although the real Marion actually did have a career of her own, albeit a chorus-line one, when Hearst met her, and was nowhere near the ninny of a wife depicted in the movie.

An even more outrageous attempt to buy stardom is gamely being perpetrated on a yawning public in the present day by one Meshulam Riklis, the massively wealthy creator of the Rapid-

American Corporation and would-be Pygmalion to a most unlikely Galatea named Pia Zadora. As Nicholas Von Hoffman
observed, Miss Zadora is a celebrity for no particular reason; she
just *is* a celebrity, which is not a bad definition of what many of
the people in *Interview* magazine are trying to achieve, though
none of them would acknowledge Pia's existence. Pia will appear
more or less unclothed at the drop of a bra—in movies,
skin magazines, or at the Cannes Film Festival. Once that happens, it becomes obvious what at least men see in her; she
is built something like a Brigitte Bardot who got caught
in a garbage compactor. She also has a preternaturally large
and yet teenaged-looking face (she is in her late twenties)
atop that nubile little frame, giving her the look, it has
been remarked, of a comely Mrs. Potato Head. Anyway, this
little package certainly did charm the wallet off of Meshulam
Riklis.

Riklis is quite a story himself. A Turkish-born Israeli, he got
to the United States via a jeep-driving (rabbi's chauffeur) assign-
ment for the British Eighth Army during the war. He put himself
through Ohio State by teaching Hebrew. Then he got a job as a
stock analyst; then he bought stock; then he acquired companies.
Riklis was a go-go conglomerateur before it became popular. At
one point he was known as Meshuggenah Reckless for his wild
and crazy ways in compiling his corporate empire. Dodging several bullets along the way, he managed to acquire, among other
properties, Schenley Industries, the liquor giant, and the Riviera
Hotel in Las Vegas. Pia now does commercials for Dubonnet,
which is owned by Schenley, and sings at the Riviera Hotel. As
she is quick to point out, she had a thriving career long before
she met Meshulam. She was one of Tevye's daughters in *Fiddler
on the Roof* at the same time that Bette Midler was in the chorus.
She made her movie debut at the age of eleven as one of the
green-faced princesses in *Santa Claus Conquers the Martians*, which
is generally considered one of the worst movies of all time. After
a string of Broadway assignments, Pia ended up, at the age of
seventeen, in the touring company of *Applause*, with Rich Little
and Alexis Smith. In Dayton, Ohio, the Italian Catholic girl met
the Israeli entrepreneur. He sent an agent to bring her to his
office. (Always a good sign of unfathomable wealth.) The rest is
history, of a sort. Riklis chased Pia across the continent for two
years, and it all had a happy ending. By their accounting, Pia
would have been glad to be a happy housewife, but Riklis, in

the manner of enormously wealthy men, was looking for new worlds to conquer. He bankrolled a movie called *Butterfly*, in which Pia plays a Lolita whose attentions are directed toward her up-country father. The forgettable plot was matched by profoundly forgettable performances. Nevertheless, Pia managed to walk away with a Golden Globe award for "new star of the year in a motion picture," beating such competition as Kathleen Turner in *Body Heat*. This was enough to upset even the jaded Hollywood community. It was not enough to give Pia any pause in her drive toward stardom. This girl *works*. The dance lessons, the acting lessons, the singing lessons—it's enough to make any princess turn the color of cottage cheese. Pia remains as fresh and wonderful as she always was. It's just that nobody except Riklis appreciates it.

There is a mirror-image tradition in which the successful female performer uses her talents to attract her rich man. For most marriers of rich men, those talents are at a subpublic level: they may very well be smashing models (or simply women of notable beauty); sometimes they are strikingly clever, or even women of kindness and character. But at the top of the scale of riches and ambition, men who want it all frequently aim for women whose achievements in the performing arts have made them famous all over the world. While one hesitates to downplay the obvious attractions of a Grace Kelly or a Rita Hayworth, it also seems obvious that part of the attraction here is the sense of immense achievement for the tycoon in doing—once again—what all men want to but no one else can. Besides the fairy-tale marriages of those two (though Rita's had no happy ending) the most famous of the recent liaisons between stars and tycoons have been Jennifer Jones–Norton Simon and Maria Callas–Ari Onassis. These matches are frequently full of *angst*—which might be something of a surprise until one reflects that they represent the concatenation of two compounds of nearly equal ego, drive, and fame. Not that things are all terrible because of money. The men delight in showering their women with the glories of wealth—Jennifer Jones getting a family collection of Indian art after she became interested in yoga, Maria the protection from the crowd and the company of the rich and famous; and they actively pursue their wives' career goals, even if, in Ari's case, they don't have any particular interest in the art. But the clashes of personality take their toll. Maria's love for Ari was only another nail in her emotional coffin, and the love of his beautiful woman has not prevented Norton Simon from continuing to take on himself all the burdens of the world and pronouncing, "In the Dostoevskian sense, I am the suffering man."

22 Giving It Away

> It's very hard to get rid of money in a way that does more good than harm. One of the ways is to subsidize people who are trying to change the system and get rid of people like us.
>
> —Laura Rockefeller Chasin

Not that it's something that most people consider at length, but the general assumption is probably that rich people regret dying more than others: they have so much to leave behind. On the other hand, many of them have the small comfort of knowing that there will be extensive tributes to the good they have done. That is what philanthropy can do for you.

When Lila Acheson Wallace died in May 1984, at the age of ninety-four, in the home she had shared with her husband in Mount Kisco, New York, she left behind what many rich people crave—immortality. She did it through philanthropy. With her husband, DeWitt Wallace, she had started *Reader's Digest* in a basement in Greenwich Village in 1922. (Surely a legacy disdained by most subsequent residents of the Village.) It was an immediate success. Today the *Digest* has the largest circulation of any periodical in the world, with thirty million copies appearing in seventeen languages; and many people still think a toilet doesn't look dressed unless it has a *Reader's Digest* on top of its tank. After her husband died in 1981, Mrs. Wallace owned all the voting stock in the company, worth an estimated $250 million.

This woman started without a silver spoon. The daughter of a Presbyterian preacher (in what other religion could you find a marriage partner for somebody named DeWitt?) she traveled throughout the American Midwest and met her future husband in Minneapolis, where she had been sent to establish a branch of the YWCA. As the *Digest* fortune rapidly accumulated, Mrs. Wallace became one of the major contributors to just about everything. Her interests were a compendium of the concerns of the upper class. She accumulated a substantial art collection, estimated to be worth about $5 million, mainly in French Impressionists—Cézanne, Chagall, Corot, Degas, Gaughuin, Manet, Matisse, Sisley, Soutine, Utrillo, and others—which she used to decorate the offices of *Reader's Digest* in Chappaqua, New York. By all accounts, Mrs. Wallace was passionate about her gardening and her art collection; she bought paintings because she loved them, although perhaps she never had The Eye that the great collectors did. "A painting is like a man," she said; "if you can live without it, then there isn't much point in having it." She gave $8 million to the Juilliard School for programs in music and drama; $5 million for the construction of the World of Birds exhibition facility at the Bronx Zoo; $2 million to the YWCA; at least $1 million to the University of Oregon, her alma mater; $1.6 million for an auditorium at the Asia Society, the Rockefeller-dominated think tank; $1 million to the New York Botanical Garden; $1 million to the Sloan-Kettering Institute for Cancer Research; $2 million to the Near East Foundation; more than $4 million to the Northern Westchester Hospital Center; and smaller amounts to the Metropolitan Opera, New York Hospital, Columbia-Presbyterian Medical Center, and a number of Presbyterian churches. When the Mount Kisco A.M.E. Baptist Church was conducting a fundraising drive and looking for contributions of $25 or $50, Mrs. Wallace sent in a check for $50,000; she spent the same sum for a shelter in Leonard Park in Mount Kisco. Altogether, she donated more than $60 million in her lifetime.

Like many of the great philanthropists throughout history, Mrs. Wallace was determined to put her mark on the things that she did. For example, when she gave $8 million to restore Boscobel, an eighteenth-century mansion on the Hudson River, she was there many days during the work, making sure that the interior decorators were giving their all and that the gardeners were planting the right flowers in the right patterns. She showed up every week to watch the progress of the restoration of the Great Hall in the Metropolitan Museum, and once it was finished she paid for flowers to be installed there every day. She gave more than $1 million to the restoration of the Abu Simbel temples in Egypt, and paid for the preservation of Claude Monet's house and grounds, including the famous lily ponds, in Giverny, France.

Lila Wallace was merely practicing a seemingly contradictory realization achieved by most wealthy people—Americans in particular—almost in conjunction with their realization of their wealth: much of the power of money is realized only in giving it away. Of course, those whose great wealth is bound up in a personally or family controlled company have life-or-death power over their employees; but at the most this comes to several dozen thousand, and managers tend to intervene between the boss and his workers. No, true power comes in the ability to dominate an institution—or perhaps a number of institutions—that have major impact on the multitudes, washed or unwashed. Art collections have the wonderful ability to impress one's peers, and patronage of art, in particular, the additional dimension of shaping public taste; but giving large amounts of money to hospitals, foundations, universities, and miscellaneous charitable organizations is a much better way to secure a good name among one's poorer fellow citizens.

The greatest of the philanthropic women have almost always spread their giving among a number of fields. The motivation, predictably, grows out of personal interests and preoccupations. Marylou Whitney is the kind of personality, through background, interest, and great wealth, that automatically gravitates toward philanthropic endeavors. But even Whitney fortunes have limits. Which ones should she favor with her attentions? These choices are largely determined also by backgrounds and personal experiences. In Marylou Whitney's case, her husband Sonny had long been involved in sports of all kinds, as well as international affairs, so it was natural that she should host one of the biggest international gatherings of 1984 as part of the Winter Olympics. The Whitneys had already done more than their share for the 1980 Winter Olympics in Lake Placid, near one of their homes. She is involved in fundraising projects for the Whitney Museum because it is in the family. Sonny's daughter died of leukemia, so Marylou has raised something approaching $8 million for a cancer center at the University of Kentucky Medical Center over the past several years—partly through television commercials that her early career as an actress help out with, and partly by auctioning off the breeding services of the Whitney thoroughbreds. When her children were young, Mrs. Whitney naturally got involved in the quality of education in the lower grades; she and Sonny have, in effect, adopted a small private school near their Kentucky home—buying books, contributing buildings, sending the teachers to Yale for additional study. (For that work she got a high school named after her in Lexington.) Mrs. Whitney also began bringing to market the homemade crafts of the women in the hills in Kentucky. Near the Whitneys' Adirondacks camp, she did the traditional local-gentry job of raising money for nearby churches and hospitals. Saratoga Springs has been practically a Whitney family town for decades; most recently, Marylou has been concentrating on a new civic center with an auditorium, a two-hundred-room hotel for conventions, and a Dance Hall of Fame.

Here are the women who have made the largest contributions in the United States, which means, in all likelihood, in the world:

—The youngest child of tobacco magnate R. J. Reynolds, Nancy Susan Reynolds, is a Greenwich, Connecticut, dowager in her seventies. In 1938, she and her siblings gave $30 million to establish the Z. Smith Reynolds Foundation, which contributes to projects in North Carolina only, mainly in the arts and education. She started the Arca Foundation herself with a gift of $11 million, and has also given more than $2 million in dribs and drabs to such causes as Planned Parenthood and the solving of the nuclear waste problem.

—Anna Bing Arnold, now in her eighties, has collected her substantial fortune from two widowings. She paid for the Bing Theater at the University of Southern California, and continues to fund a wide range of programs in the Los Angeles area, including theaters, child care centers, museums, arts education, and population control.

—Since 1919, the recently deceased Helen Clay Frick was the sole controller of one of the great nineteenth-century robber-baron industrial fortunes, that accumulated by her father Henry

Clay Frick, the "Coke King" of Pittsburgh. It was she who established the Frick Collection in the mansion her father built on Fifth Avenue in Manhattan, and her Helen Clay Frick Foundation runs an art reference library in New York, supports Episcopal Church causes, and operates a museum of Renaissance art in Pittsburgh.

—Enid Annenberg Haupt, as we have seen, concentrates her charitable inclinations on matters vegetable. Since 1978 alone, her contributions to the New York Botanical Garden have come to more than $10 million, and she has planted hundreds of cherry trees along Park Avenue, a street not greatly lacking in horticultural distinction to begin with.

—Rose Fitzgerald Kennedy, the matriarch of the rapidly fading Kennedy dynasty, has run the Joseph P. Kennedy, Jr., Foundation since her husband's death, doling out millions to programs for mental retardation (one of her daughters was afflicted) and social institutions.

—Estée Lauder, together with her two sons, funds the Lauder Foundation, which does such things as donating playgrounds in New York City and contributing to social agencies, museums, medical research, and education, all to the tune of more than half a million dollars a year. In October 1983, the family announced a $10 million gift to the University of Pennsylvania in the name of Estée's late husband Joseph to establish an institute for management and international studies.

—Frances Lewis, together with her husband Sydney, has been involved in the creation of Best Products, the discount retail chain headquartered in Richmond, Virginia. The Lewises gave $6 million for a west wing for the Virginia Museum in Richmond, as well as some fifteen hundred pieces of art. In 1972, they gave Washington and Lee University $9 million for a new law school building, and another spare few million to Virginia Union University, a black school in Richmond.

—Alice Tully, who got her money by being the granddaughter of Amory Houghton, the founder of Corning Glass, and is now a much-honored octogenarian in New York, has not only contributed Alice Tully Hall to Lincoln Center, but has made major grants to Alliance Française, New York University Medical Center, the New York Humane Society, the Save the Children Federation, and a number of wildlife organizations.

—Ruth Chinitz Uris and Joanne Diotte Uris are the widows of Harold D. Uris and Percy Uris respectively, the principals in the

Uris Building Corporation, a major Manhattan construction firm. They have given $10 million for a new educational facility at the Metropolitan Museum, $2 million to Lenox Hill Hospital, and $2.5 million to Columbia University.

—Marajen Steveck Chinigo is another of the female publishers. She owns the Champaign (Illinois) *News-Gazette*, which makes her small potatoes as a publishing force but an extremely rich woman. She gave $5 million to the University of Illinois and $1 million to the City of Faith at Oral Roberts University.

—Doris Duke, in her early seventies, has combined a storied and, increasingly, an eccentric life with some substantial charitable contributions. In World War II she gave her Hawaiian estate, Shangri-La, to the United States Navy for use as an R&R stop for officers returning from Pacific combat duty. She is also the sole contributor to the Newport Restoration Foundation, which has saved much of the colonial heritage of the Rhode Island sailing port.

—Helene R. Foellinger, yet another newspaper publisher, is president of Fort Wayne (Indiana) Newspapers, and like her counterpart in Champaign, a major donor to the University of Illinois, her alma mater.

—Mary Lasker, well into her ninth decade, another of the grandes dames of New York society, has contributed millions from her husband Albert Lasker's Chicago advertising fortune to various charitable endeavors, including hundreds of thousands of flowers to New York City, but concentrating on medical research. "You have to be alive to enjoy flowers," she remarked.

—Cordelia Scaife May, in her middle fifties, has a major chunk of the gargantuan Mellon fortune. In the lee of a rather miserable life, including a husband who committed suicide after he was indicted for financial irregularities connected with his tenure as district attorney of Pittsburgh, she has become a fervent supporter of leftist causes, thus making herself appear even stranger among the ranks of the very wealthy. Her Laurel Foundation backs a number of social agencies, especially in population control, concentrated in western Pennsylvania.

—Margaret McDermott, the widow of a founder of Texas Instruments, along with her daughter Mary supervises two family foundations that her late husband Eugene set up. They've given $1.25 million to Stevens Institute, his alma mater, for a technology center, $1.25 million to M.I.T. for scholarships for students from Texas, and $200,000 to Southern Methodist University for a theater. Margaret McDermott has also been one of the largest donors to the Dallas Museum of Fine Arts.

In 1982, a recession year, Americans donated slightly over $60 billion to charity, more than $48 billion of that from living individuals. What are all these people doing donating all this money? It is distinctly a United States phenomenon. There are simply not that many Europeans who retain the personal wealth to give money on this scale. Moreover, the quasisocialistic cast of most European governments has long since encouraged the specious feeling that government is somehow giving the populace things for free out of its own generosity. Most developing countries, especially those in Latin America, are saddled with long-entrenched oligarchies who make their own rules, which seem to include a blanket prohibition on any activities in the public interest. But the single greatest inducement for Americans to give money away is the Internal Revenue Service, which allows philanthropists to deduct the full amount of their contributions from their income—a savings in the top tax bracket of 50 percent. But whatever the reasons, anyone acquainted with the world of philanthropy realizes that Americans are easily the most generous people in the world. "It was in the United States that I learned how to give, how to participate in the society," says Suni Agnelli.

The most important recent trend in charitable giving is a tendency to give it away while one is alive. "No one wants to die rich," *Forbes* proclaimed recently in an oracular tone. There is an increasing sensitivity to public relations, with the consequent realization that it is bad form to spend all of one's entire fortune on conspicuous consumption. Philanthropy lends purpose and seriousness to your life. Finally, giving while one is still around allows control of the expenditure; it has always been one of the maddening disabilities of great wealth that someone else is eventually going to be able to do whatever they want with it. (There is no recorded theological speculation on whether this causes annoyance to the souls of the departed.) Brooke Astor, for example, has made no secret of the fact that she is raiding the principal of the Astor Foundation—to the tune of some $80 million so far—despite the family's historic preference to pass it along to the next generation, because she does not want to see it fall into the hands of people neither she nor Vincent knew.

It has also become increasingly *fashionable* to give a building to a college, a medical center, a performing arts institution. As we have seen, much of the social circuit in New York and elsewhere revolves around dinners and dances that are a sort of peer-pressure operation to raise funds for a bewildering array of institutions, diseases, and just about any cause that could possibly arrange to have money spent on it. These are known collectively in the trade as "guilt dinners." The MO can be surmised from the comments of Art Buchwald, whose humor in this case arises from his deadly accuracy, at a dinner in 1982 honoring Mark Handler, the president of Macy's. "Some of you may be wondering why the Cystic Fibrosis Foundation is honoring this great humanitarian," Buchwald said, "and I am proud to give you the answer tonight. Mark Handler sells tables. When Cystic Fibrosis was looking for someone who could fill this gigantic ballroom, the name Mark Handler repeatedly came up. As one member of the board put it, 'There isn't a Macy's supplier in the country that would refuse to buy a table if we told him we were honoring Handler. Companies who are doing business with Handler will have to buy a table. Companies who *want* to do business with Handler will have to buy *two* tables. Companies who are going bankrupt because of Macy's will have to buy *three* tables in the hopes they can get well again. With Handler as our honoree we can blackmail every dress manufacturer on Seventh Avenue. The advertising agency that handles the Macy's account will have to buy a table. The advertising agency that is trying to steal the account from the other agency will buy four tables.''

Except in the summertime, there is at least one of these events virtually every night in New York, and sometimes, during the height of the fall season, up to four events in a single day—at a single place, the Grand Ballroom of the Waldorf-Astoria. In October and November 1983 alone, according to one report, no fewer than sixty-eight fundraising events took place there, including Episcopal, fundamentalist, Catholic, and several Jewish events; a good number of popular diseases; several hospitals; and opera, Boys' Clubs, the Philharmonic, the Olympics, and the American Committee on Italian Migration. To a lesser extent, similar events are going on throughout the other major American cities, especially Los Angeles, Chicago, Dallas, Houston, and of course, in season, Palm Beach. Most of these affairs are put together by professional party-giving counselors who charge up to $25,000 or $30,000 for putting on a show that frequently grosses over $200,000 and sometimes much higher. An important contributing factor at the major banquets for substantial charitable causes is the corporation; even though the share of corporate giving to charities in the United States is only 5 percent of the $60 billion total, they are useful because they are identifiable and concentrated sources of the money to purchase an entire table. And much of the purely business-related circuit of fundraising is therefore dependent primarily on the corporate clout and connections of the honchos being "honored" at the affair, as well as the skill of the party-givers in ferreting out the right friends.

As fundraising has become big business, the role previously held by the great social hostesses and Junior League young women has concomitantly shrunk. This does not mean that women have no role, of course. A great part of the reason that anyone shows up for these events is that there is a large group of women who have spent much of their lives and their husbands' or fathers' money creating a look and wardrobe for themselves—not something that they can wear to the office, even if they work. The dependable impulse to see and be seen remains a major reason for the cohesiveness of the charitable class.

Moreover, the day of the great charity gala, nearly always put on by a socially prominent and, of necessity, a very rich woman, is by no means gone. The local gentry of many cities of the country, as we have seen in the sections on the arts and on debutantes, gathers in a predictable seasonal round to show its hearts and its gowns at a number of fundraising events. These affairs, until not long ago, were crucial to the social stability of a provincial American city; a young woman worked or did not work on, attended or did not attend, the charity ball at the country club based almost entirely on who her parents were, with minor nods toward her appearance and social graces. This sort of thing still exists; charitable and philanthropic endeavors will always rely on an inner circle of dedicated supporters and a wider circle of friends of theirs for support. However, in recent decades the really big charity extravaganza has more and more tended to be the production of a single woman rather than the once ubiquitous "committee," and it can put her on the national or international social map, vaulting her well over the lesser lights who used to be important.

Such an event is the Carousel Ball thrown in Denver each October by Barbara Davis for the Children's Diabetes Foundation, which she started seven years ago when she learned that her daughter had the disease. What made that impulse more than a family concern was the family involved: Barbara's husband Marvin Davis is easily one of the richest men in the world, with a huge position in his privately held Davis Oil and ownership of half of 20th Century Fox studios. As a result of the clout of her bulldog husband and her own year-long preparations, Mrs. Davis's idea has, within those few years, become not only one of the largest and richest fundraising events in the world, but a genuine stop on the international circuit—something that Denver had not been. In 1983, for example, the event attracted Henry Kissinger, Gerald R. Ford, Jimmy Stewart, Dolly Parton, Raquel Welch, Lucille Ball, Diana Ross, Princess Yasmin Aga Khan, Eppie Lederer (Ann Landers), the John Johnsons of the black publishing empire from Chicago, the William Coorses of the beer industry, and about twenty-five hundred other guests, five hundred of whom sat at two-thousand-dollars-a-person "Golden Circle" tables. It is hard to find a place for that many partygoers, so Mrs. Davis rented Currigan Hall, which is otherwise used for conventions and trade exhibitions. Then she carpeted the entire hall and brought in Walter Scott, an Academy Award–winning set designer. Scott hung a carousel with twenty-four fiberglass horses from the ceiling, and shipped in such items as temple scenes from *The King and I* to serve as the backdrop for a silent auction of, among other things, six mink coats, a Mercedes, several gift certificates for $1,500, and walk-on parts in television shows. Scott did not even want to estimate the cost of the thing. It was underwritten entirely by Marvin Davis, whose instructions to Scott when asked how much could be spent were, "The rule is that you please the little lady, that's your job." Of such incisiveness are charitable careers made.

Sarah Pillsbury, heiress to the flour fortune, is part of a substantial portion of the current generation of wealthy inheritors who need to do something with their money. What she and her brother George have both done is to create philanthropic organizations dedicated to the easing—or in some cases the destruction—of the capitalist structure that their forebears built. She has put some chunk of her inheritance—as with other rich women, nobody wants to say how much—into the Liberty Hill Foundation, based in Santa Monica, near Los Angeles and not far from Westwood, the charming area where Sarah Pillsbury has set up her movie and TV production company. They support things like prison reform, women's equality, and homosexual rights. Miss Pillsbury graduated from Yale in 1973 and moved to Los Angeles because she wanted to see what Los Angeles was all about. Who doesn't? "I was fairly certain I would pursue some sort of career in film," she says, "but I also wondered what went on in Los Angeles politically. And fairly soon after I got out here, I hooked up with a few other people who had inherited wealth—who also had a history of making contributions to the kinds of progressive social-change–oriented projects that I was involved with."

George Pillsbury had already started the Haymarket Peoples Fund. The movement that they are both loosely associated with started in 1971 in Philadelphia with the Bread and Roses Community Fund, which was specifically created as an alternative to the United Way. Those who are unkind have called the prime sponsors of such organizations fat kittens. Knowing Sarah Pillsbury would disabuse anyone of the notion that she is an unthinking rich girl. She is a *thinking* rich girl. The world is not a bitter place to rich people, but it is a place that takes constant reassessment. Miss Pillsbury, for example, knows people of inherited wealth who have moved to Los Angeles for the sun and the fun and the newness, who have then decided that it is no place to raise children—"the values that people in Los Angeles have concerning wealth are so warped." Sarah Pillsbury herself would not want to bring up a child in Beverly Hills. But that is for the future. For now, she has sparked an "alternative philanthropy": it makes even less difference than a serious, centimillion-dollar philanthropy, but it is charting a path that more and more of her fellow philosophical heiresses will follow. In small amounts, Liberty Hill has donated money to push nuclear disarmament, rent control, opposition to police abuse, "education" about Central America, South Africa, and the Philippines; to oppose hunger, rapacious developers, battering and general maltreatment of women. This is an intelligent, small-scale contribution to the battle against the forces that keep people down these days. Sarah Pillsbury intends to "assist people in any way that we can to be involved in the process of just empowering people, of making their lots better—or see what it takes. Maybe they fail, but they learn something, and they're no longer as ignorant or apathetic as many Americans are."

Then there is Yoko Ono. Besides buying full pages in the *New York Times* to wish their public Christmas greetings, she and the late John Lennon seem to have evolved from their lying-in-bed-for-peace days into a much more typical kind of philanthropy.

In October 1983, Miss Ono announced that her Spirit Foundation was donating a historic waterfront mansion in Virginia on 22 acres, a 25-acre site in Ireland, 120 acres at another Virginia site, $500,000 in cash, a 1965 Classic Phantom Rolls-Royce, a collection of lithographs by Lennon, and musical instruments owned by both of them for the benefit of a foster home program, Central Park, and orphans in Ireland and Liverpool. The donation was being made, she said, "in apology as a member of the human race and in memory of war casualties of the world."

The really extraordinary charity fête of recent memory was held in Washington on February 17, 1984, and featured an international cast of hundreds of movers, shakers, dress designers, watch manufacturers, President and Mrs. Reagan, nobles of various stripes, fashion models, and even doves imported from North Carolina and placed in cages on tables during a luncheon fashion show. (They were drugged to keep the fluttering down.) The entire weekend's series of events cost each guest $5,000. "Five-thousand-dollar tickets—that's not an abnormal thing," said Lynn Wyatt, the effervescent and universally known Houston hostess who spent a year or so putting the whole thing together. "People spend $5,000 every day here for politicians." And this was different. It was hardly for a politician—it was for a princess. It was the establishment of the Princess Grace Foundation, an institution that the elite of several continents developed after her untimely death, for the support of the arts. (More precise goals have not yet been agreed upon.) The foundation was aiming to raise $1 million right that weekend. Not everybody was expected to come up with $5,000 for the whole weekend, of course, and fewer than two hundred did. Fortunately, there were various bargain-priced ticket combinations from $500 to $1,500 for the weekend's events, which kicked off with a Friday night reception at the White House, then dinner, a luncheon fashion show Saturday, the crowning gala Saturday night, and finally an anticlimactic brunch at the State Department on Sunday.

Part of the reason that Lynn Wyatt was such a perfect choice as the hostess was that she was old buddies with the Grimaldis from all those pine-scented nights in the south of France. Her famous Yellow Rose of Texas balls at the house in Cap Ferrat were begun at the request of Princess Grace herself. So in 1982, when all this round of Grace celebrating started, Lynn Wyatt had already offered a lavish dinner, as well as overnight accommodations, to Princess Caroline at the stately manse in River Oaks. The beneficiary then was the International Shakespeare Globe Center, one of the late princess's favorite causes. Princess Caroline, stepping up into her mother's place in the socially impeccable and financially incredible charity-party round, hadn't stayed with the Wyatts for long, because then it was on to a huge reception given in New York by Harry and Leona Helmsley in their Palace. But on the other hand Lynn Wyatt was hardly insulted, because others who might aspire to her rank as philanthropic hostess had already been forced to give their bashes for the Shakespeare fund without Princess Caroline. Among them were Caroline Hunt Schoellkopf at the Mansion on Turtle Creek, Ann and Gordon Getty in the Pacific Heights showplace, and Mr. and Mrs. Louis Cabot up in Boston. Such is the pecking order of powerhouse party-giving.

So Lynn Wyatt has long had the inside track for the Princess Grace Foundation through her friendship with the family. But there are other reasons as important. One is her great personal wealth, which enables her to pick up a few spare tens of thousands here and there without discomfort, and to set the example for her friends. And rich friends are another crucial attribute of the would-be international charity hostess; when Josephine Hudson blew in from Houston for the gala, she told a reporter, "Lynn's a friend of ours, and we just said, 'What the heck, why not go.' " Just being a Texan is a great help, since there are no groups of citizens extant as happy—or as financially able—to fly somewhere for a party and a boosterish cause at the drop of a hat. Lynn Wyatt has been on the circuit long enough, and has honed her rich southern girl breeziness to such a pitch of appeal that she can invite the really big guns—like Betsy Bloomingdale and the powerhouse advertising woman Mary Wells Lawrence —and be on good terms with the likes of Princess Beatrice of Savoie (daughter of the last king of Italy), Sarvenaz Pahlavi (niece of the last shah of Iran), Contessa Christa Odiel (great-granddaughter of a queen of Spain). She also knows how to pick out her potential donors and to treat them with honeysuckle sweetness—a skill that achieved donations of forty cases of Moët & Chandon, a fashion show by the Italian manufacturer Genny, and the underwriting of $100,000 of the party's cost by Piaget, which also donated a watch of similar value for a raffle. Finally, it is of considerable importance that the party-giver possess The Look, as the Internationally Best-Dressed Mrs. Wyatt so clearly does. The mere presence of such a hostess guaranteed that the lengths gone to would be extraordinary even for the internationalities. And the event did lend itself to those little touches. Besides the doves on the tables and the little tulip bouquets on the backs of each chair at the Saturday night gala, the toilet bowls available during the fashion luncheon were refilled with shredded carnations after each flush.

23 | POWER HOSTESSING

LYNN WYATT is justifiably famous for her lavish and memorable parties—the Western-outfit bash for the Yellow Rose of Texas, the black-tie party at Gillies for the premiere of the movie *Urban Cowboy*, and a few hundred others that people in her circle could run down in an hour or two. There are a few qualities to which she attributes her success: she loves people. She is a perfectionist. And she loves to be amused. She wants to do "things that are actually different and amusing and not just charitable. I mean I know so many people who do it so much better than I do, and for me to really get involved in something like that—number one, I [have to] feel very strongly about the cause, and number two, it has to be something that is a little bit unique, either the theme or something that's never been done before or, you know, something that might give it a different twist, and I think it becomes something much more amusing."

This is no mere personal hedonism, she wants it known, nor even a simple ambition to have everyone love her, although

surely there is something of that. It is also that the people liable
to attend these affairs genuinely have their choice of whatever
they want to do of an evening—"they're flying off to Atlantic
City or Rio," is the way Mrs. Wyatt puts it—and they need a bit
of urging to attend yet another charitable function. Moreover,
once you get a reputation for Lynn Wyatt's bankable combination
of great personal wealth, energy, interest, and charm, you become catnip to every ambitious director of development for miles
around; she solves this problem by simply saying no, even for
the use of her name, unless she is interested enough to do a
major job. As the figures on fundraising suggest, she has perceived a substantial increase in the number of charity events.
"The thing of big, huge parties, balls and things, private balls,
are no longer being given," she said.

> And so people who gave those balls are now working on chari-
> table—and even those, it's not exclusive because anybody who
> pays can go. [However,] usually the friends of that person . . . go
> to that person's charitable ball. So in a way it has taken the place
> of the big enormous private galas. Well, I think that in the world
> situation, it just sort of made it in bad taste to be throwing all this
> money away just to have a great party and just to have a good
> time; whereas people can still have a good time but at least they
> feel like they're giving their money to something more substantial.
> . . . I'm not saying there aren't any—there are still wonderful kind
> of parties. There are less and less in Paris.

Not that Lynn Wyatt succumbs to the vulgar trend herself. She
gives plenty of parties for her friends. Dinner parties of twenty
or thirty or fifty are common. Just about anyone of any celebrity
who passes through Houston has been invited to stay over at
the mansion, from Mick Jagger to Stavros Niarchos.

Marylou Whitney is a sort of friendly competitor of Lynn Wyatt's
in the hostessing-for-fun-and-philanthropy sweepstakes, but she
is much more in the classic old-line mode, the WASP goddess
well above the tumult of lesser mortals even while she is observing and entertaining them. She too has noticed the increase
in charity events: "These people [who have just moved to New
York, especially rich foreigners], they want to do something and
it's very interesting to me that—I suppose they want to be social
and they don't know who to go with and to see, and they buy
tickets to all these different balls and charity events and meet

people and then they can have some social status. I have no idea, but I assume that's what it is. But it's very nice for all the charities." Mrs. Whitney herself, of course, has no such base motives in her charitable endeavors, having already achieved as much social eminence as is possible in the inchoate modern whirl.[33] Her methods of picking among the plethora of worthy causes can be taken as a guideline to the similar choices that the wealthy of any known generosity must constantly make. As we have seen, the charities are related to her and to her husband by family tradition, family diseases, geography, and sometimes simply by random choice. She does not stint. Her memberships, boards, clubs, and awards run to two full single-spaced pages on her "dossier." "If you want something done, ask a busy person," is one of her sayings.

Mrs. Whitney is nothing short of incredible as a hostess; indeed, she may be the last of the great "society"-forming hostesses in the United States. Where Lynn Wyatt puts on the occasional extravaganza, like the Princess Grace gala, Mrs. Whitney does two of nearly that size every year, at the Kentucky Derby and at Saratoga. Then she does her occasional special, such as the little party she gave in Sarajevo two days before the beginning of the 1984 Winter Olympics. It was part of the tradition, really since she had given what she called "the only really big party" at the Lake Placid Olympics—a concoction of silver snowflakes, plastic igloos, and icicles, an orchestra, and bottomless champagne. For Sarajevo, Marylou had connections through the Whitneys, who are supposed to have done some secret favor for the Yugoslavs after the end of World War II; they came in handy when the first hall she thought of was found wanting, and the grandiose Parliament House was borrowed instead. She invited four hundred guests—kings, presidents—and shipped over all the liquor and champagne from the United States. She also sent an advance party consisting of Virginia Douglas, her personal secretary, and two decorators to put the whole thing together. One of the disadvantages of the Third World is the general un-

33. Not that she does not have to defend her eminence occasionally, like a ballplayer being challenged by a rookie upstart. Before Queen Elizabeth II visited Bluegrass Country in 1984, her host oil heir William S. Farish and his wife Sarah, a du Pont, invited people to small dinners with the queen on the four nights of her stay—but failed to include Mrs. Whitney. The British press reported that she smoldered upon learning of the slight, which Farish thereupon amended by announcing the Whitneys would be invited to a small reception with Elizabeth on her last day.

availability of the florists, drapery peddlers, and other specialized service people that Marylou Whitney generally depends upon. She made do with ribbon, flags, votive candles, and whatever flowers she could find; local strolling violinists provided the music. It was the sort of display that has doubtless been missing from Sarajevo since the salad days of the Austro-Hungarian Empire. It cost Marylou Whitney somewhere between $25,000 and $50,000. But who's counting? as Suzy would ask.

Much of Mrs. Whitney's energy, not to mention her sense of self, is bound up in these extravagant and wondrous occasions. "I love to stage a party," she says, and indeed the fiddling with the glasses seems suddenly less studied, and the tongue flicks a little faster around the words as she talks about it. "It's really like a stage setting. I plan it months in advance [in fact, she is famous for hatching the design for her next parties at the Derby and Saratoga the day after the last one], and it's such fun—I draw pictures of it on the table, what everything should look like, and then I have the men on the farm in Kentucky and the caretakers in Saratoga, and I get them all together and I get them to volunteer to help me with such things, and it's really much more fun than getting the professionals. We make our own things. They have a lot of fun doing it and it's just a fun project. It's almost like putting on a play. And if it's successful, it's almost as if you've had a play that's successful." Her parties have been known to turn a simple ballroom into a fanciful Versailles or a circus, complete with tumblers, food booths, fortune-tellers, and merry-go-rounds. In 1980, the Saratoga party theme was the Saratoga potato chip; in 1981, the light bulb, which was invented somewhere nearby; in 1982, "Young in Heart," with guests being awarded the short-lived faddish deely-boppers as favors; in 1983, "Floral Fete." The Kentucky Derby dazzler in 1983 had a Victorian theme: porcelain cherubs were installed in all the archways of the pool house, the big house was hung with old lace, exotic birds peered over the festivities from their cages, the centerpieces of all the tables were little maypoles, and everyone got a vermeil bookmark as a favor. Some of the biggest names in the country, and beyond, were present, like Henry Kissinger, Beverly Sills (both houseguests), the Nelson Bunker Hunts, senators, business owners, and others of that ilk. Princess Margaret showed up at the Derby party one year, and Queen Noor of Jordan (the former Lisa Halaby, of Princeton University) has said she might attend a future Derby party.

Naturally, everyone desperately wants to be among the 175 tiptoeing through Mrs. Whitney's Kentucky tulips and the 225 invited to the Saratoga fling. The awareness of this bitter fact is a great burden on Mrs. Whitney's shoulders. "That's hard, it's awfully hard," she says, frowning slightly at the pain she is causing all those poor social climbers. "There are always people that you have to leave out. That's part of the whole thing. You can't invite the whole world. When we give parties in Saratoga, we have more people outside than inside. The town people are standing there waiting, lined up on both sides. The city police now keep them back so that our guests can get out to their cars." Fortunately there are other occasions for invitations, as Mrs. Whitney's life is literally one round of entertainment, a gauzy, stylized whirl from one perfect setting to the next (though there is, one can readily believe, a great deal of detail work between the parties). "I do give a lot of parties," she says with the wide-eyed sincerity that rich women affect.

In Kentucky or Saratoga, I give parties almost every Sunday night. It's just a little informal thing; sometimes I cook, and sometimes I have somebody come in to cook, and I never know which way I'm going to do it, and we sit around the indoor pool and watch old movies—oh, we have eighteen to thirty people and we show old movies like Fred Astaire and Ginger Rogers and things like that, and it's kind of fun. Then, I'm coming back here [to Manhattan] on the thirtieth [of October 1983], and I'm having thirty-two people for dinner before a little dancing group that we're going to, and then I go to Kentucky on the seventh, I have—no, the ninth, I'm having people coming in for a seated dinner-dance there and that will all be very pretty. I'm having all the decorations done for that, I'm even having the placecards done. Then I go to Saratoga, and on the fifteenth we have a dinner-dance there for about a hundred people—seated. We have an awfully pretty party in Saratoga, it's a darling party. On the twenty-third of December, I have my closest friends come with all their children, and it amounts to about fifty people, and we meet in an indoor swimming pool and the tables are all set for Christmas. . . . And then I have a very dear friend who gives a Christmas birthday party for me on Christmas Eve, and no one can bring a present, they have to write a poem. . . . A week from today, I'm giving a luncheon for fifty people for Matilda Cuomo [wife of New York Governor Mario Cuomo], a seated luncheon in Saratoga. I want her to meet my Saratoga friends because she's involved with very, very interesting people. . . . So I'm giving her a luncheon, and then on the following Saturday I'm having my daughter, who wanted to have the christening of her little child, . . . so we're having the christening at the little chapel and the Episcopal priest is coming to christen the child. Then we're going to go back around the pool, and everything is going to be ready, and we're having a seated dinner there. And then afterwards we'll have a movie. So we have things pretty well arranged. . . . So it keeps on going and going and going. And then the next week we go up to the Adirondack Mountains to the hunting lodge. My children all want to be there, my grandchildren arrive from England, and my children all arrive because there's skiing. So we'll have a lovely Thanksgiving, I hope.

All this is recited without notes of any kind.

There will never be another Babe Paley, and the circumstances surrounding her death in 1978, at the age of sixty-three, can well stand as an epitaph for that height of style that she represented. For Mrs. Paley had actually *planned the details of the luncheon for guests at her own funeral.* Indeed, she had planned two, one for winter and one for summer. In the event, she died in July, which meant it was the chicken *à l'estragon.* Waiters stood at the entrance to the manor at Kiluna Farm, the Paley estate on the North Shore of Long Island, with trays of champagne and Ladoucette Pouilly-Fumé, her favorite wine. The cutlery was in wicker baskets, inside napkins folded to look like flowers. The last touch for her hundreds of friends to remember her by were the centerpieces, Chinese porcelain bowls filled with black cherries, which Babe Paley idiosyncratically preferred to flowers. Trademark centerpieces may not be the greatest memorial to leave the world, but it is better than not being remembered at all.

There will always be with us those cavillers who inquire exactly what value there is to small-S society in all of this—whether Marylou Whitney really ought to be indulging her precious whims at the horse farm when there are children starving in the next Appalachian hollow. Some of her biggest parties are strictly private; there are no proceeds going to anyone, except for the vermeil bookmarks. They are much more closely related to the parties attended by her husband's relatives of three generations ago, consisting of lavish "fun" for its own sake, than they are to the ordinary run of events that size these days, which are almost uniformly dedicated to one or another of the fashionable disabilities or ennobling institutions. As one might well expect of a philosopher of hostessing, Mrs. Whitney has long since salved her conscience on this score. Fortunately, she has the benefit of a long line of rich persons' thinking on the topic; and "society" being precisely the lavish expression of homogeneity, all such thinkers—from the infamous squanderers of the Gilded Age, through the Barbara Hutton types of the depression, and in an underground way to the present—have come to the same conclusion. That is, simply, that *throwing parties is good for the economy.* "Some people say," observes Mrs. Whitney,

"Look at the waste of this, think of the money you could have given to the poor," and I say, "This helps the community." The women go out and buy new dresses [thereby presumably aiding the *haute couture* industry of upstate New York], the men will have their tuxedos pressed [she laughs], they might buy a new bow tie, or buy a new pair of socks or whatever—I don't know that they do very much for the clothing business. However, when you do a party, you're hiring caterers and cooks and waiters and waitresses and bartenders. The food has to be bought locally, and if you're going to have three hundred people at a party, there will be a lot of food consumed, and a lot of drinks; it helps the liquor store, it helps the grocery store. And *everyone* goes to the hairdresser, I mean a few of the men might have their hair cut at home, but the women *all* go to the hairdresser, there's no doubt about that. And it helps the jeweler, whether it's costume jewelry or whatever. And then, some people like to arrive with people driving them in cars or whatever. It does help the community in many, many ways, because you spend a lot of money in the community. So it's not— it's giving a lot of people a lot of jobs. An untold number of people. There's the people who clean up, the people who you rent the tables from, the people who you rent the chairs from and the tablecloths from, all those rental people that have all those rentals— the glasses, the china, the linens, the florist.

It is reassuring, in a way, to know that in these days even a hostess of Mrs. Whitney's stature does not actually possess service for several hundred, as her predecessor social queen bees did.

Fortunately, all of this sweaty beneficence has its reward in the feudal allegiance of the locals. In Saratoga, Mrs. Whitney allows, "I don't receive my guests inside, I receive them outside so I can talk to all those lovely people. They're so dear. They've all become such good friends of mine. Their children come up and they bring me a rose.[!] They kiss me. After twenty years, the townspeople have become such really good friends. I don't know them by name, I know them by face. They come every year. It has to be put in the paper when we're having a party. . . . They'll stay there for three or four hours watching people coming and going. It started to sprinkle last year and I felt so sorry for them. I said, 'Oh, dear God, I can't let it rain on you—I don't know what to do, I can't let you come in.' Well, the rain stopped—it only sprinkled a little bit. But I thought, 'Oh, this can't happen,' because they just are so dear—lovely."

Very few people throw parties on the scale of Mrs. Whitney's anymore. At least, very few talk much about it, although the Palm Beach social circuit and the occasional bash in New York measure up rather nicely to the impressive standards set in the old days. Everybody complains about the lack of good help and the high price of sterling. But as we have seen, there is plenty of money at the disposal of potential hostesses. No, what we have here are changing mores: a general democraticization, with the attendant disrepute of the rich county family of Mrs. Whitney's ilk, and, especially, feminism. No woman really wants to admit anymore that she has nothing better to do than to spend an entire day supervising preparations for a dinner party, as Marjorie Merriweather Post habitually did.

"The whole thing has changed," Pamela Harriman told the *New York Times*. "Women aspire to be political leaders, not social leaders." Nowhere is this more evident than in the case of Mrs. Harriman herself, the daughter of an English lord of a generation (she is in her sixties) in which women were meant to be purely ornamental. Her series of illustrious marriages—first to Winston Churchill's son Randolph, then on to the late Broadway producer Leland Hayward—having climaxed in an alliance with the ancient W. Averell Harriman, one of the most respected and richest of grand old diplomats, it was only natural to expect that she would quickly assume a dominant position in Washington society. Which is a rather peculiar mixture of political hustlers and influence-peddlers (and buyers) with the respectable old-line types like the Harrimans themselves, but also with rules of its own. People thought, in other words, that she might well become a social arbiter of Washington something like Miss Post, and before her the likes of Alice Roosevelt Longworth, Evalyn Walsh McLean (one-time owner of the Hope Diamond), Perle Mesta ("the hostess with the mostest"), and Cissy Patterson, the free-spirited publisher of the old *Washington Times-Herald*. The breeding was right, for not only was Pamela Harriman born correctly, she had already run a famous salon in London during her first marriage. Her acquaintances there had included Kick Kennedy's (Jack's tragic sister) exclusive set; and when she married Harriman in 1970, one of her first acts was to join the exclusive Middleburg Hunt.

Pamela Harriman did indeed become a notable in Georgetown, but not quite in the way anyone expected. She used her husband's money and position not to establish a regular social gathering place for herself to preside over, but to set herself up as the honcha of a political action committee. She does have people over, but her guests amidst the fabulous Impressionist paintings and antique Chinese porcelains are uniformly utilitarian types— though not lacking in the glamour engendered by power—whose counsel and contacts give her personal PAC as much clout as those run by small trade organizations. In so doing, Mrs. Harriman expresses the elitist, high-minded, internationalist, liberal leanings of the school of benevolent millionaires of the eastern Establishment represented so prominently by her husband. But the method is different from the past methods of a woman of that class. Mrs. Harriman is actually pushing for certain policies in her own right and twisting arms to raise money for them, when in a previous incarnation she would merely have been the sponsor of the gathering place where the powerful came to relax. "It's terrible to be so concerned about money, don't you think?" she asked a reporter with classic upper-class self-amusement after one fundraising tour in 1982.

Mrs. Harriman is representative of a general shift in the sensibility of the Washington social scene. As elsewhere, much of the entertaining in the capital, which has always been lavish, has shifted to the corporation—where, among other advantages, the stockholders and customers can pay for it. Not that nobody gives parties at home anymore. Katharine Graham tosses affairs for eighty or more at her Georgetown town house, and Evangeline Bruce, widow of the late ambassador David K. E. Bruce and mother of the tragic Sasha, hosts brunch regularly in *her* Georgetown showplace for the delectation of politicians, writers, and visiting celebrities. Mrs. Bruce, who in addition to her experience as an ambassador's wife had the rare advantages of being raised abroad as the daughter of a Foreign Service officer, told the *Times* that she is not especially delighted with the opportunities for a rich, stylish woman in Washington: "I don't think any gathering in Washington includes the main ingredients of a salon. . . . The tone has to be light, humorous, witty, and the more elusive the reference, the more prized. In Washington we [she means "they"] don't go in for elusive statements. We are not particularly well-read and therefore even the deft allusions are lost. The thinking is that salons should be run by women because women are considered able to conquer egotism better than men—they take the time to be sure that everyone shines, they are more likely to keep their own talents in the background. . . . In a salon, you can't be ponderous, egocentric. Anything other than a lucid, witty, graceful style is simply not allowed. That doesn't sound like Washington, does it?"

24 | Climbing

The Citadel

THE IMPLICATION of the demise of the Washington hostess is that "society" itself is crumbling. Certainly, there is nothing left like the monolithic structure once presided over by *the* Mrs. Astor, or the various Mrs. Vanderbilts, or Mrs. Fish. The center began not to hold with the dislocations of World War I, and then the sex, drugs, and jazz of the twenties. Still, residual snobbery and prejudice carried "society" through the thirties and forties. Finally, it developed that no one really cared much anymore; "society," defined as a collection of people of the proper background and taste, simply withered away. It was replaced by what might more properly be called fashion than society, although it hardly matters what it is called. For the people who are in it, it matters a great deal; for those outside, it is generally a matter of no importance. By its very nature, however, the world of "society" is for many of the world's richest people the most fascinating and important game of all.

There was a time when "society" claimed to be a guardian of proper behavior; that time is long past, although it is still important for those aspiring to join its ranks to behave appropriately. At its best, this grouping of people who are rich, well-bred, and talented serves as a fundraising adjunct of great American institutions, primarily the great causes of New York, which have been summarized as "the library, New York Hospital, and both Mets, opera and museum." At its worst this is an endless round of one-upmanship played by people who really have nothing else to play at. There is a central core, an "A list," of people who, because of background and social concentration, are bade to appear at all the proper events and who toss a few of them themselves. It also helps if the daddy's rich and the mama's good-looking.

The best way to indicate one's in-group status is not merely to attend the expensive benefits, which are of course open to everyone with a thousand dollars or whatever (although it's not much fun to show up without knowing anyone). Rather, one must begin to be invited to the cozy dinners in private homes, given, as Marylou Whitney puts it, for "eighteen or thirty people." Mrs. Whitney herself is at the top of the list of hostesses— a position she takes pains to ensure by inviting both Aileen Mehle ("Suzy") and Charlotte Curtis, the two most important chroniclers of present-day "society," to her aerie on Fifth Avenue. She is so well funded; so perfectly compacted of proper family, show biz and impeccable marriage; so tasteful; so *amusing* (which does not have much to do with being funny); so kind, and so generous that she is very nearly a universal favorite, and the parties at 834 Fifth are among the most important in New York. When Nancy Reagan stopped in New York late in 1982, Marylou Whitney was at the helm of the command-performance private dinner she attended. Nancy's sidekick Betsy Bloomingdale was there, of course, and the others included next-door neighbor Mary French (Mrs. Laurance) Rockefeller, Douglas Fairbanks, Jr. (as socially respectable as any Hollywood type can get), Gloria Vanderbilt escorted by Bill Blass—Nancy was wearing a Blass—Jerome Zipkin, Trini Fierro (the wife of Alfonso Fierro, a banker from a family synonymous with money in Spain), and Countess Consuelo Crespi.

Among the other key hostesses and/or guests in New York are Alice Mason, a real estate broker—she recently sold A. Alfred Taubman an apartment in 834 Fifth for $4 million—who, it was reported in the fall of 1983, had already at that time planned her dinner dates for the next six months, and who has also hosted presidential-quality private dinners (but in her case, unusual for this crowd, for Jimmy Carter, a *Democrat*); Mica Ertegun, the interior-decorator wife of record baron Ahmet Ertegun and, according to William F. Buckley, Jr., "one of the most beautiful and interesting women in the world"; Drue Heinz, wife of H. J. Heinz II; Mercedes Kellogg, the Iranian-born (stepdaughter of Empress Farah Diba's uncle) wife of a retired diplomat; Patricia Buckley, wife of William F.; Mary Lasker and Brooke Astor, both widely admired for their obviously genuine concern for their charities; and Gloria Vanderbilt, who puts together a glitzy spectacular every now and again.

For Texas and the south of France it is, of course, Lynn Wyatt, considered a little flashy, partly because of that magnolia voice. In San Francisco, Ann Getty has dominated the social landscape for years with her dinner parties for from eight to eighty—frequently a musical evening because of Gordon's interests—but she and Gordon are now spending six months a year in their Fifth Avenue apartment so she has a better base for her assaults on the East Coast bastions of philanthropy like the Metropolitan Opera (vice-chairman), Metropolitan Museum (trustee), the National Endowment for the Arts, and the National Gallery. And of course any invitation from a Rockefeller is a command performance.

These are the old-line people, the ones you really can't go wrong with. They tend to be matched by a horde of lesser but sometimes richer lights, who have the advantage of novelty. Among these are Carroll Petrie, who was the Marquesa de Portago when Milton Petrie, the crusty octogenarian department store and Toys-Я-Us tycoon, married her in 1979; Judy Taubman, a staggering, Israeli-born, seven-language-speaking beauty who has pretty much taken Palm Beach by storm recently (fueled by the immense fortune of husband A. Alfred Taubman, who developed shopping centers, bought into the Irvine Ranch, and recently took over Sotheby Parke Bernet); and Susan Gutfreund, the good-looking wife of John Gutfreund, managing partner of the investment-banking firm of Salomon Brothers, who is generally accused of trying to buy her way into social preeminence, and with considerable success. (For example, the Gutfreunds recently moved their base of operation to 834 Fifth, buying the late Revlon founder Charles Lechman's apartment for $6.5 million.)

And just who gets invited to all these spectacular dinner parties, *intime* and yet earthshaking? As always, the key to making a dinner party amusing is to create a volatile mix. These days that tends to include the dress designers, hairdressers, makeup artists, and other caterers to female appearance who are valued for their interest in that kind of thing. A second important group is powerful government officials, with Henry Kissinger apparently enthroned permanently as the most valuable of all; Alexander Haig has also become popular recently. Businessmen of verve and great corporate dash are fine too, with the likes of Avis's David Mahoney and the NFL's Pete Rozelle much in demand. There will always be a place for stylish, charming, wellborn women—somebody like Amanda Burden, an attractive heiress, and it doesn't hurt if like Amanda she has been married to a politician, is the daughter of the late Babe Paley, has been linked to Kennedys in rumor, and is vice-president for architecture and design of the Battery Park City Authority. Depending on the crowd, celebrities might be acceptable; Mick Jagger and especially his ex-wife Bianca have made all sorts of scenes over the years, and they—Mick especially, since Bianca has gone very upscale—add a *frisson* of excitement to any table. Andy Warhol is in the same category. There are also celebrity writers. The late Truman Capote set the standard in the sixties with his court-jester role to Babe Paley; George Plimpton has always been of the proper background; and Norman Mailer has achieved a sort of transcendent celebrity that makes him just fine for just about any occasion.

Then there are the omnipresent characters that *W*, the fashion paper, has called walkers—known more usually as extra men. Since it has always been considered decadent for even a very rich man not to work, and no such prohibition applies to his wife, it is a matter of simple logistics that she will frequently find herself mateless for important social events—even if her husband would want to attend, which is questionable in many cases. In many cases as well, men approaching infirmity are precisely the types that younger women marry for money and stability, and the elderly husbands are often indisposed. Fortunately, there are always extra men around. Marylou Whitney, whose fathomless social energy would wear men much younger than her octogenarian husband to a frazzle, has twice traveled all the way to Thailand for a visit with her buddy, Queen Sirikit, in the company of well-known walker (as well as a PR agent) Budd Calisch.

But the greatest of these is Jerome Zipkin, and his career and influence tell a good deal about what holds "society" together. Zipkin, who lives on the income of inherited Park Avenue properties and somewhat resembles a swankly attired Pillsbury Doughboy, is best known for being Nancy Reagan's escort in New York and Washington. He is described as a master of the arcane art of the *entre nous* aside, which is simply to say that he likes to gossip as much as do the ladies that he flutters among. And he can sit through the same number of long lunches. His companions love his smooth-but-bitchy delivery and his near-perfect availability. He is tremendous on fashion commentary; "Jerry's got that eye for perfect detail," Betsy Bloomingdale has said. The ladies who lunch also much appreciate his ability to track the social comings and goings: if you've just dashed in from St. Martin and need to know if Nan's available for dinner next week, if Jacqueline's in New York, or where Susan got her sable, Zip is the one to ask.

But the trait valued above all is his unvarying selflessness. "He never burdens you with his problems, is always concerned with yours," fashion doyenne Nan Kempner put it once. For the rich, and especially for rich women, life involves an endless realization that most people are out to try to take advantage of you. Zipkin *never wants anything*! He just gives what is needed. For one of the few things that a rich person cannot buy, especially in this day of unthinking egalitarianism, is the acknowledgment that she is especially admirable. Zipkin, and the best of the other walkers, provide that homage.

Social Climbing

Don't bother with the men. You'll only make the wives jealous. Concentrate on the key women, and if you play your cards right you'll be a success.
—LORD WEIDENFELD TO ARIANNA STASSINOPOULOS

There are two ways of achieving social presence, which correspond to what can be thought of as two different types of "society"—namely, the glitterati and the self-consciously serious.

There is considerable overlapping and a good deal of confusion beween the two, and even within the classic social-climbing mechanism of fundraising for worthy causes, there can be a great deal of difference in style. One is flashy, self-promoting, and spotlight-loving, while the other aspires to be Old Rich even if it is not, and the worst that can happen is to get one's name in the papers for a purely social occasion. For object lessons in how to go about achieving a place in "society" these two ways, we turn once again to Texas, the empire of the nouveaux.

The proper way to go about social acceptance is illustrated by Anne Hendricks Bass. Like many of the important rich women of Texas, Anne Bass does not fit the stereotype of the spoiled daughter of a crude oilman. Born in Indianapolis to a prominent and well-to-do surgeon, Anne Hendricks was educated at private schools, studied Italian literature at Vassar, took a world tour, and then very politely got down to business by becoming an executive trainee at Bonwit Teller. She was an assistant buyer by the time she married Sid Richardson Bass. Sid is the oldest son and the manager of the family fortune—the largest nuclear-family fortune in the United States after the Hunts'—which started in oil, branched into the stock market, real estate and hotels, and is now estimated to be worth a total of something between $2 and $3 billion. Sid Bass is not your typical Fort Worth billionaire, either. He went to Andover and Yale; then, after he married Anne, out to Stanford to study business. (Managing the family fortune shrewdly isn't a genetic trait.) Anne kept herself busy by joining the Junior League and designing art programs for schoolchildren in Palo Alto. When they moved to Fort Worth to settle down, Anne blossomed into the perfect rich man's wife: mothering their daughters, laying out their garden with nonpareil landscaper Russell Page, raising orchids, joining art societies and, most portentously, picking up the daily ballet lessons she had abandoned when she went off to Vassar. As the Basses whirled between civic activities and empire-building in Fort Worth and the small, private art collections they delighted to visit in Europe, they frequently stopped in New York where they joined the Museum of Modern Art. On one of the stops in New York, Anne's interest in ballet led her to the out-of-town volunteers' section at the School of American Ballet. Naturally, the board expected to hit up the oil-drenched Basses for some major money. Anne tricked them all; she put on her solid midwestern look and buckled down to fundraising for the school's first benefit. It was far from the usual lavish fashion-show-cum-tax-deductible-lunch routine. Anne Bass just ran through her address book filled with rich chums, found people from Texas, Pennsylvania, and California, used them to find other people, and piled up a huge amount. Next, the school persuaded her to become chairman of the fiftieth anniversary fundraising drive for $15 million. It took three months to overcome Anne Bass's reluctance; but the school finally prevailed, and the drive rang up some $6.5 million within two years. The world of generous women had a new heavyweight.

Out of an entirely different mold is the incredible Carolyn Farb, whose fame has been gained, many in the world of style would say, by G. T. F.'ing—going too far. For one thing, Carolyn Farb has much too obviously made her personal fortune—about $30 million—through a rapid series of creative marriages and strategic divorces. With her immediate million-dollar annual allowance upon her marriage in 1977 to developer Harold Farb, Carolyn set about crashing Houston society. "I'm interested in a lot of very different things—cancer research, the Archives of American Art, lots of things," she says. "A city is judged by its arts, and I think it's extremely important that we keep everything moving along. I am just immersed in it. I have a lot of energy. I get up early, and I kind of like not to have enough time in the day."

The divorce was a masterstroke. It rid Carolyn of Harold, who was not only a *nag* at home but slightly ridiculous in public, with his endless tycoon-sings-Gershwin act; but even more important it set her up as obviously, and irrevocably, an independent locus of wealth. Everyone knew that Carolyn Farb could now choose her own events to organize, to support, and to browbeat her friends into attending. She had attained the position of a pillar of the social-charitable establishment—a sort of modern-day equivalent of the matriarchs of the Old Testament. She had, first of all, The Look, Texas style, and the sweetness. She thought more and harder about what she was doing on the charity circuit than anybody else did. Judging from Harold's complaints, giving money away—to fashionable charities, and fashionable clothiers—is *all* she thinks about. She doesn't mind conceding that anything is fair game for copying if it enhances her events. Even Houston had hardly seen anyone with the sudden clout, the sheer tiger determination of Carolyn Farb. Within a year or two, she had a wonderfully open field for her O.T.O.'s (one-time-only's), as she calls her unique events. Breaking money barriers was one mark of her success; it is one of Carolyn Farb's proudest boasts that she was the first woman in Houston to charge $10,000 per table at a single fundraising event. Mrs. Farb was also, she is proud to claim, one of the first to incorporate fashion designers into her events.

However, big is better only when it is within the bounds set by the *arriviste* but now firmly entrenched Carolyn—at least by her own lights. The $10,000 figure stood only until the following spring, when a benefit for the Houston Symphony sold tables for $15,000 at a benefit in Bayou Bend marking the hundredth birthday of the late Ima Hogg.

By 1984, supporters of the Lyric Theater in Houston were asking a very noticeable $25,000 per table for a benefit starring Frank Sinatra. This was not taken in very good grace by Carolyn Farb. She gives the distinct impression that she believes these people are competing only for glory, drying up funds that might otherwise be given to other, perhaps worthier causes. "It can turn you off," she pipes. But it is, she realizes, the price of leadership to be imitated, challenged, even ridiculed. You set up your achievements and others try to knock them down. The importance of what she is doing, and her prodigious appetite for detail and socializing, carry Carolyn Farb well beyond the slough of petty jealousy.

She is certainly aware that there is what she calls politics in the worlds of art and fundraising in general. She says that she does not go out of her way to ask people, reporters for example, to pay attention to her little extravaganzas. However, she is what might be called considerate to a fault; she makes herself available to questioners of all stripes, treats reporters of no special social background with some politeness, and even returns telephone calls. And she is rather too full of her public achievements for anyone to believe that she is not carefully trying to create an image for herself. She is happy to read a passage from a book called *In America*, which refers to her as a "fun heiress with a Farrah Fawcett hairdo," and another she was interviewed for called *The Ultimate Seduction*, which is about people utterly dedicated to their work. She is part of the social-celebrities-writing-about-social-celebrities quadrille in *Interview* magazine; and she notes that her appearance at the royal wedding was chronicled by a local television station.

This accessibility is generally interpreted in the social circuit she aspires to dominate as sheer personal promotion, which is not supposed to be done for nearly so unselect an audience. Indeed, it leads to disasters such as the distressing article in *People* magazine in 1983 that referred to Carolyn Farb as "a silken social climber with a yen for outrageous consumption." Now, a woman in Carolyn Farb's position of aspiring charity doyenne is not normally interested in what any magazines say except *Town & Country, Architectural Digest,* or *Interview.* Nevertheless, it is a mark of how significantly social-climbing strategy has changed that a hatchet job in a big-circulation magazine caused Carolyn considerably more distress than the cattiness of her fellow committee members. "People in New York were very upset and embarrassed," she says. "They just denounced that magazine. Now, I do enjoy *People.* They just happen to have a bureau here that's very negative. Those were just terrible things they said. That is just not the reality. I just came across as somebody just looking in her closet. They used a picture that I never said they could use for that article. Well, I suppose this is just something you have to take. There are lots of forces that get envious or green. And I guess when you have a divorce, you have to expect to get publicized."

Then there is social climbing that has not even the filmy veneer of social usefulness. It has only untethered ambition and energy, combined with the practically unlimited resources of a man who, generally, has made the fortune himself and is happy to indulge his wife's schemes. Such a rare combination of elements was present for Mitzi Newhouse.

By the accounting of Richard H. Meeker in his recent biography of S. I. Newhouse,[34] Mitzi was fully up to the task of complementing the mindless determination and acquisitiveness of her husband, whose disdain for the ideas and the people of the newspapers he dealt in stood out even among the antisentimentalists of the publishing fraternity. Nowhere has there been a clearer example of the power of sheer money and labor to achieve social acceptance; nor of the crucial role of publicity, among a group that ostensibly disdains the opinions of the masses. S. I. doted on his wife and children, and it was largely with her

34. *Newspaperman: S.I. Newhouse and the Business of News* (New Haven and N.Y.: Ticknor & Fields, 1983).

interests in mind that he purchased the Condé Nast magazine conglomerate.

Its crown jewel was *Vogue*, the powerful fashion arbiter. It had been of major social importance since the days of Condé Nast himself, a legendeary *bon vivant* of the early days of café society and even more influential through the seminal stylish magazine *Vanity Fair*. S. I. apparently tried to make the purchase of Condé Nast coincide with their wedding anniversary; he used to say that as he was out strolling with Mitzi one evening along Park Avenue, "she asked for a fashion magazine, so I went out and got her *Vogue*." Their apartment itself had been an earlier emblem of Mitzi's social ambitions; around 1940, they had moved to a fourteen-room duplex at 730 Park Avenue—across the hall from Richard Rodgers, in the same building as several Farkases, and across the street from several Rockefellers and the Marshall Fieldses. This allowed Mitzi renewed access to the Manhattan she had missed as Newhouse ran the *Staten Island Advance*, the first bead in his necklace. For her amusement, while he was on the road compiling his newspaper kingdom, S. I. also provided an eighty-acre estate in the New Jersey foothills, private schools for the boys, all the clothes she wanted, annual trips to Florida and Europe.

But all this was nothing compared to *Vogue*. Mitzi acquired herself a seat on the board of directors and a permanent place in the circle that whirled in and out of the Colony Club, Sardi's on opening nights, and the fashion and society columns. She took over La Côte Basque—with the Pavillion and El Morocco, part of the previous generation of restaurants that couldn't be missed—for a party in honor of Estée Lauder attended by Diana Vreeland and C. Z. Guest. She showed herself adept at the rapidly changing rules of what was "fun" in proper society by staging, in the wake of Truman Capote's masked ball at the Plaza, a party solely for people standing five feet or less. This rather remarkable ascent in the strange circle of mid-sixties fashion society was heavily promoted by *Vogue* itself. In June 1964, Mitzi made her own pages, in the "People Are Talking About . . ." feature. The piece stands as a sort of lexicon of rich fashion talk. Mitzi was called "pastel, fragile, with the look of Belleek porcelain." She was "easy, organized, amused, with a feeling for the amenities of life;" "a woman of astonishing energies, she takes special pleasure in fashion, French furniture, American abstract paintings, dixieland jazz, opening nights at the theater, and her six grandchildren."[35] In the lock bet of the year, Mitzi made the best-dressed list. She scaled the social heap and she remains there—now in Palm Beach, where as a widow she has begun to get involved in a few charities, as they are an important part of the social life.

Charity is not, however, Mitzi's proclivity, and she never pretended it was. When her husband, a notorious tightwad when it came to charity, decided late in life to donate $15 million to Syracuse University for an entire communications center, Mitzi pronounced the idea "outrageous"; it was one of the few times in Sam's life that he ignored her. Even more telling was her behavior when the New Orleans repertory theater group founded by her sister-in-law limped into bankruptcy in 1973. Although the debts amounted to less than $100,000, the Samuel I. Newhouse Foundation, of which Mitzi was a director, made no move whatever to rescue the group. Later that year, though, she cheerfully handed over $1 million to the much higher-profile Joseph Papp to make his New York Shakespeare Festival a regular part of Lincoln Center. "I know I'm going to get a great big bang out of this little contribution I'm giving today," Mitzi said—doubtless thinking that the bang would be heard loudest in the world to which she so desperately aspired.

35. It is fascinating to note that Edie Sedgwick made "People Are Talking About" as a "youthquaker" slightly more than a year later, in August, 1965. Now this was a substantial change in the type of person achieving social-fashion stardom. *Vogue* treated Edie as a sort of early-day Cornelia Guest, sieving her peculiarities into the same consistency of prose as that expressing Mrs. Newhouse's peculiarities. Edie was "white-haired with anthracite-black eyes and legs to swoon over . . . shown here arabesquing. . . . In her deep, campy voice, strained through smoke and Boston, she said: 'It's all I have to wear.'" Although Edie's well-publicized association with the drug "underground"—it was becoming less so all the time—contributed to her departure from the pages of *Vogue*, the amalgamation of the fashionable and the precious with the camp continued unabated, under the winking chandelier of great wealth.

PART 5
The Problems
of the Rich

25 | THE CURSE

> We found out that everyone he gave money to basically terminated their friendship.
>
> —CANDI WOZNIAK

ONE MORNING in February 1981, Steven Wozniak, who in three years had made a nearly unimaginable fortune by inventing key components of Apple Computers, crashed his new Beechcraft Bonanza just after taking off from a tiny airport not far from his home in the Santa Cruz Mountains, south of San Francisco. He and Candice Clark, a young woman he had met shortly after the bitter breakup of his first marriage, were on their way to San Diego to pick up their wedding bands from Candi's uncle, a jeweler. Wozniak had only had his flying license for ten weeks and was not certified to fly the airplane. In the plane with Wozniak and Candi were her brother, Johnson Clark, and his girl friend, Janet Valleas. All but Janet Valleas were knocked unconscious on impact—a blessing for them, since the effect of sudden unconsciousness is to rob the mind of the images that immediately preceded it. Wozniak had amnesia for five weeks. Candi Clark's shattered cheekbone had to be replaced with a stainless steel rod, and she lost the hearing in her right ear, nearly lost an eye, and had her left forefinger sewn back on in five hours of microsurgery. Janet Valleas remained conscious through the horror of the airplane crash. The troubles of all of them were just starting.

The pain of the crash and the other burdens of her outwardly blessed life have affected Candi Wozniak. She lives a life of great luxury and loneliness. Money has afforded her the curse of endless contemplation. While Steve was off during the day, tinkering around with some random modification of an Apple computer or putting together one of the peculiar art-for-the-masses sorts of deals that he became noted for, Candi remains in splendid isolation on their fourteen-acre ranch with her son, the Hispanic nursemaid, the caretaker with the high-powered rifle, the swimming pool, the reservoir where she can paddle her kayak when she rouses herself to it, the waterfall, the six-hundred-ampere generator, the turrets, and the llamas grazing on the hillside. On clear days she has an almost unimaginably beautiful view across Monterey Bay to Point Lobos, but for much of the year her world is bounded by the fog that rolls relentlessly through the crags and hollows of Summit Drive. She is, she says with her characteristic painful honesty, "kind of stagnating a little bit here." She has little drive, she finds. Her life is marked by events like the weekly arrival of her tennis instructor.

Like everyone else from California, Candi Wozniak acts it. She speaks slowly—drawls, actually—and moves with the lazy grace of those who have been born into sunshine. She adores her son, treats the nursemaid with friendly command, answers the telephone with briskness and worry. She is troubled: in her early thirties, she is married to one of the wealthiest men in the United States, a man whose eight-figure financial dealings she regularly reads about in the newspapers. Candi Wozniak was a rich kid to begin with. She uses such locutions as "upper-lower class" in describing Wozniak's previous wife, the sort of phrase that bespeaks considerable reflection on money and its effects. She speaks without embarrassment of a life of privilege before her marriage to Wozniak—the half-dozen apartment buildings her family owns, the trips to Europe when the other kids in even her affluent neighborhood were going only to Disneyland, the training of an Olympic kayaker as obviously the sort of life that can be afforded only by those with immense resources. She was, in short, raised to be the wife of a wealthy man.

The giddy saga of Steven Wozniak—Woz, as even his wife

calls him—has within a few years become part of the legend of modern America, and more specifically, of golden California. The peninsula below San Francisco harbors the greatest concentration of high-technology firms in the world. They spring up like mushrooms in the fantasy cellars of Silicon Valley, a walled-in world of no weather but perfect weather, no little girls but "valley girls," no cars but BMWs, no towns but quaint towns, no people but white people, no voices but quiet voices, no crooked teeth, no frowns, no crying babies, no forgetfulness, no fatigue, no irritation, no perspiration, no death. Hundreds of thousands of people shuttle through this dream landscape ceaselessly, effortlessly, like the data they so assiduously process. The high school nerds of the entire nation flock here to work for—and eventually, in their dreams at least, to start—the hundreds of fledgling computer-related firms. Commonly, they exchange thoughts and gimmicks with one another, so that the entire valley is webbed with a network of percentages in each others' companies, and everyone miraculously waxes rich along with everyone else. Many of them have grown rich through Apple Computer, and none so blindingly and romantically rich as Steven Wozniak, the co-founder and resident tinkerer of Apple, the inventor of the floppy disk, the bizarre idealist who grafted high-tech onto rock-and-roll to produce those most peculiarly 1980s California phenomena, the US Festivals.

Steve Wozniak and Candi, who takes care of the complex family accounts and tries to rein in her husband's more quixotic impulses, are the distillation of all the pressures that immense wealth can bring as it abruptly falls upon otherwise normal people.

"Money—the family is ruined now because of it," says Candi Wozniak, still delicately pretty after the accident, as she curls into the chair like any other dreamy, feline young mother on the West Coast.

The airplane crash: my brother and his girl friend were in the plane with us, and Steve was pilot, and he crashed. We were seriously injured. Steve was unconscious, I was unconscious, my brother was unconscious. So we really have no memory. . . . Anyway, my brother's girl friend was not unconscious, and she experienced the crash, and had a nervous breakdown because of it, and she also had whiplash in her neck. And so the thing that happened was that we were paying for all of her medical bills. Anything she asked for, we paid, unconditionally. This went on for about a year. And then, somehow, because of communications difficulties—she apparently didn't like asking and justifying her expenditures, although with an insurance company you have to justify your expenses. She would send us a copy of the bill, and we would pay it—we thought it was no big deal—you know, unconditionally. And then, she basically wanted a settlement, but didn't really tell us. And so we didn't give her a settlement. So she wrote a demand letter for two million dollars. And so my brother—he was our favorite brother—he lived with her; he wasn't really part of this, but he was on her side. He wasn't part of the demand letter-writing . . .[He felt he had to support her.] We wish that he had moved out. So anyway, it got very messy, so Steve basically rejected the demand letter, and that's when she filed the lawsuit. So it's now been three years and it's still in the process. She claims her life is ruined; we claim that she's a mental case, and that she doesn't want to get well because she wants money. My brother's life is ruined; she isn't very healthy mentally, and so it drags him down. Now we have Christmas and Thanksgiving, and there's a void. . . . There was no insurance. In a situation where there's insurance, it alleviates things. But this is directly Steve, and so that makes it a little more sensitive. . . . Our point in the whole situation was, well, if she *asked* for some money, if she asked for a settlement, we could have talked about it. But she wrote a demand letter.

This is our side of the story, of course. But we respond favorably to people who ask us for money—or we did at the time, we responded favorably to people who asked. Now we're slowing down on that. . . . [For example,] Steve had this movie theater in town, and he had his employees, and he had to close the theater. He sold it. And all the employees were poor, and they wanted money— they all wanted new cars. So he bought them new cars.

[At that time,] he was giving ten thousand dollars to everyone he knew—anybody who asked kind of thing. So now he slowed down on that. . . .

The reason we slowed down is because we found out—this is an interesting point too—that everyone he gave money to basically terminated their friendship. Somehow they felt funny about the fact that—I mean, they felt embarrassed, or something, that they have this money. They don't feel good about it. So anyway, he's no longer friends with basically anyone he's given money to— unless it's in return for something. Or if it's a birthday gift, then it's no big deal. Even if it's a significant birthday gift. But if it's something like all the people at his theater got their ten thousand dollars—none of them. . . . And so we decided if we want to keep our friends, we can't give them any money. And we found that that actually seems to work: we keep our friends better if we don't give them money. . . . Even if they ask for money when they're desperate, they're still no longer friends.

They're all—quote—loans, and none of them have paid it back.

Nor is it only Candi Wozniak's family relations, or casual acquaintances, that have suffered from the curse of money. "I had a girl friend who was my best girl friend," she relates.

Steve lived in a house down that way when we got married. And so we let my girl friend stay in that house. And then problems came up. She was single and had two kids, and I wanted to take care of her. We had the means to take care of her. I was always taking care of her, basically, all my life. At one time I bribed my father to let her be manager of one of our apartment buildings—things like that. I took care of her all my life—not all my life, but for a while. I liked her, and I wanted to do things that weren't a big deal for me but would help her out. She lived in Steve's house, and then problems arose when she got a boyfriend. I basically didn't approve of him, and so that created problems. I didn't want her to live in our house now that there was this man, an able-bodied man that could take care of her. The situation got very nasty and very bitter. I evicted her through legal proceedings from the house. . . . It was the whole idea that I had control of her life. Because I didn't like her boyfriend and I thought that since she had a boyfriend—it was her choosing, and now he could take care of her. So they could pay rent. That was how it came down. So she didn't feel that was fair. And so basically our relationship just terminated, and that was because of money. Because I had the power of veto. And if she's chosen this man, that's fine, it's her life, so now she has her own life with this man. But as long as her life was with mine, it was on my terms. And it was a very powerful situation, and I had the power. It was nasty. . . . It's unfortunate. A lifetime friendship is terminated, basically forever, because there were things said that will always be there. And it is because of money—because we had the means for her to live. As long as it's on my terms—

Had we not been able to give them a house, it would never have happened. . . . I missed her terribly.

Candi Wozniak's entire life is dominated by the brute fact that she has access to much more money than anybody she knows—essentially, an unlimited supply. Much unlike her husband, she consciously keeps her friendships among people she has known all her life, to dodge the likelihood that new acquaintances find her most attractive quality to be her wealth. Beneath the fragile exterior is a cool intelligence that tends to make mincemeat of the objections of those around her. As she came to control the life of her former best friend, so she has become the young matriarch of her siblings through her possession of the means to alter their lives radically. She successfully lobbied Woz—"against his better judgment"—to refinance the apartment buildings owned by her brothers and sisters, which gave them a little spare change; or, as she puts it, "not a lot of money, but enough for them to buy houses." That was, of course, a favor to them, not having to deal with banks; but it was also a business arrangement to the long-term advantage of the Wozniak fortune. She has made the decision to do no more for her family: "They're all quite comfortable—own their own homes and have jobs that they enjoy. Maybe they dream about not working, but they might not realize that having a job that you enjoy is more desirable than not having a job. Having a job you enjoy is a desirable thing, and a lot of people don't have that choice, they don't know that it's—

"Like for me, sometimes I get a new project; I sometimes think about getting into some real estate deal, or some kind of a project, because without a job—like at Apple, when I was working at Apple [as an accountant], it was very hard, but I liked it."

Now, it is her only continuous occupation, aside from motherhood, to keep tabs on Woz's money. Her training in accounting, on top of an entire life spent in the bosom of plenty, made Candi a perfect candidate for the role of watchdog over the somewhat disheveled state of Wozniak's finances.

The major factor in Woz's financial complications was the disastrous breakup of his marriage to Alice Robertson in 1980. Candi is profoundly disgusted with her predecessor. "I feel very bad for Woz," she says. "He's not a playboy and she is. He expected to be married forever, and as soon as they got a little money she started running around and staying out all night. She just treated him badly." Perhaps even worse than Alice's emotional maltreatment of Woz, in Candi's book, was her profligate ways when it came to money. "She's not capable of financial decisions," Candi says in her measured tones that belie the bitterness of her thoughts. "She's just not very bright, not well educated." She is, however, rich. Not only did Wozniak endow her family substantially while they were married, but she gained a settlement worth something like $40 million when they were divorced.

With the fact, if not the emotional residue, of that unpleasantness behind them—it obviously galls Candi that the easygoing, unworldly Wozniak stays in close touch with Alice—Candi has turned with a sort of wry resignation to the business of curbing her husband's more quixotic impulses. Clearly, she does not expect an overnight reformation of the man who lost roughly $10 million on each of two US Festivals, gargantuan celebrations of high technology and the quasimusical emanations of such groups as Van Halen. Wozniak's performance in organizing those extravaganzas led his manager of the first one, rock promoter Bill Graham, to characterize the computer wizard pungently as "an innocent *putz*." This is not an aspect of the Woz's personality—it may, in fact, be his entire personality—that Candi would appear to have much of a chance to eradicate. It does make them one of the odder couples even in California, for Candi's preoccupation with money runs precisely in the opposite direction to her husband's. He is amazed and amused by it; she fears it. He drifts with it; she fights it. Sometimes she loses this struggle badly. During the 1984 Olympics, she was arrested for scalping tickets to the popular gymnastics events. She was selling them for $200 apiece, nearly three times their face value. The police reported that Mrs. Wozniak protested her arrest on the grounds that her husband had donated $100,000 to the Los Angeles Olympics Organizing Committee and, in return, had been given more than $15,000 worth of tickets. Under the terms of the donation, however, the tickets had to be either used or given away, but not sold. Of course, the antiscalping ordinances are generally honored in the breach; Candi was more careless than venal to get caught hawking her ducats at a markup. But the incident is a fascinating illustration of her ceaseless struggle to counteract what she considers Steve's bizarre openhandedness.

"We just gave fifty thousand away to somebody," she says in the casual tone of those long on close terms with wealth.

It was this musician guy who wanted to make an album. See, the thing is, people wear Steve down, so he finally goes yes, and to shut 'em up he gives 'em a check. And so some other one came up and wanted money—another fifty thousand to make an album— and he said no to them; he said, "I just gave this to someone else, so we'll see if they make an album, and see if I get my money back." But chances are they won't make a bit. And he doesn't feel happy about that, but he felt that it was the only way he could get him off his back.

He says, "I'm not a bank"; but then he does bankroll these outrageous festivals—which I totally disagree with. I was very evidently against that. I was just not happy about the whole situation. . . . But if he makes this incredible fortune that he's dreaming of, then he says he's gonna do another one. There's nothing I can say about it. But I could take a more active role in it. . . . If you can't beat 'em, join 'em. I proved I couldn't beat him last time. So if he does make enough to finance another festival, then I will take an active role in the financial environment. I think if I took an active role he would certainly lose less money; but he would still lose money. . . . When you have that kind of money floating around— but Steve lets the lawyers handle all the lawsuits. He doesn't think about it—which is a healthy attitude to have. . . .

Candi Wozniak thinks of nothing else.

It naturally sounds unsporting, ungrateful, and downright outrageous to hear rich people complain about the problems of their lives. Certainly, money eradicates many of the problems of just folks: rich people do not have to worry about starvation, about sending the kids to college, about buying whatever clothes they want, or about burning themselves out in a job they hate. What rich people *do* have to worry about, as Candi Wozniak could tell you, is almost entirely connected with the fact that they have money in the first place. Every aspect of their lives is colored by wealth: they must protect it, pass it along to their children, explain it to the curious and to themselves. Their possession of it makes them a target of people who are greedy, criminally minded, or merely annoyingly curious—not to mention journalists. There is a more insidious danger to wealth as well. It allows one to control the physical world, other people, and time itself. This immense power can turn on its possessor. It puts rich people in a position to be, like Tom and Daisy Buchanan, "careless people" who "smashed up things and creatures and then retreated back into their money or their vast carelessness, or whatever it was that kept them together, and let other people clean up the mess they had made." Money is wonderful for creating self-sufficiency, but there are great numbers of people who do not especially appreciate their own company.

26 | The Rich Need Safety Nets Too

My life was never destined to be quite happy. It was laid out along lines which I could foresee almost from my earliest childhood. It has left me with nothing to hope for, with nothing definite to seek or strive for. Inherited wealth is a real handicap to happiness. It is as certain a death to ambition, as cocaine is to morality. If a man makes money, no matter how much, he finds a certain happiness in its possession, for in the desire to increase his business he has constant use for it. The first satisfaction and the greatest, that of building the foundation of a fortune, is denied him [i.e., *the man of inherited wealth*]. He must labor, if he does labor, simply to add to an oversufficiency.

WILLIAM K. VANDERBILT

SARAH KIMBALL PILLSBURY has some of the oldest wealth in the United States. The family's grain company was established in 1869 in Minneapolis, creating a fortune for them well before the other massive millionaires of the nineteenth century had come to the attention of the American public. For as long as there has been a Minnesota, Pillsburys have been business and political leaders there, not to mention social leaders in Palm Beach and throughout the United States. Sarah's father, George Sturgis Pillsbury, ran his own investment advising firm and became a state senator, in addition to manning his hereditary position on the board of the Pillsbury Company; her uncle John Pillsbury was chairman of the Northwestern National Life Insurance Company.

Sarah Pillsbury grew up in the gilded suburb of Wayzata; it is a time she depicts with the golden glow associated with the childhood in the Ingmar Bergman movie *Wild Strawberries*, before all the bad stuff happens.

In Sarah Pillsbury's case, nothing bad ever did happen. She grew up delighting in her parents and in her siblings. It was, by her description, a household rather reminiscent of the Kennedys', without the undercurrent of possibly ill-gotten gains or the overt push to succeed in national politics. It was perfect. The children were all very competitive with one another. Sarah Pillsbury jokingly describes herself as "my mother's clone." "Thanksgiving was a big day," she recalls. "We were very lucky. We had a lot to be thankful for." Though her parents are Republicans, they were, she says, socially progressive. The children were imbued from birth with the sense that, as rich people in a world full of poor people, they had a special obligation and destiny. Sarah Pillsbury went to Yale as her father had before her. She moved to Los Angeles because she thought the city was intriguing and different—one can hardly fault her observations—and is now involved in trying to sell movies and television shows. Her firm is now producing a film with rock star Madonna. She and her partner have an office amidst the easy prettiness of Westwood, not far from the campus of UCLA, and when lunchtime comes they drop down to the store on the first floor that serves sandwiches of relentless vegetable integrity. As she notes, life can be very easy in southern California. Sarah Pillsbury is also strikingly handsome, in the almost clichéd way that one thought had disappeared with Katharine Hepburn: long-limbed, with a face not only pretty but marked by an obvious intelligence and curiosity. Her jaw moves with an energy that suggests she is creating the words as well as the ideas that she talks about. She is blonde and slightly unkempt, in a charming way, of course, although she would very obviously despise being thought merely charming. She wears the uniform of her class—pearl earrings and a simple gold chain around her neck—and adds to it the casual charm of southern California's less ostentatious residents, in the form of pink pants and a white shirt. She is well endowed financially, physically, and, one might almost venture to say, spiritually. As Audrey Hepburn once noted about Cary Grant, there is absolutely nothing wrong with her.

This paragon of intelligence, charm, and rightmindedness has spent much of her adult life in psychoanalysis.

"I think you'll find across the board among people with inherited wealth a desire to do something with that wealth," says Sarah Pillsbury.

And I think that often that's quite a burden for people. Because when you turn twenty-one, it's a very tough time of life anyway. . . . You've gone to college, and you're wondering what you're going to do with your life, and all of a sudden you're not just wondering what you're going to do with your life—you're wondering what you're going to do with your life in the context of all this money, and what you should do with the money. You're trying to think about what your career is going to be, and there are too many decisions and too many choices. Having to get out of bed every morning and go to work is an organizing factor for the vast majority—ninety-five percent of this country, probably. And the drive to work is also a very important psychological drive; so you can just imagine that it does affect people fairly deeply, not to have that as an organizing factor—and yet to feel that they have to amount to something, that they perhaps have some reputation to uphold. And that they have this money; and they may, like I, have been told all their lives that they were damned *lucky* to have all that money. Which only proceeds to make them guiltier.

So I think therefore you sometimes find a lot of people with inherited wealth who have been tracked into some of the "new age" activities. This extends to those people who give all their money away to some *guru*. They feel that they are—quote—cleansing themselves, doing something responsible with their money, and also making—it's very convenient, it's like hitting three or four birds with one stone. But you could also say it's putting all your eggs in one basket, to use another cliché. In a less extreme fashion, you find a lot of people with inherited wealth who have been very involved with self-improvement; and often that's connected to sort of a spirituality. And I think that there's a way that they're wounded—and their wounded spirits are in tune with this feeling that our *society* is sort of sick. So they get involved a lot of times well beyond the self-improvement—hoping to change the world: make it an entirely new world. Not just changing what they might see as more external and material things, but spiritual things.

I, on the other hand, am much more of a materialist, from the standpoint of believing in the impact of material things on people's lives. . . . Though I'm also, I don't think this is a contradiction, psychologically oriented—to a great extent because when I was going though some of the confusion [of early adult life], I went to a psychiatrist, to try to get to the bottom of this. All of these feelings of guilt and indecision, etcetera, were combining to make me fairly depressed and nonfunctional, I think, in my early twenties. I think that there's also another manifestation of it—the more traditional or old-fashioned theories of third generations not amounting to very much, and playboys, and that kind of escapist activity. . . . And certainly that escape route is the route that John Paul Getty took—he's, as you know, in a coma. I don't see that [suicidal behavior] among the women I know.

My view is shaped to a certain extent by the people I know who have inherited wealth. And I tend not to believe when I meet people who have inherited wealth and seem very comfortable with the way they spend their money and completely at ease with the way they live. For example, I know some women with inherited wealth who have no difficulty in totally sharing that wealth with their husbands. I see them at the "wealth workshops," we call them, that the [Liberty Hill] Foundation sponsors that deal with money and spouses, money and loans, and money and careers; and [these women] hear those kind of questions and quickly say, "Oh I'm past that" or, "That's never been a problem." Perhaps it's because I'm too much of a materialist to not believe that money is not a factor—particularly living in a society where there is such an enormous value placed on money. So even though I see [rich] people who are different from other people I described, I always think that if you could get to the bottom of it, you'd find a bit of [the same problems].

Sarah Pillsbury's view, in short, is that great inherited wealth inevitably has a massive impact on the personality of its possessor—in effect, that neurosis and guilt are natural byproducts of money. She believes that no one escapes the scars; that those who say they have are only repressing their guilt, and one either deals constructively with money or crazily with it, but in either case one pays an emotional price for the "lottery of birth." That is a phrase from a booklet written by Sarah Pillsbury's older brother George, which informs its target readership, those with great unearned wealth, that "inherited money presents problems of all kinds."

Self-Help for the Heir Who Has Everything

More or less in passing—it's not something really to discuss with people who aren't involved—Miss Pillsbury mentioned "wealth workshops." On the face of it, it may sound a bit absurd to hold self-help sessions to confront the problems of wealth, much as women would hold consciousness-raising sessions. Absurd or not, the practice is not unknown. In the case of Miss Pillsbury's Liberty Hill Foundation, and her brother's philanthropic groups in New York, the aim is politicization as well as emotional stability. Not so with Gideon Inc., an organization in San Francisco whose founder, inheritance millionaire and est graduate Rob Martin, promises to enable the troubled possessor of unearned wealth to come to terms with his disability. The eventual goal is the realization that Martin came to about himself after a decade of wrestling with the burden his wealth placed on his psyche—his twenties, in line with Miss Pillsbury's timetable—that "the real me I had been looking for was all of me, including my money." Those fighting such demons will not balk at the thousand-dollar fee for the training weekend.

While on the topic of self-help training, one might as well note that courses in how to marry a millionaire remain as popular as ever. One of the most popular is given by Joanna T. Steichen, a psychotherapist in New York, who has set herself the pleasant task of trying to enable more women to suffer the problems of the wealthy. Her suggestions are, for the most part, common sense: a woman needs first to acknowledge what she is after, then put herself in harm's way by joining charitable organizations, the right clubs (especially sports ones), and the right company.

Shrinks and the Rich

A much more common role for psychiatry, as Miss Pillsbury's analysis suggests, is to serve as an emotional truss for those already afflicted with inherited wealth. Historically, psychiatry has always been a plaything of the upper middle class, and to a somewhat lesser extent of the very rich. Sigmund Freud's work has long been criticized for its built-in assumption that the problems of wealthy women in Victorian-era Vienna—the group that provided virtually all his experimental subjects—could be extrapolated to the general population. One of the earliest American converts to the infant science of psychoanalysis was Edith Rockefeller McCormick, who not only inherited a great deal of her own money from her father, John D. Rockefeller, Sr., but married the scion of the International Harvester fortune. She became a fanatic partisan, living in Switzerland for several years to study with Jung, then claiming when she returned to Chicago that she had acquired the secret to curing tuberculosis and a host of other diseases. Her extensive psychoanalysis certainly liberated her inner life. Eventually it led her to astrology and reincarnation, including the theory that she had once been Akn-es-en-pa-Aten, child bride of a pharaoh. She also participated in numerous scandalous affairs with a string of male secretaries, squandering most of her fortune on high living, and leaving half of what remained upon her death in 1932 to the last of the lovers, a Swiss. As we saw previously, psychoanalysis has since become practically a family tradition among the current generation of Rockefeller cousins.

The phenomenon of the children of the rich undergoing intensive psychoanalysis almost as a rite of passage into adulthood has blossomed since the sixties, especially in the United States. Before that, psychiatry was called the Jewish Science for understandable demographic reasons; even after World War II, it was something undergone primarily by upper-bracket Jewish women in big cities, the group stereotyped by William Styron's hilarious depiction of Leslie Lapidus in *Sophie's Choice*. Lingering anti-Semitic sentiments, the sexual connotations of psychiatry, and a feeling that upper-class women should be able to take care of themselves combined to restrict analysis to the radical fringes. All that changed with the explosion of interest in "countercultural" phenomena beginning twenty years ago. As usual, it was the rich who were in a position to engage most thoroughly in the manifold opportunities for new forms of recreation, creating a whole new class of service people who included not only psychiatrists but gurus of all stripes, as well as a number with no stripes at all. Moreover, in the past ten years—beginning with Burton Wixen's 1973 book *Children of the Rich*[36]—it has for the first time become fashionable to discuss the distinct problems of the rich in public.

As anyone who has passed a newsstand within the past decade realizes, money in all its manifestations has shamelessly become the favorite subject of written matter, and one can see the recent public discussion of the problems of rich people as an odd variation on this theme. The topic received formal apotheosis in 1984 when it was not only the subject of a panel at the annual meeting of the American Society for Adolescent Psychiatry but was covered in the *New York Times*. One of the key performers in the small field of the craziness of the superrich was there—

36. N.Y.: Crown Publishers, 1973.

Dr. Roy R. Grinker, Jr., from Chicago. Grinker has been instrumental in advancing Wixen's theory that the "golden ghetto" they are raised in affects rich brats mainly by depriving them of proper role models in their formative years. His characterization of the syndrome of rich folks' neuroses is worth repeating at some length as a sort of classic statement of how tough it is to grow up rich and sane:

> The group to which I refer in this paper are generally not the children of hard-working immigrant parents who "have made it rich" in the new country but are the grandchildren of that group, who were not very good parents but were good models. The parents, the second generation, are usually closer to their own parents in values and ideals, having lived with poverty or financial struggle and work-ethic attitudes. They, too, may struggle hard, although their goals may be power or fame as well as amassing more wealth. Generally, the parents of the patient group have been close to their own parents and, although often clinically ill, suffer primarily from typical neurotic conflicts, such as depression, phobias, compulsions, oedipal neuroses, and the like. Often raised by servants, this second generation still had much close contact or at least knowledge of their parents and their values.
>
> Their children, on the other hand, the third generation, although also usually raised by servants, tend to see little of their parents, have fewer and less clear role-models with which to identify, are much more aware of the immense monies available, and are surrounded by friends and servants who often value money and possessions more than anything else. In general, their parents are busy and socially active, travel a great deal, and leave the child-rearing to servants, who are often fired when the parents jealously feel that their children are too attached to them. Thus, there is also a great turnover in parenting figures. Not only do these children have great freedom, but they have relatively little consistent discipline. Their relationships with friends are relatively superficial and, because their friends usually have the same background, tend to reinforce their values or, rather, lack of values.

Grinker characterized the rich patients he has seen as "emotional zombies" and contended their lives were marked by "chronic failures, symbiotic attachments of great ambivalence, and absent, perverse, or compulsive sexuality." They show "easy frustration, self-centeredness, shallowness, rage, vindictiveness, lack of shame or embarrassment, low empathy, little tenderness. . . . They are indecisive; have few interests except clothes and beautiful cars and people; lack involvement with others or have relationships that are abruptly and regretlessly broken off . . . have magical-omnipotent expectations; and are megalomanic, hypochondriacal, and exhibitionist." With all that misery, it is fortunate indeed that the rich at least have a little money to distract from their problems.

If you're wondering who the very rich remind you of psychologically, it is the very poor. "Their similarity to children of the poor is startling," writes Grinker. "The poor are a special group and suffer from discrimination; often their parents provide inadequate child-rearing or are despised by their children and are therefore poor models for adult behavior. The parents of the poor are often absent, depressed, action-oriented, angry, and antisocial. The poor tend to feel frustration, hopelessness, and boredom, cluster in groups of people like themselves, have a low tolerance for frustration and little empathy, and have a poor sense of self." The main differences between the very rich and very poor, he concludes, are that the poor are more antisocial and—the other side of the coin—much less approved of by the people around them.

Although they have not had a great deal of experience in studying the very rich specifically, psychiatrists have still managed to indulge their perennial impulse to coin catchy phrases for the conditions they uncover. John Levy, director of the C. G. Jung Institute in San Francisco, came up with *affluenza*. This state, discovered during research paid for by a prominent businessman who realized the disheartening lack of knowledge in this area, is marked by the symptoms of lack of motivation or self-discipline, suspiciousness, boredom, guilt, and low self-esteem.

The villainess in all of this, as in most of psychiatry, is of course the mother; and the specter of being an unfit mother, of loving your things and your position more than your children, thus becomes yet another pitfall for the rich women of the world. The shrinks speak primarily of the mere absence of the proper motherly attention as the crucial factor in later psychological problems. This happened literally in such situations as those of Barbara Hutton (whose mother apparently committed suicide) and Gloria Vanderbilt. More to the point nowadays is the padding between rich parents and their children allowed by the existence of servants, boarding schools, and the breadth of childhood and adolescent activities available to those with great resources. Naturally, many very rich people are careful not to allow these things to separate themselves too much from their offspring; such women as Marylou Whitney and Lynn Wyatt, despite their immense fortunes and the spectacular busyness of their lives, go out of their way to ensure that their children are intimate parts of the fabrics of their lives. But rich women tend to be much busier and more preoccupied than the merely middle class, so if the impulse for either parent or child to drift apart germinates at all, it can grow rapidly. In some cases the women are such paragons, or such driven terrors, that the children are painfully obvious in their attempts to dodge their destinies by removing themselves, sometimes physically, from their parents' sphere. It was the general impression among family and friends that Sasha Bruce's miserable self-image rose largely from the overwhelming, seven-language, diplomatic-hostess stylishness of their mother. Recent revelations about Ethel Kennedy's quirky imperiousness seem to go a long way to explaining the troubles of her children.

Throwing It All Away

As with everything else, mental health is a matter subject to the winds of fashion, which are felt strongest on the lonely plateaus of wealth. In the sixties there was a vogue, as Sarah Pillsbury notes, for giving away one's wealth to religious sects for the sake of purification. Alfred B. Ford, the nephew of auto-company magnate Henry Ford II, joined Hare Krishna and put several million dollars of his inheritance into the purchase of a huge auto-money estate in Detroit; joined in the purchase, in blissful irony beyond all that is human, by Elisabeth Luise Reuther, daughter of the longtime president of the United Auto Workers and thus the heiress of one of the Fords' greatest opponents. Eastern religions of all types, self-help communes like Esalen, political apocalypse engines like the Symbionese Liberation Army of Patricia Hearst, nihilistic abuse of drugs and sex—all were cheerfully adopted by a generation of wealthy heirs for whom the previous useful avenues of expression, such as political conservatism, social snobbery, devotion to the Episcopal church, or even a sunny debauchery, seemed very pallid stuff beside the possibilities suddenly open before them.

In California, New York, London, or Rio de Janeiro, the seekers after self-knowledge or thrills at that time drifted to a wonderful new underground of "Dr. Feelgoods," who might or might not have had medical degrees but certainly did have access to previously untasted combinations of drugs. At the time it was assumed, at least by the willful and really crazed, that the amphetamine combinations being proffered both gave you new insights into yourself—especially your sexual capabilities—and made your body better. It certainly *felt* better. The experiments of Timothy Leary and Ken Kesey had given speed and LSD an irresistible tang of both fast-social and intellectual acceptability. One of the largest LSD-manufacturing rings ever discovered turned out, upon FBI investigation in 1972, to be financed by William Mellon Hitchcock, beneficiary of a $160 million Mellon family trust. There were a number of doctors, known in select circles, who were conducting their own experiments and even preaching the glory of the stuff. In Manhattan, the Warhol crowd gravitated to the fashionable East Side office of Dr. Charles Roberts. All the shots were of course very expensive; and while, drug people being what they are, that did not necessarily guarantee a financially exclusive clientele, Dr. Roberts developed an inner group who rushed right through the burnouts jamming the waiting room and received their buttocks shots immediately, as well as getting to relax in his sauna and, indeed, take in whatever paramour they might like along with them. Dr. Roberts also kept an office far out on Long Island, and one summer he was invited along to keep the starry crowd sparkling on a jaunt up to the Kennedy compound in Hyannis. These were the days, of course, when the president of the United States himself was getting his drugs as well as his women delivered directly to the White House— amphetamine injections from Max Jacobson, as well as painkillers for his back and procaine injections. The sky was the limit. Since the towering decadence of the Roman Empire, there has never been a better time to be rich and crazy.

Society's Sanitaria

When the time came for concern on the part of those who had provided you in the first place with the money for these excursions into the world of mind-expansion, there was never a place as perfectly socially acceptable as the Silver Hill Foundation in New Canaan, Connecticut. When Anne-Marie Rasmussen, the housemaid from Norway who married Steven Rockefeller, found herself acquiring the rootlessness and uncertainty associated with great wealth, this retreat in the folds of the wealthy New York suburbs was the logical place. Anne-Marie understood it to be a sanitarium for "many important people from enlightened backgrounds." She shortly departed when the doctors' "very personal questions" about her sex life left the still-countrified young girl "horrified." (Questions from New York psychiatrists about her families, genetic and marital, proved equally unsettling, and she reported later that she found attending Kenneth's and Elizabeth Arden's much more soothing and interesting than the more arduous ways of finding inner peace.)

Silver Hill has seen the likes of Rita Hayworth, Standard Oil heiress Rebekah Harkness, Joan Kennedy, and Truman Capote, frequently for the treatment of drugs and alcohol; or in the case of Edie Sedgwick, simply because she was exhibiting signs that her father, who was *really* troubled, interpreted as bizarre. The family sent Edie there because her brother Minty had been there before; he later was there again, when he committed suicide. "Silver Hill was very swish in my time," recalled Virginia Davis, a "classmate" of Edie's.

> Some rich lady kept donating her Hitchcock furniture . . . originals. Every year she would redo her house and Silver Hill would get all this fine furniture. Edie was in the main house. Everyone had private rooms; I think it was something like a thousand dollars a month to stay there, not including psychiatric care. [This was in 1962.] In those days they had no maximum-security facilities, and they claimed not to take anyone who was seriously disturbed—no psychotics or schizophrenics or alcoholics. Of course, half the younger crowd there—the people in their forties—were alcoholics, and they could wander down to the Silvermine Tavern any time they wanted and get crocked. I mean, who was to stop them?
>
> Silver Hill was like a country club when Edie and I were there. We were served at dinner, all very proper, from the left, and dinner attire was required. We goofed off and had a grand time. After lunch Edie and I would go into town and she would spend thousands of dollars charging stuff. I mean, thousands! Maybe not at one shot, but a few hundred one day and then a few hundred the next. If you stayed at Silver Hill, the New Canaan merchants would extend you unlimited credit.

A place on the honor roll of major philanthropists must be reserved for Robert Brinkley Smithers, whose foundation is the only one in the world devoted entirely to combatting alcoholism.

Smithers is an IBM heir who has a great deal of sympathy for the problems of the rich. So much, in fact, that he tried to renege on a pledge of $10 million he had made to Manhattan's Roosevelt Hospital because the place refused to honor his demand that the money be used solely for "people from my walk of life, plus employed alcoholics." Smithers's reasoning was simplicity itself: "Rich people have more problems than poor people, especially the women. The children grow up and leave; they have servants; they have no strong hobbies. So they have drinks at lunch; play bridge; have some more drinks. Then their husband gets home and they have a couple of cocktails with him. These poor women drink themselves into addiction. I've seen this firsthand. . . . You take a Park Avenue dowager rubbing shoulders and eating with people she considers below her—she just wouldn't stay in that kind of treatment program."

27 | Rich and Really Crazy

THE WEDDING of Ethel du Pont, "the most beautiful and eligible wealthy bachelor girl in America," to Franklin D. Roosevelt, Jr., had the aura of myth from the beginning of their romance. It was really a Montague-and-Capulet situation. The du Ponts were possibly the most right-wing of all the clans of great wealth in the country. They were key bankrollers of the Liberty League, an organization convinced that "That Man"—President Roosevelt—was psychotically trying to sell out the United States, and their fortunes along with it, to the rabble or Russia or both. For those reasons, but even more because of the intense publicity glaring on the wealthy during the depression, the two golden young people conducted a clandestine romance; FDR, Jr., gallantly broke a photographer's camera after he snapped her picture, and he slipped across the state line to visit her at her ancestral home, Owl's Nest, while he was nominally visiting Harvard classmates outside Philadelphia. Finally, on June 30, 1937, they put all obstacles behind them and were married in

Christ Church Christiana Hundred, the tiny home church of the du Ponts. Thirteen hundred people were invited to the reception. The wedding gifts filled two large rooms and an upstairs hall at Owl's Nest. The pressure of public interest was so great that an entire news bureau was set up in the Hotel du Pont in downtown Wilmington specifically for the wedding, as well as a press tent near the church, with fifty telegraph operators tapping out every detail of the nuptials. "If the lighthearted scenario continues as it has begun, they should live happily ever after," wrote *Time* magazine.

The reporter could scarcely have injected a crueler irony on purpose. After the marriage, things settled down considerably— for a while. The couple had two children and lived, to all outward appearances, a normal if high-toned married life, with Roosevelt beginning his law career and getting into politics. Then, in 1949, he divorced her. (Following another divorce, the president's son went on to marry, in 1970, Felicia Warburg Sarnoff, a scion of one of the greatest of the German-Jewish banking families of New York and the ex-wife of Robert W. Sarnoff, the chairman of RCA.) Ethel married again a year after her divorce—Benjamin S. Warren, Jr., a socially prominent attorney from Detroit—and had another child by him. That marriage did not do very well, either. The couple separated for a while, but early in 1965 they were reconciled, for the time being. Their ten-year-old son was off at boarding school in New England. Mrs. Warren had been under psychiatric care, off and on, for years, and had been hospitalized several times, the last, late in 1964, at Silver Hill. But she had a vacation in Florida early in 1965; her friends said she was in good spirits and looking forward to the marriage, scheduled for June 12, of her son Christopher du Pont Roosevelt to Rosalind Havemeyer. On the morning of May 25, 1965, Mr. Warren, as usual, left their home in Grosse Pointe Farms for the trip to his Detroit law firm. At nine in the morning, Martha Weber, a maid, served Ethel Warren breakfast in bed. She found her gloomy and complaining of feeling ill. At about ten, Miss Weber failed to get a response when she called her mistress. She tried Mrs. Warren's bathroom door and found it locked, then called the family doctor and the police. The heiress was found dead, hanged by the neck from a braided bathrobe belt looped over the shower-curtain rod in a bathroom on the second floor. Her will left most of her $10 million estate to her sons and their future children. A codicil, filed three months before she killed herself, cut off her husband from any inheritance.

The du Pont heiress was unusual among women of her class and generation—not in finding life not worth living even amidst all the glory money can buy, but in doing something so definite about it. As with women throughout the financial spectrum, rich women do not commit suicide with anything near the frequency of men. It does happen, naturally; at around the same time, Fernanda Wanamaker, an heiress to the Philadelphia department store fortune, jumped out of a Manhattan residential tower after a life of considerable confusion. To outside or even inside observers, these women grew up typical of the rich women of their generation: they internalized the mores that still held their class firmly in its grip—the du Ponts were notoriously among the archest of conservative families in the United States—but discovered in middle age that those mores had ill prepared them for the changes, and then the emptiness, of life in the modern world. Much more common than suicide is the pattern of women of that age slowly drinking themselves into oblivion, or of turning to increased eccentricities. In the current generation of the wealthy, however, the self-destructive impulses seem to appear much earlier and spread throughout the woman's psyche much more quickly. Being a wastrel, dodging responsibility, has historically been the province of the sons of the third generation and beyond, the men who, like William K. Vanderbilt, found themselves destined never to be quite happy. But in the area of rich craziness too, women have been liberated.

Among the most notorious of the self-destructive rich girls of the current generation are Patty Hearst, Edie Sedgwick, and Sasha Bruce—all of them, significantly, from families that have had wealth for at least four generations, all from stock that contributed significantly to the institutions of the Republic, all under great pressure from parents, school, or general background to do *something*. On their fragile shoulders the already terrific weight of growing up in the fluctuating American society was redoubled by the fact that their personal history could be identified so easily with the agony of society as a whole.

Obviously, much that happened to Patty Hearst was not her own, or her parents', fault; had she not been dragged screaming from Steven Weed's apartment that memorable day, by all odds she would have grown up to be another quiet blip in a family that has been notable, since W. R. Hearst himself, mainly for dissolution. Nevertheless, the ease and thoroughness of her conversion to radicalism was symptomatic not only of the troubled minds of many rich kids during the 1960s, but of the specific deficiencies in her parents. Patty's father, Randolph Hearst, suffered, like his four brothers, in the bloated shadow cast by their father William Randolph Hearst; the great man was an absentee father nearly as well known by the public at large as by his sons, a parent who could not decide whether they ought to have a good time or buckle down.

Randy opted for a good time: he could generally be found much more easily on the golf course than in the editorial offices of the newspapers he nominally ran. He was a heavy drinker as well. When, at the age of fifty-five, after a breakdown in Mexico of indeterminate provenance, he finally got around to taking an active role as publisher of the *San Francisco Examiner*—one of the worst big-city newspapers in the United States—he alternated between catatonic despair at falling circulation and vigorous energy that included new awareness of the problems of the ghetto. The latter phase was his "Little Brown Brothers thing," Patty sneered, with her awareness of her father's fundamental fear of change. That was before the kidnapping; afterward, as Tania, her taped message denounced him as "a corporate liar," addressed him as "Adolf," and urged him to tell the truth about how the Fascist state he ran was destroying the world.

Patty's scorn could better have been aimed at her mother, Catherine Campbell Hearst, a stiff-necked convent girl whose main interests in life were maintaining "the Hearst tradition" (not, in general, something to brag about), trying to curb Randy's peregrinations, "bettering" herself, performing good works, and in particular attempting to rescue the University of California, of which she was a regent, from what she perceived as forces of darkness that were organizing demonstrations, promulgating drugs, and inducing "immorality and Communism on campus." By the time of her kidnapping, Patty was not only distant from her mother's unblinking insistence on social propriety, she was part of that very evil structure at Berkeley. Although in a mild-mannered way, she was probably closer to the philosophy of the SLA than to her own parents' ways of thinking.

By now Patty Hearst's incredible experience has become an emblem for modern America, and more specifically for the state of the rich woman in modern America: her kidnapping in 1974, being dragged away screaming from her boyfriend's apartment; her reemergence as the carbine-toting bank robber; the fiery death of most of her cohorts in their Los Angeles hideout; her clenched-fist salute as she was driven off to prison; the later revelations of sophisticated brainwashing, rape, constant terror, mindless obedience. In short, the terrors that plague the subconscious of rich women—kidnapping, disgrace, the fantasy of "class suicide"—became real for her. It is fascinating to note that the entire bizarre episode ended with Patty Hearst devoted to the sort of life that one would confidently have predicted for her before her abduction—with variations, such as her marriage to Bernard Shaw, the man who was appointed her bodyguard after her release from prison in 1977, which any self-respecting analyst could perceive as a standard reenactment of her need for authority figures along the lines of her captors, or presumably her Fascist father. She lives in Westport, Connecticut, the quintessential upper-crust suburb; her husband is now director of corporate security for the Hearst Corporation; and Patty's deepest dreams in life are to care adequately for her daughter and to bear a son. As for her ordeal, she has told a reporter in her best *pukka* fashion, "I don't dwell on it. When you go through any kind of traumatic situation, it's just healthier to get on with your life, and not woe-is-me it." She is delighted to live on the East Coast because "there are a lot of cuckoos who live in California." Patty Hearst's reversion to her heritage is so completely a boomerang from her revolutionary days that she contemplates working—it would presumably be in one of the Hearst properties, such as *Town & Country*—only through the distant haze of suburban maybe-someday contentment. "I don't want to work with children at home," she told an interviewer. "That is my radical idea these days. You don't have to work *and* have children." Only she has improved on the rich girl's background: raised by governesses herself, she devotes her own person to her child.

Neither Alexandra Bruce nor Edie Sedgwick was rescued for bourgeois normalcy by outside agents; their demons could not be removed by lawmen.

Alexandra Bruce—Sasha—was the late-life daughter of David K. E. Bruce, who was at various times the United States ambassador to France, West Germany, and the Court of St. James, chief negotiator at the Paris peace talks on Vietnam, first American ambassador to Communist China, and permanent ambassador to NATO. Although Bruce was descended from an old and once very rich Tidewater family, the contemporary fortune came only from his marriage in 1926 to Ailsa Mellon, the daughter of Andrew Mellon and sister of Paul Mellon, and at the time unquestionably the richest woman in the world. That marriage brought Bruce an outright personal gift of $1 million from Andrew Mellon and a dowry of $10 million.

The result was that upon birth (to a later wife of Bruce's) in 1946, Sasha was endowed with a $1 million trust fund, with much more to come. Educated at fashionable St. Timothy's School and at Radcliffe, Sasha nevertheless early on exhibited distress that was apparently induced by the distance of her adored, somewhat avuncular father and the uncertainty of maintaining her impressive, fashion-plate mother's love. Her response was to engage in a series of bizarre sexual affiliations—getting raped by a black man she invited to her room in Cambridge, living in London with a sleazy Greek dealer in stolen icons, and finally holing up in the family ancestral mansion in Southside Virginia, Staunton Hill (a gift to the children made possible by Ailsa Mellon's bequest to David Bruce on her death in 1959), with another Greek national of dubious pedigree. In November 1975, Sasha was found dead of a bullet wound to the head under a tree on the estate. Her boyfriend, Marios Michaelides, was indicted in Virginia but escaped to Greece, where charges were brought against him but later thrown out of court.

Edie Sedgwick was a St. Tim's girl also—she left in 1959, two years before Sasha Bruce arrived—and a product of the same Harvard circle, although Edie was in art school, not Radcliffe. She was raised on a California ranch dominated by her father, Francis Sedgwick, a Boston Brahmin gone west and turned into a sculptor, outdoorsman, and outrageously indiscreet womanizer, among whose intended conquests were at least several of his own daughters, including Edie. Edie exhibited signs of mania from an early age and had to be installed for a time at Silver Hill (mainly because she had embarrassed her father, and the stay did not do her any obvious good). After she came down to New York from Cambridge, Andy Warhol discovered her; for a time during the effervescent mid-sixties, just at the cusp of the incredible explosion of creative, bizarre, and tragic behavior, Edie was the leading light of his underground troupe, the queen of all the

Chelsea girls, the inspiration of Bob Dylan's "Just Like a Woman." Edie was part of that breathless time in Manhattan when the Beautiful People took over the social world. At the leading edge, the Warhol alternative-culture explosion was essentially a rich girls/poor boys sort of thing.

The book *Edie*,[37] which does an excellent job of re-creating the heady atmosphere of that bubble in time, contains a telling summation of the core of the excitement from Richie Berlin, a daughter of Richard Berlin, the president of the Hearst Corporation, who grew up amidst the glitter of Manhattan at 834 Fifth Avenue. "What fun she was to be with!" Richie Berlin remarked about Edie:

> All my friends are the most divine mixture of horrors. Darling, you have no idea what it was like, to get up, get into a Donald Brooks dress, put my Zuckerman coat on, get my gold shoulder earrings out, get my Margaret Jerrould pumps on, and go around with Edie to Lord & Taylor's on the ground floor with my paranoia and tell them I'm rich. . . . "Mrs. Richard Berlin's daughter. No, don't be silly! I don't carry identification with me. You can call up all the stores; they know me instantly. I've *got* to have those things," and those things would start coming down the chute. Edie would go with me on the "trips"—a Hedda Hopper, a shoplifting tour. She'd pop those eyes at them—the storekeepers waiting for the merchandise to be packaged, and I'd always be waiting for that click to come down the tubes telling the manager that we were to freeze at the counter. My picture was on the cash register of the Notions Department of Bloomingdale's. To go into a store was like Broadway. This was it! You'd go in and you're up for the Academy Awards on the ground floor. It was their number against yours. There was nothing to make you feel marvelous like a quick purchase. Bath products. A little of this, a little of that. Edie didn't care. She'd say, "Listen, we'll go and get these fabulous things. We can trade them for cash for Dr. Roberts."

Aside from a clinic in brand-name dropping, Miss Berlin's account of those wild and woolly days illustrates the fantastically materialistic nexus of that crowd of vaguely artistic poseurs. Like her predecessor Baby Jane Holzer, Edie's celebrity was based on a reputation for extravagant consumption. She rode around in rented limousines and hosted staggering parties at her grandmother's apartment on Fifth Avenue. She spent eighty thousand

37. By Jean Stein, edited with George Plimpton (N.Y.: Knopf, 1982).

dollars in six months. Unfortunately, Edie's career, whatever it was exactly, conflicted with her deep infatuation with the drugs that were at the heart of those days of utter disbelief in all that had gone before. Like her siblings, she was psychologically disturbed, something apparently spurred by her father's nearly insane quest for female conquests. Edie wavered between a sort of spacey virginity and pharmacologically induced promiscuity before she died following a blizzard of sex, drugs, and rock and roll at the age of twenty-eight. She broke just like a little girl.

Not every troubled millionairess comes to a satisfyingly horrible end; many simply live out their lives in various phases of large-scale peculiarity. We have seen Cordelia Scaife May retreating into the icy splendor of her aptly named home Cold Comfort since the suicide of her husband, Pittsburgh district attorney Robert "Dixie" Duggan, just six months after they were married; she devotes her life to charitable causes somewhat alien to rich women of her generation, like population control. In Cambridge, Massachusetts, Sandra Ferry Rockefeller—she doesn't use the "Rockefeller" anymore—lives as a virtual recluse, admitting only her music therapist and her psychiatrist. Doris Duke has done such charmingly eccentric things as having her hair teased into an afro and singing in the choir in a black Baptist church some twenty-five miles from her massive estate in Hillsborough, New Jersey. But for a full-length portrait of the congeries of problems that all too frequently trouble the aging girls out of the golden ghettos, we can turn to this telling description by Craig Unger of the Standard Oil heiress Rebekah Harkness as her dance company and her fortune drifted irrevocably away from her:

> Now, without a public presence, she increasingly insisted on being surrounded by others. Drinking and drugs became more of a problem. One suitor during those years compared her to Norma Desmond, the aging beauty played by Gloria Swanson in *Sunset Boulevard*. At night, people sat in the Grand Hall of her 30-room estate on the Hudson and watched old movies. Rebekah rarely made it to the final scene without dozing off. But there, in the 45-foot-long room with its 30-foot-high ceilings, its two grand pianos, its sofas and chairs covered with yellow and gray silk and velvet, Rebekah and her entourage were always well protected, if isolated. The chauffeur was armed in case an intruder barged in. A barbed-wire fence ran around the perimeter of the estate. At times the group was stranded, as all three cars—the two Mercedeses and the

Harkness Blue Rolls—were out of commission. The windows and doors were left open, even in the rain, which poured in and ruined the rare Oriental rugs. Guests used Dom Pérignon to scrub down the tiles in the swimming pool. The dog gnawed away at priceless *objets d'art*. By 1976, the entourage was always there. Even when Rebekah didn't eat at home, the grocery bills would top $2,000 a month. The servants had eight-course meals. A cat ate filet mignon. But the giddy, driven, disciplined energy that was Rebekah's hallmark disappeared—except when she was accompanied by her famous black doctor's bag or when her special Pink Drinks and Blue Drinks were being served. The face-lifts no longer concealed her years. More than anything, she feared getting old. In the bathroom, guests occasionally came across one of Rebekah's hypodermics. Presumably, it had been used for the shots of vitamin B—shots that used to make some of her dancers soar—or for testosterone injections, which had given her voice its new husky tenor. In 1977, Rebekah entered Silver Hill . . . for several months to recuperate from her problems with alcohol and drugs.

28 | WHAT GOES WITH THE TERRITORY

MINERVA MASON is easily the premier hostess of Jacksonville, Florida, and one of the best-known and most sought-after women on the international social-and-charitable scene. She is an utterly charming person; nobody goes into the hostess business without being charming, but Minerva Mason is one of those people whom you would be profoundly disappointed to find was faking it; it would demolish your confidence in your powers of interpersonal perception. She is a honey blonde, done in a little more casual way than the porcelain heads of New York; and her manner has the unguarded way of the sweet, middle-class, perfectly groomed young woman that she once was. The honeysuckle voice is irresistible—as it is no doubt worked on to be, but one is happy to ignore the possibility that it has been socially enhanced. She dresses rather simply in the middle of the day, and the only sign that she has been one of the richest women in the world is the bird's egg of a diamond on her hand. And the surroundings, of course. In 1972, Minerva and Raymond K. Mason bought Epping

Forest, a historic sixty-acre estate with a mile of waterfront on the St. Johns River just south of downtown Jacksonville. Epping Forest was begun in 1926 by Alfred I. du Pont, under the supervision of the late Edward Ball, his wife's brother; Ball became the dictatorial trustee of the Alfred I. du Pont estate upon his death, building the relatively modest fortune into a $2 billion empire of timberland, banking, real estate, and railroads, and managed until he died in 1981 to preserve his own control over the funds despite the objections of those who thought that a "charitable foundation" ought to be making a few attempts to give money away.[38]

The somewhat peculiar selection of Jacksonville for the estate was due to the fact that at the time it was the southern terminus of the railroad; it enjoyed a brief vogue before Palm Beach and Miami took its place as a desirable winter home. The house is approached through an impressively gloomy stand of cypress and live oaks dripping with Spanish moss; it would make a wonderful set for a Hitchcock movie. The foreboding building contains twenty-five rooms and fifteen thousand square feet, not to mention such mementoes as the modern Moroccan rug in the entrance hall (a gift from King Hassan II of Morocco on the occasion of a visit by his daughter, Princess Lila Merian, and her entourage) and, in the music room, the modern Persian rug that was a gift from Ardeshir Zahedi, former Iranian ambassador to the United States, for the visit of *his* daughter, Princess Mahnaz. Out back, however, all is sunshine and the fat lazy river and the fat lazy smell of pine and sweet plants. Minerva Mason is, by all indications, the happiest woman in the world showing off her formal gardens; her delight in her good fortune, for she was not born to it all, is palpable. "Listen, you might as well use it," she says, smiling. One feels good for her. She shows off the pool house she designed in a modification of the eclectic Mediterranean styling of the big house: "You have to let them know what you want; these architects all want to build monuments to themselves." Don't we all!—and Mrs. Mason gets to. Her husband can be seen in *his* monument to himself, the second story of the boathouse that he has had enclosed and made into an office. The golden sun smiles through the massed trees and marks the gardens with sculpted shadows. The dock is big enough for half

38. Epping Forest is a small English town that was the ancestral home of the Balls; it became much better known a few years later as the staging area for the D-Day invasion.

the Atlantic fleet. This is where (to cite only the most important of the luminaries who have visited the Masons at Epping Forest) President Gerald Ford and secretary of state Henry Kissinger had lunch with Anwar Sadat of Egypt at a summit meeting in 1975. (When Ford was voted out of office, the Fords and the Masons took an around-the-world trip together.) Mrs. Mason has the scrapbook with all the pictures.

There has also been tragedy. Twenty years ago, when the Masons were living across the river in their smaller (a relative term) house, their youngest son, then five years old, disappeared. The natural thought was that he had been kidnapped; the Masons were not as rich and famous as they became later, but they were already rich, and well known in Jacksonville. For three days they searched, but mostly they waited for a ransom note that never came. Then the child was found drowned. Raymond Mason has not been back to church since. But for Minerva Mason, the finality of the drowning was at least preferable to the anguish of uncertainty. You can live with something that's final, she says.

They Can Take It from You

This is the ongoing anxiety at the heart of being rich: that it can all be taken away from you by some unaccountable act of God or man. The condition of wealth makes one more intensely aware than one's poorer brethren of the inherent instability of the world. To run a risk of oversimplification, it can be said that if men are generally charged with the making and expansion of the fortune, it falls to the women to worry about and protect it and its beneficiaries. There are psychic and social risks to being rich, as the rich are always happy to tell you; but the first and greatest fear—for the unfairness of death and leaving it all behind has generally been accepted—is over the physical threat of kidnapping and attack.

Ever since the Lindbergh child was snatched in 1932, the fear of such attacks has dominated the thinking of the rich. With the widespread poverty of the time, combined with the romanticization of the Bonnie-and-Clyde types, kidnapping did indeed become a common sport. A gang came to Montreal in 1931 intending to grab Sam Bronfman, but was dissuaded when one of their number was arrested for rape; they returned to Canada three years later and kidnapped John Sackville Labatt, the brewer.

After a period of relative quiet through the war years and afterward, kidnapping came very strongly back into vogue in the early 1970s. In 1972, two gangs of kidnappers, one Greek and one German, were arrested on charges of plotting to abduct John F. Kennedy, Jr.; that same year, Amanda Mayhew Dealey, the daughter-in-law of the president of the *Dallas Morning News*, was released after a $250,000 payment to her kidnappers, who were then arrested; in 1973, J. Paul Getty's family paid $2.9 million after Italian kidnappers mailed his severed ear to a Rome newspaper; Patty Hearst was kidnapped in 1974, spurring a long string of copycat crimes; and in 1975, kidnappers, also caught later, returned to an old favorite target and extorted $2.3 million for the release of Samuel Bronfman II.

The problem has not evaporated in the mellower 1980s. Edith Rosenkranz, the wife and bridge partner of a founder of Syntex, the conglomerate that manufactures birth control pills and other drugs, was grabbed from a Washington, D.C., hotel in July 1984 during a bridge tournament—something that would be difficult to pull off when the couple remains in their exclusive Mexico City neighborhood, walled in and patrolled by armed guards. She was driven around the city for two days, then released after her husband dropped off a suitcase with $1 million in it. A Houston man who said he was trying to save his securities business was arrested.

In November 1984, three men were arrested in connection with an apparent plot to kidnap Paul McCartney's wife Linda in a "military-style raid" on their heavily guarded farm in southern England and hold her for a ransom of $12.5 million.

European-style abduction is an especially serious problem, since the kidnappers frequently have political as well as financial goals in grabbing members of the industrial classes. The ear-slicing episode was replayed late in 1983. This time the victim was Giorgio Calissoni. In November, he and his mother, Anna Bulgari Calissoni, had been taken from their fifteen-hundred-acre estate near Rome by Sardinian gunmen. Anna is a first cousin of Gianni Bulgari, head of the famous jewelry house, who himself paid a ransom of nearly $2 million for his release after he was kidnapped from his car on a Rome street in 1975; their family is considered among the wealthiest in Italy. Mother and son were released in December after the family, convinced by the message of the ear, paid a ransom of some $2.4 million (or, even more impressive in Italian currency, four billion lire). The Calissoni kidnapping served as a reminder that Italy—though it seems calmer on the surface than a few years ago when there seemed to be Red Brigades terrorists lurking around every crooked corner—remains a dangerous place for the wealthy. "The security question is still there; we haven't sort of forgotten," says Susanna Agnelli, the outspoken woman who is under a double whammy in the dangers of being rich department, since she is not only an heiress to the omnipresent Fiat automotive empire—her brother Gianni is chairman—but also a politician of high profile, and therefore one of the best-known women in the country. "It was a bigger problem a few years ago, but it still is a problem. As in everything, you know, one tends to get into the habit of things, of taking precautions. [She has a personal bodyguard and travels in an armored Fiat.] Now, when I went to Colombia, the security problem is even worse. I went around with five bodyguards; so when you come back to Italy it seems, well, everything here is marvelous and free. . . . But there are still quite a lot of kidnappings in Italy." Indeed; the Calissoni incident brought the total number of people kidnapped for ransom in Italy in 1983 to thirty-two. Which is a lot, even if down from the rate in the late 1970s, when kidnappings were rolling along at a clip of sixty a year.

Robbery and burglary are constant threats for the wealthy. In November 1973, the year after the beginning of the idyllic alliance between Leona and Harry Helmsley, they awakened in their Palm Beach apartment to find an intruder in a gas mask leaning over their bed. Leona screamed and they managed to knock the attacker down, but when they chased him they were both stabbed. Leona spent seven days in intensive care with a collapsed lung, and with her typical ebullience she now shows female reporters her chest scar. The intruder got away without jewelry but also without capture. Most other rich robbery victims have received wounds only to their material possessions and their sense of security. Cat burglars removed $780,000 worth of Marylou Whitney's fabulous jewelry collection from the Saratoga house on the night of August 6, 1967; luckily she was wearing $175,000 worth to dinner at the time. In 1974, burglars stole six paintings, including an Eakins, a Hopper, and two Winslow Homers, from the Hirshhorns' Connecticut estate while they were in Florida; three men were arrested and the paintings recovered unharmed.

A gunman who followed Mrs. Henry J. Kaiser into the lobby of her United Nations Plaza apartment building yanked a $500,000 diamond necklace from her neck as she was returning home alone from a party at Studio 54 for Elizabeth Taylor in March 1978. The following year, Estée Lauder and members of her East Side town house staff were tied up by three gunmen, who looted $1 million worth of jewelry. Thieves took $190,000 worth of jewels from a safe in Babe and William Paley's Long Island estate in 1963. Nearly that much worth of gems was stolen from the Begum Aga Khan just before her son, Aly Khan, married Rita Hayworth; Aly compensated in a way by giving Rita what she described as "the largest diamond in the world." Georgia Rosenbloom Frontiere returned home from a victory in Atlanta by her Los Angeles Rams in October 1981, to find that burglars had pried open a double wooden door to her home and carted away two color television sets in her Cadillac Biarritz. Anne and Sid Richardson Bass were confronted by two armed men as they drove up to their home outside Fort Worth one evening in November 1980; but they were released without injury or loss when a burglar alarm went off and a police car drove up to the home within the minute.

A special variation struck Carolyn Skelly, an oil heiress who lives in the mansion Bois Dore near Newport's Narragansett Avenue. In August 1984, a new maid stole more than $2 million worth of her jewelry. Mrs. Skelly did not even know it was missing until the police, alerted by the maid's husband, returned it to her.

"You can't live in fear," says Minerva Mason. But many very wealthy people deliberately curtail their activities in order to remain as obscure as possible, primarily on the out-of-sight-out-of-mind theory of protection from the knaves and fools of the world. Typical of this school is Josephine E. Abercrombie, the five-times-divorced daughter of oilman J. S. Abercrombie (he invented the blowout preventer) and owner of oil operations, land around Houston, and part of the Cameron Iron Works. In response to a request for an interview for this book, her secretary wrote: "For security purposes and on the advice of professionals in the security field, Mrs. Abercrombie keeps a very low profile, and she feels that incorporating her biography in this book would be most detrimental to this purpose."

For those who elect to remain in the public eye—whether because their business demands it, or more likely in the case of the women because it's so little fun to have money if you can't show it off sometimes—substantial security precautions are of crucial importance. The first rule, as Mrs. Abercrombie's consultants advised her, is to keep details of your daily life out of the press. This will not deter well-organized professional criminals, but it does cut down on the likelihood of casual attacks and petty harassment. Anyone who has tried to find an address in a town like Palm Beach soon comes to the obvious conclusion that wealthy suburbs are designed to discourage those who do not know exactly where they are going. It took an organized protest by local workmen and postmen in 1970 to get the residents of Hobe Sound even to post house numbers at the end of their driveways. Wealthy people do not ordinarily list their home addresses in telephone books or *Who's Who*; even the *Social Register*, which is among the better sources for locating at least old monied families, frequently contains only the name of an estate rather than a street address. Even those wealthy women who are always in the society columns maintain standing agreements with guests, and especially with reporters, that their addresses and telephone numbers do not become generally available. They avoid publicizing their travel schedules. Minerva Mason does not do television interviews, for fear of giving would-be burglars too much information. Joan Irvine Smith is so paranoid about potential kidnappers that she moves from house to house in Orange County to confuse them. Countess Aline de Romanones arrived at a 1984 reception before a performance of *Rigoletto* by the English National Opera in Manhattan wearing a baseball jacket to cover her emerald necklace.

Those who do make their homes a matter of more or less public record—for example, by hosting charitable parties for paying guests recorded by the media—are required to maintain elaborate security installations. After Leona Helmsley was stabbed, she began traveling only with a bodyguard, and she mentioned in a number of interviews that now she wears only replicas of her jewelry in public. It can be assumed that any substantial estate has at least one armed caretaker on duty at any one time, and more at night. Minerva Mason states simply that she has "tremendous security," especially because a young grandson lives on the compound; James the butler and Wilbur the driver live on the grounds, and there are substantial electronic systems making it extremely unlikely that anyone could get close to the house without invitation. Lynn Wyatt says that being known for great wealth "does change how you live. Kidnapping and robbery and burglaries, that kind of thing, I'm very aware of it all the time.

I try to be very careful. I'm warned a lot by my husband, by friends of ours." Her house is practically an institution, standing in broad-shouldered splendor right at the entrance to the River Oaks Country Club, presenting no problems of geography for any potential criminal. But it is guarded by a thick wall surrounding the four acres, doubtless backed by sophisticated electronics. The entrance is only through a long, narrow, one-way side driveway with an electronic gate on the street side; and at the end, past the masses of garbage bags generated by such an establishment, are signs advising the visitor not to leave his car without honking and waiting for an attendant, for fear of the dogs. One who drives around the sprawling living complex of Electra Waggoner Biggs, admiring the barbecue tent and the landscaped pool, is suddenly confronted by a workman with a lopsided grin—a refugee from *Deliverance*—inquiring exactly what the purpose of the tour might be. Assured that Mrs. Biggs has issued the invitation, he notes with an apology tinged with suspicion, "It's required of the help that we check." It's hard to imagine a felon getting far from a crime scene on the Waggoner Ranch.

The siege mentality that the rich are forced to adopt in the United States is even more pronounced in a country like Italy, with its much more sophisticated and more politically motivated criminals. The disappearance of *la dolce vita* has been widely noted; no one wants to look rich. Said Countess Consuelo Crespi at the time of the Moro kidnapping crisis in 1978, "In Italy now you want to feel rich and look poor." It was reported at the time that there were twenty thousand professional security guards in the country rented out to the wealthy, and that Italians annually bought $7 million worth of German shepherds as watchdogs.

The Good Witch of the North

A less dangerous but more consistently irritating byproduct of being known as a rich woman is the endless appeals for funds from strangers. They pour in by the bushel—directly to the woman's address, to the companies she owns stock in, to her husband's company, to her divorce lawyer, or in the case of Helen Hunt Schoellkopf, simply to "Oil Heiress, Texas, U.S.A." It is another part of the lives of the unbelievably rich that they have in common only with each other. They develop thick skins about it, become very careful, and sometimes even have to laugh about

it. "You can just go through the most incredibly—I mean, sometimes it's fun," says Lynn Wyatt.

> Sometimes I'll get a five-page, hand-written letter that just says
> one paragraph, one page after another, everything that's hap-
> pened—and I know that they're just sending the same letter off to
> the next episode of "Dynasty" or "Dallas," because it sounds like
> a soap opera. But there are occasional charities that I haven't heard
> of that I will call and check on and find out that they're legitimate,
> and I will send them some money, just because I feel sorry for
> them or I think they need it. But more times than not, I will check
> into something, and sure enough it's a bunch of baloney. I'm not
> anybody's fool, let's face it. But at the same time I have a heart,
> and I have on occasion done that to people I just don't even know—
> I've just sent them some money, knowing I'll never see it again
> and sort of feeling good about doing it. . . . But I get ones I don't
> give to all the time. And, you know, don't even answer them. And
> it makes me mad in a way, because when I think of the energy
> that that person took to sit down and write a five-page, handwritten
> letter, the imagination—they could go get a job with that same
> kind of exertion of energy, with that same kind of imagination. I
> say "tough."

Suni Agnelli gets the same kind of appeals "all the time, all
the time. There's a complete madness: for instance, 'I want to
buy an apartment for my daughter; would you please send me
fifty thousand dollars.' Or, 'My son has to go to university and
he has to take the train; it takes him so many hours; please send
me an old car.' That kind of thing, if I can, I always say 'Yes,'
because I understand. But when they say, 'Could you send me
fifty thousand dollars?' I generally answer, 'Even *my* daughter
doesn't have an apartment for fifty thousand dollars.' It depends.
Sometimes people ask you for something which is possible, and
logical, and then I try to help them. But when they sort of think
that because you're called Agnelli, you should be saying yes to
any request you get, well—" Disdain. Wanda Ferragamo, on the
other hand—another wealthy woman from Italy with an international reputation—never gets such requests; apparently there
is no particular reputation for great wealth, or perhaps her secretary screens them thoroughly. Electra Waggoner Biggs passes
everything along to the family foundation, and makes a point of
telling everybody how little of the ranch's wealth is actually in
her hands. She still gets massive volumes of begging letters. It
goes with the territory. There must be an entire underground

out there busily scribbling letters to rich people—another fascinating example of the power they exert over the popular imagination.

Nor is it strangers alone that besiege the rich woman with requests. Candi Wozniak can tell you that; so could Barbara Hutton. "You can't believe the depths to which some people will stoop for money," the Woolworth heiress remarked plaintively in another of her honest-to-a-fault phases. "People have blackmailed me all my life and I never did anything to deserve it. I always make the mistake of believing that people are like they appear to be. Yet it turns out I'm always wrong." Like Mrs. Wozniak, many of the rich restrict their friendships to lifelong friends who would, in theory at least, not presume to ask for money. Others seek acquaintance and love solely among those with at least a few million, who feel no need to ask. Rich people who tread outside those relatively safe areas are liable to the sort of depredations visited upon Hutton, who disastrously mixed an immense longing for love with her admitted blindness toward seedy motivations. The highly developed fear of being taken advantage of is another of the personality traits that mark the rich woman.

Etc.

The problems of the rich can take peculiar forms that would not normally occur to anyone without a few million. There is an entire class of problems that might be lumped under the rubric of "resentment." We have seen the knocks that young scions, who might not even be aware of their financial clout, take from their schoolmates; one thinks of the Rockefellers' bewilderment at jokes about free gasoline. One of the more intriguing complications of wealth in recent memory involved a New York suburbanite named Gene LePere, who suffered every traveler's nightmare when, in 1983, she was stopped by Turkish customs officials in Izmir and thrown into prison for a month on a charge of smuggling "antiquities"—three stone heads that she insisted she bought from a street vendor for $20. Mrs. LePere's maiden name is Hirshhorn; she is a daughter of the museum donor by his first wife. The family, in a state of incredulity and desperation, batted around the possibility of using influence to spring her. One of the ideas was to ask Olga Hirshhorn, the tycoon's fourth wife, to invoke her friendship with Sukru Elekdag, the Turkish ambassador to the United States, with whom she has played tennis in Washington. But on consideration the family feared that the Turks might assume that Gene LePere had some connection to the Hirshhorn Museum, which she does not, and conclude that she did indeed have motivation to try to smuggle valuable pieces out the country. Olga Hirshhorn was not asked to intercede. (Gene LePere was eventually freed on bail and skipped the country.)

Some women, like some men—more commonly those of the current generation—dislike publicity because they are genuinely interested in being left alone, in being like everyone else.

And just overall, rich women in general are chary of publicity not only because it is dangerous or troublesome in other concrete ways, but simply, in effect, because it exists. It can be so *common* to have one's name in the wrong newspapers. It is this impulse that for so long supported the system of social press agents, and which still is largely responsible for the success of publications such as *Town & Country, Interview, W,* and Harold Farb's *Ultra* in Houston. Those are safe because they *understand*; they are written, if not by wealthy women themselves, at least by women who know wealthy women, admire them, and would like to be in their place. Ultimately, many rich people deeply resent publicity because it so frequently seems to them wrongminded. Electra Biggs feels the townspeople her family have done so much for don't understand what they've gotten. Marylou Whitney thinks some people don't understand the kind of money her apparently frivolous parties pump into the community, nor do they appreciate that children with "names" have to work harder to prove themselves. Carolyn Farb is sure that the local bureau of *People* magazine is simply out to get her for no good reason, and that she has been maliciously depicted as a "social climber" when all she wants to do is help the community. This is why Jerome Zipkin is so popular, why the convicted murderer Claus von Bülow is still a fixture at the best parties: they understand.

29 | THE WORST PROBLEM of BEING RICH

IN APRIL 1984, Minerva Mason suffered through the worst thing
that can happen to anyone with money: she lost it. We are not
talking about utter poverty here, of course. The Charter Company, the firm that her husband Raymond K. Mason had created
out of a small family lumberyard in Jacksonville—a firm which,
in the process of acquiring two oil refineries, a large insurance
company, a newspaper, and several major magazines, had rewarded Mason with 2.7 million shares that in 1979 reached a
total value of well over $100 million—this wonderful concoction
collapsed unceremoniously and filed for bankruptcy. Aside from
the avalanche of slurs from businessmen who appear to have
just been waiting for the mighty Mason to be humbled—Raymond Mason was, in effect, accused of fudging his earnings
reports to keep investors and banks in the dark and of maintaining his personal ownership to the detriment of the stockholders' interest—the family faced the ignominy of having to sell
their wonderful, beloved Epping Forest. It sold for between $7

million and $8 million, so at least they won't have to worry about affording another house. But the memories, the views, the adulation, the power! —all gone with the disappearance of the marvelous estate. The children, who lived in the compound, will have to move too. The house is scheduled to be turned into a yacht club, which will at least preserve most of its glory. But it will no longer be the Masons' in trust for the rest of the world.

Minerva Mason, who after all came from middle-class roots and is still well above that station, is being no Scarlett O'Hara about her forced dispossession. "It was easy," she said in May, pausing in the middle of the enormous job of organizing the museumful of contents for transportation or sale. "Living here was like living in an institution. It's just an anachronism. I'm delighted to be moving. We thoroughly enjoyed it; but now it's gone, and we want to grow." Growth in the immediate future was to be in the direction of a house—"not with twenty-five rooms"—in one of the beach communities, half an hour's drive to the east of central Jacksonville, and perhaps also to a condominium in the middle of the city. The kids already have their new houses. They won't starve either. Mrs. Mason is not liable to be kicked off the boards of the dozens of philanthropies that she serves, and will still get her awards for community service and her name in the newspaper.

But it will not be as often. And how many visits from world statesmen, or even their daughters, can be expected to arrive in pomp at a condominium in downtown Jacksonville? There is something of a hollow sound to Mrs. Mason's stiff-upper-lip attitude toward the loss of Epping Forest; the lady doth protest too little. Two months earlier, she gave no hint of annoyance in the burdens of maintaining it; there was only pride in her bearing as she pointed out the pool house she had designed, the masses of azaleas that she was anxiously nursing back from a disastrous freeze, the dock at which she had arranged with her friend the labor leader for union members to construct an extension to keep President Ford's shoes dry. Nor does her chipper attitude at losing the estate jibe with the tone of the booklet, listing Epping Forest's wonders, that she composed for distribution to her thousands of visitors—a booklet that is now only an elegy to the Masons' dreams of empire:

Epping Forest is a Florida landmark, rich in history, charm, and grace. It is listed in the National Register of Historic Sites, and is significant architecturally for its structure and landscaping. In many ways Epping Forest represents much that is Florida, and parallels the evolution of business in the region. [The irony should not be missed as the estate slips through the Masons' fingers along with their own business.]

The story of Epping Forest has many fascinating chapters. Each room has a story of its own and an individual character that makes it a special experience for all who have had the opportunity to tour Epping Forest.

Painstaking care has been given to preserving this architectural masterpiece with historic integrity, while at the same time adapting it to modern living. The Masons share with other appreciative friends the illustrious heritage which is so important in Florida's history, as well as the rare beauty of museum quality within the walls of Epping Forest. . . .

Almost half a century ago when the plans for Epping Forest were on the drawing board, an acorn motif [the symbol of the Charter Company] and stone owls [the sacred bird of the goddess Minerva] were incorporated into the design. It almost seemed predestined that Minerva and Raymond Mason and their family would eventually make Epping Forest their home.

THE WORST PROBLEM of BEING ANYBODY: LOOKING FOR LOVE

30 in ALL THE WRONG PLACES

Love between a man and a woman is debilitating and counterrevolutionary.
—ABBY ROCKEFELLER

To be young, beautiful, and rich obviously puts a woman in the role of a highly desirable sexual object. To be old, ugly, and rich does the same thing, but with the emphasis on the desirable rather than the sexual. It has always been the greatest curse of the rich woman that the source of men's attraction toward her is never entirely clear. For rich men the reverse is no problem: they expect to be loved for their money; they *want* to be loved for their money. It is a relatively commonplace matter for a rich man to be taken to the cleaners in a divorce, the way Carolyn Farb took her Harold for $30 million. This is annoying, but hardly a disgrace. When it happens to Barbara Hutton, though, the world pities and disdains her.

Love with a Titled Stranger

Partly, of course, this is because it happened to poor Barbara six times out of seven marriages. (Cary Grant was the sole gentleman.) It is also because she carried suckerhood to ridiculous extremes: she was married to Porfirio Rubirosa for fifty-three days and gave him roughly one million dollars worth of gifts and two and a half million in cash—or approximately $66,000 for every day of the marriage. It is easy to say that Barbara should have known better; her own grandfather, F. W. Woolworth, whence the fortune descended, wrote to his brother from Switzerland in 1909, "These cheap titled foreigners over here are all after the American girl and her money. You must respect their good judgment in hoping to acquire both money and a fine-looking wife. But the American father and mother have their troubles if they are not sympathetic with this sort of courtship." But Barbara was part of an American rich girl's fad that rolled on strong for fifty years or more and continues in an attenuated form into the present. These girls—or their mothers—answered the question of what a rich girl wants in a marriage very simply: social position. (In latter days this impulse was mixed with a desire for "true love," which frequently amounted to a sexual attraction to an exotic foreigner.)

The parade began as early as 1874, when Jennie Jerome of Baltimore married Lord Randolph Churchill and eventually became the mother of Winston. The same family acquired a richer catch in 1895, when Consuelo Vanderbilt was wed to the Duke of Marlborough, bringing along a $2.5 million dowry and a guaranteed $100,000 a year; she spent her wedding morning in tears and her fifteen years of marriage in dismay, a sacrifice to her mother Alva Vanderbilt's social ambitions. That same year Mary Leiter, heiress to a Chicago fortune, married Lord George Curzon, the future diplomat. May Goelet's dowry was an incredible fortune in New York real estate when she wedded the Duke of Roxburghe in 1903. By those times, American millionaires and European nobles were on an integrated social circuit through the pleasure domes of England and the continent, so such matches were easy to arrange.

It continued through the 1920s and 1930s. All the American girls in Hutton's circle seem to have been madly in pursuit of foreigners of questionable morals and tin titles. (It did not work the other way across the sexual gap because male commoners do not acquire their wife's title.) The famous gossip and hostess Elsa Maxwell became famous largely for her ability to match specimens of the two groups. Porfirio Rubirosa married both Hutton and Doris Duke; Louise Van Alen married both of the marrying Mdivani brothers, Alexis and Serge. Little known today, Mrs. Harrison Williams, generally described as one of the most fashionable and beautiful women in her prime—the thirties and forties—not only married Count Edouard von Bismarck and Count Enrico de Martini, but did it despite the handicap of starting as the daughter of a stablehand at a farm in Lexington, Kentucky, with the unpromising name of Mona Strader. She started the ball rolling by marrying the owner of the farm when she was eighteen years old, then ensured her fortune by snatching Harrison Williams, a utilities tycoon, from under the nose of a friend of hers who had been affianced to Williams and entrusted Mona to keep Williams entertained while she went to Paris to buy her trousseau. Mrs. Williams ended up leaving an estate of $30 million when she died in 1983, well into her eighties.

It continued after the war as well: Kathleen Kennedy, the golden girl of that gold-plated family, married the Marquess of Hartington, who was killed in the war, and then died herself in a plane crash with her subsequent lover, the Earl Fitzwilliam (who, in a switch from the typical pattern, was actually richer than Miss Kennedy). Virginia Fortune Ryan, heiress to another of the great nineteenth-century New York fortunes, married the Earl of Airlie in 1952. Much more recently, Cecil Amelia Blaffer of Houston, Texas—no hick, as she will point out—took as her third husband Prince Tassilo von Fürstenberg, ex-husband of Clara Agnelli and father of internationalites Egon and Ira. Her reaction: "I'm very proud to bear my husband's name, and naturally I get a great kick out of it. But in America I'm just Mrs. Fürstenberg. In France I'm known as Madame de Fürstenberg. In Germany and Austria, however, I'm Her Serene Highness with all the responsibilities it calls for." Count Boni de Castellane, who at the turn of the century captured Anna Gould, daughter of the stock manipulator Jay Gould and sister of the Riviera developer Frank Jay Gould, frankly summarized the operative principle of many of these matches when he remarked, "It was very simple—our eyes met, our hands met, our lips met, and our attorneys met." (After their marriage was subsequently dissolved by the attorneys, Anna went on to even greater heights by marrying the Duc de Talleyrand.)

The count's bald-faced cynicism may have been the sentiment on the side of the fortune-hunting Europeans, but for the American girls, like Barbara Hutton, it was frequently mixed up with sex and love. The dangers of mingling such impulses with what should properly be a business and dynastic arrangement appeared all too clearly in the case of the tragic Martha Crawford.

Heiress to a Pittsburgh natural-gas fortune of some $75 million, Sunny grew up sheltered and shy, a trait that made her classmates at the Chapin School and St. Timothy's think her less than bright. Perhaps they were right. In 1957, when she was twenty-three and he was twenty, Sunny married Prince Alfie von Auersperg over the vociferous objections of her mother, Annie Laurie, who wanted her daughter to marry a "boy next door" type, which meant at least an American and ideally someone with some money, standing, education, and a good job. Prince von Auersperg had none of those but standing—and great looks, which clearly won Sunny. For his part, Alfie doubtless loved Sunny, but he also loved her money and other women. He was exactly the type of European catch that some American mothers have pursued for their rich daughters, while the rest have feared them as fortune-hunters.

Alfie turned out to have no intention of modifying his habits, which included African safaris and other women, to preserve the marriage. Sunny got out of that with her fortune relatively intact; but her next choice, though similar, had more drastic consequences. This was the infamous Claus von Bülow, whose title and background were dubious but whose charm and ambition were unquestioned. Gradually it became clear that Sunny's money, her Newport palace, and her person were not enough for Claus: he wanted out, but he wanted the money too. In 1979, she suffered the first of her mysterious comas; she has never recovered from the second, in 1980, and remains brain dead in a New York hospital. Claus was convicted of attempted murder in 1982; the verdict was overturned by the Rhode Island Supreme Court in 1984; but in early 1985, the attorney general's office announced that he would be retried. In the meantime, free on $1 million bail, von Bülow has remained much in evidence on the social circuit while—confirming the worst fears of fortune-hunting among the defensively rich—he pays lawyers to fight for part of Sunny's fortune. Shortsighted as always, society ignores the threat and attends Claus's parties. It's so *déclassé* to bring up a murder conviction to a person's face.

Like marriages among rich Americans, the transatlantic trade in love and money has suffered its share of bizarre variations in recent years. Perhaps the most striking ended in June 1984, with the imprisonment of Michael Telling, the second cousin of the incredibly wealthy British businessman Lord Vestey and himself the beneficiary of a substantial family trust. Telling was convicted of manslaughter after a jury found that he had "diminished responsibility" when he killed his Californian wife of seventeen months, Monika, and chopped off her head so he could keep a part of her with him. One could hardly blame Telling. In their brief union, Monika, an alcoholic and drug addict, told the people on their merry-go-round of wild parties in a downright Castellanean manner that she had married him only for his money. Adding insult to insult, she publicly taunted him for his sexual inadequacy while she proved to a good number of their friends, both male and female, that she suffered under no such disability herself. Of course, he should have known better: even before their marriage, he testified, he happened upon her rolling on the living-room floor with a neighbor's wife.

The Grand Illusion

The impulse to marry an exotic foreigner—the Cornelia Guest syndrome—is only one aspect of the malignant illusion among rich young women that their money removes the normal obstacle to marrying a poor man one is *really, really* in love with. Brought up, by and large, to believe they can have anything they want, rich girls all too frequently find that is not a very useful guideline when investing in commodities, like husbands, that change radically over time. The intriguing poet turns into the moody alcoholic; the ambitious stockbroker becomes resentful and emasculated over his wife's fortune; the international businessman connives to divert the wife's money.

Even more complicated are the difficulties faced by the daughters of a family like the Rockefellers, where the combination of fame and fortune is liable to intimidate even the strongest of potential suitors. The women of this fourth generation all married quite young, and their choices had predictable upper-crust names: James Case, John Spencer, Robert Pierson, William Strawbridge, Charles Hamlin. In each of those cases—five out of seven women cousins married in the 1950s and early 1960s—the marriage broke up within a decade or so. The brothers could not understand their daughters' marital difficulties; there were obviously no money problems, the men were proper and respectable and decent, no great tragedies marred the courses of the marriages. What neither parents nor children had at first taken into account was that emotional ease might be incompatible with the traditional notion of marriage among the rich, which had always been predicated on the primacy of the fortune and the family and not on the happiness of the women involved. When the woman has the money, the problem is compounded because of the reversal of traditional roles, what David Rockefeller, Jr., referred to as "the odd fact of having more power than their men"; and it is made even worse by the feminist temper of the times, since the heiress is unlikely to defer to everything her poorer husband would prefer. Said Dr. Lucy Waletzky, "When I got divorced [from Dr. Charles Hamlin in 1969 after five years of marriage], I went into analysis. I wanted to find out about myself. My first husband had been a good person. There was something wrong with *me*. I didn't know how to think things through. I didn't know how things worked. I didn't know how anything related to me as a Rockefeller." Many of the young Rockefeller women, in fact, had acted out of a feeling similar to Laura's: "I got married when I was nineteen because it was a way to lose the name. I copped out." Perhaps also active was the feeling that Laura had confided to a friend, that her name and fortune were so formidable that *nobody* would want to marry her. Indeed people do want to marry women like her, but mostly for all the wrong reasons; the very ordinariness they seek in their men is screened because ordinary men would not attempt to penetrate the barriers of wealth.

As Sarah Pillsbury observes, it is a rare young woman of property who has not—at least by the time she has been married for a while—been struck and concerned by the formidable presence of the sacks of money in bed, as it were, beside her and her husband. One consequence of women's increasing financial sophistication has been the decrease in "poor little rich girls" who end up giving away much of their money for love. Not that the phenomenon has disappeared completely, of course—witness Sasha Bruce's lavish presents, like Jaguars, to her no-count lovers. But it seems much rarer and more under control. For one thing, not many families today leave total control of great fortunes to young girls. For another, young women today are the first generation really to take a serious interest in the workings of their fortunes, and in how the money ought to be spent beyond the purely personal arena. Women like Sarah Pillsbury and—more radically—Abby Rockefeller have combined a sophisticated appreciation of the power of money with their feminist convictions to become young wealthy women of a strength unprecedented in previous generations. (Abby's great contribution to the movement was a seminal article, "Sex: The Basis of Sexism," in which she argued that men's stronger and therefore less discriminating need for sex led them to keep women oppressed, in order to keep the supply of sex readily available.) Whatever the dynamic, the most notable recent victim of serious fortune hunting was male: Steven Wozniak, who made something like $100 million almost overnight and gave $40 million away to his first wife. Today, with the divorce between technological invention and finance, the true innocents who need protecting from fortune hunters are young men.

Gigolos and Fortune Hunters

The great danger in rich women's generous impulse to indulge their love by paying for their man is, of course, that the payment is all he is interested in. This phenomenon has, perhaps, existed as long as women have had their own fortunes. Henry James novels are fraught with the dangers of the sophistication and venery that a girl of great fortune faces in Europe—obviously a fear well founded. American men too have been known to marry for money. The rich young thing is beset from all sides.

In the saddest cases, such as those of many of James's heroines and of the real nineteenth-century heiresses, the woman not only finds her money squandered but suffers public humiliation at the hands of her husband, who frequently despises her as the creator of his own dependency. Count Boni de Castellane spent $3 million of Anna Gould's money in five years, but that did not stop him from showing her how badly he felt at the "sacrifice" he made in marrying an ugly woman: when he was not out sleeping around, he was supposed to have forced Anna to pin a thousand-dollar bill to the bed curtains every time he made love to her.

With all these obvious warning signs around, what could possess these foolish young women to throw themselves away on obvious fortune hunters? It would seem that in some cases the answer must be, simply, sex. Porfirio Rubirosa had not only the smoothest style on two continents—tough but smooth—he also featured equipment that became the stuff of legend. It became a common practice among the internationalites to call for the "Rubirosa" when you wanted pepper ground onto your meal. Rubi was constantly pursued by women of all levels of class and wealth who wanted to check out these rumors for themselves. Everyone from a string of movie stars to such international rich women celebrities as Tina Onassis, Evita Perón, and Brenda Frazier went out of their way to sample his pleasures. According to C. David, Barbara Hutton, who said being near Rubirosa was enough to put her "in a lather," described Heymann, . . . "priapic, indefatigable, grotesquely proportioned. His lovemaking secret is that he practices an Egyptian technique called *Imsak*. No matter how aroused he becomes, he doesn't allow himself to complete the act. What he enjoys about it is the sense of control he achieves over his own body while exciting the woman beyond control, beyond the threshold. His pleasure derives from totally arousing his partner while he remains aloof, the absolute master of the situation." No doubt there has been something to the theory that it is the technique as well as the charming accents that recommend Europeans and Latins to American heiresses.

But perhaps more than anything it is the need for love, and finally just for company, that puts some rich women in the position of paying with their fortunes and their dignity for men. How else is one to explain such a marriage as that of newspaper heiress Helen Bonfils to her uneducated, foul-mouthed, thirty-years-younger chauffeur, Edward Michael "Tiger Mike" Davis? Or of Rebekah Harkness's attraction, in her last years, to the two homosexuals who were to receive such a large portion of her estate? The tradition of paid companions goes back, at least by etymology, to the Parisian dance halls of the early years of the century, when *gigolos* were simply tango partners for hire. They were, of course, generally younger, prettier men hired by older, none-too-attractive women, and after World War I the term came to be applied to such combinations whether they took place inside a dance hall or not. For a time in the 1930s, there was even an aboveground and more-or-less respectable operation called the Guide Escort Service in New York that provided Ivy League–caliber young men to go out with lonely society women. The same function has also long been performed by "extra men." It is expected that rich women will fade into old age in genteel widowhood, with the occasional flirtation in proper society their only romantic diversion. Those who want more are treated with bitchiness and contempt by those around them. Barbara Hutton's last years were a constant odyssey in the company of handsome, feckless men three decades her junior, who shamelessly cheated her and then gossiped behind her back. The older she got, the more desperate and pitiful she became. Her last fling, at age sixty, was with a twenty-four-year-old Spanish matador named Angel Teruel. Although she hated the brutality of bullfighting, she followed him for months from one *corrida* to the next. She eventually spirited him away for two weeks in Marbella, an assignation that left Teruel with a Rolls and a $75,000 diamond ring and Barbara with an increasingly gaunt look and the ill wishes of the Spanish press.

Their Own Kind

One logical escape from the conundrum of who loves you is, theoretically, to marry only a wealthy man; since the rich tend to hang together, this turns out to be a practical thing to do as well, and it becomes the actual route chosen by the bulk of fantastically wealthy heiresses. The flaw in this thinking is that rich men are, conversely, catnip to virtually all women. And not only does great wealth provide the attraction, it also provides the means with which to capitalize upon it. Money makes sex, like life in general, easier. There is a considerable body of academic study suggesting that rich men have a more vivid interest in sex than their less affluent fellow citizens; in at least one study there was a direct link found between the increase in income and philandering, although the chart topped out at a relatively modest income level, so it is probably not fair to conclude that a massive fortune automatically means a correspondingly gargantuan sexual appetite. However, in many cases that is obviously true. Men who are rich, whether they made it themselves or inherited it, generally acquire a sense of the power that money brings; and this would clearly extend to a power over women as well. Thus, whether a woman is rich and marries a rich man to avoid possible exploitation, or starts out middle class and then finds her husband has become rich, she is more than likely to end up with a husband who has the motive and the opportunity to screw around.

The most direct way for him to indulge that predilection, naturally, is to buy it outright. There is a good suspicion that rich men enjoy call girls not merely because they don't get enough sex at home, but because they don't get enough variety. "The lower-class man has not experienced an expensive call girl and may have never even seen one," writes John F. Cuber, a sociologist at Ohio State University. (We will leave unexplored the question of what a sociologist at Ohio State knows about it.) "The reason is not merely that he doesn't have the money to spend in this way, but rather that he has not learned to need or want the sophisticated and richly embellished sex at which the call girl is adept." Some idea of what embellishments might arise can be culled from the late Vicki Morgan's unrefuted testimony in her "palimony" suit of 1982 that the late Alfred Bloomingdale, the department store heir and a member of President Reagan's kitchen cabinet, enjoyed such diversions as working himself up to a drool by whipping naked women until they wept.

Vicki Morgan is a good example of the type of fun young women, generally of no particular background, education, or talent, who serve as fodder for the fantasy factories of such places as Manhattan, Beverly Hills, London, and Marbella. They can be seen in discos (or whatever they are called currently), in apartments obviously beyond their means, around pools and on yachts. They may well be aspiring actresses or models, though their chances of reaching those goals are predictably poor. For a long time, offers of employment in those fields have been sufficient to persuade such young women to shuck their virtue. More recently, the offer of stylish drugs, generally cocaine, has been the coin of the fantasy-sex realm. Vicki Morgan was more serious, and more professional, than most. Through three marriages by her mid-twenties—two to older, wealthy men and one to an actor—and assignations with notorious financier and womanizer Bernie Cornfeld as well as Bloomingdale, Vicki never worked a day in her life, except at the ultimately debilitating job of pleasing rich men. She testified that she accepted Bloomingdale's offer to buy her out of her first marriage so that she could become his mistress. There seems little argument that virtually everything she did was to sell herself for money—a lot of money, with expense checks of up to $18,000 a month from Bloomingdale, not to mention clothes and stylish houses. With the filing of the palimony lawsuit, Betsy Bloomingdale, the tycoon's wife and herself a member of Nancy Reagan's circle of ladies who lunch, ended the gravy train. Since those who live by the wiggle die by the wrinkle—Vicki was partial to drink and Valium, and it was beginning to show in her late twenties—there were no replacement sugar-daddies in immediate view. She was forced to move in with Marvin Pancoast, another unemployed drifter she had met while they were fellow patients at a community mental health center, and he clubbed her to death with her son's baseball bat out of frustration with her endless demands.

What impact the publication of these sordid details may have had upon the grieving widow can only be imagined,[39] but it took Betsy only a few months to resume her full schedule in the society party world. It has, of course, long been a commonplace that men of property maintain mistresses on the side and that their wives, whose purpose has traditionally been procreation rather than recreation, in turn maintain a silence. Such sophistication is a cultural institution among the wealthy of Europe, much to the distress of American heiresses like Sunny Crawford, who had had no initial intention of allowing her Austrian prince, Alfie von Auersperg, his head. Boy, was she wrong. Barbara Hutton ran into the same problems all the time. The sex goddess Rita Hayworth faced the angst of her Mohammedan prince running around *before the wedding*. For what it's worth, Susanna Agnelli believes that the younger men of Italy, at least, are becoming increasingly discreet about such behavior: "Italian men know they have to be careful today," she has said. "I think it's good that they understand the suffering that women have always felt when vice versa happens."

Historically, the development of the American manufacturing fortunes and then of a transatlantic society grafted European mores onto the American upper class. It was generally accepted that enough money to keep all concerned in style meant that infidelity was acceptable. William Randolph Hearst was able to conduct most of his adult life with his much younger mistress Marion Davies, who became his hostess at San Simeon and even a confidante of his children, to the apparent distress of no one except his wife Millicent; when he asked for a divorce to marry Davies in 1922, her answer was a flat no and a quick trip to Tiffany to buy the most expensive pearl necklace in the store; she even won an agreement that W. R. would spend a substantial amount of time with her at home until the boys were grown.

It is self-made men that have been notoriously the most aggressive pursuers of sex outside the home, as they are of every-

39. Her only word on the subject came in December 1984, when she testified briefly in the drawn-out palimony proceedings that she knew nothing of any agreement with Miss Morgan and insisted—breaking into tears—that their thirty-six-year marriage had been a happy one.

thing else. H. L. Hunt was perhaps the foremost example in our time of the close association between financial and sexual conquests in the same man. His recent biographer, Harry Hurt III, concludes that Hunt's predilection for philandering gave him the same sort of feeling of his own invincibility that his accumulating oil fortune did. When his eldest son Hassie began exhibiting the roundabout thinking and fits of rage that would result in his lobotomy and institutionalization, Hunt's cure was to keep Hassie well supplied with compliant women—a number of whom had to be paid off for the outrage and sometimes physical injury they suffered at Hassie's hands. But, Hunt being Hunt, he went beyond the usual rich man's feeling that conquering women was akin to conquering the world. He not only wanted to sleep with women, he wanted to produce families with them, because he was convinced that he had a "genius gene" and would be doing the world a favor. That compulsion led to the great strain of the three different families; as with most other strange sexual escapades among the very wealthy, it seems to have done little to affect the public estimation of the man. But the embarrassment inherent in H. L.'s bizarre escapades may have had a permanent effect on the next generation. When his sons took over the family enterprise, they insisted that their employees be staunchly faithful to their wives; at one point Herbert Hunt engaged a private detective to follow around a part-time consultant who was supposed to be philandering.

Aristotle Onassis was a man bigger than life in almost all aspects except physical height. His creation of an immense fortune from scratch during World War II was matched in its daring and its attention to detail only by his love life. Ari claimed that his great goal in life, alongside achieving immense wealth, was to find the perfect mate. Naturally, to do so he had to sample the candidates in great detail. Beginning at the age of sixteen, when he arrived in Argentina to escape the marauding Turks and to begin acquiring his fortune, Onassis went out with all the women he could, and graded each of them in ten different categories, ranging from receptivity and dress to love of the sea and love of parents. Along the way he made some stunning conquests. Perhaps the greatest was Eva Perón, whom he first met during World War II and seduced in 1947 in her villa on the Italian Riviera; after their congress, Evita cooked him an omelet, and he gave her a check for $10,000 to donate to charity, leading him later to describe the breakfast as "the most expensive I have ever had." At the age of forty, Onassis finally married for the first time, selecting the seventeen-year-old daughter of one of the rival Greek shipping clans, Tina Livanos. Tina's tenure came to an end with the appearance of Maria Callas, the high-strung diva, whom Onassis pursued by describing his cluttered love life in such a way that it made her proud to be the culmination. Tina went on to marry the marquess of Blandford and then, in a move that shocked Onassis, she wed his lifelong rival Stavros Niarchos. It had been only eighteen months since Tina's sister Eugenia, who had also been married to Niarchos, died on Spetzapoulos under mysterious circumstances, including physical injuries and barbiturates. Onassis, of course, went on to the towering achievement of marrying Jacqueline Kennedy, where he got his come-uppance—a premarital agreement guaranteeing separate bedrooms and immense sums at Jackie's disposal.

Jackie, for an ethereal thing apparently more interested in clothes than in sex, has been involved with two of the biggest sexual marauders of the twentieth century. Her first one was, of course, John F. Kennedy, the greatest debunkee in recent history, who was harder on his women than he was on Castro. The sexual lives of Jack and Teddy—Bobby was a conspicuous exception in his militant profamily orientation—were based largely on their father Joe, the ambassador and creator of the family fortune. In his dealings with women as well as with money, suggests Collier and Horowitz's recent biography of the family,[40] Joe Kennedy established a simple rule that his sons would emulate all their lives: the rules didn't apply to the Kennedys. They could, and did, do anything they wanted. Jack used to tell young women staying at the Hyannis compound that they should lock their doors because "the Ambassador likes to roam at night," and it was not at all clear that he was jesting. Friends of his daughters and wives of his cronies alike had to physically beat Joe off. His affair with Joan Crawford was only one of the numerous infidelities that he virtually flaunted in front of Rose, who became something of a hollow shell as a result of the continuous slaps in the face. Jack Kennedy said once in a discussion about his family, "My mother is a nothing."

Kick Kennedy, Jack's sparkling, ill-starred sister, was as con-

40. *The Kennedys: An American Drama* (N.Y.: Summit Books, 1984).

fused by the outrageous philandering as the sons were warped by it. Once when she was in a discussion with some English friends, someone unknowingly made a disparaging remark about another man's extramarital adventure. "That's what all men do," Kick said sharply. "You know that women can never trust them." Her friends found themselves forced to argue with Kick that a second woman was not necessarily an expected part of every marriage. With the ambassador as a role model, Jack came to consider women as nothing more than appendages useful for reaffirming a man's reality. Before his marriage to Jackie, the bachelor legislator slipped a different stewardess or secretary into the Georgetown house every evening, and never bothered to learn their names.

Jackie, of course, was different—a Farmington-Vassar debutante from an old family with an Auchincloss stepfather and his Newport estate. But it was apparently Jack's very resemblance to her own father, the notorious rake "Black Jack" Bouvier, that made him so attractive. Unfortunately, Jackie's romantic streak allowed her little insight into what life with Jack was going to be like. She was no social dummy, and within months was quite aware that Jack was sneaking out of parties with other women and running down to a specially kept nest in an apartment house on the Potomac for trysts involving permutations of his Senate colleague George Smathers and groups of young things who naturally flocked around a young, rich, good-looking senator. "After the first year they were together," a friend said later, "Jackie was wandering around looking like the survivor of an airplane crash." It only got worse when Jack attained the White House and had the use of the Secret Service to procure his women. Regular visitors included Marilyn Monroe ("I think I made his back feel better"), Judith Campbell, the mobster moll, and Mary Meyer, sister-in-law of *Washington Post* editor Ben Bradlee, then *Newsweek*'s White House correspondent, who introduced Kennedy to marijuana and joked with him in the White House bedroom about being stoned when the time came to push the button. For casual diversion, there was a matched set of blondes in the secretarial pool whom Jack and his pals referred to as "Fiddle and Faddle" and Jackie called "the White House dogs." Jackie took the high road as best she could. When she found panties in a pillow slip, she handed them to Jack and said in her best finishing-school tones, "Here, would you find who these belong to. They're not my size."

(The Kennedy women tended to be spoiled by their close relationship with their father, much as the Annenberg daughters
were. After Peter Lawford's marriage with Pat broke up, he
remarked, "I always felt that her love for her father took prec-
edence over her love for me.")

The difficulty of marriage to Arab men is legendary, and one
is hard put to decide if it makes it better or worse that they have
the legal right to multiple marriages. A few of the wrinkles of
marriage to Westerners will appear in the section on divorce,
below. As far as marriages within the tribe go, it is safe to say
that with a very few Westernized exceptions, Arab women do
not have very high expectations and are not surprised. Myra
Davies, the Welsh trainer of the horses of Sheikh Nasser ibn
Sabah al Sabah, the ruler of Kuwait, remarked, "Being married
to an al Sabah isn't like being a wife as we understand it. It's
like being a brood mare."

What is a rich woman to do, then, with this impossible situation?—the money that makes her the object of such irresistible
pursuit also subjects her to alliances with either fortune-hunters
or hunters of other women. For guidance we turn to Leonora
Grosvenor, a debutante, a beauty, a mother, and the sister of
perhaps the richest property owner in England. Leonora was
rather a shy thing when she first visited Shugborough, the country pleasure palace of Patrick, the fifth Earl of Lichfield; hence,
although Leonora had no particular claim to the freewheeling
peer, she was rather dismayed to find Dewi Sukarno, the earl's
main squeeze of the time, "much in evidence." Leonora decided,
however, that Lichfield's breezy charm and aristocratic connections (he is a cousin of the queen's) more than balanced his sexual
notoriety: "I'd always said that I wanted to marry a challenge,
not someone nice and safe." She got all of that and more; Lichfield travels incessantly, being a society photographer in the Lord
Snowdon mode, is reportedly rude to Leonora and the staff, and
gets into public scrapes such as asking several models to strip
for video auditions so he could choose subjects for a nude calendar. Leonora deals with the situation in probably the best way,
with resignation. "One has to look forward and beyond," she
told *People*. "And one has to have faith and trust. I do. I hope
he does."

Or, for a little more practical advice, one might heed Maggie van Zuylen, the sophisticated pal of the emotionally unsettled Maria Callas. "Never create jealous scenes," she said. "Be unfaithful. The greatest, the most effective jealousy scene you can create is a nicely publicized affair on the side. A man can't go on being interested, especially sexually interested, in his wife, if he feels too secure in her."

Perhaps the most important thing for the rich woman to remember, though, is that she is a rich woman first and a lover second. Once again, it is being rich that is the full-time job. Her loves and marriages are welcome diversions from the serious business of being rich, but if she lets them become more important than her wealth itself, she runs the risk that she will have neither love nor money for long.

31 | Divorcing for Dollars

By 1979, Sheikha Dena al-Fassi had had enough. Now, she must have been aware from the beginning that this was not going to be an ordinary marriage. Actually a coal miner's daughter, she was sixteen and working in a shop in Piccadilly—under her own name, Diana Bilinelli—when she was discovered by the al-Fassi clan. Living in London, she can hardly have missed the presence of the hordes of Arabs who ran around buying all the jewelry, cars, and apartments they could find; and she must have noticed from the first that Mohammed al-Fassi, whose brothers brought him into the store to meet the smashing Italian girl, was treating her rather like just one more of those precious commodities. It was surely flattering that he would simply up and follow her back to Milan when she returned home three months after their meeting. She insisted on marriage, like a good Catholic girl, and it worked. In March 1976, they were married in Los Angeles.

Probably in the beginning Dena had no very good idea of the oceanic dimensions of the al-Fassis' wealth or of the incredible way it was accumulated: Mohammed's father, "Dr. Sheikh," a Moroccan whose business was best described as magic, had actually been jailed in Saudi Arabia as an enemy of the kingdom in 1970, just before he managed to marry his daughter Hind to Prince Turki bin Abdul Aziz, over the apoplectic protests of Turki's brother, the future King Fahd. Though not an especially sophisticated young woman, Dena was not slow to notice the ridicule heaped on her husband and his brothers, whose boorishness was as outsize as their wealth: Sheikh Tarek was expelled from Geneva's prestigious Collège du Léman for attempting to run over the headmaster with his Ferrari, while Mohammed once came down from his family's three-floor suite in that city's Intercontinental Hotel and strode through the massively formal lobby in his pajamas, spitting pistachio shells onto the carpet. She was appalled when Mohammed, after buying a three-acre estate on Sunset Boulevard in Beverly Hills for $2.4 million in cash, decorated it in nouveau bordello, hiring an Egyptian artist to daub the genitalia on the garden statues in red, and had his own portrait painted on the bottom of the pool. She was bewildered when he adopted a little girl in Uruguay and a diseased little boy in Turkey. She was outraged when he married a young American, Victoria Sosa, while she was on a trip to Europe and Saudi Arabia, and then after discarding her married an Arabian girl named Ibtissam in a three-night, $5-million bash in London that Dena read about in the papers while she was in France. Finally, three years after her own wedding, she began to be legitimately terrified as bodyguards followed her even into the bathroom and prevented her from seeing the couple's four children. In 1979, she got in touch with lawyer Marvin Mitchelson.

Divorce is the ultimate act of a rich woman. Through it, she finally achieves financial independence and hence social independence, in the sense both of being able to sleep around and of deciding utterly on her own which charities and businesses her money will go toward. And when she remarries, it is this time as a peer of the rich man that she still seeks.

Mitchelson sued al-Fassi for $3 billion, and in 1983, when she was twenty-four years old, he won nearly $85 million for Dena, the biggest court-ordered divorce settlement in American history. Collecting it has been another matter. Dena does have the Sunset Boulevard estate; but she can live there only in a small guest house, for the mansion itself was gutted in a fire that an ex-chauffeur set to cover up the theft of hundreds of thousands of dollars worth of artworks, and now Dena lives amidst the ruins, more like Miss Havisham than the richest divorcée in history. All over the world, Mitchelson has colleagues looking out for the two Boeing 707s, $70 million worth of jewelry, thirteen Rolls-Royces, and a $15 million yacht—all of them property of al-Fassi subject to liens. In 1984, a judge ruled that the sheikh still owed his ex-wife $81.5 million. Indeed, al-Fassi had been so shrewd at squirreling away his assets that when Sheikha Dena first went to Mitchelson, she had to pay his $50,000 retainer in jewelry. Nor has the sheikha had any better luck repossessing the children. In 1983, she tracked them to the Martinez Hotel in Cannes, but the sheikh and the kids had checked out the day before, and father and children are now presumed to be safely ensconced in Saudi Arabia. "I'm very happy," Dena said after the settlement. "I was sure that he would make a fair judgment. But the money is nothing to me. It's normal to me. My mind is on my children and to get them back."[41]

Actually, al-Fassi was not even the biggest Arab fish Mitchelson has tried to fry. That would be none other than Adnan Khashoggi, who does a good imitation of the richest man in the world—although Khashoggi eventually managed to get out of the frying pan. Soraya, his English-born wife, divorced the international businessman and arms dealer in 1974; then, with Mitchelson in her corner, sued him for $2.4 billion. Sadly, it was thrown out of court in 1981. Soraya has not had an easy time of it. Like Vicki Morgan and Roxanne Pulitzer, who at various times were both Mitchelson clients, Soraya found life off the gravy train disappointing. In 1982, at the age of thirty-nine, she married a twenty-one-year-old American, Arthur Rupley. The union lasted only eight months and ultimately ended with Soraya unsuccessfully in court again, this time trying to get a London judge to throw

41. Sheikh Mohammed al-Fassi's well-deserved obscurity was invaded in the middle of 1984 by another agent of the courts. A former State Department official who performed heroically in the last days of Vietnam named Walter Reed Martindale III was indicted on a charge of conspiring to knock off the sheikh. According to the indictment, Ibrahim al Rawaf, a Saudi businessman with whom Martindale set up a company in Washington after the war, paid him at least $40,000 to line up a plot to kill al-Fassi. Martindale allegedly went so far as to scope out the sheikh's $3-million spread outside London, purchase an Uzi semiautomatic rifle and line up a group of French and Cuban assassins to help him out. There was no assertion in the indictment why Rawaf might want al-Fassi dead, but his outrageous performances over the years have probably induced at least passing homicidal dreams in many Saudis.

Rupley in jail for contacting her in violation of a court order.

Mitchelson not only whirls through the most famous of divorces involving those madcap characters in Hollywood—Marlon Brando, Mick Jagger, three different divorce suits (two by the same woman) against the late Beachboy Dennis Wilson, the much-married Alan Jay Lerner, and Rhonda Fleming, for whom he once promised he would win "all the bidets in Europe"—he takes on the even richer characters who live in Tinseltown's reflected glow. In 1983, he asked half of Dr. Jerry Buss's estimated $250 million, plus $100 million damages, on behalf of Veronica Buss, claiming that both of them were married to different people when they tied the knot in Tijuana. He collected $10 million for Mary Entenmann upon her divorce after twenty-eight years of marriage to the scion of the coffee-cake dynasty. Not all his clients are famous, he has said; "many of them are anonymous multimillionaires."

Mitchelson is, of course, a multimillionaire in his own right as a consequence of his success in separating wives from their rich husbands and rich husbands from their money. He is also a reputation waiting to happen for some other jealous, struggling divorce lawyer, a prospect he views with his usual disabused clarity. ("That would be a Tylenol headache of the worst sort.") He makes no secret of the ephemeral nature of his marriage to Marcella, an Italian blonde he met on Capri some twenty years ago. He sees her, he says, for a few minutes in the morning, and at parties—such as the one thrown by Roy Cohn, another counselor to the rich and famous, for Marcella in 1983 on the occasion of the opening of a show of her paintings. Rather typically, Mitchelson flew into New York escorting both Marcella and Dena al-Fassi. In return for such attentions, the hot-blooded Italian in her has inspired Marcella to such touches as invading a Sunset Strip restaurant to grab a hairpiece from Mitchelson's dining companion of the day and dump it in her fettucine.

The lawyer is duly preoccupied with his women. On his office ceiling, he has a lighted reproduction of the face of the Botticelli Venus on the half shell. The glory of his product! Free, rich women! "I love women," he has told an interviewer. "I am committed to their civil rights. I not only care about them, but if there's nothing in the law that provides for them, I want to create something that will provide for them."

His greatest creation—perhaps the most telling invention in the history of rich women, at least since seduction—is of course the concept of palimony. The genius of the idea is the final quantification of a woman's time and attention. Not merely for her body, but for her entire sexual being and her warmth, a woman is entitled to be kept. Merely being a woman should be a career, a full-time job and a well-paying one. It is the final apotheosis of the key underlying rule of all the great rich women throughout history: love is money.

Bibliography

Adler, Bill, *The Kennedy Children* (N.Y.: Franklin Watts, 1980).

Agnelli, Susanna, *We Always Wore Sailor Suits* (N.Y.: Viking Press, 1975).

Anger, Kenneth, *Hollywood Babylon* (N.Y.: Bell Publishing Co., 1981).

Ash, Mary Kay, *Mary Kay* (N.Y.: Harper & Row, 1981).

Babcock, Judy and Kennedy, Judy, *The Spa Book* (N.Y.: Crown Publishers, 1983).

Babyak, Blythe, "The Reagan Court's First Fop," *Washington Monthly*, December, 1981, pp. 50–55.

Barnes, John, *Evita* (N.Y.: Grove Press, 1979).

Barron, D. Susan, "Reviving the Rituals of the Debutante," *The New York Times Magazine*, January 15, 1984, p. 26.

Baer, Jean, *The Self-Chosen* (N.Y.: Arbor House, 1982).

Baumgold, Julie, "Lunch at Le Cirque," *New York*, April 18, 1983, pp. 139–148.

Bender, Marylin, *At the Top* (Garden City, N.Y.: Doubleday, 1975).

Bender, Marylin, with Monsieur Marc, *Nouveau Is Better Than No Riche At All* (N.Y.: Putnam, 1983).

Best, Hugh, *Debrett's Texas Peerage* (N.Y.: Coward-McCann, 1983).

Birmingham, Stephen, *Duchess: The Story of Wallis Warfield Windsor* (Boston: Little, Brown, 1981).

————, *The Grandes Dames* (N.Y.: Simon and Schuster, 1982).

Blandford, Linda, *Super-Wealth: The Secret Lives of the Oil Sheiks* (N.Y.: William Morrow, 1977).

Brenner, Marie, "The Class Menagerie," *New York*, September 19, 1983, pp. 30–34.

Brooks, John, *Showing Off in America* (Boston: Little, Brown & Co., 1979).

Browning, Dominique, "Dominique in Full Bloom," *Town & Country*, February 1984, p. 167+.

Buckley, William F., Jr., *Overdrive* (Garden City, N.Y.: Doubleday, 1983).

Cameron, Roderick, *The Golden Riviera* (London: Weidenfeld & Nicholson, 1975).

Carr, William H. A., *The du Ponts of Delaware* (N.Y.: Dodd, Mead, 1964).

Chaney, Lindsay and Michael Cieply, *The Hearsts: Family and Empire—The Later Years* (N.Y.: Simon and Schuster, 1981).

Coles, Robert, *Privileged Ones* (Boston: Little, Brown and Company, 1977).

————, *The Kennedys: An American Drama* (N.Y.: Simon & Schuster, 1984).

Collier, Peter, and Horowitz, David, *The Rockefellers: An American Dynasty* (N.Y.: Holt, Rinehart and Winston, 1976).

Cowles, Virginia, *The Astors* (London: Weidenfeld and Nicholson, 1979).

de Marty, Diana, *The History of Haute Couture 1850–1950* (N.Y.: Holmes & Meier, 1980).

deButts, Mary Custis Lee and Rosalie Noland Woodland, *Charlotte Haxall Noland* (Middleburg, Va.: The Foxcroft School, 1971).

Dempster, Nigel, *Princess Margaret* (N.Y.: Macmillan, 1981).

Devi, Gayatri and Santha Rama Rau, *A Princess Remembers* (Philadelphia and N.Y.: J. B. Lippincott Co., 1976).

Evans, Hilary, *Harlots, Whores & Hookers* (N.Y.: Taplinger Publishing Co., 1981).

Goldberg, Herb and Lewis, Robert T., *Money Madness* (N.Y.: William Morrow, 1978).

Goldsmith, Barbara, *Little Gloria . . . Happy At Last* (N.Y.: Alfred A. Knopf, 1980).

Grinker, Roy R. Jr., "The Poor Rich: The Children of the Super-Rich," *American Journal of Psychiatry* 135:8, August, 1978.

Gunther, Max, *The Very, Very Rich and How They Got That Way* (Chicago: Playboy Press, 1972).

Halberstam, David, *The Powers That Be* (N.Y.: Alfred A. Knopf, 1979).

Harrop, David, *World Paychecks: Who Makes What, Where and Why* (N.Y.: Facts on File, 1982).

Heymann, C. David, *Poor Little Rich Girl* (N.Y.: Random House, 1983).

Hoving, Thomas, "101 Top Collectors," *Connoisseur*, September 1983, pp. 108–118.

Hurt, Harry III, *Texas Rich* (N.Y.: W. W. Norton, 1981).

Kanner, Bernice, "Guilt Dinners," *New York*, December 5, 1983, pp. 127–141.

Kelly, Tom, *The Imperial Post* (N.Y.: William Morrow, 1983).

Kornbluth, Jesse, "The Rise and Rise of Arianna Stassinopoulos," *New York*, July 25, 1983, pp. 32–38.

Koskoff, David E., *The Mellons* (N.Y.: Thomas Y. Crowell, 1978).

Lasky, Victor, *Never Complain, Never Explain: The Story of Henry Ford II* (N.Y.: Putnam, 1981).

Lundberg, Ferdinand, *The Rich and the Super-Rich* (N.Y.: Lyle Stuart, 1968).

McTaggart, Lynne, *Kathleen Kennedy: Her Life and Times* (Garden City, N.Y.: Doubleday, 1983).

Meeker, Richard H., *Newspaperman: S. I. Newhouse and the Business of News* (New Haven and New York: Ticknor & Fields, 1983).

Mellen, Joan, *Privilege: The Enigma of Sasha Bruce* (N.Y.: Dial Press, 1982).

Morella, Joe and Epstein, Edward Z., *Rita: The Life of Rita Hayworth* (N.Y.: Delacorte Press, 1983).

Newman, Peter C., *The Bronfman Dynasty* (Montreal: McClelland and Stewart, 1979).

O'Brien, Robert, *Marriott: The J. Willard Marriott Story* (Salt Lake City, Utah: Deseret Book Co., 1977).

Ramsey, Lynn, *Gigolos* (Englewood Cliffs, N.J.: Prentice-Hall, 1978).

Rasmussen, Anne-Marie, *There Was Once a Time* (N.Y.: Harcourt Brace Jovanovich, 1975).

Rottenberg, Dan, "The Most Generous Living Americans," *Town & Country*, December 1983, pp. 197–204+.

Selznick, Irene Mayer, *A Private View* (N.Y.: Alfred A. Knopf, 1983).

Silk, Leonard and Mark, *The American Establishment* (N.Y.: Basic Books, 1980).

Stadiem, William, *A Class By Themselves: The Untold Story of the Great Southern Families* (N.Y.: Crown Publishers, 1980).

Stassinopoulos, Arianna, *Maria Callas: The Woman Behind the Legend* (N.Y.: Simon and Schuster, 1981).

Stein, Jean, edited with George Plimpton, *Edie: An American Biography* (N.Y.: Alfred A. Knopf, 1982).

Thompson, Jacqueline, *The Very Rich Book* (N.Y.: William Morrow, 1981).

Thorndike, Joseph J. Jr., *The Very Rich* (N.Y.: American Heritage, 1976).

Unger, Craig, "The Heiress: The Untold Story of Rebekah Harkness," *New York*, June 27, 1983, pp. 24–45.

Wagner, Walter, *Money Talks* (N.Y.: Bobbs-Merrill, 1978).

Wallace, Irving, et al. *The Intimate Sex Lives of Famous People* (N.Y.: Delacorte Press, 1983).

Whitney, Cornelius Vanderbilt, *High Peaks* (Lexington, Ky.: The University Press of Kentucky, 1977).

———, *Live a Year With a Millionaire!* (Lexington, Ky.: Maple Hill Press, 1981).

Whitney, Marylou, *Cornelia Vanderbilt Whitney's Dollhouse* (N.Y.: Farrar, Straus and Giroux, 1975).

Wiseman, Thomas, *The Money Motive* (N.Y.: Random House, 1974).

Wright, William, *Heiress: The Rich Life of Marjorie Merriweather Post* (Washington, D.C.: New Republic Books, 1978).

Wright, William, *The Von Bülow Affair* (N.Y.: Delacorte Press, 1983).

PERIODICALS

Andy Warhol's Interview
Architectural Digest
Art News
Business Week
Dallas Times-Herald
Denver Post
Forbes
Harper's Bazaar
Houston Post
Jacksonville (Fla.) Times-Union
Kansas City Star
Los Angeles Times
Miami Herald

New York
New York Times
Newsweek
Palm Beach Daily News
Paris Match
People
Philadelphia Inquirer
San Francisco Chronicle
Time
Town & Country
Vogue
Wall Street Journal
Washington Post

Index

Roosevelt, James, 35
Rosenbloom, Carroll, 42
Rosenbloom, Steve, 42
Rosenkranz, Edith, 351
Rosenstiel, Lewis, 150
Ross, Diana, 152
Rothschild, Baroness Philippine de, 24
Rothschild, Baron Guy de, 39
Rothschild, Baronne Olimpia de, 126, 225n
Rothschild family, 24, 27, 29, 125, 126
Roussel, Thierry, 26
Royster, Vermont, 72
Rozelle, Pete, 309
Rubenstein, Howard J., 83, 85
Rubinstein, Helena, 18, 113, 115
Rubirosa, Porfirio, 36, 363, 368–369
Rupley, Arthur, 380–381
Rupley, Soraya Khashoggi, 380–381
Ryan, Virginia Fortune, 364

Sabah, Sheikh Nasser ibn Sabah al, 376
Sadat, Anwar, 350
St. Laurent, Yves, 120, 126, 225, 228
Sakowitz, Bernard, 134
Sakowitz, Louis, 134
Sakowitz, Robert, 134
Sakowitz, Simon, 134
Sakowitz, Tobias, 134
Salama, Princess, 76n
Sanford, Mary, 146, 185, 252
Scaife, Richard Mellon, 30
Scarborough, Anne Ford, 175, 176, 198
Scavullo, Francesco, 228
Scevers, Bobby, 47
Schatz, John Michael, 116
Schermerhorn, F. A., 247
Schiaparelli, Elsa, 120

Schoellkopf, Caroline Hunt, xiv, 12, 13, 14, 16
Schoellkopf, Helen Hunt, 355
Scott, Marion du Pont, 48
Scott, Walter, 291
Sedgwick, Edie, xiv, 142, 161–162, 211, 216, 316n, 337, 341, 343, 344–346
Sedgwick, Francis, 344
Selznick, David O., 233
Selznick, Irene Mayer, 233
Semerjian, Madell, 198–199
Shakespeare, William, 68
Shapiro, Irving, 28
Shaw, Bernard, 343
Shouse, Catherine Filene, 274–275
Shouse, Jouett, 274
Sian, Sally Aw, 79
Sidamon-Eristoff, Anne Phipps, 33
Silliman, Henry H., 28–29
Sills, Beverly, 299
Simon, Norton, 280–281
Simpson, Abby Rockefeller, 32
Simpson, Marilyn Milton, 32
Sinatra, Frank, 84, 187, 313
Singer, Isaac, 180, 181
Singh, Charan, 76
Sirikit, Queen of Thailand, 238, 310
Skelly, Carolyn, 353
Smith, Joan Irvine, 55–58, 354
Smith, Norma, 235, 236
Smith, R. E., "Bob," 37
Smith, Vivian L., 37
Smithers, Robert Brinkley, 337–338
Sofia, Queen of Spain, 17
Sorensen, Ted, 272
Sowell, Anne Windfohr, 33
Spencer, Ivor, 146
Spencer-Churchill, Lady Sarah, 174
Spencer-Churchill, Winston, 204